METHODS AND ISSUES IN SOCIAL RESEARCH

METHODS AND ISSUES IN SOCIAL RESEARCH

JAMES A. BLACK
and
DEAN J. CHAMPION
University of Tennessee

JOHN WILEY & SONS, INC., New York • London • Sydney • Toronto

Library of Congress Cataloging in Publication Data:

Black, James A
    Methods and issues in social research.

    Includes index.
    1. Social sciences—Methodology.   2. Social science research.
I. Champion, Dean   J., joint author.   II. Title.

H61.B476   300'.1'8   75-26659
ISBN 0-471-07705-4

Printed in the United States of America

10 9 8 7 6 5 4 3 2 1

Book Designed by Angie Lee

PREFACE

Since World War II the volume of social research has burgeoned. Various social science professional associations have expanded their memberships at overwhelming rates. As these disciplines have become increasingly popular, a wider variety of subareas within each has developed accordingly.

Presently, the diversity of interests characterizing each of these fields has necessitated the development and elaboration of several strategies designed to collect, analyze, and interpret information common to each. Needless to say, different interest areas, even within the same field, have frequently required the construction and application of unique measuring instruments, methods of data collection, specific statistical tools for analytical purposes, and particular approaches or study designs in order for investigators to fulfil their research objectives.

This book is designed to assist a broad variety of social researchers to achieve their quest. It does not purport to be comprehensive or all-encompassing in its discussion and treatment of research strategies, however. Nor should it necessarily be viewed as a manual for "ready-to-apply-and-interpret" individuals who seek easy solutions to their research problems. Although several key research strategies and their respective advantages, disadvantages, and suggested applications are presented in some detail, the reader should not be misled into thinking that the research process is a simple one, even for seemingly facile research problems. There are many problems that the investigator must face and many decisions that must be made as each phase of research is entered. As a somewhat logical sequence of activities to be performed, the research process may be viewed as a chain that is no stronger than its weakest link. This book has as one of its foremost objectives, therefore, a dedication to help novice and professional social investigators alike to become increasingly aware of some of the more important kinds of in-puts, often unplanned or unanticipated, which can contaminate the quality of their respective research enterprises.

This text may be seen as serving a multiplicity of research interests. Its sole assumption is *that the reader has some limited familiarity with social scientific literature.* No procedures are discussed here that require anything but the most elementary mathematical and/or theoretical skills. It is practical in orientation and elementary in its presentation. The following aims have functioned as our guidelines for each chapter discussion.

1. To acquaint and/or refamiliarize students with the traditional scientific approach and its accompanying benefits as well as restrictions. Among other things, these include conservatism, objectivity, and a willingness to pursue knowledge of any kind through the application of ethical and legitimate means.

2. To present several of the more commonly applied research strategies used by social scientists for gathering information and manipulating it. Interviewing, observation, and questionnaire construction and administration are included among such strategies. Others include sampling procedures and various types of scales for the measurement of social and/or social psychological variables (e.g., Likert summated rating techniques, Osgood's semantic differential, Guttman's technique for assessing the unidimensionality of a measure, and Thurstone's "equal-appearing interval" measurement work). The content analysis of secondary source material and ethnomethodology are also treated briefly.

3. To provide the student with easily understood examples (both hypothetical and from relatively current professional literature) to illustrate some of the practical applications of such strategies and some of the potential implications of their use relative to one another.

4. Finally, to present research strategies as a fund of tools from which to draw in order to answer particular social scientific questions. We feel that a balanced perspective is necessary for most, if not all, social researchers in their selection of such strategies. Some professionals in the various social science disciplines have consistently adhered to hard, data-gathering methods that emphasize quantitative procedures to the point of excluding entirely the so-called software or soft, data-gathering techniques for acquiring information. Other professionals have assumed the opposite posture in the selection and use of their data-gathering and analytical tools. We firmly believe in and hope to project the balanced philosophy that recognizes the benefits of all research instruments, whether they be basically quantitative or basically qualitative. Therefore, we have sought to highlight some of the more important weaknesses and strengths inherent in

each strategy throughout the succeeding chapters. The simultaneous application of hard and soft methods is not discouraged, and the complementarity between each category of techniques is implicitly, if not explicitly, stated in our subsequent discussions of these.

The organization of this book is a mutual endeavor and we share equally the responsibility for its nature and orientation. Although all chapters were mutually analyzed and criticized, in the actual writing, Black prepared Chs. 1, 2, 3, 9, 10, and 12, while Champion prepared Chs. 4, 5, 6, 7, 8, and 11.

J. A. B.
D. J. C.

CONTENTS

METHODS AND ISSUES IN SOCIAL RESEARCH

PART 1
FUNDAMENTAL DIMENSIONS OF SOCIAL RESEARCH

CHAPTER 1
THE RESEARCH PROCESS

One of the most important features of the training of research scholars is the acquisition of skills required to conduct sound scientific investigations. The major purpose of this text is to contribute to that training by introducing you to a broad range of research methods employed in the social sciences. Because scientific inquiry involves more than the development of technical skills, however, we have a further objective. That is to present procedures in a context that will enable you to select appropriate research strategies, whatever they may be, on the basis of their relative merits and limitations as scientifically useful undertakings.

Before turning our attention to the variety of topics that need to be mastered to make suitable methodological decisions, several fundamental features of the research process need to be understood. In this introductory chapter, it will be beneficial to address ourselves to five related matters so that we can:

1.   Acquaint you with the most characteristic qualities of scientific research.   Asking questions in a scientifically useful way is not simply a form of sophisticated inquisitiveness. Those qualities that serve to separate scientific inquiry from other ways of seeking information need to be understood.

2.   Delineate the major objectives of scientific inquiry.   One of the most interesting yet underemphasized aspects of scientific activity is the extent to which it is organized to achieve certain goals. Although some of these objectives are accepted by all scientists and some are taken for granted by many, others are highly controversial. Each, therefore, deserves attention.

3.   Identify the major targets of social research.   Social scientists do not seek answers to the countless behavioral riddles they encounter from day to day in a haphazard, hit-or-miss fashion. Rather, there is an underlying unity to the questions they ask that is designed to shed light on selected dimensions of human conduct. The targets of social science investigations are important because they promote a more or less integrated look at the same general sectors of human life over time. Furthermore, they encourage the introduction of a more stable foundation from which to engage in interdisciplinary research.

4.   Place in sharp relief some of the major ethical problems posed by social science research.   To a degree, scientific inquiry confronts obstacles similar to those encountered by any sort of persistent investigation. When the targets of the investigation are humans and their relations with each other, matters seem only to be compounded. Special problems arise for the investigator as well as for those investigated.

5.   Erase some frequently held misconceptions about social research.   A number of quaint and indefensible notions about the research process abound in the thinking of those unfamiliar with what such activity actually entails. Because they tend to discourage many from taking a more active part in the accumulation of scientific knowledge, these distortions must be corrected early.

THE NATURE OF SCIENTIFIC RESEARCH

We are continually seeking knowledge of how our social lives came to be as they are. From simple questions raised by children that cry for enormously complex answers to the relatively elaborate questions posed by social scientists that insist on simple responses, our inquisitiveness is insatiable. But the fact that all of us ask questions about our social lives does not make the questions scientific. In fact, as Lazarsfeld (1972) cautioned, "the question-and-answer business" that occurs in our daily social discourse is considerably different from that which goes on as a part of scientific activity. As he suggested, "In social intercourse, it is most likely that what is important for our respondent is important also for us who have made the inquiry" (Lazarsfeld, 1972, p. 184). Therein lies the crux of the difference between scientific inquiry and everyday social discourse. Questions are asked and answers given in the course of normal social behavior that will "contribute especially to a mutual understanding of the present situation" (Lazarsfeld, 1972, p. 183). Inquisitiveness, essential as it is to the research process, is by no means its sole ingredient. Other conditions must be met before our desire to find answers to our questions can be considered scientifically relevant.

CHARACTERISTICS OF SCIENTIFIC RESEARCH

Numerous attempts have been made to capture those characteristics which, when taken together, comprise the major elements of scientific activity. For the most part, there is little variation of any significance among these efforts. All would probably tend to agree with Willer (1971, p. 132) that scientific thinking is "empirical, rational, and abstractive." Positing similar criteria but addressing himself more specifically to those characteristics of sociology that make it scientific, Harry M. Johnson (1960, p. 2) observed that sociology has the following characteristics of science:

1. It is *empirical*; that is, it is based on observation and reasoning, not on supernatural revelation, and its results are not speculative. In the early stages of their creative work, all scientists speculate, of course, but ideally at least, they submit their speculations to the test of fact before announcing them as scientific discoveries.

2. It is *theoretical*; that is, it attempts to summarize complex observations in abstract, logically related propositions which purport to explain causal relationships in the subject matter.

3. It is *cumulative*; that is, sociological theories build upon one another, new theories correcting, extending, and refining the older ones.

4. It is *nonethical*; that is, sociologists do not ask whether particular social actions are good or bad; they seek merely to explain them.

Other scholars such as Kerlinger (1965) and Rose (1965), although not necessarily agreeing with Johnson about the extent to which sociology meets these criteria, rely on essentially the same principles as those most characteristic of scientific research. What each seems to be saying is that *scientific research consists of obtaining information through empirical observations that can be used for the systematic development of logically related propositions attempting to establish causal relations among variables.*

The definition makes it increasingly clear that scientific fact gathering is different from other types in at least two important ways: (1) a reliance on certain methods of gathering information; (2) an orientation to the achievement of specific goals.

THE IMPORTANCE OF METHODS

Few have stated the need for methods more clearly and eloquently than Arnold M. Rose (1965, p. 11). As he pointed out, "Facts do not simply lie around waiting to be picked up. Facts must be carved out of the continuous web of ongoing reality, must be observed within a specified frame of reference, must be measured with precision, must be observed where they can be related to other relevant facts. All of this involves 'methods'." To familiarize you with the range of methods available to the social science investigator today is the primary reason for our writing this book.

THE IMPORTANCE OF SCIENTIFIC GOALS

To concentrate exclusively on methods ignores a second central aspect of scientific fact gathering. Our inquisitiveness must be characterized by more than technical precision; it must be focused toward the realization of specific objectives. We have tried to remain sensitive to this point throughout the text. Decisions about which research techniques to employ and about the sorts of usefulness the results of our studies can be expected to have must be made against a special background. That background must stress the goals of scientific inquiry. It is, therefore, advantageous to examine these goals more closely.

GOALS OF SCIENCE

Gouldner (1970, p. 491) observed that, "The nominal objective of any scientific enterprise is to extend knowledge of some part of the world." There is probably universal agreement with such a lofty pursuit. It would be difficult *not* to embrace it. But knowledge is not expanded easily. It is built up over time, through the painstaking interlocking of sometimes disparate sets of research findings. Only gradually do the bits and pieces of information generated by research combine to form that formidable phenomenon we call a "scientific fact." And only through the most disciplined thinking are these facts linked together in various abstractive ways. So, although it can more or less be taken for granted that we are all motivated by a desire to extend knowledge, most of the research actually undertaken is directed at achieving more specific objectives. As a rule, scientifically useful knowledge aims to be (1) *descriptive,* (2) *explanatory,* and (3) *predictive.* A fourth and admittedly controversial objective of research is to provide a sense of understanding or *awareness.*[1]

DESCRIPTIVE INFORMATION

Basic to all scientific inquiry is description, *a cataloging or classification of the range of elements seen as comprising a given subject matter domain.* Most investigators tend to regard description as the least difficult of all scientific activity. For that reason, there is frequently less attention devoted to discussions of the various facets of description than is warranted by its extreme importance to other scientific pursuits.

Actually, useful description is not as easily attained as it might at first appear. Two criteria must be met in any system of classification to render the descriptive information contained in it suitable for other scientific purposes. In practice, these can create some difficulty. Data that are classified must at some point be assessed on the basis of their (1) exhaustiveness and (2) mutual exclusiveness. Exhaustiveness has been achieved when all the elements requiring attention have been identified and a place has been found for each item in the system of classification. Mutual exclusiveness occurs when each item can be unambiguously placed in no more than one location in the system.

In addition to these elementary but stringent demands, descriptive information must parallel and contribute to the achievement of the remaining objectives of science. Unless descriptions are useful for *explanation, prediction, and awareness,* they are of little value *no matter how closely they approximate the demands of exhaustiveness and mutual exclusiveness.* Of course, as descriptive data move closer and closer to concerns such as explanation and prediction, more and more demands are made on them. Questions about the appropriateness of the methods used to obtain the data are raised, as are questions about the degree to which such findings address themselves to particular conceptual interests. It is not too far off the mark to contend that the respectability attached to a fact that is scientific stems as much from the critical scrutinizing it has undergone as from anything else. In subsequent chapters, questions pertaining to such matters as the *reliability* and *validity* of data will be raised.[2] These and other demands (to be discussed) that are made on descriptive information in scientific activity will serve to show that the path from a "fact" to a "scientific fact" is a deliberately treacherous one. Therefore, the researcher should be as familiar with how findings obtained from a given investigation can be utilized for other scientific pursuits as with the technical skills required to answer a particular empirical question.

SOME DIRECT USES OF DESCRIPTIVE INFORMATION

There are three ways in which descriptions are directly related to other scientific objectives:[3]

1. Descriptive information can focus directly on a theoretical point. In the social sciences, for example, data demonstrating the existence of the central conceptual interests of investigators are eagerly sought. The presence of norms, values, statuses, social class, role relations, institutions, sanctions, and so forth cannot be taken for granted but must be verified through empirical observations. When descriptions lead directly to such verifications, they are especially useful. Not only are investigators interested in determining the number of contexts within which such findings are applicable, they are interested in portraying them more accurately.

2. Descriptive information permits the extension of the concepts of a given theoretical perspective to findings that document predictions made in the theory. Much of social science research is not meant to expand on the knowledge of a system of thought so much as to point out that the ideas contained within its boundaries are capable of being used to say something about areas of social life not directly spoken to in the theory.

3. Descriptive information can highlight important methodological aspects of data compilation and interpretation. Frequently, the factual data gathered in social investigations are meant to increase our awareness of the relative accuracy of our measuring devices. "Knowing" that certain things have an influence on our behavior is not necessarily being able to test them empirically. With the increased precision that comes from more sensitive measuring devices, we are capable of focusing in a more sophisticated way on problems only casually treated previously in our scientific thinking. As a consequence, our ability to accumulate further knowledge is significantly broadened.

These uses of descriptive information are certainly sufficient to accord it a central place as a scientific objective. Especially in disciplines such as sociology where much of the research done is of an essentially descriptive nature at this stage of development, description is not to be slighted or dealt with casually. When investigators argue, as they frequently do, that there is too much description, they probably mean that there are too many factual data that do not lend themselves to other scientific goals. It is precisely because of the inattention paid by investigators to the overall relevance of their findings that description is often inadvertently relegated to a position of secondary importance in the conduct of social research. One way to elevate descriptive information to its proper place as a significant scientific objective is to stress the use of such data in the development of typologies.

TYPOLOGIES

To order information in such a way that data are more directly consonant with the other uses that must be made of them, investigators usually rely on one or another form of classification. Lazarsfeld and Barton (in Lazarsfeld and Rosenberg, 1955, p. 84) specified the basic requirements for the classification of open-end responses helpful in ordering data from other sources as well:

1. *Articulation:* The classification should proceed in steps from the general to the specific, so that the material can be examined either in terms of detailed categories or of broad groupings, whichever are more appropriate for a given purpose.

2. *Logical correctness:* In an articulated set of categories those on each step must be exhaustive and mutually exclusive. When an object is classified at the same time from more than one aspect, each aspect must have its own separate set of categories.

3. *Adaptation to the structure of the situation:* The classification should be based on a comprehensive outline of the situation as a whole—an outline containing the main elements and processes in the situation which it is important to distinguish for purposes of understanding, predicting, or policy-making.
4. *Adaptation to the respondent's frame of reference:* The classification should present as clearly as possible the respondent's own definition of the situation—his focus of attention, his categories of thought.

Probably the most significant form of classification insofar as building scientific theories is concerned is the construction of types and typologies. A type is a "selective, purposive simplification, constructed in terms of certain criteria and constituting a bridge between a theoretical approach on the one side and empirical observations on the other. A typology is a collection of types having certain characteristics in common but also sufficiently different to be distinguishable from one another" (Caldwell and Black, 1971, p. 66).

Numerous examples of typologies can be found in the social sciences along with discussions of the procedures for their construction. It is not our intention to go into detail about the relative merits and limitations of the various sorts of typologies that do exist. Neither do we want to examine the procedures for their development. Ferdinand's (1966, p. 42) observation that "there is no base other than intuition for accepting or rejecting them" is probably as accurate an assessment of our progress in this area as can be found. That should in no way detract, however, from the importance of classifying data in some typological form as an empirical step toward the building of theories.

It is clear, though, that there are types of factual information that can be of considerable value to social science research activities without having a direct bearing on the expansion of knowledge in these areas. Their place as descriptively useful information in a scientific sense is considerably more tenuous and uncertain than that. Still, because they either generate subsequent data that prove to be directly useful or facilitate the gathering of such data, these types of information should not go unheeded.

SOME INDIRECT USES OF DESCRIPTIVE INFORMATION

More is involved in the generation of scientifically acceptable information than deciding whether or not given data are useful. Facts do not always present themselves to us in ways that easily enable us to retain or discard them on these grounds. In at least two instances, facts should be seen as potentially relevant.

First, there are those pieces of information that are simply "interesting." A datum that has no directly forseeable use can be put aside for reflection at some future time. Sometimes the results of a particular study are sufficiently disquieting intellectually to command attention in a more systematic and controlled way. We are frequently reminded, in fact, that several far-reaching scientific discoveries have been made because investigators were unwilling to discard information that, at the time, had no demonstrable scientific utility. Unfortunately, there are no recognized or established procedures for knowing whether such facts will eventually prove to be of some significance in comprehending the world around us. Beyond the sensitivity and inquisitive luck associated with the creative talents of the researcher, we have little to guide us. Consequently, this type of information, regardless of its ultimate contribution to our research activities, is inevitably only indirectly related to the advance of knowledge.

Second, there are certain types of information that promote the promulgation of descriptive facts by facilitating the process of social research. One of the first things learned by those who conduct scientific investigations of persons' social lives is that there are numerous kinds of information which, once one is familiar with them, greatly enhance the data-gathering process. These are very important to research activities and can save considerable time and avoid costly mistakes. Two examples of this type of information are:

1. Knowledge of the respondents. Any information which alerts investigators to conditions that respondents take for granted as defining their conduct in given social contexts enables the investigator to design research in a more suitable fashion. This is especially so when dealing with groups of people whose very identity is, in significant measure, formed out of a mutually shared specialized knowledge. Such groupings may be either "conforming" or "deviant," highly organized or only informally bound together, easily recognized or known only among themselves. Criminals (especially those in institutions) and various occupational and professional groups such as doctors, lawyers, jazz musicians, teachers, and corporate executives, for example, relate to each other in special ways. More important from the standpoint of the researcher, they also relate to outsiders or others in special ways as well. Lawyers, for instance, who spend much time asking questions of one another are so attuned to question-asking behavior that a researcher who approaches them with questions of a hypothetical nature will more than likely end up serving as an adversary rather than as a scientific investigator.

In addition to providing valuable insights into ways of designing research to take advantage of those things respondents find important in their daily discourse, this type of information can be used to enhance the position of the investigator vis-à-vis the respondent. It does so, in effect, by letting others know that the investigator has more than a fleeting familiarity with their daily activities. Indications that one has "been around," "knows the ropes," or otherwise has a feel for those in a particular social context from which information is being extracted can contribute immeasurably to obtaining the types of data more directly linked to the scientific problems of central concern to the investigator. Time devoted to obtaining facts that will establish a researcher's credentials or in some way legitimize that person in the eyes of the respondent is seldom wasted.

2. Knowledge of the setting. Although it sounds sufficiently obvious to preclude mentioning, information about the settings in which people are found can be as relevant to the acquisition of data for scientific purposes as information about the respondents. Particularly when the setting is highly organized with its own internal bureaucratic and normative structure it is useful to know something about it in order to gain easier access to needed data. In another context, one of the authors has suggested several factors that are important in getting into organizations. They illustrate the sorts of advance knowledge that can save enormous amounts of time and energy (Champion, 1975: 124–26):

Does the researcher have a sponsoring agency to work through in contacting organizational officials? Studies which are funded and sponsored by such organizations as the Ford Foundation, the National Institutes of Mental Health, the U.S. Office of Education, the Russell Sage Foundation, and the National Opinion Research Center (the University of Chicago) seem more likely to be in the position of obtaining cooperation from target organizations than an unfunded study conducted by an obscure professor at a small college. The prestige of the sponsoring institution obviously lends credence and legitimacy to the study and carries significant weight in eliciting the cooperation of the organization to be studied.

Does the researcher have direct access to organizations through friends or professional associates? Often the influence of friends enables the researcher to enter organizations and obtain the required information. Much depends on the position of the friend in the organization and the influence of the professional associate.

What degree of formal approval is required for the project? Bargaining with hierarchies of authority in bureaucratic organizations is a delicate matter. Often, studies approved at one level in the hierarchy are subject to disapproval or rejection at a higher level. In a proposed study of the social organization of a bank, I was introduced to the bank president through an influential acquaintance. The basic elements of the study were explained to the president in detail; he seemed agreeable and gave me tentative assurance that the study would take place. He said that he would have to "touch base" with the personnel officer "just for the record" before final approval could be given. Two weeks later, the president informed me by letter that he did not feel that the study would be in the best interests of his bank.[2] No other explanation for the refusal was given.

Which type of approach is used by the researcher to contact organizations initially? There are an infinite number of approaches to be taken by investigators for contacting organizations. The researcher's "sales pitch" may emphasize the benefits which may potentially accrue to the organization. Or the investigator may ask the organization to "help" him in an altruistic sense. Students working on doctoral dissertations or master's theses (or other research papers at the undergraduate level) may facilitate the achievement of their research objectives by using this type of appeal.

What is the length and complexity of the proposed study? Does the researcher wish to study staff members on the job over time through nonparticipant observation? Does he plan to interrupt their daily work routine by asking them questions when he chooses and by otherwise interfering with the efficiency of the performance of their work operations? Does the researcher require repeated examination of the organization over time such as is common in before-and-after research designs? Will the employees be subject to social manipulation in some experimental fashion, or will their interpersonal relations with other staff be placed in a state of flux?

To what extent will the research instruments used be viewed as threatening to organizational officials? In a very real sense, tests and measures of individual, interpersonal, and organizational variables are *learning experiences* for employees as respondents. There is some justification for managers of organizations to believe that social scientists will raise questions which their staff members may not have considered relevant before their exposure to the research instruments. Specifically, questions pertaining to job satisfaction, the nature of supervisory practices, and the openness of communication channels might generate enough interest among employees so that they might begin asking the same kinds of questions of their own organizational officials.[3]

Record (1967:38) suggests that

the unease with which any organization, especially if it operates in sensitive or controversial fields, is likely to view research projects by outsiders is not hard to explain. Findings critical to the organization may cause it to lose face, force, friends, or funds. Critiques by noneducationists of school curricula and teaching methods, for example, particularly after Sputnik, roused public concern and drew a defensive reaction from the education establishment. A private social work agency lost contributions of volunteer services and money to a rival organization in a California community when the rival publicized a few critical comments contained in the report of an academic researcher who had received the cooperation of the first agency making the study.

How much anonymity is guaranteed the participating organization? Many organizations hesitate to become involved in social research because of the possibility that the researcher may reveal their identity and someone may turn an otherwise innocent piece of social research into a bad bit of publicity. In fact, some researchers, by virtue of their university or college affiliation and geographical location, may refer to a local company anonymously, still leaving no question in the minds of readers as to the identity of the company cited. Many investigators provide written guarantees to target organizations that all published accounts of information derived from them will be utilized in an anonymous fashion. References to these organizations will be vague, such as a "small metal-working firm in the Northwest" or "a small liberal arts college in the New England area."

Not every one of these factors will be operating in a given project, of course. Some will be extremely crucial in one study and have little or no bearing on another. Nevertheless, simply by taking into account these organizational features of the setting in which research is to be conducted, an investigator can save considerable time and needless bother.

EXPLANATION AS A SCIENTIFIC AIM

As we examine the various aims of scientific inquiry, it is evident that they are related in such a way that it is hazardous to stress one or another of them at the expense of the rest. There is a point beyond which descriptions, when placed in a certain context relative to each other, cease to be viewed as descriptions and become viewed as explanations. Explanations are difficult to distinguish from predictions under certain conditions. Still, there is a certain excitement that comes with being able to *explain* something. Our ability to interpret data so that some segments of our social lives are rendered more comprehensible is an especially rewarding undertaking. For some, it is the *sine qua non* of scientific activity; to explain is to expand our knowledge of the world around us. We, however, are inclined to draw back from such a compelling view of explanation, preferring to see it as one of several activities toward which our research activities are directed. A more balanced view can be obtained by looking at what is actually involved in explanation and considering how dependent it is upon other scientific pursuits.

Explanation has a number of meanings, so it is important that its scientific usage be clearly understood. To the scientific investigator, *explanation is achieved when relationships can be demonstrated between specified causes and effects*. Borrowing the words of Rescher, "In explaining a fact, we place this fact in the context of others in such a way that they illuminate its existence" (1970, p. 2). Fundamental to explanation, then, is its *relational* nature. There must be *both* facts to work with *and* some plausible conceptual mechanisms by which they can be linked together. When *explaining* facts, we must account for why they must be considered relative to one another; we must contribute to a *comprehension* of them by pointing out *why* this form of existence occurs.

That brings the task of explanation down to a dual set of problems. On the one hand, there is the problem of relating facts to one another. In sociology and kindred disciplines, the relational units of analysis are called *variables*. Variables have several qualities central to explanation. They represent features of social life that are *changeable*, such as age, sex, race, social class, education, occupation, and so on. Furthermore, they can assume *any one* of a designated set of values. Discerning regularities among them, when certain conditions have been met, increases an investigator's confidence in the possibility of making generalizations beyond the immediate data. Finally, they can be arranged in a certain *time order* with respect to each other, enhancing the prospects for asserting cause-effect relations among them. Much more needs to be said about demonstrations of causal relations among variables, and Chapter 2 explores these problems in detail.

On the other hand, there is the problem of the *comprehension* of the linkage among the relationships. This illumination of the existence of facts is, of course, the basic stuff of *theories* of social life. Again, the range of topics vital to an appreciation of the place of theories in the research process is sufficient to command the attention of an entire subsequent chapter (Chapter 3).

PREDICTION

Prediction is *an effort to foretell future occurrences on the basis of past information*. When that information takes the form of a scientific law, confirming a universal pattern of regularity in the relations among variables, predictions can be highly accurate. Because the social sciences have nothing approaching a law-like statement, predictions are correspondingly inaccurate. Consequently, there has been less attention to the formulation of protocols designed to handle prediction problems.

   Scientific predictions must be fashioned within the context of established theoretical premises. These, in turn, are encased in carefully etched descriptions. It would be presumptuous, indeed, to expect that prediction could develop independently of progress made in these related areas. No amount of rhetoric is going to alter the fact that sound prediction rests upon appropriate descriptive and explanatory knowledge. As a result, most of what follows is designed deliberately to enhance these latter scientific objectives under the assumption that such practices will invariably lead to greater predictive accuracy.

AWARENESS

In looking over the fruits of their labors, social scientists are seemingly forever frustrated by their inability to generate laws of social behavior. For some, that time will come only when social science disciplines fashion their research activities after those of the natural sciences. For others, that time will never come because it will never be possible to establish parameters that permit cloture about the enormous, ever-changing complexity of social life. Neither those who argue for the application of formal criteria of scientific adequacy along the lines of the natural sciences nor those who embrace a distinctively social science perspective with awareness as a major component have been able to mount a convincing position. As Gross (1959, pp. 531–32) observed:

> The first group is guided by the faith that a science of social be-
> havior is possible, a faith that is sustained despite the absence of any
> well-confirmed law of social behavior. The second group is guided
> by the faith that carefully interpreted descriptions of social events
> will provide a greater understanding than any attempt to imitate the
> methods of natural science.

There are, however, several disquieting features about the notion of
awareness or understanding as a goal of scientific research. As portrayed by its spokesmen, it is an especially *subjective* pursuit. Reynolds
(1971, p. 7), for example, suggests that ". . . a sense of understanding is
provided only when the causal mechanisms . . . have been fully
described. If a person feels ambiguous or uncertain about an explanation, it is because some part of the causal linkage has been omitted
from the description." Others, too, have stressed similar subjective
qualities (Stinchcombe, 1968; Gouldner, 1970). Gouldner (1970, p. 493)
strikes at the core of the position in distinguishing between
knowledge for information and knowledge for awareness. For him,
"Knowledge as awareness . . . has no existence apart from the persons
that pursue and express it."

Such an argument is compelling in its simplicity. Maintaining that
scientists are persons, aware of information and responding to it, advocates of this orientation more quickly make a distinction between
men and *information*. For us, such a distinction is not so easily drawn.
We fail to see how the concepts used by sociologists are actually set
apart or removed from them as men. It is perhaps the most elemental
observation in all of sociology that society, or science, or social behavior, or any other abstraction has no existence apart from those
sharing some mental view about it. Knowledge as information is no
different from knowledge as awareness in that regard. The formal criteria used to assess the scientific adequacy of data and ideas are as
much inside men, a part of them, as any other social facts. Besides, as
we have already pointed out, facts become scientific because of the
way they are used, not because we are aware that they exist.

To strike a delicate balance between the social world as we think we
see it and the social world as it actually is enables us to acquire the
sort of knowledge sought through our scientific research. As Rescher
(1970, p. 7) noted: "Scientific explanation is not a matter of a heuristic
design to make something *understood* by any person or group, but
the creation of a context-free body of machinery for rendering things

understandable.'' Pleas for a subjective awareness on the part of scientific investigators do not, as presently developed, lend much to such pursuits.

They fail to do so largely because they have not specified the precise mechanisms for moving from *subjective* to *objective* interpretations of data. All objectivity means is that there are preexisting criteria that have been agreed upon by those seeking answers to questions. Otherwise, it would not be possible for one investigator to verify the findings of another's research. A far greater measure of certainty that our interpretations are extrapersonal or objective comes from knowing that they proceed according to established and shared canons of scientific adequacy. Unless and until those persons promoting awareness as a primary thrust of the scientific enterprise can explicitly delineate how others besides the investigator are to be made aware of the investigator's own personal sense of understanding (Reynolds, 1971), their views will necessarily remain vague, ambiguous, and based on extralogical considerations (Gross, 1959).

We do not find much substance in such an alternative, and throughout the text we will caution against expecting much in the way of calculated scientific worth from research designs and procedures placing an undue amount of emphasis on awareness.

GOALS OF SCIENCE: AN OVERVIEW

In presenting the major objectives of science, we have emphasized the following points:

1.   The Interrelatedness of the Objectives of Science.   At times, it is very difficult to distinguish the precise point at which one discontinues the pursuit of one goal and undertakes the quest for another.

2.   The Mutual Importance of the Goals of Science.   One of the most important things to learn from an analysis of the goals of science is that they differ predominantly in terms of degree, not kind. Recognition of that makes it extremely hazardous to conjecture about which one is more important than the others. Little progress can be made in any long-range scientific inquiry without careful and unrelenting attention to all the goals. Attempts to place them in some hierarchy of importance are of dubious worth.

3.   The Contribution of Scientific Goals to Making the Social World Comprehensible.   Of all the things in science that are difficult to achieve, none poses such formidable problems as establishing scientific facts. Putting these facts together in an understandable manner is an extremely painstaking task.

We look askance at those who feel they already know so much about science that they need not be bothered with such mundane topics as what scientific activity is all about. Even the most sophisticated research scholars make glaring mistakes when their vanity pushes their humility aside. More often than not, that only leads to mistakes that could have been averted by a thoughtful review of the fundamental features of their undertaking.

TARGETS OF SOCIAL INVESTIGATIONS

Very early in the chapter it was noted that answers are not sought to scientific questions in a capricious, hit-or-miss fashion. There is an underlying integration to these inquiries that permits sustained concentration on selected features of human conduct. Most investigators find it useful to raise questions within the broadly established boundaries of their disciplines. This facilitates the achievement of scientific goals in three ways by (1) providing conceptual unity, (2) encouraging empirical persistence, and (3) promoting replication studies.

CONCEPTUAL UNITY

Political scientists, sociologists, psychologists, economists, anthropologists, and others all tend to orient themselves to the world around them in terms of certain conceptual interests shared with their colleagues. Sociologists, for example, are inclined toward assessments of human conduct within the context of the ways in which people interact. Status, role, institution, norms, sanction, community, stratification, and complex organization represent but a few of the dominant conceptual concerns explored by sociologists. Hosts of variables have been identified and examined to ascertain the extent to which our conduct is shaped by relations among them. Gradually, we are coming to know more of the impact of social factors on our lives.

By maintaining a sharp sensitivity to unexamined or insufficiently tested dimensions of these shared perspectives, investigators can be more confident that their questioning will have a more direct and foreseeable impact on the accumulation of scientific knowledge.

All of this is not to say that there are no differences among social scientists in given disciplines in focusing on topics exposed for empirical resolution by their perspective. Indeed, quite the contrary is true; differences abound. To be fully cognizant of the reasons particular topics are approached in certain ways and given special priorities in the work of given investigators, it is necessary to be aware of these differences in orientations (Cole, 1972).

EMPIRICAL PERSISTENCE

To the extent that it can be identified even in the broadest sense, conceptual unity provides the basis for persistent empirical attention to problems that are agreed upon as having scientific utility. Unfortunately, there is all too little empirical persistence evident in the research activities of social scientists. Recurrent pleas to adhere more firmly to "intellectual craftsmanship" usually stress the need for closer scrutiny over longer periods of time to a manageable set of research topics (Feldman, 1971; Merton, 1957; Mills, 1959; Reiss, 1969).

Where this advice has been heeded, and it all too infrequently has been, productive results have been obtained. A case in point is found in examining the studies that have inquired into the dynamics of the social stratification system. Not only have we come to know more about the existence of vertical and horizontal dimensions of social stratification, we have been able to locate important areas for continuing research through a conceptual refinement of our knowledge. Concepts such as situs, which focus on the horizontal clustering of occupations, have permitted a much closer look at some important sociological problems (Pavalko, 1971, pp. 140–55).

REPLICATION

The greater the degree of conceptual unity and empirical persistence, the greater the likelihood that replication studies will command a more prominent place as worthwhile scientific pursuits. Except for research on a few selected topics such as delinquency, community power, voluntary associations, small groups, and so forth, most of which constitute continuity studies rather than strict replications, little has been done with this type of investigation. Sociologists seem to have a penchant for constantly breaking new ground, relegating replication studies to a less prestigious position. There may be plausible reasons for this in certain areas where, for example, there are few noteworthy studies to replicate. Similarly, data gathering and analysis techniques may have progressed rapidly, making replications less valuable. But where theoretical and methodological considerations permit, more thought should be given to the contributions that can be made through such studies.

ETHICAL ISSUES IN SOCIAL RESEARCH

Objectivity on the part of the social investigator is a necessary corollary to acceptable research, but the difficulties encountered in achieving it are many. Not only are there problems in regulating the personal biases of the investigator, some of which we have alluded to, there are value-related problems that arise from the social context within which research occurs. Drawing a sharp and easily recognizable line between objectivity and ethics is, in the final analysis, very difficult. Our intent in doing so here is to emphasize some problems endemic to the inquisitiveness of social scientists that are not usually considered when the focus of attention is on objectivity. Whereas objectivity alerts us to the values held by an investigator in relation to his *subject matter,* ethics spotlights an investigator's relations with other participants in the research process. As Goldner (1967, p. 264) suggests, "Ethics, then, is an especially interpersonal concept."

More specifically, *issues of ethics are those that arise out of the social context in which research occurs.* Sensitivity to the possibility of these intrusions on the acceptability of scientific information is vital to the overall quality of investigations in the social and behavioral sciences. There are at least four discernible types of interpersonal relations that pose potential ethical dilemmas: (1) relations with those sponsoring the research, (2) relations with those permitting or supporting access to sources of data (whether from documents or respondents), (3) relations with other investigators connected with the project, and (4) relations with the research subjects themselves.

RESEARCH SPONSORSHIP

The issue of research sponsorship is faced by those whose research depends on some form of funding. Investigations by students and the relatively small, independently pursued projects frequently engaged in by social scientists are, when unfunded, not subject to such concerns.

When research is funded, it is in the form of either a contract or a grant. Contracted research specifies the nature of the work to be done, the time period for its completion, and what can be done with the findings by an investigator. Furthermore, contracting agencies advertise their projects, directly soliciting interested parties. Finally, contract research usually centers about topics of current interest requiring immediate information to solve practical problems. Given the highly structured nature of contract research and the explicitly stated expectations of the agencies, the primary ethical question posed is the initial one of whether the investigator wants to operate within the confines of such restrictions. Researchers must answer to their own satisfaction ahead of time the question of whether they are willing to withhold findings of interest to the scientific community. Controls exercised by the contracting agency do not always permit the free and uninhibited publication of research findings. Investigators under contract must be aware that the scientifically useful features of their work may be subservient to the policy interests of the contracting agency. That does not mean that plausible reasons cannot be found by social science researchers to conduct contract research. Indeed, as Horowitz (in Denzin, 1970a) acknowledges in assessing the reasons for the involvement of social scientists in Project Camelot, an ill-fated investigation into social and political change of Chile sponsored by the United States Army, there is a variety of reasons for such involvement.

Research funded through grants has many features not found in contracted projects. First, the expression of interest is initiated by the investigator rather than the agencies. Second, problems to be investigated are not so specifically delineated as they are in contract research. Granting agencies such as the National Science Foundation, the Department of Health, Education and Welfare, the National Institutes of Mental Health, and so on are prone to state their objectives in the broadest possible way to attract a wide range of scholarly interests. Finally, while requesting acknowledgments for financial support, granting agencies do not prohibit publication of the results for consumption by the scientific community. For these reasons, such agencies are usually accorded a higher priority by scientific investigators.

For some, the difference between contracts and grants is seen as a difference between applied and pure research. We think that time-worn distinction serves more to detract from the central issues than to illuminate them. That is owing, in part, to the fact that the distinction rests on the motivations of the investigators and the agencies. Nagi and Corwin (1972, p. 6) argue that "more fundamental distinctions between basic and applied research can be made when criteria are based on the types of knowledge produced rather than on the researcher's values and attitudes or the sponsor's mission." They indicate that the manner in which the data are classified and the type of question being asked determine whether the research is of one type or the other. Their views are consistent with our own in maintaining that it is the *way* data are used rather than the labels attached to data *after* they have been used that determines whether they are pure or applied.

APPROVAL OF SPONSORS

Anyone who has gone through the process of obtaining approval from someone to carry out research will be quick to acknowledge that it is imperative to establish effective working relations with those in positions to permit or deny access to data. Whether the investigator is requesting time with individuals from whom to elicit information through questionnaires, interviews, or observation or is seeking access to files and documents containing the desired data, certain ground rules usually have to be understood in advance. There will have to be understanding about at least the following points:

1. **The degree of anonymity to be accorded to sponsor needs to be determined.**   Some sources do not mind being identified; others do. In either case, the way in which the sponsor is to be identified in published results should be understood in advance. Investigators usually are as vague as possible about their sources of data. Information taken from schools or courts or house-to-house surveys in cities elusively identified as being located in a particular region of the country can be found in great abundance in sociological journals and books. Such considerable caution is not necessarily warranted. Only that degree of anonymity felt to be appropriate by the sponsor and the researcher is required. There are no hard and fast rules for determining that, of course. But that does not alter the fact that it is a matter which must, in each research project where it arises, be settled in a mutually understood way.

2. **Procedures for handling data in ways to assure the degree of anonymity guaranteed must be broadly stated.**   Usually this involves a statement to the effect that the data will be coded and tabulated in such a fashion that given individuals and/or situations will not be identifiable.

3. **Decisions must be made about indicating to the sponsor the nature of the project.**   As a rule, there is no need to go into the particular scientific reasons for wanting to get the kinds of information one is after. Saying something simple and straightforward and using terminology the sponsor understands, especially if the person is not familiar with the technical jargon used to discuss the problem with one's scientific colleagues, can do much to answer the almost inevitable question: Why is this being done? As the debate on disguised observation in sociological research suggests, these questions are not resolved simply (Erikson, 1967; Denzin, 1968).

4. **It is important to know whether and in what form findings from the study will be available.**   As with the other points listed above,

there are numerous ways to handle this problem. In part, its resolution is closely related to the types of decisions that have been reached in connection with other facets of obtaining approval to carry out a project. Where it is feasible and does not violate any guarantees of confidentiality between investigators and other participants in the process, a final draft of a completed research project should be made available to those granting original access to the information.

RELATIONS WITH OTHER INVESTIGATORS

Among the most neglected topics in the ethics of social research is that covering the conduct of investigators in a project vis-à-vis one another. We suspect the lack of attention is attributable in part to the fact that many social scientists do not fully appreciate the total range of interpersonal relations having an impact on their activities. Insofar as it can be maintained that research is not completed until findings have been published (or at least submitted) for appraisal by one's colleagues, interpersonal factors effecting the flow of information toward this can be considered ethical in nature.

When individuals are pursuing problems independently, say out of some personal inquisitiveness or to satisfy course requirements or complete thesis or dissertation topics, these issues are not present. Increasingly, though, the active researcher finds that the conduct of scientific inquiry takes place with the joint collaboration of others (Nagi and Corwin, 1972). In such a context, certain questions must be resolved to permit more systematic attention to the problem at hand. Who has the right to use the data and for what purpose? In what manner are the findings to be published as articles or books? Where are the findings to be published? Who will assume what responsibilities in preparing the materials for publication? In what order are collaborators to be identified? These are examples of the kinds of problems that require early attention. Many of them can be, and frequently are, avoided by the formal designation of each investigator according to the tasks assumed. That is, they are identified as "principal investigator," "research associate," "statistical analyst," "consultant," "research assistant," and so on.

Even with these status distinctions, ambiguities arise. All that can be done as a rule is to be as sensitive as possible to potential interpersonal difficulties such as these in advance. There are no firmly entrenched rules for their resolution. Consequently, it is hazardous to take it for granted that all the participants in a project share the same views about how to handle them. It is, at the same time, conjectural to assume that each of the investigators attaches the same priorities to each of the questions or, for that matter, is equally aware that there are certain matters to be agreed to. Only when such ambiguities have been addressed and clarified very early can a minimum amount of friction be expected among joint collaborators.

RELATIONS WITH SUBJECTS

Of all the ethical issues, there has undoubtedly been more concern for the protection of subjects than for the others. Over the years, professional associations such as the American Sociological Association and the American Psychological Association have devised codes of ethics to govern obtaining information from individuals. Granting agencies, too, expect explicit statements and documents in this regard from investigators prior to approving studies. In fact, most universities and many departments in which research involving human subjects is conducted have committees that review procedures to safeguard against any intrusions on personal privacy or inflicting any physical or mental harm. Cautious researchers will invariably want to check on the rules of their respective organizations and incorporate them as a routine feature of the initial planning of an investigation.

MISCONCEPTIONS ABOUT SOCIAL RESEARCH

It should be clear that scientific research embraces a broader spectrum of considerations than mere fact gathering. The keen and perceptive reader will, in addition, be struck by the fact that there were some things we have *not* discussed and others that received but a casual glance. That is because there are several widely held notions about research that have little credibility. To place these misconceptions in sharper relief against the views espoused so far, it is advantageous to examine some of the more prominent and persistent ones briefly. Because they sometimes serve to divert attention away from the excitement of doing research, they need to be properly understood. Their continued influence can only distract those who might otherwise be motivated to participate actively in the accumulation of scientific knowledge. Those selected for discussion include:

   1. The misconception that one is either a theorist or a methodologist. Social scientists are frequently divided into two groups— those who sit in their offices and think about the world outside and those who go out and gather the facts. C. Wright Mills (1959) depicted these disparate activities as "grand theory" and "abstracted empiricism." Such gross oversimplifications fail to do justice either to the process of gathering data or to thinking about data. Sound social research demands that an investigator have a working familiarity with both. It is beside the point whether given scholars have more of an affinity for one than the other of these activities. What is important is the realization that neither can the appropriate methods be selected nor the goals of science achieved unless an investigator has a working familiarity with each range of concerns.

Not only does this misconception blur the importance of the interrelatedness of theoretical and methodological problems, it narrows the range of informational items that come to be viewed as facts. As a result, information that could be of some promise in resolving problems is frequently ignored. Only recently has there been much sustained interest in secondary analysis and the use of documents as important sources of scientific data, for example. Also, suprisingly few investigators have viewed journal articles as data which, when examined according to carefully devised coding and classificatory procedures, yield valuable insights into the scientific adequacy of our knowledge (Feldman, 1971).

2. The misconception that one is either a teacher or a researcher. It is the exceptional person who is capable of moving easily from the demanding atmosphere of the classroom to the hectic pace of day-to-day research activity. Most of us prefer to give priority to one or the other during any given period of time. Most of us are probably a little better at one of them because we feel more comfortable engaged in that type of activity. To accept those inclinations is not to maintain that a choice must be made between being a teacher or a researcher, however. As with the previous misconception, such a stance seriously distorts what scientific inquiry actually entails.

Once it is realized that data can include more than responses to questionnaire and interview questions or various types of observational conclusions, it is easy to envision ways in which the various kinds of documents and journal articles used by most teachers in their lecture or seminar preparations can be handled in scientifically useful ways. The best teachers are always raising questions and sorting through information in ways designed to expand on the knowledge of the subject matter being considered. By the same token, the best researchers are constantly seeking ways to communicate to others the ways in which data extend our comprehension of social life.

3. The misconception that research is either basic or applied. None of the preconceived ideas dismissed in this section will be harder to dispel than the one maintaining that the only justifiable and worthwhile research for social scientists to involve themselves in is basic. Investigations of an applied nature are by and large relegated to a position of lesser importance. One of the factors contributing to the perpetuation of this distinction is the set of definitions given to these activities by the National Science Foundation. According to that agency (Vollmer, 1972, p. 67), basic research includes "original investigations for the advancement of knowledge that does not have specific objectives to answer problems of sponsoring agencies or companies, although these investigations may be in fields of present or potential interest to the sponsoring organization." Applied investigations constitute "research activities on problems posed by sponsoring agencies or companies for the purpose of contributing to the solution of these problems."

In a sense, Vollmer's distinction parallels an earlier one made in this chapter between grant or contract research funds. Both, however, take as their point of departure the interest of the sponsor (Vollmer, 1972). Neither the intent of the investigator nor the nature of the results obtained is seen as having any direct bearing on the matter. Consequently, an insufficient amount of attention is paid to the fact that the way data are *used* has as much bearing on whether they are basic or applied as the reasons for their having been accumulated in the first place. In the final analysis, what is important is what has been done with the findings. There is little, if any, hard evidence to permit any more than the most speculative conclusions about the relative contributions made by basic or applied research findings to the expansion of scientific knowledge.

4. The misconception that the social sciences are inherently more difficult than other sciences. The argument is frequently advanced that research in the social sciences is much more difficult than in other sciences because human behavior is so complex. Tullock (1966), however, points to several flaws in such reasoning. First, he maintains that such a posture is basically evidence of an ignorance of research in other fields. Second, he argues, any attempt to claim that the social sciences must resort to different methods than others clouds what is meant by methods. Insofar as it means "making the best possible use of man's mental endowments" (Tullock, 1966, p. 166), it applies to *all* scientific activity. To the extent that it means that the methods of one discipline do not necessarily lend themselves to use in another, there are variations in other fields as well as in the social sciences. As Tullock (1966, p. 167) correctly observes, close scrutiny of what investigators are actually doing in various disciplines will erase any doubts that there is a single "scientific method" employed by them. As a discipline matures, it is increasingly likely that its techniques of data gathering will be less and less applicable to others.

Finally, Tullock (1966, pp. 167–68) argues that there is little to commend a position which grants *special* difficulty to the social sciences because the subject matter is people. As he puts it, "Every branch of science deals with some special class of phenomena; that is how we divide the general field of human knowledge into branches. In each case the special phenomena under investigation present special problems which are met nowhere else."

It is easy to argue along with Tullock that those who embrace this misconception need to acquire a healthier skepticism about the inherent difficulties associated with social science research activities. We have tried to take a step in this direction by viewing several problems in the context of ethical issues. Whether that or some other way of viewing them is endorsed, it is clear that serious questions can be raised about the degree to which scientific inquiry poses more insurmountable problems when related to social life than are raised anywhere else.

SOME CONCLUDING REMARKS

In addressing attention to the five broadly related topics outlined in the introductory section to this chapter, we have frequently returned to the observation that doing scientific research is neither as simple as gathering facts nor limited to learning techniques to facilitate such activity. At the same time, research is not so difficult that it can be grasped by only a selected few. Not everyone will obtain the same intrinsic satisfaction from engaging in scientific investigations, of course. For some it will always prove challenging and stimulating, even if demanding; for others it will necessarily be laborious and occasionally even tedious. There is no reason for anyone to be frightened away from comprehending at least the basic dimensions of scientific inquiry, regardless of how they react to it later.

In the remaining chapters of this section, our focus will be on several topics only briefly mentioned so far. Chapter 2 looks closely at the problem of causes. There follows in Chapter 3 a careful consideration of the place of theory in social research. And in Chapter 4, we will pinpoint some major research designs used in the accumulation of data.

SOME QUESTIONS FOR REVIEW

1. What is the difference between scientific inquiry and questions asked in normal social discourse? Illustrate with several examples.

2. Beyond inquisitiveness, what are the characteristics of scientific research.

3. Discuss both the direct and indirect uses of descriptive information in scientific research.

4. Of what value are typologies in achieving the goals of science?

5. Carefully explain the difference between scientific and other forms of explanation. What are the dual problems involved in the task of explanation?

6. Discuss the pros and cons of awareness as a scientific goal. Suggest ways to go about resolving the issues presented in the controversy.

7. Identify and discuss the targets of social research.

8. What is meant by an ethical issue? Distinguish between ethics and objectivity in social research. Why is such a distinction important?

9. Discuss the types of interpersonal relations that pose potential ethical dilemmas.

10. Identify the various ways in which social research is misconceptualized. Find examples from the literature in the social sciences illustrating each misconception. How can they be overcome?

FOOTNOTES

1. Reynolds (1971, pp. 4–9) uses the term typologies rather than descriptions and includes control as a goal of scientific knowledge.
2. See Chapter 7 for a discussion of these problems.
3. See Kuhn (1962) for a somewhat different statement of these points. We have deliberately avoided casting these problems in the context of what he calls "normal science."

BIBLIOGRAPHY

Blalock, Hubert M. *Theory Construction: From Verbal To Mathematical Formulations.* Englewood Cliffs, N.J.: Prentice-Hall, 1969.

Buckley, Walter. *Sociology and Modern Systems Theory.* Englewood Cliffs, N.J.: Prentice-Hall, 1967.

Caldwell, Robert G. and James A. Black. *Juvenile Delinquency.* New York: Ronald Press, 1971.

Champion, Dean J. *The Sociology of Organizations.* N.Y.: McGraw-Hill, 1975.

Cohen, Morris R., and Ernest Nagel. *An Introduction To Logic and Scientific Method.* New York: Harcourt, Brace, 1934.

Cole, Stephen. *The Sociological Method.* Chicago: Markham Publishing Co., 1972.

Denzin, Norman K. "On the Ethics of Disguised Observation," *Social Problems* 15 (1968): 502–506.

———. *Sociological Methods: A Source-Book.* Chicago: Aldine, 1970(a).

———. *The Research Act: A Theoretical Introduction to Sociological Methods.* Chicago: Aldine, 1970(b).

Erikson, Kai T. "A Comment on Disguised Observation in Sociology," *Social Problems* 14 (1967): 366–73.

Feldman, Kenneth. "Using the Work of Others: Some Observations on Reviewing and Integrating," *Sociology of Education* 44 (1971): 86–102.

Ferdinand, Theodore N. *Typologies of Delinquency.* New York: Random House, 1966.

Goldner, Fred H. "Role Emergence and the Ethics of Ambiguity." In *Ethics, Politics, and Social Research,* edited by Gideon Sjoberg. Cambridge, Mass.: Schenkman Publishing, 1967.

Gorden, Raymond L. *Interviewing: Strategy, Techniques, and Tactics.* Homewood, Ill.: Dorsey Press, 1969.

Gouldner, Alvin. *The Coming Crisis of Western Sociology.* New York: Basic Books, 1970.

Gross, Llewellyn. "Theory Construction in Sociology." In *Symposium on Sociological Theory,* edited by Llewellyn Gross. Evanston, Ill.: Row, Peterson, 1959.

Hill, Karl, ed. *The Management of Scientists.* Boston: Beacon Press, 1963.

Horowitz, Irving Louis. "The Life and Death of Project Camelot." In *Sociological Methods: A Sourcebook,* edited by Norman K. Denzin. Chicago: Aldine, 1970(a).

Johnson, Harry M. *Systematic Sociology.* New York: Harcourt, Brace, and World, 1960.

Kerlinger, Fred. *Foundations of Behavioral Research.* New York: Holt, Rinehart, and Winston, 1965.

Kuhn, Thomas S. *The Structure of Scientific Revolutions.* Chicago: University of Chicago Press, 1962.

Lazarsfeld, Paul. *Qualitative Analysis: Historical and Critical Essays.* Boston: Allyn and Bacon, 1972.

Lazarsfeld, Paul, and Morris Rosenberg, eds. *The Language Of Social Research.* New York: Free Press, 1955.

McCain, Garvin, and Erwin M. Segal. *The Game of Science.* Belmont, Cal.; Brooks/Cole Publishing, 1969.

McCall, George, and J. L. Simmons, eds. *Issues In Participant Observation.* Reading, Mass.: Addison-Wesley, 1969.

McCormick, Thomas C., and Roy G. Francis. *Methods of Research in the Behavioral Sciences.* New York: Harper, 1958.

Merton, Robert K. *Social Theory and Social Structure.* Rev. and enlarged ed. New York: Free Press, 1957.

Miller, S. M. "The Participant Observer and 'Over-Rapport'," *American Sociological Review* 17 (1952): pp. 97–99.

Mills, C. Wright. *The Sociological Imagination.* New York: Grove Press, 1959.

Nagi, Saad Z., and Ronald G. Corwin. *The Social Context of Research.* New York: John Wiley, 1972.

Pavalko, Ronald M. *Sociology of Occupations and Professions.* Itasca, Ill.: F. E. Peacock, 1971.

Phillips, Bernard S. *Social Research: Strategy and Tactics.* 2nd ed. New York: MacMillan, 1971.

Record, Jane C. "The Research Institute and the Pressure Group." In Gideon Sjoberg's (ed.) *Ethics, Politics, and Social Research.* Cambridge, Mass.: Schenkman, 1967.

Reiss, Albert J., Jr. "Whither the Craft," *Sociological Inquiry* 39 (1969): 149–54.

Rescher, Nicholas. *Scientific Explanation.* New York: Free Press, 1970.

Reynolds, Paul Davidson. *A Primer in Theory Construction.* Indianapolis: Bobbs-Merrill, 1971.

Rose, Arnold M. *Sociology: The Study of Human Relations.* New York: Alfred A. Knopf, 1965.

Selltiz, Claire; Marie Johoda; Morton Deutsch; and Stuart W. Cook. *Research Methods in Social Relations.* Rev. ed. New York: Henry Holt, 1959.

Sjoberg, Gideon, ed. *Ethics, Politics, and Social Research.* Cambridge, Mass.: Schenkman, 1967.

Stein, Maurice, and Arthur Vidich, eds. *Sociology on Trial.* Englewood Cliffs, N.J.: Prentice-Hall, 1963.

Stinchcombe, Arthur L. *Constructing Social Theory.* New York: Harcourt, Brace, Jovanovich, 1968.

Tullock, Gordon. *The Organization of Inquiry.* Durham, N.C.: Duke University Press, 1966.

Vollmer, Howard M. "Basic and Applied Research." In *The Social Context of Research,* edited by Nagi and Corwin. New York: Wiley-Interscience, 1972.

Willer, Judith. *The Social Determination of Knowledge.* Englewood Cliffs, N.J.: Prentice-Hall, 1971.

CHAPTER 2
CAUSATION

It is one thing to maintain that the thrust of scientific activity is toward the attainment of description, explanation, and prediction. It is quite another to establish causal relations among variables. And it is yet another problem to develop theoretical schemes made up of propositional statements of relations among variables. Although the dual problems of determining causes and developing theories are intimately bound together in the long run, each necessitates separate attention. In this chapter, our focus will be on several topics related to the problem of causation. Included among the issues raised are:

1. The nature of causation.
2. Characteristics of variables.
3. Criteria for establishing causation.
4. The problem of spuriousness.
5. Alternative strategies for assessing causes.
6. Problems of cross-cultural research.

THE NATURE OF CAUSATION

When we say that one variable, A, is the cause of another, B, what do we mean by our statement? That B could not have taken place without A? That B can be expected invariably to follow A? That A is the only cause of B? Or do we mean that A causes B but is one of several causes? That B is quite likely to occur after A but not invariably so? These and other questions make it imperative to arrive at a clear conceptualization of the concept "cause" at the very outset.

We will forego the consternation and bewilderment that usually accompany arguments over what the concept of cause means from various perspectives, whether social science research activity should ever be oriented toward a search for causes, and so forth.[1] Suffice it to say that a major driving force behind nearly all of our research activity is the hope of locating factors that make a difference or have more of an impact on the behavior being examined than other factors. It is that force, spoken or unspoken, usually referred to as causal analysis, that sparks the inquisitiveness so essential to the research enterprise.

Causation is best viewed in probabilistic terms. That is, *the likelihood of a given event or occurrence taking place will depend on the likelihood that other specified conditions are present or have occurred to some degree.* Taken to the bottom line, research inquiring into the causes of social behavior begins with finding variables and designing ways to examine if and in what ways they are related. The task begins with acquiring a working familiarity with the nature of variables. For as we shall see, some caution must be exercised in pinpointing certain features of variables in order to assess their relations to one another.

VARIABLES

At the very heart of social research are variables. Variables can be defined as *relational units of analysis that can assume any one of a number of designated sets of values.* Causal analysis requires that more be taken into account about variables than their quality of variance. To understand the central place of variables in causal analysis, several of their relational features need to be examined. Among the many distinctions utilized by scientific investigators, the following emerge as the most essential for our purposes: (1) their discrete or continuous quality, (2) their time order, and (3) the forms by which relations among variables can be assessed.

DISCRETE AND CONTINUOUS VARIABLES

To conceptualize a variable as *discrete* is to view it as being made up of parts or categories that are separate and distinct. Age, at least as it is used most of the time, is a discrete variable. No matter how one chooses to divide it, each of the various categories comprising the variable age are separate and distinct from the rest. Sex, too, is such a variable. Years of education, years of employment, and so on are also variables. In fact, most social science research contains at least some variables that are treated as though they were comprised of discrete categories.

There is no rule that says that a variable is irrefutably discrete. Its quality of discreteness is *imposed* by the investigator. One can rely on tradition, common sense, or whatever to conceive of a variable in such a manner. But it would certainly be erroneous to assume that it was a preestablished condition. As with all scientific activity, it is a fact carved out of reality and shaped to suit the needs of the investigator. That makes it all the more imperative that the investigator be imbued with the scientific nature of the research enterprise.

Variables can also be classified as *continuous*. When we wish to treat a variable in this manner, we treat it as though there were no clear demarcation among its categories. One way to think of continuous variables is in terms, again, of the variable age. We sometimes like to talk about "growing older" or "becoming more mature." Each is a way of looking at age, but each tends to portray the variable as a continuing process. There are no precise or easily distinguishable boundaries between one age category and the next. Age, when viewed from such a vantage point, becomes a continuous variable. By the same token, sex, when used in a way that means something other than being a male or a female, can be a continuous variable. Take, for example, the quality of "sexiness" of "sex appeal." This is not a quality one either has or does not have. Rather, it is possessed in varying degrees. There is no explicit cutoff point for examining "sex appeal." Its various components tend to mesh together into some indistinguishable, unified web.

Nothing keeps an investigator from taking a variable previously conceptualized as discrete and treating it as continuous. In delinquency research, for example, some researchers have chosen to conceptualize delinquency as a continuous variable rather than as a discrete one. An individual's conduct is thus seen as being either more or less delinquent than someone else's.

Whether a variable is treated as discrete or continuous has some bearing on the way research can be designed to test its causal significance with respect to other variables. Not only must statistical procedures and research strategies be formulated to accommodate the variables, studies must be designed which gather data in accordance with the discrete or continuous qualities. It is usually more difficult to obtain measures in quantitative terms of continuous variables than of discrete variables. It is because of this that we find in most of the research undertaken by social scientists that an individual is either delinquent or nondelinquent, married or single, employed or unemployed, has completed certain levels of educational attainment or has not, and so on. These contingencies, in turn, play heavily into any assessment of the overall scientific utility of data compiled relating to a given set of variables.

TIME ORDER

In addition to being viewed as discrete or continuous, variables are characterized according to their relation to one another in time. Such a distinction enables us to specify variables as being *independent, dependent,* and *intervening.* They can be understood only in relation to one another. Independent variables are those that affect other variables but may have no relation to one another. One's age, sex, and race may influence the likelihood of engaging in certain other behavior patterns. Who marries whom, to use a simple illustration, is highly dependent upon these factors. People of approximately the same age, opposite sex, and same race, tend to marry one another. But age is not dependent upon race or sex, nor race upon sex or age, nor sex upon age or race. They are variables that are independent of one another but related to specified *dependent* variables, in this case, marriage.

Dependent variables are those affected by independent variables. That is, they will vary according to variations in our independent variables. As one gets older, it is less likely that one will marry. Males are far less likely to marry other males than they are females. And whites are far more likely to marry whites and blacks, blacks. Marriage is, then, portrayed in these examples as a dependent variable.

As with the distinction between discrete and continuous variables, the distinction between independent and dependent variables is a choice made by the investigator. At least this is so insofar as there is no violation of the natural time-order relations between them. Variables can be independent in one study and dependent in another.

Intervening variables are, just as the term indicates, those that lie between independent and dependent variables in time. To illustrate how intervening variables operate, suppose we want to ascertain the relationship between a person's sex and the severity of sentences imposed by a judge. A fairly widespread view is that females tend to receive more lenient sentences than males simply because they are females. And suppose that, in fact, upon initial examination of data collected to answer the question, there is strong support for such a view. But one's knowledge of the factors influencing a judge's sentencing practices point to the possibility that sentencing severity is rather strongly influenced by the defendant's prior criminal convictions and the number of offenses with which he or she is charged currently. Prior criminal convictions and number of offenses with which currently charged (bills of indictment) are *intervening* variables. They may help account for the original relationship between sex and sentencing severity. Consequently, to appreciate whether females are treated more or less leniently by judges than are males, data pertaining to these intervening variables must be obtained and the original relationship examined in light of them (see Figure 2-1).

One of several possible things can occur as intervening variables are introduced into the picture. First, the original relationship between *A* and *B* might remain the same. Second, the original relationship may disappear. Finally, the original relationship between the independent and dependent variables may be reduced but not entirely eliminated.

Intricate procedures and vocabularies have been developed to assess the impact of adding additional variables to the analysis of two-variable relations (Hyman, 1955; Lazarsfeld and Rosenberg, 1962; and Rosenberg, 1968). At this point it is probably more important to become familiar with the basic time-order distinctions denoted by the

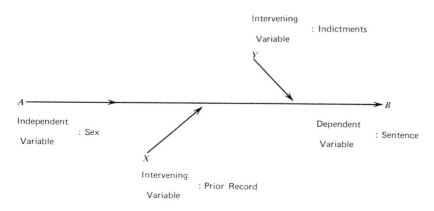

Figure 2-1.

terms independent, intervening, and dependent than to tackle these rather complicated dimensions of the problem.

FORMS FOR ASSESSING RELATIONS AMONG VARIABLES

As if thinking about variables in terms of their discrete or continuous qualities and their time order were not enough, there is a further problem for investigators to consider. It is one having to do with the *form* the relationship is to take. In other words, just *how* are the variables related? It will not do to say simply that variable *A* is related to variable *B*. That tells us very little. Does that mean that as *A* changes, a change can be expected in *B*? If so, what kind of change can be expected? Will *B* increase as *A* increases? Will it decrease? Will it increase for a time, then decrease? Will *B* increase or decrease in the same proportion to increases or decreases in *A*? Or will *B* change more rapidly than *A*?

Orienting ourselves to the *form* the relationships among variables take will bring us closer to providing answers to questions such as these. Hage (1972) delineates three forms that the relations can assume: (1) linear form; (2) curvilinear form; and (3) power function form.

When the relationship between variables is conceived of as linear by investigators, it means that as variable *A* changes, there will be a corresponding change in variable *B*. A *positive linear* relationship occurs when an increase in *A* "causes" an increase in *B*. A *negative linear* relationship is found when a *decrease* in *A* is followed by a corresponding increase in *B* (see Figure 2-2).

The relationship between *A* and *B* is considered *curvilinear* when *B* changes in a direction corresponding to changes in *A* up to a certain

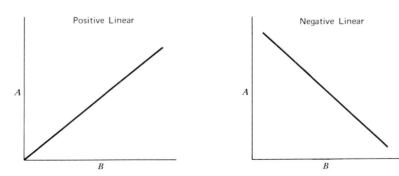

Figure 2-2.   Linear relations.

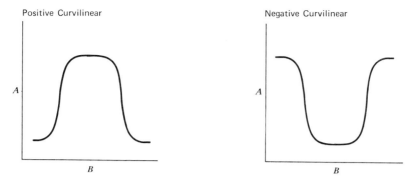

Figure 2-3.   Curvilinear relations.

point, then reverses itself. Curvilinear relations are positive when, as *A* increases, *B* increases up to a point and then begins to decrease. They are negative when the opposite occurs, i.e., *A* decreases, *B* decreases for a time, then begins to *increase* (see Figure 2-3).

When relationships are conceptualized as power functions, it points to the fact that changes in one variable produce changes in the second variable at an accelerated rate (see Figure 2-4).

Paying attention to the form of the relationship between variables enables investigators to move a considerable distance beyond mere demonstrations of association. Only as it becomes possible to say something about the *form* of the linkage in one or the other of the above ways, is it feasible to comprehend just what the relationship means.

Coming to grips with the nature of variables is only the beginning of the quest for causes. An understanding of the variables' various

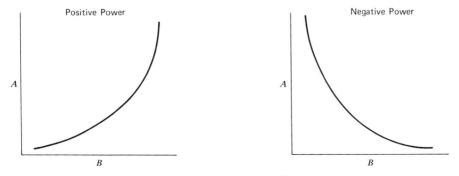

Figure 2-4.   Power function relations.

characteristics, although pointing us in the right direction, is nothing more than a step along the way to establishing causal relations among them. Three additional problems immediately present themselves to us: (1) criteria for establishing causation; (2) spuriousness; and (3) alternative approaches to causal analysis.

CRITERIA OF CAUSALITY

As a matter of course, there are at least three conditions that must be met to establish a causal relationship between two variables. First, there must be an association demonstrated between them. Several ways of demonstrating an empirical association are available to an investigator. Some of the more important and frequently used of these will be discussed below. According to most accepted practices, appropriate statistical procedures are employed for these purposes.

Second, the variables must exist in a particular time order. The independent variable must precede the dependent variable in time. Determining the time order between variables is not always an easy task. Many times, in fact, it is *assumed* without ever being carefully documented. Even when it is apparently a simple matter, problems can arise. In studies of alcoholism, for example, it is very difficult to know which comes first, the alcohol or the problem (Roebuck and Kessler, 1972, p. 164). In studies of delinquency and broken homes, it is difficult to know which comes first, the breakup of the home or the delinquency. The list could go on and on. Investigators must make every effort to see that the time order of variables can be empirically established. When time order is especially important, it might be necessary to rely on study designs that have the resolution of the problem built right into the study design. Panel studies, experimental designs, and various other strategies have this advantage, as we shall soon discover.

But demonstrating that variables are related in some statistical way and in a definite time-order sequence does not complete our task. To posit a causal relationship requires that yet a third condition be satisfied. It must be shown that the relationship between the two variables persists when other variables that precede them in time are controlled for. In other words, in demonstrating cause, it is necessary to prove that there are not other variables which could plausibly account for the relationship.

A word of caution must be introduced at this point. It is not our contention that *all* preceding variables must be accounted for, desirable as that would be. What is important is that those which are felt to have some bearing on the problem should be examined to assess their effect on the relationship. And it must be understood that we are concerned with variables that *precede the other two in time*, not intervening variables that might lead to a more refined comprehension of the problem.

Some authors, such as Hyman (1955), suggest that causal analysis requires the inclusion of intervening variables. Others, like Hirschi and Selvin (1967), maintain that it is possible to speak of causation between two variables without the introduction of intervening ones. These latter authors point out that "holding a match to a pile of leaves is a cause of their bursting into flames, even if one cannot describe the intervening chemical reactions" (1967, p. 38). Our position is in accord with Hyman and others who prefer that more than two variables be included in discussions of causal relations. After all, it makes quite a difference whether the leaves are wet or dry!

If one fact stands out from the rest by now, it is that a considerable amount of ingenuity and deliberate thought must accompany all efforts to establish causal connections among variables. Still, as simple and as few in number as the conditions for establishing cause are, there is much evidence that they are abused and ignored by even the most respected and experienced researchers. Hirschi and Selvin (1967) detected six different "false criteria of causality" in their evaluation of research inquiring into the causes of delinquency. Briefly, they noted that investigators:

1. Falsely assume that to be causal, relations between two variables must be perfect. Social life is sufficiently complicated that social science researchers almost invariably endorse a multiple causation stance. Seldom, if ever, do investigators expect to find a perfect, one-to-one relationship between variables. As a result, it is incorrect to dismiss relations that are less than perfect as noncausal.

2. Falsely assume that causal relations are equivalent to characteristics. As Hirschi and Selvin point out (1967, p. 123), characteristic does not mean important. Variations that occur on a relatively infrequent basis are, in effect, not characteristic variations. They might still be important variations in the sense that they are demonstrated differences. It is incorrect to assume that important variations are characteristic of the population being studied.

3. Falsely assume that variables whose relations are restricted to a specific social context can be used to comprehend relations between similar variables in other contexts. By restricting the context, an investigator is seeing to it that certain things do *not* vary. As Hirschi and Selvin (1967, p. 125) so trenchantly observe, "no investigation can establish the causal importance of variables that do not vary."

4. Falsely assume that intervening variables eliminate the original causal relation observed between two variables. Mention has already been made of this type of problem. All that needs to be said here is that variables which add to our overall comprehension of an original relationship do *not* diminish the importance of the original relationship.

5. Falsely assume that, to use Hirschi and Selvin's words, "measurable variables are not causes" (1967, p. 130). Oddly enough, after paying what seems like an almost inordinate amount of attention to problems related to ways to measure variables empirically, some researchers feel that the "real" causes of social phenomena lie somewhere beyond the grasp of social science methodologies. How that position is ever documented is, of course, not answerable.

6. Falsely assume that relationships between variables are dependent upon other variables and that the independent variable is not a cause of the dependent one. To assume that each independent variable is, by itself, capable of causing some form of variation in a dependent variable is incorrect. It is to assume, in effect, that unless something can, by itself, produce an effect in another variable, it cannot be seriously considered as a cause.

Because of the ease with which even the most sophisticated researchers fall prey to these incorrect ways of thinking about causal relationships, the novice must be instructed to review any and all criteria used to demonstrate causality carefully and constantly.

SPURIOUSNESS

To assert that a relationship between two variables is spurious means that it has occurred by accident and does not imply a causal connection at all. A purported relationship between the two variables is due to conditions other than their observed connection. Fire trucks, for example, are usually found at fires but cannot be said to cause them. Their relationship is an artifact of other relationships that have preceeded both of them in time.

Because the possibility always exists that demonstrated associations between variables are spurious, investigators like to examine their findings carefully. An important ingredient in assessing the relations between variables for the possibility of spuriousness is the knowledgeability of the investigator regarding the topic being researched. As Hirschi and Selvin (1967, p. 87) point out:

> Testing for spuriousness should be relatively simple. In any field of investigation there are not more than a few plausible counterexplanations of observed results. The investigator familiar with past research can, therefore, include many of the necessary variables in the design of his study and, when he comes to the analysis, can determine whether they account for his results. He need not consider all possible antecedent variables.

Spurious relationships, then, are not to be confused with incomplete variable analyses. Spuriousness is a special sort of inaccuracy because it represents a relationship that is a by-product of each variable having been affected by a third.

ALTERNATIVE APPROACHES TO CAUSAL ANALYSIS

Social scientists long ago abandoned the idea that there was a single cause for each effect. There is almost universal agreement that numerous factors combine to "cause" something to happen. As has been seen from our discussion of variables, these factors frequently relate to one another in rather complex ways. Unless investigators have some initial grasp of the social world, causal analysis can prove enormously frustrating. Partly because of the potentially overwhelming nature of the task, most researchers prefer to conduct their operations relative to one or another frame of reference. (See Chapter 3 for a further discussion of frames of reference.) Not only does it provide a framework within which to develop systematic linkages among variables and concepts, it permits a decided narrowing of the range of theoretically relevant items to which attention must be paid empirically.

Just as frames of reference do much to establish the broad range of intellectual problems to be studied, they dictate in turn the range of possible approaches for engaging in causal analysis. Although not completely locking an investigator into any certain type of analysis at the exclusion of others, frames of reference do much to determine the overall scientific strategy chosen by investigators to isolate those things that make a difference to some facet of social life.

Frames of reference enable us, when they are carefully developed, to recast interesting facts as variables. Furthermore, they enable questions to be posed in terms of relationships among variables. Then, as we have already pointed out, the process of causal analysis begins in earnest. Different research strategies are formulated to a significant extent out of the way variables and their relationships are conceptualized by researchers as they view the social world from a particular frame of reference. Yet, regardless of the investigator's frame of reference, all alternative approaches to causal analysis can be broadly classified according to whether they follow experimental or nonexperimental canons of data collection.

EXPERIMENTAL RESEARCH

In the experimental type of research, investigators are able to examine accurately the effect that certain variables have on others through the systematic introduction of them into the research context. As a result, it is possible to measure directly their impact on existing social conditions. *Control over the research situation* is the key to experimental research. Because of the appeal of obtaining highly accurate findings, numerous types of experimental designs have been developed. These will be taken up at some length in Chapter 3.

NONEXPERIMENTAL RESEARCH

Many of the problems of interest to social scientists are not amenable to the sorts of controls utilized in experimental designs. As a rule, social researchers cannot go around introducing variables into ongoing social activities in order to satisfy their scientific curiosity. Therefore, it has been necessary to devise various ways of controlling for the effects of variables in more symbolic ways. Various types of *nonexperimental* (or *quasi-experimental*) techniques have been devised over the years to ascertain the effects of independent and intervening variables on dependent variables. One approach is, of course, to employ statistical procedures.[2] A second is to employ some type of matching procedure in the research design. A third is the introduction of what is known as "test variables." More recently the analysis of covariance,[3] path analysis,[4] and chain analysis[5] has been developed to enable researchers to manipulate variables in nonexperimental ways. Procedures have also been developed to ascertain the interaction effect that different variables might have on dependent variables and on one another in certain social contexts.[6] Some of the more important and fundamental of these strategies are discussed in some detail in Chapter 4.[7] What needs to be understood here is that all approaches are designed to eventually achieve a common objective: *The accumulation of data that will establish linkages among variables in accordance with the basic criteria of causality.* There is no particular reason to think that any one or another of them is more or less acceptable as scientific inquiry than the rest.

A NOTE ON CROSS-CULTURAL RESEARCH

A central feature on the scientific perspective is its *universality.* Knowledge about events or activities that is restricted to a particular society, important as it is, does not automatically move us closer to demonstrating the universal applicability of our findings. Even in those circles where a quest for scientific "laws" is not embraced as a major objective of the scientific enterprise, the ability to generalize beyond the boundaries of our own societal context is crucial to an overall comprehension of social life.

Sociologists have been especially reluctant to move beyond the confines of their own countries, nonetheless. As Everett C. Hughes observes, "We invented ethnocentrism. Now we have fallen into it." (1971, p. 477). To offset this methodological (and, all too often, theoretical) preoccupation with data gathering restricted to settings in the investigator's own society, recent years have witnessed increased interest in the acquisition of data from foreign settings as well. But as Marsh (1967) is quick to point out, much of the research in foreign settings falls short of the mark as *cross-cultural* research in the strict sense of the term.

To Marsh (1967, p. 11) "comparative sociology" as he prefers to call it, "is restricted to the *systematic and explicit comparison of data from two or more societies."* Most of what passes as cross-cultural or comparative social research is, from this vantage point, not really comparative at all. Rather, it constitutes no more than research carried out in foreign countries. The consequences of this are readily seen:

> . . . the cross-societal comparison tends to be implicit rather than explicit, and the real burden of systematic comparisons is often left to the reader. There is, then, a real danger that as more sociologists shift their attention from their own societies to others, we shall have a spate of studies on individual societies and a somewhat haphazard accumulation of noncomparable cases. This would leave us little better off than we are now in terms of explicit cross-societal analyses. (Marsh, 1967, p. 17).

Procedures for conducting cross-cultural research have not been carefully developed. This might be expected, given the general lack of interest in such research. Some general steps to take and questions to be posed can be put forth here, however, as tentative guidelines for the interested researcher to start from. These suggestions are based on Marsh's *Comparative Sociology* (1967, p. 21–43), in which he designates a highly general "codification schema" for engaging in cross-cultural research.

A PROTOCOL FOR CROSS-CULTURAL RESEARCH

STEP 1: Establish a basis for classifying the societies in question. Marsh, for example, advances a strong argument for making distinctions among societies on the basis of social differentiation. Indicators of social differentiation were developed and societies rated along a seven-point "Index of Differentiation" scale. Other possibilities for classification might include such things as urbanization, technological development, and so forth. The important point is that the basis for comparing societies as similar or dissimilar must be made very explicit. It is a fact to be established and not an assumption to be made, as is so often the case.

STEP 2: Figure out what it is about the societies in question that is to be investigated. In other words, what is the *dependent variable?* Is the focus of the study a comparison of two societies in terms of suicide rates? Delinquency? Drug use? Adolescent rebellion? Is an investigator interested in examining variations in occupational patterns? Differences in the acceptance of contraceptive devices? Patterns of kinship? Without extending the list of questions any further, it is clear that the dependent variables used need not be confined to some narrow range of topics. Whatever attracts the attention of investigators in a single social order is capable of being studied on a cross-cultural basis.

STEP 3: Formulate categories for codifying data. Marsh (1967, p. 42) suggests that there are four logically possible categories for this purpose. These are replication, universal generalization, contingency generalization, and specification.

a.   *Replication* occurs when the societies are found to be *similar* on the basis of procedures taken in *Step 1* and there is no variation obtained in the dependent variable.

b.   *Universal generalization* occurs when societies are found to be *dissimilar* on the basis of findings in *Step 1,* and there is no variation between or among them in terms of the dependent variable.

c. *Contingency generalization* is established when the societies are dissimilar, and the dependent variable is shown to vary according to the basis for determining similarity and dissimilarity.

d. *Specification* is found when the societies are found to be similar, and yet there are differences among them in the dependent variables, or the societies are dissimilar and the dependent variables vary among them, but not in relation to the basis for comparison.

It is not possible to know whether this protocol is the only one or the best one from which to begin systematic cross-cultural research. Because it does allow for some degree of codification, though, it is probably as appropriate as any other approach to the problem. Where the stumbling blocks are encountered is at the point of actually obtaining the types of data to put into the overall categories in the schema. Measures for many dependent variables are more or less "culture bound" and as limited ethnocentrically as the vision of the investigators. Obtaining comparable *data* poses complex questions that take us far beyond this discussion. It can only be hoped that significant strides will be made in this area in the near future.

SOME CONCLUDING REMARKS

Fundamental to the research process is a search for causes. As the materials in this chapter indicate, the task is at one and the same time simple and complex. It is hoped that enough has been discussed to provide an overall view of the place of causal analysis in scientific research without presuming too much knowledge on the part of the reader.

But, as was pointed out at the outset, more is involved than a capacity to think in these terms. Before serious thought can be given to designing and executing a research project, something needs to be known of the place of theory in the research process. It is to that topic that our attention is turned in the following chapter.

SOME QUESTIONS FOR REVIEW

1. Define causation. How important are variables to causal analysis?

2. Distinguish between discrete and continuous variables. What bearing does treating a variable as discrete or continuous have on designing social research?

3. Discuss the importance of viewing variables in terms of their time order. Compare and contrast intervening, independent, and dependent variables.

4. Identify the forms that relations among variables take. Of what importance to causal analysis is knowing about the form of relations among variables?

5. Specify the criteria for determining causality. Discuss the sorts of misapplications of these criteria that can occur in social science investigations.

6. What is spuriousness? Why is it a special form of inaccuracy?

7. Distinguish between experimental and nonexperimental research. What types of nonexperimental research designs are available for research into the targets of social research?

8. What is meant by comparative sociology? Review the steps for engaging in cross-cultural research.

NOTES

1. For literature that takes up some of these issues, consult the following:
    Robert Brown, *Explanation in Social Science* (Chicago: Aldine Publishing Company, 1963).
    Morris R. Cohen and Ernest Nagel, *An Introduction to Logic and Scientific Method* (New York: Harcourt, Brace and Company, 1934).
    Bernard S. Phillips, *Social Research* (New York: The Macmillan Company, 1971).
    Karl R. Popper, *The Logic of Scientific Discovery* (New York, Science Editions, Inc., 1961).
    Walter Wallace, *The Logic of Science in Sociology* (Chicago: Aldine-Atherton, 1971).
2. For a discussion of the more basic procedures, see Dean J. Champion, Jr., *Basic Statistics for Social Research* (Scranton, Pa.: Chandler Publishing Co., 1970).
3. Allen L. Edwards, *Experimental Design in Psychological Research* (New York: Holt, Rinehart & Winston, Inc., 1967).
4. Otis Dudley Duncan, "Path Analysis: Sociological Examples," *American Journal of Sociology* 72 (1966): 1–16.

5. Harrison C. White, *Chains of Opportunity: System Models of Mobility in Organization* (Cambridge, Mass.: Harvard University Press, 1970).
6. Leo A. Goodman, "On the Multivariate Analysis of Three Dichotomous Variables," *American Journal of Sociology* 71 (1965): 290–301.
7. Only those requiring no special training in statistics will be covered.

BIBLIOGRAPHY

Hage, Jerald. *Techniques and Problems of Theory Construction in Sociology.* New York: Wiley-Interscience, 1972.

Hirschi, Travis, and Hanan C. Selvin. *Delinquency Research: An Appraisal of Analytic Methods.* New York: Free Press, 1967.

Hughes, Everett C. *The Sociological Eye.* Chicago: Aldine-Atherton, 1971.

Hyman, H. H. *Survey Design and Analysis: Principles, Cases and Procedures.* New York: Free Press, 1955.

Lazarsfeld, Paul F., and Morris Rosenberg. *The Language of Social Research.* New York: Free Press, 1962.

Marsh, Robert M. *Comparative Sociology.* New York: Harcourt Brace Jovanovich, 1967.

Roebuck, Julian, and Raymond G. Kessler. *The Etiology of Alcoholism.* Springfield, Ill.: Charles C Thomas, 1972.

Rosenberg, Morris. *The Logic of Survey Analysis.* New York: Basic Books, 1968.

CHAPTER 3
THEORY IN SOCIAL RESEARCH

There are those who feel that once a theoretical problem has been identified and a research strategy formulated there is little to do but gather data and examine them in the light of theory. Such people ignore much that is basic to the relations between the theoretical and data-gathering aspects of scientific inquiry. Theoretical concerns are part and parcel of the constant thinking that must accompany any project. It is not by accident that this chapter has been entitled "Theory *in* Social Research." More needs to be done to integrate theory and data gathering than listing the benefits that will derive from attention to both, important as it is to know these.

Because this is a text in which the primary focus is on procedures for conducting social research, our concern here will be to present those facts of theory building most directly linked to the process of empirical investigation. We have neither the intention of discussing the relative merits and shortcomings of a variety of theoretical perspectives nor of critically assessing theoretical positions espoused by social theorists. And we certainly are not going to posit any theoretical premises for others to research. Rather, this chapter will stress one fundamental feature of any sound investigation: *Research is conducted within the context of a way of thinking about data that places specific demands on the data if they are to have any scientific utility.* The way of thinking about data normally encompasses what is loosely referred to as "theory." In the final analysis, the specific demands placed on data by these theoretical and conceptual concerns are what enable us to distinguish these thoughts as scientific. *Thus, we are permitted to move from speaking of facts to discussions of scientific facts.* Although it is certainly true that no theory can stand before scientific facts that contradict its assertions, it is equally true that facts are of dubious theoretical value if they fail to conform to established canons of scientific adequacy. Just as there are facts that theories must fit, so, too, are there rules of scientific thought before which the facts must pass muster.

There is no established way to guarantee that there will always be a proper blending of the theoretical and empirical dimensions of the research process. Interestingly, although the interrelatedness of theory and research is widely endorsed, considerable latitude is permitted in the extent to which such interrelatedness is actually attained. it is usually the case that correspondingly less weight has been given by researchers to procedures that achieve interrelatedness by a route stressing theoretical bases for acquiring facts than to procedures that focus ·on refinements in data-gathering and analysis. With the hope that an appropriate balance can be struck between these concerns, this chapter will concentrate on the following related topics:

1. What is Theory?   Numerous answers, some of them especially disconcerting, can be found to this question. Naturally, the extent to which one's research is seen as being theoretically relevant will be determined by how it gets answered.

2. What are the criteria for determining whether given systems of thoughts constitute "theory"?   Theories are not developed by adhering strictly to a set of criteria reflected in formal definitions of the theories. They are generated out of a combination of pragmatic as well as ideal considerations. Unless this is understood, data accumulated by social science researchers are subjected to demands that are, at this point, too rigorous and unrealistic.

3. How do theoretical constructs become operational? There is frequently a tendency to overlook the technical procedures by which investigators proceed from the empirically relevant aspects of theoretical statements to putting them into operation. Being able to appreciate the connection between answers to questions on a questionnaire or in an interview and the abstract commentary of a theory is essential. Even though this is largely uncharted ground, sensitivity to the types of problems encountered here is most important to the integration of theory and research.

4. What are some of the major issues related to the testability of theories? The theory-building process is a complex one with several identifiable dimensions. Misunderstandings and disagreements often arise out of the different postures taken by investigators with respect to them. Two dimensions in particular seem to pose special problems for those engaged in empirical research, and they need to be focused upon. These are (1) deduction and induction and (2) theoretical models.

It is on these that our attention will now focus.

WHAT IS THEORY?

Numerous answers can be found to the question of what constitutes a theory in the social sciences. Several answers hinder effective attempts to develop a facility for combining theoretical and empirical activities in the research process and, as a result, should be disposed of immediately. Three such views are particularly troublesome: (1) theory as unsubstantiated ideas; (2) theory as mystique; and (3) theory as confirmed postulates.

THEORY AS UNSUBSTANTIATED IDEAS

One view enjoying wide currency holds that theories are seldom little more than unsubstantiated and usually incomprehensible ideas in the minds of professors out of touch with "reality." Most often theories are seen as being totally unrelated to the give and take of day-to-day living. By not addressing "relevant problems" such as how to get a job, make ends meet financially, have a happy married life, keep from getting into trouble with the law, overcome personal tragedies, and so on and on, theories are seen as having no demonstrated utility. Only when they can be shown to make living "better" can theories be taken seriously, according to this view.

Data accumulated to extend scientific knowledge must, however, transcend the immediate and more or less private concerns of people. What enables one person to find work may put another out of a job. What permits some to overcome life's tragedies proves ineffective when others are concerned. The unique, idiosyncratic things we do are an insufficient basis from which to assess the nature and importance of a theory. It is to the recurrent, the regular, the patterned features of social life that social science inquiry is directed. Although a healthy skepticism is involved in establishing the empirical support for systematically developed ideas, it should not give way to a cynicism that automatically dismisses the place of theory in research activities by concentrating on the unique.

THEORY AS MYSTIQUE

For those accepting another view, much that passes for theory represents simply ideas for which no empirically relevant operational procedures have been formed. Such a view imbues theory with an almost mystical quality. Investigators set about to obtain factual information bearing on a theoretical premise only to be rebuffed for not capturing the ever-elusive "essence" or "heart" or other unmeasurable quality of the subject under scrutiny. Some social scientists can even be found who embrace this view. Once a phenomenon is measurable, it ceases to be *theoretically* relevant (Hirschi and Selvin, 1967, pp. 130–33). In effect, to those holding this view, that which is theoretical is apparently that which defies empirical scrutiny. Consequently, no matter how much research is undertaken, it will be "theoretically" irrelevant or, at best, of secondary importance.

THEORY AS CONFIRMED POSTULATES

Finally, it is frequently contended that there are, strictly speaking, no systematically related propositions in sociology that even begin to conform to a theory. There are no firmly established laws of social behavior, no integrated sets of universally acknowledged and empirically documented sets of propositions from which to posit new relations for study or predictions. When the usual criteria are applied to our ideas, they fall so short of meeting them that it would be frivolous to dignify the ideas as theories. For all their brilliant, innovative, provocative, and heuristic value, social science ideas are too fraught with inconsistencies, too loosely formulated to be seriously dealt with as established systems of thought. Furthermore, even those perspectives that rest on the most sketchy and assorted empirical foundations contain sizable amounts of speculation. To make matters worse, what little support there is for a given perspective usually contradicts the partially tested and verified evidence marshalled in defense of other perspectives.

Little will ever be done to bring theoretical and empirical interests together if undue emphasis is placed on the fact that few, if any, empirically confirmed laws of social life exist in the literature of the social sciences today. Untested and even untestable assumptions will continue to be a feature of all social theories. What matters is not that theories will be based in part on speculation but that the amount of speculation will grow smaller and smaller as more and more factual observations are compiled to support what were previously speculative observations. By the same token, it is the relative emphasis given to the assumptions contained in theories as opposed to other elements that is significant, not that theories rest on certain assumptions. Everyone takes some things for granted that do not require direct empirical testing.

Taken together, these views impede serious progress toward integrating theoretical and empirical activities in the research process. Those who fall prey to them will probably find that neither their ideas nor their data are of much scientific value. But to discredit such notions is still not to say much about the nature of theory. We are brought once again to our original question: What is a theory?

SOME DEFINITIONS OF A THEORY

A theory is a set of interrelated constructs (concepts), definitions, and propositions that presents a systematic view of phenomena by specifying relations among variables, with the purpose of explaining and predicting the phenomena (Kerlinger, 1965, p. 11).

. . . a set of hypotheses which form a deductive system; that is, which is arranged in such a way that from some of the hypotheses as premises all the other hypotheses logically follow. The propositions in a deductive system may be considered as being arranged in an order of levels, the hypotheses at the highest level being those which occur only as premises in the system, those at the lowest level being those which occur only as conclusions in the system, and those at intermediate levels being those which occur as deductions from higher-level hypotheses and which serve as premises for deductions to lower-level hypotheses (Braithwaite, in Selltiz, Jahoda, Deutch, and Cook, 1959, p. 480).

... a theory is a set of logically interrelated statements in the form of empirical assertions about properties of infinite classes of events or things (Gibbs, 1972, p. 5).

... a theory should contain not only concepts and statements but definitions—both theoretical and operational—and linkages, again both theoretical and operational. The concepts and definitions should be ordered into primitive and derived terms and the statements and linkages should be ordered into premises and equations (Hage, 1972, p. 172).

To these, we will add our own definition: *A theory is a set of systematically related propositions specifying causal relationships among variables.* This particular conceptualization of a theory has certain advantages from the standpoint of its methodological implications. These can be better understood after some related issues have been introduced. Not the least among these problems is the enormous gap between definitions and the theories themselves.

It is understandable that students usually experience some difficulty in grasping from definitions what a theory is. That is attributable in part to the fact that there are so few theories from which examples can be drawn for illustrative purposes in the social and behavioral sciences (Gibbs, 1972; Hage, 1972; Kuhn, 1962; Reynolds, 1971). Never having "seen" a theory, so to speak, students find it both too tedious and too abstract to relate these definitions to the systems of ideas they actually ponder. All too often, what passes as "theory" is related to definitions of theory in only the most imaginative, far-flung way, if at all. We do not mean to say that definitions have no value. Of course they do. We mean only to emphasize that the desire to integrate theory into the research process is not achieved merely by providing definitions, no matter how explicit and refined they are. To accomplish the task, an appreciation of theory is needed that is more sensitive to the current state of theory development in the social science.

COMPONENTS OF A THEORY

Theories start out as ideas. How well formulated they are in terms of precision, clarity, and thoroughness will vary a great deal. By the same token, how closely they approximate established fact when they are conceived will vary considerably. Yet, as our definition of a theory indicates, it is the extent to which ideas conform to basic demands of proposition formulation that determines whether or not they will assume the stature of theory. Satisfying these demands is no simple task. Many ideas are simply not of a caliber or quality to remain standing after an assessment of their scientific utility. That does not mean that ideas should be discarded and forgotten when they fail to pass muster. Quite to the contrary, some ideas are so far-reaching in their identification of major areas of human behavior and so removed from the context of prevailing systems of thought that the scientific community cannot adjust readily to them. The works of Freud and LeBon are examples of such ideas, as are those of George Herbert Mead.[1]

Numerous factors might contribute to the failure of scientific activity to respond easily and naturally to these types of ideas. Methodological techniques might not have been developed that are sophisticated enough to test them. Logical systems of thought might have to be reformulated to exhaustively examine the interval consistency of the ideas. And, after considerable exposure to empirical data, the ideas might have to be significantly modified or altered. Thus having served their purpose as stimulants to raising more pointed and refined questions, they can be abandoned for their more carefully pondered offsprings.

IDEAL CRITERIA

It is generally agreed that sets of ideas must conform to the following criteria to be theoretically acceptable:

1. They must be logically consistent. There can be no discernible internal contradictions.
2. They must be interrelated. There can be no statements about phenomena that are unrelated to one another.
3. The statements must be exhaustive. That is, they should cover the full range of variations concerning the nature of the phenomena in question.
4. The propositions should be mutually exclusive. There should be no repetition or duplication.
5. They must be capable of being subjected to empirical scrutiny. Unless they can be tested through research, there is no way to determine their scientific worth.

Whenever ideas have been sufficiently refined to meet these most basic but demanding criteria, they can be said to be theoretical in the strictest sense of the word. As it becomes possible to state the ideas contained in a theory in a more codified manner, the theory assumes a quality of elegance. *Elegance* is usually arrived at through the utilization of mathematical formulas in which given universally shared symbols come to replace the more cumbersome and less precise words used in normal discourse.

Furthermore, as the theory gets refined through the processes of mutual exclusiveness and exhaustiveness, it can take on a quality of parsimoniousness.[2] *Parsimony* is achieved by relying on the smallest number of propositional statements to cover the widest possible range of phenomena. Parsimony seeks to avoid redundancy. A word of caution needs to be interjected: Avoiding redundancy does not mean opting for the more simplified of two theories. There are occasions when a more complicated theory will be chosen because it more closely approximates the realm of social life being examined (Wallace, 1971, pp. 112–14).

PRAGMATIC CRITERIA

Almost without exception, the major ideas in the social sciences fail to meet the basic demands of theories as set forth here. As we have already indicated, this is precisely the point at which many have chosen to begin paying no more than lip-service to the connections between theory and research. Until recently, little has been done to work systematically toward the resolution of the many unanswered questions in this area. There are increasingly encouraging signs that this omission is being corrected, albeit slowly and with numerous differences of opinion on many of the issues.

It is probably best to assume an especially pragmatic position about theory-building in the social sciences. There seems no better way to begin than by taking the ideas that exist and ascertaining what needs to be done to move them closer to the theoretical ideal expressed in our definitions of theories.

Most of the theoretically relevant ideas in the social sciences are broadly grouped into general configurations referred to as "frames of reference", "schools of thought", "perspectives", "orientations", or "approaches". What each configuration does is identify major dimensions of social life that merit study. Each has its own particular ideas and assumptions from which questions to be answered are formulated. Each has at least a few basic concepts that serve to identify those who use them extensively as being of one persuasion or another. Each is in the process of developing sets of "empirically applicable" (Gibbs, 1972) assertions that permit the identification of variables that can be put into operation and tested empirically. And each has its own following of scholars. As Gibbs trenchantly observes, "sociologists wittingly or unwittingly write for cliques" (Gibbs, 1972, p. 58).

None of these configurations of ideas can be said to have moved very close to establishing the logical rigor and conceptual consistency required of theories. Similarly, none has provided an exhaustive or thorough statement of those aspects of social life they propose to have knowledge about. And, certainly, none can be said to enjoy the comfort of solid factual support.

Both the excitement and the frustration of research in the social sciences comes from this theoretical quagmire. It is exciting because there are so many directions to choose from in charting areas of scientifically fruitful research over extended periods of time. It is frustrating because unless the investigator is acutely sensitive to the actual state of scientific thought related to the questions being posed, the overall quality of completed studies can be misinterpreted or ignored by others. Worse yet, it may not even be fully appreciated by the investigator.

The complex and worthwhile task of delineating the theoretically promising features of the various substantive frames of reference dominating contemporary sociological thought will have to be left for others (Hage, 1972; Hagedorn and Labovitz, 1973). Right now, more important then isolating the major proponents and components of functionalism, social conflict, interactionism, and so on, is the job of suggesting a means whereby *any or all* of them can be more understandable from a methodological standpoint.

For the novice in social research, it is appropriate to suggest a tentative scheme for identifying the major components of theoretical ideas in the social sciences. Such a scheme includes the following types of differentiation:

1. Assumptions and ideas. Assumptions and ideas consist of basically untestable premises about the nature of selected aspects of social life. Functionalism, for example, as exemplified in the works of Talcott Parsons (1951) and Parsons and Shils (1954) assumes that there are social systems characterized by tendencies toward boundary-maintenance and equilibrium. Interactionists, on the other hand, assume that social reality occurs as a result of negotiated transactions among participants in social interactions. To the extent that these assumptions are embraced, it is done in the course of taking certain things for granted. In either case, assumptions provide the basis for ideas about the nature of social life.

   2. Frame of reference. Essentially, frames of reference identify the major dimensions of social life that will be subjected to empirical scrutiny by advocates of this approach. In certain instances, such as functionalism, these dimensions are rather extensively spelled out (Merton, 1957). In others, such as conflict or interactionist thought, there is a less explicit but nonetheless roughly identifiable delineation of significant areas of inquiry.

   3. Concepts. Concepts are simply abstractions that serve to organize our thoughts and experiences into manageable mental entities. Concepts vary greatly in terms of their precision, scope, clarity, and acceptability. Examples of concepts are group, interaction, institution, sanction, and community, to name just a few.

   4. Variables. Several features of variables have already been alluded to in previous chapters. They are relational units of analysis that can assume any one of a number of designated sets of values. To the researcher, being able to obtain data that reflect variables strikes at the very heart of social research.

   5. Propositions. Once ways have been found to measure variables empirically, they are *capable* of being formulated as relational statements or propositions. That is not to say that they *will* be. Therein lies a major distinction between searching for causes and developing theories. Statements of relations between or among variables are called propositions.

   6. Theories. The end-product of these considerations is theories about social life. To obtain these systematically related propositions specifying causal relationships among variables is the ultimate objective of social science research activity. These pragmatic criteria are illustrated diagrammatically in Figure 3-1.

   Arrows or similar signs that might be suggestive of some rigid time order among these components have deliberately been avoided. There is no special order to the development and relative influence of the components. It is quite impossible under most conditions to state with any degree of certainty, for example, whether frames of reference come before concepts. They develop together, each contributing to the other's clarity and expansion. By the same token, variables sometimes precipitate research that gives rise to concepts rather than being carefully deduced from preexisting conceptual interests. And so it is with variables and propositions, propositions and concepts, and so forth.

Differences in degrees of theoretical sophistication can also be observed in the various areas of specialized interest in social science disciplines. Some areas of concentration such as demography have highly refined variables and techniques for their measurement. In areas such as deviance and sociology of law, there are few highly refined variables and even fewer advanced ways to measure them. Yet they are areas in which several frames of reference with markedly different conceptual interests can be found.

Notwithstanding the somewhat flexible time-order relation among these elements, there is much for the budding investigator to learn from Figure 3-1. First among these lessons is the recognition that there are certain aspects of theory building that are only indirectly related to the technical aspects of empirical research. Frames of reference, ideas, assumptions, and concepts are not directly testable in and of themselves. Some terms may not even be defined clearly, if at all. Our confidence in these dimensions is based on the extent to which data collected and examined in connection with variables and the testing of hypothesized relations among them meet standards of reliability and validity. Further confidence derives from the extent to which we can generalize from them. These matters, in turn, rest on more strictly methodological considerations. As Gibbs (1972, p. 53) observes, "a theory may be testable even though some of its component terms designate vague, undefined notions."

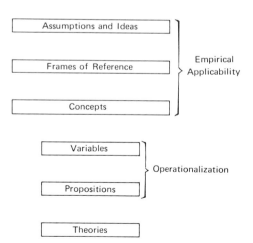

Figure 3-1. Pragmatic components of social science theories.

That introduces a second lesson to be learned: The entire burden of testing theories does not rest exclusively on the shoulders of researchers. To appreciate more fully the responsibility of theorists to the enterprise, we have capitalized on a distinction made by Gibbs between "empirical applicability" and "operationalization." According to Gibbs (1972, p. 45), empirical applicability extends beyond the "technical" problem of reliability and becomes a matter of central importance to theorists:

"... in formulating a theory that comprises assertions about quantitative properties, a theorist must specify formulas and procedures for their application. Each such specification is a tacit *assertion* of empirical applicability, and that assertion is part of the theory, not a technical consideration as sociological theorists in the grand tradition would have it."[3]

Furthermore, he indicates:

"In specifying formulas and procedures for their application, the theorist asserts not only that sufficient agreement in the values computed by independent investigators will be realized, but also that the requisite data can be secured. If requisite data are not available in published form or cannot be gathered because of limited resources, the formulas are not empirically applicable."

Whether or not theorists will heed this division of labor in the future will bear watching. It is clear that as much effort will be needed on that side as on the methodological side if any meaningful integration of theory and research is to be achieved.

It would be incorrect to think that this division of labor relieves researchers from any responsibility whatsoever, though. Far from it. Hage (1972, pp. 92–99) provides some direction for the researcher in this regard:

There are three important techniques for specifying theoretical linkages. The first is to specify the intervening variables. Frequently, these can be found by a rapid review of the literature. The second technique is to specify very general statements called premises or assumptions from which we derive the reasons for a particular lower-order statement, variously called theorem, corollary, or hypothesis. The third technique consists of thinking aloud, as it were, about why two or more variables might be interrelated.

But if empirical applicability is a major component of theoretical thinking, operationalization is its counterpart to the researcher.

Identifying the particular questions or observations or documents seen as measuring a variable strikes at the very core of social research. The operations connected with obtaining suitable data pose, as we shall see in later chapters, many complicated and frequently intractable problems for investigators. Knowing, for example, how to word questions in a questionnaire, how many questions to ask, what order they should be placed in, and so forth can be extremely crucial in acquiring scientifically useful data. Even though they are of vital importance to the overall reliability and validity of data, however, operational procedures are not, as Gibbs again cautions (1972, p. 53), the end that is sought. Rather, they constitute the *means* by which testability or empirical applicability is attained.

A specific protocol for carrying out these operational procedures has not been developed to everyone's satisfaction in the social sciences. Until recently, in fact, relatively little attention has been paid to the problem (Blalock, 1969; Coleman, 1964; Hage, 1972). Recalling our previous discussion of various forms by which relationships among variables are assessed (linear, curvilinear, power function), as well as our other observations about variables, several distinct ways of specifying operational linkages can be identified. Hage (1972, pp. 99–110) discusses three: (1) the use of trace lines; (2) tables; or (3) by asking a series of specific questions about the variables and their relationships to one another. Only one of these—trace lines—will be examined here.

TRACE LINES

One way to conduct operational procedures is by presenting results in graphic form, as in Figure 3-2.

As variables become more and more refined and complex, different types of lines can be used. For example, an examination of several dimensions of the variable Y in the curvilinear or normal curve shown in Figure 3-2 could be illustrated as shown in Figure 3-3. A legend would simply be added to specify which trace lines corresponded to which dimension of variable Y.

In sum, it must be recognized that there are several basic criteria before which ideas must be paraded if they are to be considered theories in a narrow sense. Furthermore, because there are no systems of ideas that can pass as full-fledged theories in the social sciences, it is futile to stop there and wait for theories to emerge. Like the facts we spoke of in Chapter 1, they have to be carved out of reality. The reality of things insofar as the state of sociological theory is concerned

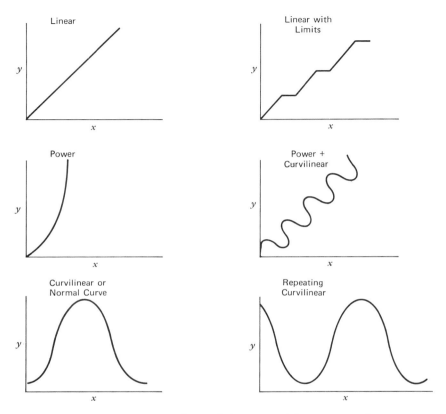

Figure 3-2. Trace Lines. Adapted from Jerald Hage, *Techniques and Problems of Theory Construction in Sociology* **(New York: Wiley-Interscience, 1972), p. 104.**

is admittedly difficult to face up to. Nonetheless, by articulating the components of sociological thought as they do exist, it is possible to see more easily where our labors need to be applied if these ideas are to be brought closer to established canons of scientific knowledge.

ISSUES RELATED TO TESTABILITY

From the above comments, it is easily discernible that more than one dimension of the theory-building process can be stressed by investigators. Not everyone agrees that it is best to begin at the same point or give equal weight to the several criteria mentioned. So far as research is concerned, perhaps the most pivotal distinctions have to do with (1) whether emphasis is placed on deduction or induction, (2) how much concern is to be given to theoretical models or forms, and (3) the purposes or objectives of theories. Disagreements and misunderstandings all too often arise when investigators stressing different dimensions of theory formulation do not sharply delineate their positions on these matters. Considerable confusion can be avoided if they are clarified.

DEDUCTION AND INDUCTION

Getting from theories to facts and back again is not only difficult, it is controversial (Blumer, 1955; Camilleri, 1962; Dubin, 1969; Homans, 1964; Merton, 1957; Parsons, 1951; Robinson, 1951). As some of the definitions cited above suggest, there are those who feel that the entire research process is initiated with theories. Deduction occurs when facts are gathered to confirm or disprove hypothesized relationships among variables that have been *deduced* from propositions. Whether there were facts that precipitated the propositions does not really matter. What matters is that research is essentially a hypothesis-testing venture in which the hypotheses rest on logically (if not factually) deduced relational statements. Because the basic outline for developing a research proposal presented in Chapter 4 is predicated on a deductive model, the step-by-step procedures employed in deductive research will not be reviewed here. Kinch (1963), Hage (1972), Schwirian and Prehn

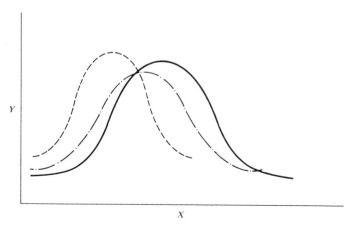

Y

X

Figure 3-3.   Multidimensional trace-line illustration.

(1962), and Burgess and Akers (1966) have all done work that exemplifies how particular hypotheses can be generated from more general and inclusive assertions.

Induction involves moving from particular instances of relations among variables to the formulation of hypotheses and from these to the development of propositions. In one or another of its forms, induction is the way most social scientists actually go about the business of expanding knowledge. Theodorsen and Theodorsen (1969, pp. 199–200) have identified two basic types of induction—*enumerative* and *analytic*. Enumerative induction, which they further break down into complete and incomplete depending upon whether information from a whole population or some position of it is being used for generalization, is the most common form of induction used in social science research today. Most often, enumerative induction involves generalizations from samples with varying degrees of representativeness. Usually, but not invariably, these generalizations are derived through the application of statistical procedures to the data. Accompanying these studies are usually statements pertaining to "probability" of generalization to larger and more inclusive populations based on findings from the sample studied.

Analytic induction, according to Theodorsen and Theodorsen, is a procedure whereby there is a case-by-case analysis of specific features to determine which conditions are *always* present prior to the occurrence of certain types of conduct. Examples of analytic induction can be found in the works of Angell (1954), Cressey (1953), Lindesmith (1968), and Becker (1953). In *Other People's Money* (1953, p. 7), Cressey outlined the step-by-step procedure that occurs in analytic induction:

1. A rough definition of the phenomenon to be explained is formulated.
2. A hypothetical explanation of that phenomenon is formulated.
3. One case is studied in light of the hypothesis with the object of determining whether the hypothesis fits the facts in that case.
4. If the hypothesis does not fit the facts, either the hypothesis is reformulated or the phenomenon to be explained is redefined, so that the case is excluded. This definition must be more precise than the first one.
5. Practical certainty may be attained after a small number of cases has been examined, but the discovery by the investigator or any other investigator of a single negative case disproves the explanation and requires a reformulation.

6. This procedure of examining cases, redefining the phenomenon and reformulating the hypothesis is continued until a universal relationship is established, each negative case calling for a redefinition or a reformulation.
7. For purposes of proof, cases outside the area circumscribed by the definition are examined to determine whether or not the final hypothesis applies to them.

Although the distinction between deduction and induction serves the important purpose of identifying opposite ways to go about theory building, most investigators find that their scientific work entails a certain amount of both. Induction probably permits more of an opportunity to see theory in a dynamic state of emergence rather than as already given, as is the case with deduction, but the issue is open to some debate. Because there is neither a rigorously developed comprehensive theory from which to deduce particular relationships for testing nor a sufficient accumulation of data to allow for systematic theory development through induction, even personal preferences for one or the other approach must remain flexible and adaptable.

Such a state of affairs poses several problems for investigators. There is, first of all, a demand for a considerable degree of creativity and imagination on the part of researchers. Both deduction and induction insist that one go beyond the statistical significance of findings to what Camilleri (1962) refers to as the "systematic import" of data. Simply put, that means being sensitive to the relevance of data to theory.

Second, there is a need for researchers to keep abreast of theoretically relevant configurations of ideas in the social sciences. Whether this can be accomplished only by joining one or another of the cliques spoken of earlier is perhaps open to dispute. But certainly to the extent that researchers are to guard against becoming raw empiricists or technicians, they must develop keen theoretical tentacles. Neither of these appeals for some degree of theoretical savvy is to be seen as being easily attained. Nevertheless, it is clear that any integration of theory and research is dependent upon them.

THEORETICAL MODELS

In moments of rare and refreshing candor, most novices face up to a perplexing question that can no longer be adroitly avoided: How do you know when you are actually reading theoretically relevant statements? After all, they do not usually present themselves to us in bold-face type. More likely than not, they tend to be interspersed among a bewildering avalanche of words designed to enhance the readability of books and articles. It is, quite frankly, almost impossible sometimes to sort out the theory from the remaining verbiage. To aid in this difficult process, it has become increasingly fashionable for social scientists to rely on *models*. Models are nothing more than *simplified systematic conceptualizations of interrelated elements in some schematic form.*

Tremendous variation can be found in schematic forms. Some researchers choose simply to set their basic theoretical tenets apart in italicized form (Homans, 1950). Others select a more condensed and simplified scheme. Merton's (1957) well-known "goals-means" scheme is a prime example of such a model. Finally, there are those who prefer to present materials in a mathematical form (Coleman, 1964).

No matter which form is chosen, models have certain advantages and disadvantages as solutions to theoretical dilemmas.[1] Among the advantages are the following:

1. Models represent pictures of theories. As such, they enable researchers to grasp more quickly and comprehensively the sorts of relations among variables posited by theories. As a result, findings deviating from these expectations can be subjected to more exhaustive scrutiny. Where no such findings exist, research designs and procedures can be formulated to compile them (Blalock, 1969; McKinney, 1966).

2. Models show more clearly the boundaries or conceptual limits of theories. By concentrating attention on the phenomena to be included in a theory, models have the effect of telling us where a theory ends. *Facts* of social life to which it is not applicable can be dismissed from examination.

3. Furthermore, models enable us to comprehend more precisely the direction of the relations among variables. Whether a given factor has a positive or negative impact on another can be readily ascertained.

Contrasted to these are several disadvantages:

1. Often persons examining a model ignore the fact that the model constitutes rather severe simplifications. In sociology, for example, there is a tendency to present extremes or polar ideal types as dichotomies. Variables tend to be conceptualized as discrete entities rather than as continuous. We study delinquents/nondelinquents, prejudice/nonprejudice, employed/unemployed, formal/informal, and so on and on. There is no particularly compelling reason why variables should not be conceptualized in terms of continuous dimensions (Blalock, 1969; McKinney, 1966).

2. Models narrow the full impact of theories in such ways that fruitful avenues of exploration opened by them risk being ignored because they are not portrayed explicitly. Merton's (1957) "goals-means" schema, for example, concentrated on differential access to legitimate avenues of success to explain various deviant adaptations. Cloward and Ohlin (1960), by combining insights from Merton with those of Sutherland (1955), were subsequently able to point out that there is differential access to illegitimate means of success as well. Thus, modification or extension of a model calls for an understanding of the phenomenon in question beyond that presented in a model.

3. Models can also give the impression of a specific time-order relation among variables even when none is intended. Sometimes the mere presentation of ideas in sequential form is sufficient for making unwarranted assumptions about problems such as time order.

4. Models tend to convey the impression that all the logically consistent dimensions have been included. This, however, is not always the case, as Blalock points out (1969, pp. 31, 34), again in reference to some logically neglected types in Merton's schema.

5. Closely related to this point is the observation that models suggest that their various elements conform to empirical reality. But no more faith can be placed in this suggestion than in the previous one. Short and Strodbeck (1965), to cite just one example, were unable to locate one of the types of delinquent gangs developed analytically by Cloward and Ohlin (1960).

6. Finally, models suffer a plight all too frequently encountered in the social sciences that is not necessarily of their formulators' own doing. Unless the language employed is sufficiently precise and widely shared, misunderstandings can easily creep into their interpretations.

Whether models hold the promise many believe they do for linking theories more closely with empirical research is as yet undetermined. Numerous differences of opinion exist in the area of theory construction, most of which are steeped in firmly established intellectual traditions (Blalock, 1969; Gibbs, 1972; Hage, 1972; McKinney, 1966; Reynolds, 1971; Stinchcombe, 1968). And as one moves closer and closer to the delineation of operational procedures for linking theoretical propositions with factual data representing variables, specific ways of accomplishing this feat quickly diminish in number. About all that is certain at this point is that the increasing emphasis on theory construction, welcome as it is, offers no panacea to the social researcher.

SOME CONCLUDING REMARKS

In addressing the several topics in this chapter, emphasis has been placed on those aspects of theory most germane to the conduct of empirical inquiry. A degree of success, it is hoped, has been achieved in striking a balance between theoretical and empirical concerns. At the very least, the way has been cleared for paying more than lip-service to these interests.

By now, though, most novices are anxious to get beyond matters pertaining to the nature and goals of scientific activity, causation, and theory. To round out the introductory section of the text, the following chapter recognizes this eagerness by examining several basic research designs. Although it is too early yet to go to the field and start "doing science," it is certainly time to move toward the drawing board.

SOME QUESTIONS FOR REVIEW

1. In what ways do views of theories as unsubstantiated ideas, mysteries, and confirmed postulates impede progress toward integrating theoretical and empirical activities in the research process?

2. Why is it so important to view theoretical activities as part of the research process?

3. Discuss the ideal and pragmatic criteria used in determining whether acts of ideas are theories. Is the distinction between them valuable? Why?

4. Apply pragmatic criteria to at least two areas of specialized interest in one or another social science. What, in your estimation, can be learned about the research needs of these areas from such an exercise?

5. Distinguish between empirical applicability and operationalization. Discuss the responsibilities of theorists to the process of testing

theories. Find examples of instances where these responsibilities are being neglected.

6. Locate examples in the literature of deductive and inductive approaches to theory building. How explicit are the procedures followed in each example? What steps are in need of further refinement? Why?

7. Examine the pros and cons of theoretical models. Find at least two such models and compare them from the standpoint of their scientific utility.

NOTES

1. For an excellent statement on this problem, see Robert K. Merton, "Introduction," in Gustave LeBon, *The Crowd: A Study of the Popular Mind* (New York: Viking Press, 1960), pp. v.–xxxix.
2. There are different views among theorists regarding the place of parsimony. For some contrasting views, see Homans (1950), Parsons, (1951), and Zetterberg (1969).
3. Italics in original.
4. No effort will be made in this presentation to assess the relative merits of these various alternatives. Suffice it to say there are complicated issues encountered no matter which one is selected.

BIBLIOGRAPHY

Angell, R. C. "Comment on Discussions of the Analytic Induction Method," *American Sociological Review* 19 (1954): 476–77.
Becker, H. A. "Becoming a Marijuana User," *American Journal of Sociology* 59 (1953): 235–42.
Blalock, Hubert M. *Theory Construction.* Englewood Cliffs, N.J.: Prentice-Hall, 1969.
Blumer, Herbert. "What Is Wrong with Social Theory?" *American Sociological Review* 19 (1955): 3–10.
Burgess, Robert L., and Ronald L. Akers. "A Differential Association-Reinforcement Theory of Criminal Behavior," *Social Problems* 14 (1966): 128–47.
Camilleri, Santo F. "Theory, Probability, and Induction in Social Research," *American Sociological Review* 27 (1962): 170–78.

Cloward, Richard A., and Lloyd E. Ohlin. *Delinquency and Opportunity*. New York: Free Press, 1960.

Coleman, James S. *Introduction to Mathematical Sociology*. New York: Free Press, 1964.

Cressey, Donald R. *Other People's Money*. New York: Free Press, 1953.

Dubin, R. *Theory Building*. New York: Free Press, 1969.

Gibbs, Jack. *Sociological Theory Construction*. Hinsdale, Ill.: Dryden Press, 1972.

Hage, Jerald. *Techniques and Problems of Theory Construction in Sociology*. New York: Wiley-Interscience, 1972.

Hagedorn, Robert, and Sanford Labovitz. *An Introduction into Sociological Orientations*. New York: John Wiley, 1973.

Hirschi, Travis, and Hanan C. Selvin. *Delinquency Research: An Appraisal of Analytic Methods*. New York: Free Press, 1967.

Homans, George C. "Contemporary Theory in Sociology." In *Handbook of Modern Sociology*, edited by R. E. L. Farris. Chicago: Rand McNally, 1964.

Homans, George C. *The Human Group*. New York: Harcourt, Brace, 1950.

Kerlinger, Fred N. *Foundations of Behavioral Research*. New York: Holt, Rinehart, and Winston, 1965.

Kinch, J. W. "A Formalized Theory of the Self-Concept," *American Journal of Sociology* 68 (1963): 481–86.

Kuhn, Thomas S. *The Structure of Scientific Revolution*. Chicago: University of Chicago Press, 1962.

Lindesmith, A. *Addiction and Opiates*. Rev. ed. Chicago: Aldine, 1968.

McKinney, John C. *Constructive Typology and Social Theory*. New York: Appleton-Century-Crofts, 1966.

Merton, R. K. *Social Theory and Social Structure*. New York: Free Press, 1957.

Parsons, Talcott. *The Social System*. New York: Free Press, 1951.

———, and Edward A. Shils, eds. *Toward a General Theory of Action*. Cambridge, Mass.: Harvard University Press, 1954.

Reynolds, Paul Davidson. *A Primer in Theory Construction*. Indianapolis: Bobbs-Merrill, 1971.

Robinson, W. S. "The Logical Structure of Analytic Induction." *American Sociological Review* 16 (1951): 812–18.

Schwirian, Kent P., and John W. Prehn. "An Axiomatic Theory of Urbanization," *American Sociological Review* 27 (1962), 812–25.

Selltiz, Claire; Marie Jahoda; Morton Deutsch; and Stuart W. Cook. *Research Methods in Social Relations*. New York: Holt, Rinehart, and Winston, 1951.

Short, James F., Jr., and Fred L. Strodtbeck. *Group Press and Gang Delinquency*. Chicago: University of Chicago Press, 1965.

Stinchcombe, Arthur L. *Constructing Social Theory*. New York: Harcourt Brace Jovanovich, 1968.

Sutherland, Edwin H., and Donald R. Cressey. *Principles of Criminology*. New York: J. B. Lippincott, 1955.

Theodorson, T., and A. Theodorson, eds. *A Modern Dictionary of Sociology*. New York: T. Y. Crowell, 1969.

Wallace, Walter. *The Logic of Science in Sociology*. Chicago: Aldine-Atherton, 1971.

Zetterberg Hans, L. *On Theory and Verification in Sociology*. Totowa, N.J.: Bedminster, 1963.

CHAPTER 4
RESEARCH DESIGNS

Research interests of social investigators are virtually unlimited. Any social setting is a potential target for scientific examination. In spite of the diversity of possible social topics and/or situations investigated, most contemporary social scientific research is characterized by some type of study plan. This plan is conventionally labeled *the research design*.

There is general agreement in the literature regarding the definition and functions of research designs or plans. For example, Kirk (1968, p. 1) and Selltiz et al. (1959, p. 50) indicate that research designs are plans that specify *how data should be collected and analyzed*. Selltiz, et al. (1959, p. 50) add that research designs should also *seek to combine relevance to the research purpose with economy in procedure*. In view of these definitions, the major objectives of this chapter are twofold:

1. **To examine several conventional research designs commonly employed in empirical social investigations.**   Given space limitations, it is not the intention of this chapter to cover *all possible* designs that may be applied in social research. Rather, several plans have been selected for discussion that appear to have the greatest degree of utility from the standpoint of their frequency of usage in the sociological literature.

2. **To compare and contrast the designs discussed in terms of some of the major advantages, disadvantages, and uses exhibited by each.** No single research design is universally applicable for all social researchers at any particular time. Each type of research design functions to allow the investigator to conduct social inquiry in different ways and at different levels of sophistication. Selecting the appropriate research design, therefore, is dependent on the *kinds of questions* an investigator wishes to answer.

Frequently, several research designs may be used in a proposed project geared to shed light on specific social questions. However, one type of research design as an alternative may be the best in a particular instance. For example, social question X may be investigated by research designs *A, B,* or *C.* The decision to select the best design of the three (in view of the social question to be answered) involves juxtapositioning the weaknesses, strengths, and functions of each research plan with the researcher's interests and obtaining the *best fit.*[1]

SOME MAJOR FUNCTIONS OF RESEARCH DESIGNS

Regardless of the *type* of research design selected by the social investigator, all plans perform one or more functions outlined and discussed below. The number of functions performed by any design largely depends upon the sophistication of it coupled with the researcher's concerns.

Perhaps the most important function of research designs is that they provide the researcher with a blueprint for studying social questions.   Without adequate drawings and plans, a homebuilder would become burdened with insurmountable problems such as where to place the foundation, what kinds and qualities of materials to use, how many workers are required, how large should the home be, and so on. By the same token, a social researcher faces comparable obstacles if he commences his study without some kind of research plan. To minimize his research problems, there are several decisions he should make before beginning his project. For example, if he chooses to study people directly, some possible considerations might be (1) a description of the target population about which he seeks information, (2) the sampling methods used to obtain his elements (people or things), (3) the size of sample, (4) the data collection procedures to be used to acquire the needed information, (5) possible ways of analyzing the data once collected, and (6) whether or not to use statistical tests, and if so, which one(s)? These problems are given strong consideration in a research proposal, prospectus, or study outline that many investigators elect to construct in advance of their research. An example of a research proposal will be presented in a later section of this chapter.

Research designs dictate boundaries of research activity and enable the investigator to channel his energies in specific directions. Without the delineation of research boundaries and/or objectives, a researcher's activities in a single project could be virtually endless. Many professors directing the work of their graduate students are probably familiar with the problem of dealing with the loose ends of an improperly planned (or unplanned) research project. With clear research objectives in view, however, investigators can proceed systematically toward the achievement of certain goals. The *structure* provided by the research plan enables the investigator to reach closure and consider any given project completed.[2]

A third function of a research design is that it enables the investigator to anticipate potential problems in the implementation of the study. It is customary for researchers to review current literature central to the topic under investigation. In the course of the literature review, they may learn about new or alternative approaches to their problems. At the same time they can acquire information concerning what can reasonably be expected to occur in their own investigations. Many articles in the professional journals, as well as specialized monographs, include suggestions for further study. More important, many authors provide criticisms of their own work so that future investigations of the same or similar topics may be improved.[3] In addition, the design can function to provide some estimate of the cost of the research, possible measurement problems, and the optimal allocation of resources such as assistants (manpower) and material.

SOME RESEARCH DESIGN OBJECTIVES

Selltiz et al. (1959, p. 50) indicate that research designs are closely linked to an investigator's objectives. Accordingly, they specify that research designs are *exploratory, descriptive,* and/or *experimental* in nature. Consistent with these types of research designs, they delineate four major purposes of social research: (1) to gain familiarity with a phenomenon or to gain insights, (2) to describe things, (3) to determine associations between variables, and/or (4) to test hypotheses. Few projects, if any, are conducted for purposes other than those stated above.

Regardless of the type of research design selected by the investigator or the objectives he hopes to achieve, a universal characteristic of any research plan is *flexibility.* It has been noted that a common function of research designs is to assist the investigator in providing answers to various kinds of social questions. A research plan conceived at one point in time is not necessarily free from alteration should unexpected conditions be encountered in a given social setting. The point of this brief discussion, therefore, is that research designs are guidelines for investigative activity and not necessarily hard-and-fast rules that must remain unbroken. This is an implicit assumption accompanying the treatment of all successive designs below.

EXPLORATORY OBJECTIVES

Research designs may have predominantly exploratory objectives. Exploratory research is characterized by several features. First, it is assumed that the investigator *has little or no knowledge about the problem or situation under investigation.* General unfamiliarity with a particular group of people or other such research target does not provide the investigator with much opportunity to focus upon specific aspects of the social situation. Exploratory research has as one of its chief merits the discovery of potentially significant factors that may be assessed in greater detail and depth at a later date and with a more sophisticated type of research design.

For instance, if a researcher wanted to study social interaction patterns of inmates in prison systems but knew little or nothing about the structure and functioning of penal institutions, an exploratory research project would be in order. A preliminary investigation of several prison settings and interviews with wardens and/or other prison officials would enable the researcher to develop a more sophisticated and specific study plan.

As a second example, if an investigator wished to analyze the content of book reviews in major trade journals as a means of determining the nature and direction of interests in an academic field over a fixed time period, he would first have to determine *which* journals contained book reviews and for what years, whether there was a sufficient number of book reviews from year to year to make such a study worthwhile, whether there were stylistic differences in reviews from journal to journal examined, and what types of categorization or classification problems he would have to overcome. (See Champion and Morris, 1973, for one application.) Exploratory studies, therefore, serve primarily to acquaint the researcher with the characteristics of his research target, whatever it may be.

DESCRIPTIVE OBJECTIVES

Much of the sociological literature is replete with descriptive studies of all types of social situations. A few examples of the diversity of social settings as objects of descriptive studies include Andreski's (1968) portrayal of military organization and society, McCormick's (1960) description of managerial unionism in the coal industry, Mouledous' (1963) description of the organization and goals of a prison social system, Whyte's (1948, 1949) descriptions of the social structure of the restaurant industry, Findikyan and Sells' (1966) examination of campus student organizations, Georgopoulos and Mann's (1962) study of hospital organization, Anderson's (1968) discussion of bureaucratic structure in school systems, Landy and Singer's (1961) study of the social organization and culture of a club for former mental patients, Flittie and Nelson's (1968) description of the occupational role of truck drivers, and Davis' (1959) examination of the cabdriver and his fares.

Although an exact tally of the number of predominantly descriptive studies undertaken during the past 30 years cannot be readily ascertained, it would appear from a cursory review of available literature that the bulk of sociological material in print to date is, for the most part, descriptive in nature.

Before universal patterns of social interaction can be delineated, there must be extensive descriptive material available about people under diverse social conditions. Descriptive studies provide researchers with a vast amount of information about many social settings. Describing certain characteristics of a sample or population of elements will enable the investigator to construct more sophisticated experimental research designs at a later date.

Contrasted with exploratory studies, descriptive designs are more specific in that they direct attention to particular aspects or dimensions of the research target. The heuristic value of descriptive studies must be considered a major contribution as well. Consistent with at least one of the objectives of research designs outlined by Selltiz et al. (1959, p. 50), descriptive studies can reveal potential relationships between variables, thus setting the stage for more elaborate investigation later.

EXPERIMENTAL OBJECTIVES

Designs with the objective of experimentation implicitly include the control of variables. The researcher experiments by observing the effects of one or more variables upon others under controlled conditions.

The use of the word *control* in social research has several connotations. In one sense, *control* means to *hold constant one or more factors while others are free to vary.* For instance, if the variable, *sex*, is believed to be a crucial factor in an experimental situation, sex is controlled by observing the differential reactions of males in contrast with females to a specific stimulus or experimental variable. An experimental variable may be a sound, an electrical shock administered to the skin, a dosage of drug, a social situation, or any other external condition to which the sample of males and females is exposed. If we control for the variable, age, this variable is said to be held constant. In other words, how do all individuals between the ages sixteen to nineteen behave compared with individuals in the age category twenty to twenty-three when exposed to a common stimulus?

A simple example illustrating the importance of controls over certain variables in an experimental study is shown in Tables 4-1, 4-2, 4-3, and 4-4. Table 4-1 shows a hypothetical sample of college students and a distributional arrangement of their attitudes (favorable or unfavorable) toward premarital sex. This table gives us some general in-

Table 4-1. Students' Attitudes Toward Premarital Sex

		Students
Attitude toward	Favorable	230
premarital sex	Unfavorable	170
		$N = 400^a$

^{a} N = total number of persons in sample.

Table 4-2. Students' Attitudes Toward Premarital Sex Controlled for Sex

		Male	Female	Totals
Attitude toward	Favorable	155	75	230
premarital sex	Unfavorable	60	110	170
		$N_1 = 215$[a]	$N_2 = 185$[b]	$N_T = 400$[c]

[a] N_1 = the first sample consisting of males.
[b] N_2 = the second sample consisting of females.
[c] N_T = the combined samples of males & females.

formation about what this sample of students thinks about premarital sex. If we wish to control for sex, we would differentiate the students into sex *subclasses*, male and female. Table 4-2 shows the students' attitudes toward premarital sex, but in this instance we have *controlled for sex*. Table 4-2 gives us a much more specific appraisal of the impact of the variable, sex, on attitudes toward premarital sex. We may even find *year in school* as a control to be advantageous as well. Table 4-3 shows students' attitudes toward premarital sex controlled for year in school. Of course, if we wanted to control for both sex and year in school, our table would be somewhat more complex and would appear similar to that shown in Table 4-4. If our sample were sufficiently large, we could legitimately derive the percentage of the actual frequency distributions throughout all cells shown in the table and determine several things about attitudinal differences of individuals compared by year in school and sex. It should be noted that continuing the addition of control variables and subdividing the table will decrease substantially the cell frequencies. For statistical analysis purposes, this makes the job of interpreting what we find increasingly difficult. The decreasing of cell frequencies not only makes it less legitimate to derive the percentage of the data we have, but for statistical and/or theoretical reasons beyond the scope of this text, any extensive data analysis becomes increasingly meaningless.

In another sense, the word *control* is used to refer to a group or an individual not exposed to an *experimental variable*. For instance, if we were to administer a drug to one group of persons and withhold the drug from another group, the group receiving the drug would be called the experimental group, whereas the other group (not receiving the drug) would be called the control group. Sometimes each in-

Table 4-3. Attitudes Toward Premarital Sex Controlled for Year in School

Attitudes toward premarital sex		Year in School				Totals
		Freshman	Sophomore	Junior	Senior	
	Favorable	40	50	65	75	230
	Unfavorable	60	50	35	25	170
		$N_1 = 100$	$N_2 = 100$	$N_3 = 100$	$N_4 = 100$	$N_T = 400$

Table 4-4. Attitudes Toward Premarital Sex by Year in School and Sex

Attitude toward premarital sex	Year in School								Totals
	Freshman		Sophomore		Junior		Senior		
	Male	Female	Male	Female	Male	Female	Male	Female	
Favorable	30	10	40	10	45	20	40	35	230
Unfavorable	10	50	20	30	15	20	15	10	170
Totals	$N_1 = 40$	$N_2 = 60$	$N_3 = 60$	$N_4 = 40$	$N_5 = 60$	$N_6 = 40$	$N_7 = 55$	$N_8 = 45$	$N_T = 400$

dividual acts as his own control. This is usually in a before/after experimental situation. A person or persons receive a stimulus (experimental variable) in one time period, and some behavior they exhibit is measured. Then in a second time period (the time interval between the first and second time periods varies widely according to the researcher's interests and the type of experiment conducted), the same behavior is noted that was observed in the first time period. The two behaviors for the same individual or group are compared to determine the effect or effects of the experimental variable. *The individual or group is said to act as (his) (their) own control(s).*

Research designs, therefore, may have exploratory, descriptive, or experimental objectives. Many research designs include elements of all three types. There is some exploration associated with description. There is some description associated with experimentation, and so on. Implicit in this discussion is that various research projects *emphasize* specific objectives but may include others by way of secondary considerations.

SOME CONVENTIONAL RESEARCH DESIGN TYPES

In this section we will examine several conventional research designs used by social scientists to answer various kinds of questions. Perhaps the two most popular research designs chosen by sociologists and affiliates of their profession are (1) the survey and (2) the case study. A third type of research design that assumes numerous forms is labeled experimental. Special attention will be directed toward several popular experimental research designs in a later portion of the present discussion.

THE SURVEY DESIGN

Survey research has been defined simply as "gathering information about a large number of people by interviewing a few of them" (Backstrom and Hursh, 1963, p. 3). Hyman (1955) differentiates between descriptive and explanatory surveys, and although no formal definition of a survey design is apparent in his work, there does seem to be implicit in Hyman's work a general consistency in the meaning of survey research with that provided by Backstrom and Hursh (1963, p. 3).[1]

It should be noted that a survey design may serve many functions including exploration, description, and experimentation. The general nature of a survey design is subject to little variation, however. We would seek to modify the definition of Backstrom and Hursh by defining survey designs as *specifications of procedures for gathering information about a large number of people by collecting information from a few of them.* There are several data collection alternatives available to the survey researcher in addition to interviewing (e.g., questionnaire administration, personal observations, and the like).

Regardless of the objectives sought by the individual survey researcher, there are several standards to which he would like to adhere. These focus primarily on the quality of the survey. The quality of a given survey, in turn, depends on (1) the number of people one is able to obtain for the study, (2) their typicalness in relation to the population from which they are selected, and (3) the reliability of the data collected from them. The first two criteria of survey quality are directly related to the problem of *sampling.*[5] Sampling means to select a few people from a larger collection of them. Since the researcher is most likely interested in generalizing the findings obtained from his sample to the population from which they were drawn, it is necessary that he select his sample of persons according to certain rules of probability theory.[6]

The third criterion of survey quality—the reliability of data—is dependent on the extent to which the researcher obtains the cooperation of persons he studies. If he asks them questions (such as in an interview situation),[7] he wants them to tell the truth about whatever they are asked.[8] Because there is no way of forcing people to tell the truth, the researcher must often relegate this dimension to the philosophical level. In essence, this means that the investigator accepts the information obtained from a survey subject to all of the potential limitations on it.

One example of survey research is a study of social class, parental encouragement, and educational aspirations by Sewell and Shah (1968, pp. 562-63). They selected at random (see Chapter 8) 10,318 Wisconsin 1957 high school seniors (about a third of the total number of high school seniors for Wisconsin that year). "Information was obtained from the respondents, school authorities, and a statewide testing program on a number of matters, including the student's educational and occupational plans, the student's percentile rank in measured intelligence, the socioeconomic status of his family, his rank in his high school class, his course of study, and the educational attitudes of the student and his family." The primary purpose of the study by Sewell and Shah was to examine the relationship between socioeconomic status and college plans.[9] The basic conclusion of their study (reflecting the explanatory nature of it as well as its descriptive aspects) was that

> . . . the correlational, causal, and cross-tabular analyses of this study substantiate, on the whole, the claim made by other investigators using less rigorous methods and less representative samples that parental encouragement is a powerful intervening variable between socioeconomic class background and intelligence of the child and his educational aspirations. While parental encouragement does not "explain" social class differences in aspirations, it contributes to the explanation of these differences (Sewell and Shah, p. 571).

Another example of survey research is a study of maternal employment and anxiety over the mother role by White (1972). In the spring of 1965, a sample of women sixteen years of age or older was mailed a questionnaire containing items about employment status, age, number of children, care provided for small children during mother's absences, and so on. Of the 15,000 population (a small community in south-central Washington), 1,092 questionnaires were returned completed. In this survey, several hypotheses were tested relating to anxiety over the mother role between employed and nonemployed mothers. On the basis of the information obtained (responses to the questionnaires), it was tentatively concluded that, as a concept, status conflict appears to be useful in the prediction of certain kinds of anxiety. Some of the hypotheses concerning middle-class and working-class mothers were not upheld, however. Therefore, the study suggested potential weaknesses in traditional notions sociologists have about the implications of particular kinds of child-rearing philosophies.

Both of these studies as examples of survey research involved contacting a sample of individuals from a larger population. On the basis of information obtained (either through questionnaire, interview, direct observation, or combinations of these data collection techniques), certain assumptions and hypotheses were subjected to test, several dimensions of group behavior were more extensively described, and several insights were achieved regarding the respective problems under investigation.

Some Major Advantages of Survey Designs

1.   The most apparent advantage of survey designs is the accumulation of information from individuals at relatively low cost to the researcher. Surveys, particularly those involving the use of mailed questionnaires (see Chapter 11), are an inexpensive means of obtaining information from large numbers of people without contacting them directly. If interviewing (see Chapter 10) is used, the costs of research soar drastically. Researchers must train persons to develop appropriate interviewing techniques and skills. Little time usually exists for such preparation. If professional interviewers are used from some research agency, potential costs per interview could run as high as $30 or more.

2. **Because large numbers of persons are usually included in a survey, generalizability to larger populations is more legitimate.** Public opinion polls of presidential elections are frequently of the survey type. Trends about population behaviors are inferred on the basis of the attitudes of the select number of individuals drawn from the larger human aggregate. One is cautioned, however, to scrutinize carefully the representativeness and/or typicalness of the sample obtained in relationship to the characteristics of the population about which inferences will be made.

3. **Surveys are flexible to permit the use of a variety of data collection techniques.** Observation, interviewing, and/or questionnaires can be used in survey designs to collect information from individuals. Which of the techniques will be used is a decision made by the researcher(s).

4. **Surveys sensitize the researcher to potential problems that were originally unanticipated or unknown.** Surveys requesting written responses and/or verbal reactions from respondents often uncover facts previously unknown to the investigator. In this sense, surveys perform an exploratory function, and serendipitous findings should not be entirely unexpected.

5. **Surveys are useful tools that enable investigators to verify theories.** The survey is one way of obtaining support or lack of support for particular theoretical notions about people.

Some General Disadvantages of Survey Designs

1. **Surveys are superficial reflections of population sentiments.** Seldom can researchers take the time to obtain in-depth information about the personal opinions and attitudes expressed by respondents, especially when questionnaires are used.

2. **Surveys, particularly political surveys, are unstable reflections of population characteristics.** Attitudes toward busing school children,

increasing or decreasing federal aid to education, and the like are apt to elicit strong reactions from prospective respondents. The major problem centers on the fluctuation of opinion about such matters, however. A survey of opinions of a sample of individuals one week may be quite different from a similar survey of the same individuals a week or two later. Speeches by political leaders, international and national affairs, management and union clashes, stock market trends, and campus discontent and disruption among other things can bring about drastic changes of opinion of a given sample of individuals. One type of survey design, *the panel design,* is indicative of attitudinal instability of a given segment of individuals. Figure 4-1 illustrates the basic structure of a panel survey design.

Panel designs are useful for revealing trends and are especially applicable during political campaigns. The information in Figure 4-1 shows a cross section or representative sample of individuals from a larger population of elements. These individuals are examined in five successive time periods regarding their attitudes toward a particular issue or political candidate. The fluctuations observed from one time period (t_1) to the next (t_2) are usually attributable to some intervening phenomenon (a speech, political decision, or some other significant political or social action). Forecasts of outcomes of elections are based on trends observed from panels of persons observed over time.

3.   The researcher has little or no control over individual responses to surveys.   Those responding differ from those who do not respond on at least one dimension—response vs. nonresponse. The potential bias resulting from such surveys (which is difficult, if not impossible, to

Figure 4-1

$t_1{}^a$ . . . . t_2 . . . . t_3 . . . . t_4 . . . . t_5

| Sample | Sample | Sample | Sample | Sample |
| observations | observations | observations | observations | observations |

Observations of the same sample of elements are made under k^b different time periods. Comparisons of opinions expressed or observations from one time period to the next (i.e., $t_1 - t_2$) are interpreted to be reflections of changes of opinions as a result of an intervening variable or variables.

---

[a] t = a given time period. The various subscripts (i.e., t_1, t_2, and so on) reflect specific time periods when observations of subjects are made.

[b] k refers to two or more time periods. It is a general symbol connoting some number from 2 to infinity.

determine) significantly limits the generalizability of one's findings to total populations from which the original samples were obtained (Clausen, 1969).

4. Statements about populations from which samples are obtained are tentative. Response is indicative of potential interest in the topic being investigated or the information requested. The researcher manipulates the data obtained by tabular and statistical analyses and arrives at tentative conclusions relative to some notion held (in some instances) about the target population. This is not really a serious disadvantage, inasmuch as social scientists (as well as *all* scientists) are obligated by their respective professional codes and orientations to regard their research findings with caution and to take into account the potential limitations accompanying research projects from start to conclusion.

THE CASE STUDY DESIGN

Although some researchers argue that case studies do not qualify as "designs" (e.g., Hagedorn and Labovitz, 1971, pp. 36–41 designate research designs in general as "the logical manner in which individuals are compared and analyzed"), case studies constitute one of the most popular types of research designs used by social scientists currently (in the context of the definition below). Foreman (1948, pp. 408–9) provides one of the clearest definitions of a case study and situations to which the definition may pertain. He says

> . . . a case study, basically, is a depiction either of a phase or the totality of relevant experience of some selected datum. When the investigator's attention is focused on development, the account is a case history. When a panoramic view of the present is obtained, case studies may be called cross-sectional or photographic. In either instance the datum may in sociological study be any of the following, taken singly or in combination: (1) a person, (2) a group of persons such as a gang or family, (3) a class of persons such as professors or thieves, (4) an ecological unit such as a neighborhood or community, (5) a cultural unit such as a fashion or institution.

He goes on to note that "case study materials may come to the social scientist by way of (a) personal documents [see Chapter 12], (b) participant observation records [see Chapter 9], or (c) third person reports [see Chapter 10]." These are discussed as various means of data collection in the chapters noted. Extensive discussions of their limitations and strengths accompany their definition and elaboration.

Because so many subareas of sociology exist presently, it is difficult, if not impossible, to provide the reader with an example of a "typical" case study design. One example from the formal organizational literature is the work of Champion and Dager (1967), who conducted a case study of a bank undergoing change as the result of the introduction of an electronic data processing (EDP) computer system. According to the authors, virtually every important facet of bank activity including employee sentiments was scrutinized carefully before, during, and after the changeover to EDP. Such data collection procedures as interviewing with tape recorders, personal observation, and questionnaire administration were used to obtain information about the nature and consequences of the change process. Background characteristics of each employee were compiled that included among other things crude approximations of personality profiles. Champion and Dager not only described the changeover to EDP in considerable detail, but they also developed a tentative distinction between those employees who appeared to adapt successfully to the changeover and those who were not adaptable to the change. *The fact that the research constituted a case study did not alter the tentative nature of the interpretation of findings.*[10]

Although definitional variations exist among social scientists regarding case studies, most would tend to agree that primary distinctions between case studies and surveys would be the *intensity* and *depth* of the investigation. Case studies are usually characterized as thorough examinations of specific social settings or particular aspects of social settings, including in varying detail psychological descriptions of persons in those settings.

A series of case studies was conducted during the mid-1950s by the U.S. Department of Labor Bureau of Labor Statistics.[11] These pertained respectively to a modernized petroleum refinery, an automatic airline reservation system, and several insurance companies. Some additional examples of case studies may be found in the work of Chinoy (1955) who studied intensively 62 automobile workers in a large factory through interviewing and participant observation; the classic investigation of the structure and process of a community, "Middletown," by the Lynds (1929, 1937); Sayles' (1958, p. 6) in-depth descriptions of workmen in hammershops, shipping departments, metal disking, and punch press departments derived from "an examination of work records, interviews, and observations of 300 work groups in thirty plants in a variety of industries"; and Argyris' (1958) case study of a bank.

Some Major Advantages of Case Study Designs

1. Case studies are flexible with respect to data collection methods used. Interviews, observation, questionnaires, and other data collection forms are possibilities for use in in-depth analyses of specific social situations.

2. The flexibility of a case study extends to virtually any dimension of the topic studied. Although a chief characteristic of case study designs is thoroughness of the investigation, specific aspects of the individual or social situation studied are emphasized while other aspects are not included. This means that although we may do a case study of a bank, for example, we focus on all important dimensions of bank activity that are important to us from the theoretical perspective we have developed. Needless to say, there are additional bank characteristics that do not logically fit into our data collection scheme. Although the Lynds (1929) studied "Middletown" in considerable detail, it is expected that certain dimensions of community life escaped their careful scrutiny. These were probably due to intentional exclusions because the particular dimension(s) in question did not fall within their theoretical and/or substantive concerns. By the same token, some dimensions were not investigated because the Lynds may have been unaware of the existence of them and/or their theoretical relevance to the purpose(s) of their study.

3. Case studies may be conducted in practically any kind of social setting. The primary factors affecting the selection of specific research sites are (a) the accessibility of elements, (b) the costs of the research, and (c) the time and manpower restrictions within which the researcher must operate.

4. Case studies offer specific instances of tests of theories. Provided that the investigator has adequately prepared a theoretical framework within which to cast his research activity, a case study may provide him with an opportunity to put one or more aspects of the theory to empirical test. As was indicated in Chapter 3, theory verification may be approached from several alternative perspectives. A case study may be viewed as a test of a more general theory to the degree that a survey design is able to achieve the same objective. Both types of research designs have their respective limitations and strengths regarding generalizability, however. A survey makes possible certain generalizations to the extent that the elements surveyed are representative of the population from which they are drawn. Similarly, a case study design has as its major concern typicalness for purposes of generalizability. An intensive case study may be equally generalizable to larger social situations or aggregates compared to the more superficial survey.

5. Case studies may be quite inexpensive, depending upon the extent of inquiry involved and type of data collection technique(s) used. Certainly a researcher's costs are kept to a minimum where data can be collected first-hand and in-depth from on-the-job experiences. It is not unusual to find researchers conducting case studies of social settings of which they are a part. This stems from the fact that their affiliation with the organization or group studied supports and helps to legitimize their research efforts. They are not outsiders and do not encounter refusals as often as outsiders.[12]

Some Major Disadvantages of Case Study Designs

1. Perhaps the most prominent disadvantage of case studies is their limited generalizability. Although case studies are conducted in such a way as to provide detailed information about social units, they are often criticized as being limited in scope and not sufficient for meaningful generalizations to be made to larger social aggregates. Again, we encounter the problem of the representativeness of the case. Of course, representativeness is a primary question in the assessment of the quality and generalizability of surveys as well.

On the theoretical level, however, it may be argued that findings from case studies lend support to or provide refutation of theories. The researcher does not regard case study findings as conclusive proof of anything. Neither does the survey researcher. Only through the accumulation of findings from many case studies and many surveys investigating similar phenomena can we begin to generate statements about the social world that have little or no exception.

2. Case studies are generally more time-consuming contrasted with surveys. Case studies frequently involve the direct participation of the researcher in the recording and collection of salient information. Some survey designs can be equally time-consuming, however, particularly those in which personal interviews are utilized as the primary mode of data collection.

A CONCLUDING NOTE ON SURVEYS AND CASE STUDIES

Illustration will perhaps make survey and case study designs clearer. Figures 4-2 and 4-3 reveal one way of looking at each design in relation to a larger social aggregate. Figure 4-2 shows that a survey derives elements from a total population. Characteristics of the sample of elements are generalized tentatively to the entire population of elements. Figure 4-3 shows a case study in relation to an "unknown" population. The typicalness of a case study in relation to some population is all but impossible to assess. However, because a social situation is involved, certain theoretical propositions and hypotheses can be put to test, again on a tentative basis.

It should be clear that both types of research designs discussed above may be used to test hypotheses. In fact, in some instances, both designs can be used to test the *same hypotheses.* Case studies appear to have greater utility for hypothesis tests about the structural and procedural characteristics (e.g., mobility patterns, status relations, interpersonal characteristics) of specific social units (e.g., organizations, small groups, cliques, communities). In addition to their descriptive value, surveys are of great utility for testing hypotheses about large social aggregates (e.g., female voters between twenty-one and thirty-

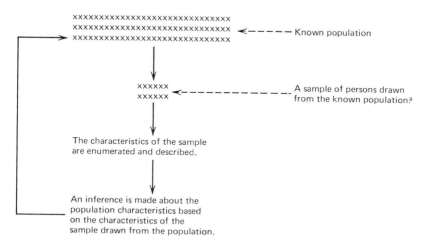

 xxxxxxxxxxxxxxxxxxxxxxxxxxxxxx
xxxxxxxxxxxxxxxxxxxxxxxxxxxxxx ◄ — — — — — Known population
xxxxxxxxxxxxxxxxxxxxxxxxxxxxxx

xxxxxx ◄ — — — — — — — — — — — A sample of persons drawn
xxxxxx   from the known population[a]

The characteristics of the sample
are enumerated and described.

An inference is made about the
population characteristics based
on the characteristics of the
sample drawn from the population.

[a] See Chapter 8 for an extensive discussion of sampling methods used for generalization purposes.

Figure 4-2.   A simple illustration of a survey.

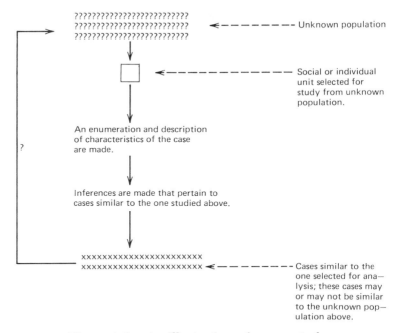

Figure 4-3. An illustration of a case study.

five, Republican attitudes toward certain community issues, prejudicial reactions of specific target groups toward certain ethnic and/or racial minorities).

EXPERIMENTAL DESIGNS

This final section on research designs is about a very large number of strategies geared to assess the effects of particular variables on people under heavily controlled conditions. All such designs that seek to control conditions within which persons are observed and analyzed may be called *experimental designs*. The totality of experimental designs in social research runs the gamut from very simple to extremely complex. Several books exist that include extensive descriptions of many kinds of experimental designs.[13]

Before commencing our discussion of various kinds of experimental designs, it will be helpful to treat briefly the subject of *control groups*. The word *control* was touched on in an earlier section of this chapter in relation to studies with experimental objectives. By way of review, a control group is defined as one that is either (1) not exposed to an experimental variable and compared with a group which is exposed to it, or (2) used as the target of research by being observed prior to an experimental variable, exposed to the experimental variable, and then observed after exposure to the experimental variable. In other words, the single control group acts as its own control.

Control groups are used in experimental designs so that the researcher may ascertain the effect(s) of an experimental variable or variables on an experimental group or groups. Reviewing again, an experimental group is one that is exposed to an experimental variable. Therefore, a control group and an experimental group can be the same group when the individuals in the group act as their own controls in response to the experimental variable over k time periods. Variations in the uses of control groups are illustrated in Figures 4-4 and 4-5.

The major problem related to the use of control groups with independent experimental groups is the degree of their similarity. Obviously, an experiment with a particular drug using a control group composed exclusively of women and an experimental group composed entirely of men will demonstrate little or nothing. If a difference in the behavior of men exposed to the experimental variable is observed where no change is observed in the control group composed of women, very little, if anything, can be said about the effects

Figure 4-4

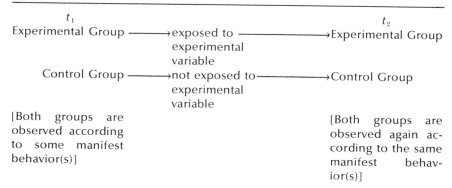

t_1		t_2
Experimental Group ———→	exposed to ———————→ experimental variable	Experimental Group
Control Group ———————→	not exposed to——————→ experimental variable	Control Group
[Both groups are observed according to some manifest behavior(s)]		[Both groups are observed again according to the same manifest behavior(s)]

Potential result: The experimental group should change (in behavior, attitude, and so on) in response to the experimental variable, whereas the control group should remain the same from one time period to the next.

Figure 4-5.

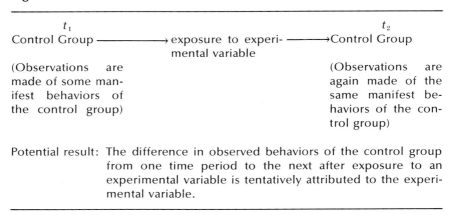

t_1
Control Group ──────────→ exposure to experi- ────────→Control Group
mental variable

(Observations are   (Observations are
made of some man-   again made of the
ifest behaviors of   same manifest be-
the control group)   haviors of the con-
                                                     trol group)

Potential result: The difference in observed behaviors of the control group
                  from one time period to the next after exposure to an
                  experimental variable is tentatively attributed to the experi-
                  mental variable.

of the drug on the experimental group in relation to the control
group because the two groups differ so dramatically regarding sex
composition. This is to say that the drug may have an effect on men,
but it may not affect the women. In fact, the drug may have no effect
at all if the change in the behavior of the experimental group is owing
to chance (which is always a possibility) regardless of whether or not
the groups are similar or different.

Researchers, therefore, attempt to equate experimental groups with
control groups on as many salient characteristics or dimensions as
possible (e.g., age, rural or urban background, socioeconomic status,
sex, years of education, and the like). Then, when changes do occur
within the experimental group but not within the control group, the
investigator is on firmer ground for tentatively inferring that a cause-
effect relation between the experimental variable and the observed
behavior change exists, and furthermore, that such changes are not
likely owing to significant differences between the experimental and
the control groups in terms of their most salient characteristics.

Apart from using each individual as his own control, there are at
least three popular methods for achieving control group-experimental
group similarities. These are (1) individual matching, (2) random
assignment, and (3) group distribution matching.

INDIVIDUAL MATCHING

Judged by many social scientists to be the most difficult method of
equating groups, individual matching involves matching each indi-

vidual in the experimental group with a person with very similar characteristics as a member of the control group. Considering the infinite number of personality variables that exist in addition to such factors as age, sex, years of education, occupation, I. Q., and so on, the task of individual matching becomes almost insurmountable. The result of such a matching method is usually to end up with extremely small samples of elements as experimental and control groups because so few people can be matched according to an extended list of salient characteristics. This is where using each individual as his own control becomes functional. This method overcomes problems of having to take into account random factors over which the researcher has little or no control (or knowledge), because each person is presumed to be *the same person* throughout successive time periods with the exception of changes in behaviors that are the targets of experimental variables.

RANDOM ASSIGNMENT

Random assignment as a means of equating groups is somewhat poor. This is because the researcher has no former or present knowledge of the salient characteristics of the randomized group members. Such a method would be comparable to taking a university faculty of size N (let's use the number, 200), and randomly (see Chapter 8 for a discussion of randomness) assigning or placing each faculty member in an experimental group or in a control group. Supposedly, the randomization of assigning faculty to each group mixes the groups substantially and overcomes any bias on the part of the researcher regarding group assignment. In reality, the true characteristics of both groups are not fully known (and may not even be partially known), and it is extremely difficult, if not impossible, to say with any degree of assurance that both groups have been properly equated.

The same problem is encountered by a researcher who would take an introductory sociology class ($N = 100$) and randomly distribute class members into two groups, one experimental and the other control. Labeling one group experimental and the other group control gives us no confidence that the groups are truely equated on any significant dimensions. The fact is there may be so much variation in student characteristics throughout the class that the researcher will not be able to know with any degree of assurance whether the difference(s) in behavior, if any, among the experimental group as a result of some experimental variable(s) are attributable to the group composition or to the experimental variable. What if the control group target behavior changes but the experimental group target behavior does not?

GROUP DISTRIBUTION MATCHING

An improvement over both of the above methods, group distribution matching involves selecting certain characteristics such as age, education, I.Q., socioeconomic status, sex, specific attitudinal similarities, and the like and locating two groups that have these characteristics distributed similarly throughout. In other words, two groups may be found that are of the same age pattern, socioeconomic pattern, I.Q. distribution, sex distribution, and attitudinal position. Selltiz *et al.* (1959, p. 107) caution that "although distributions on single factors are equated, the groups may actually be badly mismatched on combinations of these factors." Extending this caution to the present discussion, the same phenomenon could possibly occur, even if we successfully were to match two or more groups on several characteristics. They could be mismatched on variables that are theoretically and/or substantively relevant but which have been excluded intentionally or unintentionally.

As examples of the three matching methods discussed above, Figures 4-6, 4-7, and 4-8 are provided for comparative purposes.

Figure 4-6

Experimental Group		Control Group
Individual[a]	Matched with:	Individual[a]
1 ←——————————————————————→		7
2 ←——————————————————————→		8
3 ←——————————————————————→		9
4 ←——————————————————————→		10
5 ←——————————————————————→		11
6 ←——————————————————————→		12

[a] This example illustrates that 12 different individuals are involved in an experiment, six comprising the experimental group and six comprising the control group. Individual No. 1 is matched (according to certain characteristics) with individual No. 7, 2 with 8, 3 with 9, 4 with 10, 5 with 11, and 6 with 12. Therefore, if an experimental variable is introduced to the experimental group and a behavior change occurs on some target variable, and if the control group does not receive the experimental variable, the difference in target behavior between the experimental group and control group will more likely be a function of the experimental variable rather than a function of individual differences between the two groups.

Figure 4-7

random assignment	Original Group ($N = 50$)	random assignment
Experimental Group[a]		Control Group[a]
Individual No.		Individual No.
48		25
2		16
40		41
32		28
.		.
.		.
.		.
$N_1 = 25$		$N_2 = 25$

[a] This example illustrates that some original N is distributed randomly throughout two groups, one experimental, the other control. The individual numbers under each column heading indicate the persons randomly placed within each group. To accomplish random assignment, a table of random numbers may be used (See Appendix A). Each person in the original group is assigned a number, and then each person is assigned to a group as his number appears in the random numbers table. The assumption is that the two groups are sufficiently randomized so as to be considered matched. But as the discussion above indicates, there is no way to ascertain the similarity or difference between the composition of both groups after random assignment.

Using Each Individual as His Own Control

Where matching of any kind is not a consideration, observations are normally taken on a group in a preexposure-to-the-experimental-variable-time-period. Then, the group is introduced to the experimental variable. Finally, observations of the group are made after the experimental variable has been introduced. Changes in specified behaviors (targets of the experimental variable) are assumed to be attributable to the experimental variable rather than to random differences on the part of the individuals participating in the experiment.

There are cautions associated with this type of plan as well. If a time interval of sufficient length occurs between each observation, any observed changes in behavior among group members may be due to

Figure 4-8

$N_1 = 100$ Experimental Group	Characteristics used for matching[a]	$N_2 = 100$ Control Group
34.1 ⟵———————	1. Average age ——————→	34.2
14.9 ⟵———————	2. Average years of edu- ———→ cation	15.3
35/65 ⟵———————	3. Male-female composi- ———→ tion	33/67
83.9% ⟵———————	4. Percentage favorable ———→ toward group (or is- sue) X	81.8%
etc. ⟵———————	etc. ——————→	etc.

[a] Note that the characteristics exhibited by each group do not have to be exact. Approximations are permissible. The researcher uses his discretion concerning what is or what is not a good fit or close match on selected variables used for matching. This matching form overcomes the problems associated with matching individual with individual. But the researcher should maintain a degree of caution concerning possible maldistributions of characteristics that may have been inadvertently omitted in the initial selection of salient variables.

extraneous factors not immediately apparent to the investigator. The maturation of the subjects, possible changes in their jobs or family lives and the like, can create false impressions of true effects of the experimental variables. The researcher must, therefore, regulate carefully the time interval between observations and do all within his power to ascertain whether or not any factors not considered initially could have intervened between observation periods to bring about the target behavior change.

Although much more space could be devoted to the advantages and disadvantages accompanying each of the methods of control discussed above, we will now move on to treatments of several conventional social scientific experimental designs.

Three major experimental designs will be discussed here: (1) the classical experimental design, (2) the after-only experimental design, and (3) the before-after experimental design.

THE CLASSICAL EXPERIMENTAL DESIGN

Goode and Hatt (1952, pp. 76–78) offer a verbal as well as a diagrammatic description of the classical experimental design. They define it by making reference to one of John Stuart Mill's methods of proof, namely, the method of difference. Goode and Hatt state that

> ... in its simple statement, it can be formulated in this fashion: If there are two or more cases, and in one of them observation Z can be made, while in the other it cannot; and if factor C occurs when observation Z is made, and does not occur when observation Z is not made; then it can be asserted that there is a causal relationship between C and Z.

Figure 4-9 below illustrates the classical design as portrayed by Goode and Hatt.

The classical experimental design may be illustrated by hypothetical sociological example. Suppose we were to obtain two samples of individuals matched on several social and psychological variables with the exception that in one group, all subjects would have a master's degree or higher level of education while the members of the other group would possess only the bachelor's degree. Suppose further that we wished to obtain responses from both groups concerning some community political issue (e.g., zoning restrictions governing the location of liquor stores, fluoridation of the city water supply, or the like). If the outcome of our investigation revealed that 90 per cent of the more highly educated group responded favorably to the proposed changes in the community (regarding any issue, for that matter), and that 85 per cent of the less educated group responded unfavorably to the same proposals, it would appear that the educational differential between the two groups was contributory toward (if not the direct cause of) the attitudinal differences clearly observed.

Goode and Hatt (1952, pp. 78–81) are careful to point out some of the major weaknesses of such a design, especially when it comes to

Figure 4-9

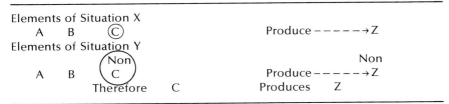

" Reprinted with the permission of McGraw-Hill Book Company, Inc. Source: William J. Goode and Paul K. Hatt, *Methods in Social Research* (McGraw-Hill Book Co., Inc., 1952), p. 77.

establishing the "proof" of the experiment. They include (1) an inability to control relevant variables in the research project, (2) lack of clarity in the causal relation between the two variables, (3) the unpredictable effect of the time factor, and (4) the oversimplification of cause-effect relations as major weaknesses of this design.

AFTER-ONLY DESIGNS

Many experimental designs intended as improvements on the classical design are, for the most part, only modifications of it (Goode and Hatt, 1952, p. 81). The after-only design seeks to compare an experimental group with a control group *after* an experimental variable has been introduced to one group and not to the other. For example, assume that two hypothetical work crews have been matched according to several important characteristics. Both groups have supervisors who allow the men much latitude in determining their own method of job performance. Assume further that in one group, the experimental group for our purposes, a change in supervisor occurs. The new supervisor over the experimental group is authoritarian and does not permit much latitude regarding job performance. Job satisfaction measures for both groups are obtained and scores tabulated and compared. Table 4-5 illustrates hypothetical data regarding the differential job satisfaction levels of the two groups.

With these figures we might assume that the supervisory change led to low job satisfaction among the experimental group members. This may or may not be true. What were the job satisfaction scores of the workers *before* the change in supervisors was introduced? Are other possible factors operating in the "after" situation that would affect the

Table 4-5. A Comparison of Job Satisfaction Scores Between Experimental and Control Groups

| | ("After" Supervisory Change) Job Satisfaction | | |
	High	Low	
Experimental Group	5	15	$N_1 = 20$
Control Group	21	2	$N_2 = 23$
			$N_T = 43$

changes in scores (e.g., a raise in pay for one group while the other group receives no raise, changes in working hours or work shifts between the two groups, and so on)?

These kinds of questions identify some of the major weaknesses of the after-only experimental design. The impact of the experimental variable on the experimental group is assessed in relation to the disparities in scores *between both groups*. The importance of after-only study designs depends in large part on the extent to which the two groups (experimental and control) are similar in social and personal characteristics. Because no matching method discussed above is infallible or perfectly effective at achieving precise matches between experimental and control groups, and because little or nothing is known about attitudinal dispositions of respective group members before obtaining measures of the target variable(s), after-only experiments should be viewed with much caution. This is especially critical when it comes to drawing tentative conclusions about causal relations between two or more variables.

THE BEFORE-AFTER DESIGN

The before-after design is a considerable improvement over the after-only design. Basically, the before-after experimental design consists of obtaining measures on some target variable or variables for at least two groups that are assumed to be matched according to certain previously specified criteria. The experimental variable is introduced to the experimental group and withheld from the control group. Measures are again taken for both groups on the target variables. This enables researchers to argue more effectively about causal relations between experimental variables and target variable changes, because the measures for both groups are compared between two separate time periods. It is assumed that the experimental group will be affected predictably by the experimental variable and that this will be revealed by comparing both the experimental and the control group scores on the previously designated target dimensions.

The control group members observed in both time periods are not exposed to the experimental variable and are expected to reflect scores similar to those they revealed in the original time period.

The principal advantage of the before-after experimental design is the ability of the researcher to evaluate experimental and control group subjects both before and after experimentation and to isolate and eliminate (or take into account, take into consideration) extraneous factors that might otherwise obscure the true effect(s) of the experimental variable. Figure 4-10 shows the before-after experimental design using an experimental and a control group. As usual, the problem of matching individuals in the experimental situation becomes a difficult task and opens to criticism the findings based on experimental group-control group comparisons.

There are many other varieties of experimental designs utilizing different numbers of control groups and randomizing the introduction of experimental variables where k time periods are involved. It is beyond the scope of this book to cover such extensions of the before-after method identified above. The reader is advised to consult specialized sources, particularly Winer (1971), for more elaborate experimental designs if needed.

The concluding two sections of this chapter will discuss in some detail the preliminary elements in the research process—research proposals and pilot studies.

A BASIC OUTLINE FOR A RESEARCH PROPOSAL

Ideally, all social research is preceded by a research proposal. A research proposal is a relatively brief statement of the problem to be investigated. It also includes specific study objectives, a representative

Figure 4-10

t_1		t_2

Experimental Group ─────→experimental varia- ─────→Experimental Group
(Observations)   ble   (Observations)
Control Group ──────────→no experimental──────────→Control Group
                                      variable

For the *experimental group,* observations on target variables should indicate changes from one time period to the next. Symbolically expressed, we should find, with respect to the experimental group, scores between the two time periods to be

$$t_1 \neq t_2.$$

For the *control group,* observations on target variables should indicate no change from one time period to the next. Again symbolically expressed, we should find scores of control group members from one time period to the next to be the same or close to the same, or

$$t_1 = t_2.$$

review of literature pertinent to the problem, a theoretical and/or substantive justification for the study, and some methodological guidelines to follow.

The research proposal is referred to by different names according to the type of research it precedes. For instance, a doctoral student preparing for a doctoral dissertation may refer to the research proposal as a dissertation proposal. A master's candidate may prepare a thesis prospectus. Others may simply refer to the proposal as a research plan, although as we have indicated, the notion of research plan is frequently used synonymously with research design. In order to avoid possible semantic problems, research plans may be viewed as integral components of the proposal or prospectus. Research plans constitute the methodological portion of the proposal.

Research proposals vary in length, complexity, and/or sophistication according to the particular standards of the investigator(s) in charge of the research activity. The format of a research proposal presented below is by no means to be considered the only way of outlining a project for social investigation. The various components included (as well as the order in which each is presented) are merely suggested as constituting a possible compilation and arrangement of the bare essentials. Many departures from the scheme below are to be expected, especially when we consider the vast array of topics of social interest as well as the diversity of researcher preferences that exists.

One way of outlining a research proposal is as follows:

1. Introduction.
2. Statement of objectives.
3. Review of the literature.
4. Theoretical structure and/or conceptual scheme.
5. Hypotheses.
6. Methodology.
7. Statement of theoretical and substantive implications.

Short discussions of each of these components are provided below. The discussions are general in nature. They are included to indicate the importance and/or significance of each section, and they are designed to be broadly applicable to projects reflecting diverse interests.

INTRODUCTION

The introduction of a research proposal should place the problem to be studied in some kind of historical perspective. The researcher should briefly illustrate the historical development of the current problem under investigation. He should also locate his particular interests in the problem fairly precisely. In short, the researcher reveals the problem to be studied and what dimension or dimensions of it will be given extensive analysis or treatment. For example, if a researcher were to be interested in studying the social and psychological effects of automation in the business setting, he might begin by describing the early origins and applications of automation in various work environments. He could follow up this historical description by discussing present uses of automation in specific settings. At this point, he could reveal his precise interests in learning about the potential social and psychological impacts of automation in contemporary businesses.

STATEMENT OF OBJECTIVES

The objectives of research projects detail what the researcher wishes to accomplish as a result of his investigative activity. What are the specific goals to be achieved? Sometimes this section is broken down into subparts to include major and minor objectives. There are primary concerns of the investigator as well as secondary ones. In this event, the researcher possibly arranges his objectives in a hierarchical fashion, listing them from most important to least important. Some proposals make explicit the distinction between major and minor (primary and secondary) objectives (goals).

There is no limit to the number of research objectives. Decisions as to how many objectives will be identified are based on the breadth of the research, the interests of the investigator, time, cost, and manpower considerations. Some studies may have a single objective, whereas other projects may have twenty or thirty of them. Although there are no limitations concerning the number of research objectives a project may have, it is possible for the investigator to bite off too much of a given problem. There is little wisdom in spreading oneself too thin, however. If a researcher has too many research objectives, he may encounter great difficulty in trying to tie together a lot of loose ends. Too many research objectives also necessitate a more complex theoretical scheme. Therefore, it is recommended that the investigator limit his objectives to a reasonable number. What is "reasonable" again depends on the time limitations, budgetary considerations, and manpower restrictions under which the researcher must work. It is possible, for example, for a single objective to involve more time and effort to achieve than ten objectives in a related study. The researcher must assess subjectively the objectives of his research to determine whether he has the capability to deal with the chosen problem effectively. It is wise to pick objectives that are challenging but not impossible to achieve.

Fairly precise statements of objectives are functional guidelines for research activity. Using the automation example cited above, vague or nebulous objectives might be "to see if the introduction of automation into an employee work setting will bring about attitudinal change" or "to see if the introduction of automation will bring about significant role changes among employees." These statements are considered vague because they fail to specify which attitudes and which employee roles are involved and affected by automation. Of course, it can be argued that an exploratory study may be loosely constructed so as to identify more specific research targets to be investigated with greater precision at a later date. But it would be more meaningful to state which attitudes of employees are considered most relevant for examination. A more specific statement of an objective might be "to investigate the impact of the introduction of electronic data processing [a form of automation] on employee depersonalization [an attitudinal variable]." This statement clearly indicates that the independent variable, automation, may be followed by a change on a specific dependent variable, depersonalization. One interest of the researcher, therefore, is to examine the relationship between these variables as a means of more accurately depicting potential implications of technological change on people in work environments.

REVIEW OF THE LITERATURE

The literature review is designed to familiarize the investigator with any relevant information pertaining to the topic being studied. Opinions vary concerning the extent to which a literature review should be conducted. Some researchers may be concerned with identifying all available literature on a given subject, whereas others are content to review literature in major professional journals for the most recent 10 year period. In a research proposal it is usually not necessary to discuss all literature uncovered by the researcher. A positive feature of a proposal literature review is to highlight representative ideas from articles and books on the subject treated. For instance, if there are 1,000 articles on a particular topic that reflect varying and opposing points of view, the investigator may select 10 or 20 of them that seem to represent the major viewpoints and conflicting opinions and/or findings. Of course, when a dissertation or thesis is involved, the expectation may be that the researcher reviews a much larger portion of literature in the final research report.

The question of how many articles should be included in a research proposal is difficult to answer in quantitative terms. If the research topic is relatively new, it is likely that little or no information exists in the available literature that bears directly on the subject. The researcher may be forced to cite available literature that is only remotely connected to the topic under investigation. For example, in the late 1950s little, if anything, was known about the impact of electronic data processing systems on school structure and administration. However, there were articles in existence that examined the impact of electronic data processing systems in petroleum refineries and airlines reservations offices. If the researcher elected to study this automation form and its impact on school systems, he would include in his review of literature information only indirectly relevant to his chosen topic. Any pioneering effort (a research project delving into previously unexplored social areas) is subject to this significant limitation. On the other hand, if there is an abundance of material in a given topic area, it is up to the researcher(s) to determine how many articles will be selected for a representative review. There are no clear-cut standards to dictate how many articles should be reviewed. Again, we return to the matter of how many are considered reasonable. Reviewing too many articles may be regarded by some researchers as superfluous activity. Other researchers may consider a particular literature review to be too scanty and inadequate. When the researcher himself feels comfortable with the articles reviewed, this subjective criterion will usually suffice.

Footnoting and referencing in literature reviews in proposals and in research reports can be handled quickly and easily by following certain conventional procedures established by such professional associations as The American Psychological Association or The American Sociological Association. Although several footnoting and referencing styles exist, some are much more simple to follow than the others. For example, "Smith (1960:223–24) indicates that . . ." is considerably less awkward than "James R. Smith, PROBLEMS OF THE INNER CITY, Holt, Rinehart, and Winston, Publishers, New York, N.Y., 1960, pp. 223–24) indicates that. . . ." Another style of footnoting is "Smith (22) indicates that . . . ." In the first instance [i.e., Smith (1960: 223–24)] a list of references consulted is provided following the proposal. The entire reference to Smith's work is included there. The second instance [i.e., Smith (22)] is indicative of a referencing system that numbers authors alphabetically. Smith (22) means that this work is the twenty-second in the list of references following the proposal. Multiple publications by the same individual(s) may be handled easily as well. For example, if Smith were to have three publications in the same year, they could be referred to as Smith (1960a), Smith (1960b), and Smith (1960c). Many journals follow these latter footnoting styles because they are quick and easy to use and enhance the readability of articles.

The literature review should have an effective summary, highlighting the important findings that bear directly upon the problem to be studied. This helps the reader to understand the relationships between the various articles presented. Of course, it is assumed that the researcher has presented the articles reviewed in a coherent fashion and has woven them together meaningfully in the main presentation. A summary following their presentation will be of great value to the reader as well as the researcher.

In the quest for scientific objectivity the researcher should make every effort to present articles (particularly in controversial areas of inquiry) that represent a balanced position. Discussing articles favorable to one point of view while ignoring those favoring an opposing point of view reflects researcher bias. This practice should be avoided because it is misleading and contrary to the canons of science.

THEORETICAL STRUCTURE AND/OR CONCEPTUAL SCHEME

In a sense this section of the research proposal is the heart of it. This is where the researcher formulates and develops an explanation for the relationships between the variables he is investigating. How does it come to be so that variables X and Y are associated with one another? Not only are the variables X and Y defined here, but their logical connection is delineated. Included here are the assumptions, propositions, and definitions the researcher uses to develop the explanatory framework upon which the entire research project rests. Subsequent research will either support or fail to support the existing theoretical framework presented here. (Chapters 2 and 3 should be reviewed, especially those sections dealing with theory construction and causality.)

HYPOTHESES

Hypotheses are logically deduced from the theoretical framework above. Within the context of the research proposal, hypotheses may be viewed as specific statements of theory in testable form. There is no limit to the number of hypotheses that can be derived from the theoretical scheme and subjected to empirical test. However, it should be noted that usually the number of hypotheses (as well as their nature) coincides closely with the objectives of the project stated earlier. In other words, by subjecting the various hypotheses to empirical test, some or all of the objectives of the research project are achieved partially or fully.

METHODOLOGY

The methodology section makes explicit the study design and constitutes the "how to do it" phase. This section includes:

1. The population to be studied;
2. The type of sampling plan to be followed;
3. The size of sample to be drawn;
4. The type of instrumentation (i.e., questionnaires, interviews, participant observation, analysis of secondary sources such as statistical records, letters, autobiographies, and so on);
5. The statistics to be used (if any) (e.g., gamma, lambda, chi square, Pearson r, and the like); and
6. The type of tabular presentation (e.g., graphs, tables, charts, figures, and so on).

The methodology section is the blueprint for researcher activity and specifies how the investigator intends to test the hypotheses, study the people, or describe social settings. The researcher is at liberty to choose from among a variety of data collection techniques and study designs as well as alternative approaches to the problem. Because so many options are available to the investigator in order to study the same problem, this fact has led some persons to label social research as an "art" as opposed to a body of strategies that have specific and limited applications.

STATEMENT OF THEORETICAL AND SUBSTANTIVE IMPLICATIONS

Although some researchers seldom give thought to the relevance of their research activity theoretically and substantively, others feel more comfortable investigating topics where several *raisons d'être* exist. If someone were to ask us the question, "So what?" at the end of our research project, what kinds of answers could we provide to demonstrate the relevance and significance of the investigation? Although there are many researchers who pursue knowledge for the sake of knowledge and give little attention to the meaningfulness of their research activity, there are others who sense an obligation to themselves and to others to defend studies they have undertaken.

Research can be assessed from several dimensions. Some people react favorably to social research if they can see immediate and direct benefits such as reducing crime, divorce rates, and psychological stress associated with urban renewal programs. Can the research help people to overcome some of their social problems? Can the results of research be of value in the solution of ecological crises? A different kind of assessment is made of social research in terms of a time dimension. Will the results of my research today be applicable 20 or even 50 years from now even though no practical value of it is apparent presently? The work of Sigmund Freud is a case in point. In his day people were quick to discard his notions of the significance of dreams, to label the id, ego, superego and libido as nonsensical. Present-day psychologists and psychiatrists (and even some sociologists) find the work of Freud not only fascinating but insightful for assisting people with various sorts of mental problems.

Research can also be assessed in terms of its theoretical value. Does this research contribute to (support or help to substantiate) existing theories of social behavior? Or does the research refute existing theoretical orientations? Couched in the context of a relation to existing social theories, research in given areas can prove to have profound significance for the nature and growth of the academic discipline.

However, it must be acknowledged that some people prefer to study a topic simply for the pleasure and interest of understanding it more fully. They are unconcerned about the opinions of others relating to the theoretical and/or practical (substantive) significance of what they do. There must be tolerance and room for all positions taken and motives reflected in the process of social inquiry.

THE PILOT STUDY

Although it is not essential for researchers to conduct preliminary investigations of more extensive projects, it seems well worth the time and effort in many instances to conduct what is known as a *pilot study*. Pilot studies are usually considered to be trial investigations of specific research problems that will be treated more intensively at a later date. Just as various products are tested on small consumer audiences prior to large-scale manufacture, distribution, and marketing, many projected social research plans are subjected to preliminary scrutiny on a small scale. For example, if it is the intention of an investigator to study a random sample of lawyers throughout the United

States, he may wish to test his data collection methods (e.g., question-naires, interviews, and so on) on some of his lawyer friends. Or, if he is affiliated with a university or college, he may obtain the cooperation of school officials to utilize classes of prelaw students to criticize what he intends to do at a later date on a larger scale.

Prior to a study of banking personnel, Champion and Dager (1967) administered questionnaires to employees of a neighboring bank of the one designated as the final research target. Through reactions of bank personnel to the wording of questions, questionnaire length, the relevance or meaningfulness of certain items, and other things, the data collection instruments were improved and modified substantially, and the administration and completion of the research in the actual research bank setting later was quite successful. The success of the study was undoubtedly enhanced by the pilot or preliminary investi-gation that helped to reveal unclear questions, awkward phrasings, and ways of approaching bank personnel most strategically.

Research projects involving the expenditure of hundreds of thou-sands of dollars (such as those supported by the Ford Foundation, the Department of Health, Education, and Welfare, and the National In-stitutes for Mental Health) cannot afford to be administered without sound planning preceding them. For instance, if the U.S. Department of Defense proposed to study factors that would influence National Guardsmen to reenlist once their military obligations were technically fulfilled, one or two National Guard units might be selected for a preliminary investigation prior to implementing a study involving hundreds of units and a substantial outlay of research funds. If the results or findings from the smaller National Guard aggregate ap-peared to be promising, then a better decision could be made to conduct a similar study on a larger proportion of guardsmen throughout the country.

If researchers are going to use interviewers (see Chapter 10) to ob-tain information, they will want to include the best interviewers available within their budgetary limitations. By the same token, if they plan to use questionnaires (see Chapter 11) as a primary means of data collection from a designated population, it will enhance the value and meaningfulness of their study if they are able to administer measuring instruments that focus clearly on salient characteristics of the group under investigation. Obtaining the reactions of a smaller sample of people who parallel the characteristics of those to be examined more intensively and on a larger scale at a later date will help to uncover potential weaknesses and flaws in the construction and content of the measuring instruments as well as illuminating various problems of approaching the target group and studying it most effectively.

A pilot study may be simple or complex. Its degree of elaboration and sophistication rest primarily on the standards, interests, and budget of the researcher involved. For example, many graduate student projects do not allow for extensive prestudy investigations. The resources of the student and/or his department may not allow for much preliminary testing of major study plans. The student (and often the professor) finds himself in the position of seeking assistance from other students regarding pilot studies and pretests. Granted, the preliminary administration of a questionnaire to a captive audience such as a class of introductory sociology students may not be the best way to determine potential weaknesses and flaws in study designs and the adequacy of measures, particularly if the design is directed toward a physician population. How capable are students of having empathy for physician roles? How capable are they of knowing what to regard as salient material to be included and what should be classified as irrelevant, meaningless, and therefore excluded? This problem is not easily overcome even by eliciting responses from a group paralleling the final target of inquiry (i.e., physicians). The investigator must learn to expect that no matter how flawless he believes his research plans to be, there will inevitably be those elements in the target sample who will regard their participation in any social project to be a waste of time, an annoyance, and an inconvenience. They will also likely be critical of questions that were improved on in an earlier pilot investigation with a parallel audience. In the final analysis, however, some initial pretest or pilot research activity is strongly recommended, regardless of the degree of similarity or dissimilarity between the group to be studied as the real thing and the group selected for the trial run.

It should be noted that a pilot study may make or break a projected research plan of larger scope. In view of what is uncovered in a preliminary investigation, a researcher may decide that little or nothing is to be gained through the implementation of a larger study. Many studies appearing in contemporary trade journals (e.g., *American Sociological Review, American Journal of Sociology, Social Forces, Administrative Science Quarterly,* and the like) are summaries of pilot research rather than reports of more extensive inquiry. In these instances, the investigator may quietly terminate the original plan and settle for an analysis of data collected from the smaller project.

On the other hand, many pilot studies show encouraging results, and more sophisticated research plans are implemented subsequently. Of course, we must not rule out the possibility that a sponsoring agency or funding foundation may alter or even discontinue research in particular topic areas as political changes at higher administrative levels occur. In this instance, the researcher finds himself knee-deep in a project for which funding has been eliminated or substantially curtailed. These contingencies must always be considered as factors that could seriously affect the nature, direction, and/or the continuation of social inquiry.

SOME SPECIFIC FUNCTIONS OF PILOT STUDIES

Any pilot study, regardless of the type of research involved and/or the intended target population, generally fulfills one or more of the following functions:

1. Pilot studies help to discover and ameliorate mechanical problems associated with interviews, questionnaires, and the like. If persons are to be queried by interviewers or through self-administered questionnaires, potential problems may be spotted such as unclear wording of questions, too lengthy questionnaires or interview sessions, irrelevant and/or offensive material, poorly printed questionnaires (if questionnaires are used), and omissions of topics that should have been included initially.

2. Pilot studies assist in developing better approaches to target populations. Researchers are usually interested in developing and maximizing rapport with respondents under any kind of data collection condition, whether it be door-to-door interviewing or anonymous mailed questionnaires. Introductory statements by interviewers or cover letters attached to questionnaires frequently have much to do with the kind of responses elicited by respondents. For example, in a pilot study of questionnaire response rate and social class, Champion and Sear (1969, p. 339) found that such things as type of postage used, type of cover letter (either an altruistic appeal or an egoistic one), and socioeconomic status of target respondents significantly affected the rate of mailed questionnaire returns from 2,700 randomly selected residents of three southern cities.

3. Pilot studies help researchers to develop meaningful methods of categorizing data to be collected. Problems of categorizing data occur primarily when researchers ask open-end questions (see Chapters 10 and 11) or use content analysis (see Chapter 12) of such documents as newspapers, letters, or diaries. In a particular election year, for example, a researcher might wish to examine the differential amounts of newspaper space devoted to covering opposing political candidates. He will have to resolve problems as to whether or not the coverage of each candidate is favorable, neutral, or unfavorable. He will also have to determine other categories by which the material extracted from the newspapers can be classified.

Equally difficult problems are encountered by researchers as they attempt to decipher lengthy replies from respondents to open-end questions (i.e., questions that request the respondent to elaborate on his attitudes and opinions on certain issues or toward specific people). A preliminary study may sensitize the investigator to recurrent attitudinal expressions that will enable him to categorize more easily at a later date.

4. One of the most important functions of pilot studies is to help the researcher to determine whether or not a more substantial investigation of the same phenomenon is warranted. It may be that a projected study contains provisions for selecting a sample of inmates from a nearby penitentiary. A preliminary investigation may reveal that permission to study these inmates will not be granted. Or, if such permission is granted, subsequent refusals on the part of inmates to participate in the researcher's study will tend to discourage further investigations, at least in that particular setting.

Pilot studies can provide the researcher with important clues to the potential significance of his ideas for explaining particular social problems. If a pilot study is relatively unproductive and fails to support the investigator's explanatory framework or theory, the larger study may be scrapped. Many universities offer their professors limited funds for mini-studies. If an application for a mini-grant is approved by the appropriate university officiating body, the professor has an opportunity to explore some of his ideas on a small scale. Mini-grants may range from $100 to $5,000 or more, but they are usually fairly small. If the professor obtains positive or favorable results from his preliminary investigations supported by the mini-grant, he is in a more strategic position for applying for more substantial grants ($75,000 to $500,000) from federal or private funding agencies or foundations.

SUMMARY

The purpose of this chapter has been to acquaint the student of social research with some of the preliminary problems associated with formulating social scientific investigations. Accordingly, research designs were defined and their objectives outlined. Specific research designs such as surveys and case studies were treated briefly with examples illustrating their respective applications in social research. In addition, several designs incorporating controls (i.e., experimental designs) were discussed, and some of their respective advantages and disadvantages were presented.

Finally, a general format for a research proposal was presented as a prerequisite to general social research projects. The pilot study was included as a preliminary step in the preparation for more extensive and elaborate research work.

Chapters 5, 6, and 7 will take up successively the problems of hypothesis testing, measurement of social and/or psychological variables, and some of the strategies for determining the validity and reliability of social measuring instruments. Each of these topics constitutes an integral part of the research process and must be considered as an important link in social investigation chains.

SOME QUESTIONS FOR REVIEW

1. What are some important functions associated with a research proposal? Can a researcher be too detailed in the construction and elaboration of a research proposal? Discuss why or why not.

2. Differentiate between exploratory and descriptive research designs. What are some major advantages and disadvantages of each. Identify three hypothetical (or real) instances from your own experience where these study designs would be appropriate.

3. What is an experimental research design? Is it necessarily better than exploratory and descriptive research designs in the investigation of social problems? Why or why not? Discuss.

4. People are often divided concerning whether to use case study designs or survey designs in their research activity. What do you see as contrasting advantages (and disadvantages) of each relative to the other? Discuss these briefly.

5. Define and discuss three types of experimental designs. In each case, cite their respective weaknesses and strengths with respect to hypothesis tests.

6. What is the "classical experimental design?" What kinds of modifi-

cations have been made in relation to it which increase the flexibility of the researcher as he seeks associations between variables?

7. What are some important objectives of pilot studies? Should they always be conducted prior to the implementation of a major research project? Why or why not? What are some potential results of conducting pilot studies?

8. Differentiate between experimental and control groups. What are their respective functions? Can a control group act as its own "experimental" group? Why or why not? Discuss.

NOTES

1. The best fit is often an *ideal* design selection. Practical considerations such as the investigator's budget, research staff, and/or the availability of research facilities (e.g., computer systems, card-punching machines, typewriters, duplicator machines, laboratories, and other equipment) are overriding factors that often force the researcher to select research design alternatives that are more reasonable in terms of convenience and economy. Also, focusing on a specific research design does not mean that a researcher must adhere stringently to a previously specified set of rules. The unique aspects of certain social settings under investigation may introduce unanticipated circumstances that require changes in one or more parts of a researcher's plan. Therefore, designs are selected and applied on a tentative basis. Barring unforeseen conditions that might arise at any stage of the research process, the design functions as a blueprint for research activity from start to finish.

2. "Completion" as used here is considered to be the technical closing of a research plan. Of course, during the process of social inquiry, it is likely that the investigator will uncover things not previously considered but which will be of sufficient importance to merit further research even within the same study. Some investigators label this phenomenon as serendipity, and they justifiably feel that their extra work is warranted considering the significance of whatever it is they find.

When the research involves a master's thesis or doctoral dissertation, for example, an implicit expectation is that the student will cover, in some detail, most of the relevant facets of his research problem. But factors such as time limits imposed on students by graduate schools for degree completion seldom allow lengthy extensions of inquiry into problems originally not included in the student's plan. Although following up interesting events that occur during the course of research activity may be quite important theoretically and substantively, research plans are designed to protect the researcher from endless inquiry.

3. For instance, the author of an article investigating the interpersonal characteristics of high school teachers may indicate ways in which his initial contacts with school officials may have been more effective. Identifying certain limitations of using interviews or questionnaires for a particular research target is an important contribution that an author makes to his own study and to those who wish to replicate it. These kinds of statements are very helpful to investigators delving into similar research problems. However, not all authors include such post factum analyses of their work and its inadequacies.

4. Those familiar with the work of Hyman (1955) should be aware that he uses cases for references to particular survey research projects as examples throughout his text. These are not meant to be equated with case studies as used in the present volume. Case studies and surveys refer to quite different design approaches to answering social questions.

5. Sampling is treated extensively in Chapter 8, and the reader is encouraged to familiarize himself with the discussion, particularly if there are plans to conduct a subsequent survey.

6. There are many kinds of sampling plans that may be selected as alternatives, but only a few meet probability sampling requirements. See Chapter 8.

7. See Chapter 10.

8. See Dean and Whyte (1958) for a discussion of this particular problem.

9. The results of this survey are given in J. Kenneth Little, *A Statewide Inquiry into Decisions of Youth About Education Beyond High School* (Madison: School of Education, University of Wisconsin, 1958).

10. Clinical psychologists might regard the intensive examination of a single patient as a "case study" in much the same sense that a formal organizational researcher views the intensive investigation of a large organization or a community researcher looks at the totality of institutions and their interrelations within a community.

11. U.S. Department of Labor, Bureau of Labor Statistics, "A Case

Study of a Company Manufacturing Electronic Equipment (Washington, 1956); "Studies of Automatic Technology: A Case Study of a Large Mechanized Bakery" (BLS Report 109) (Washington, 1957); "Studies of Automatic Technology: A Case Study of a Modernized Petroleum Refinery" (BLS Report 120) (Washington, 1957); "The Introduction of an Electronic Computer in a Large Insurance Company," (October, 1955); and "A Case Study of an Automatic Airline Reservation System (Report 137).

12. A "closed" national guard unit was opened to social scientific inquiry as the direct result of the fact that two social researchers interested in studying the guard were also members of the national guard unit. They were not defined as threats to the guard system. On the other hand, unknown quantities such as obscure social researchers encountering guard officials in a haphazard manner with similarly harmless intentions will often be turned away abruptly without explanation.

13. Two excellent sources exhibiting numerous examples of experimental designs are Donald T. Campbell and Julian C. Stanley, *Experimental and Quasi-experimental Designs for Research* (Chicago: Rand McNally and Company, 1963) and B. J. Winer, *Statistical Principles in Experimental Design,* (New York: McGraw-Hill, Inc., 1971).

BIBLIOGRAPHY

Anderson, James G. *Bureaucracy in Education.* Baltimore: The Johns Hopkins Press, 1968.

Andreski, Stanislav. *Military Organization and Society.* London: Routledge, 1968.

Argyris, Chris. "Some Problems in Conceptualizing Organizational Climate: A Case Study of a Bank," *Administrative Science Quarterly,* 2 1958: 501–520.

Backstrom, Charles H., and Gerald D. Hursh. *Survey Research.* Evanston, Ill.: Northwestern University Press, 1963.

Champion, Dean J., and Edward Z. Dager. "Some Impacts of Office Automation upon Status, Role Change, and Depersonalization," *Sociological Quarterly,* 8 1967: 71–84.

———, and Michael F. Morris. "A Content Analysis of Book Reviews in the *AJS, ASR,* and *Social Forces,*" *American Journal of Sociology,* 78 1973: 1256–1265.

———, and A. Sear. "Questionnaire Response Rate: A Methodological Analysis," *Social Forces,* 47 1969: 335–339.

Chinoy, Ely. *Automobile Workers and the American Dream.* Garden City, N.Y.: Doubleday, 1955.

Clausen, Aage R. "Response Validity in Surveys," *Public Opinion Quarterly,* 32 1969: 588–606.

Davis, Fred. "The Cabdriver and His Fare: Facets of a Fleeting Relationship," *American Journal of Sociology,* 65 1959: 158–165.

Dean, John P., and William Foote Whyte. "How do you Know if the Informant is Telling the Truth?," *Human Organization,* 17, 1958: 34–38.

Findikyan, N., and S. B. Sells. "Organizational Structure and Similarity in Campus Student Organizations," *Journal of Organizational Behavior and Human Performance,* 1 1966: 169–190.

Flittie, Edwin, and Jan Nelson. "The Truck Driver: A Sociological Analysis of an Occupational Role," *Sociology and Social Research,* 52 1968: 205–210.

Foreman, Paul B. "The Theory of Case Studies," *Social Forces,* 26 1948: 408–419.

Goode, William J., and Paul K. Hatt. *Methods in Social Research.* New York: McGraw-Hill, 1952.

Hagedorn, Robert, and Sanford Labovitz. *Introduction to Social Research.* New York: McGraw-Hill, 1971.

Hyman, Herbert. *Survey Design and Analysis.* Glencoe, Ill.: The Free Press, 1955.

Kirk, Roger E. *Experimental Design: Procedures for the Behavioral Sciences.* Belmont Calif.: Brooks/Cole Publishing Co., 1968.

Landy, David, and Sara E. Singer. "The Social Organization and Culture of a Club for Former Mental Patients," *Human Relations,* 14 1961: 31–41.

Lynd, Robert, and Helen M. Lynd. *Middletown.* New York: Harcourt Brace Jovanovich, 1929.

Lynd, Robert, and Helen M. Lynd. *Middletown in Transition: A Study in Cultural Conflicts.* New York: Harcourt Brace Jovanovich, 1937.

McCormick, B. "Managerial Unionism in the Coal Industry," *British Journal of Sociology,* 11 1960: 356–369.

Mouledous, Joseph C. "Organizational Goals and Structural Change: A Study of the Organization of Prison Social System," *Social Forces,* 41 1963: 283–290.

Sayles, Leonard. *Behavior of Industrial Work Groups.* New York: Wiley, 1958.

Selltiz, Claire, Marie Jahoda, Morton Deutsch, and Stuart W. Cook. *Research Methods in Social Relations.* New York: Holt, 1959.

Sewell, William H., and Vimal P. Shah. "Social Class, Parental Encouragement, and Educational Aspirations," *American Journal of Sociology,* 73 1968: 559–572.

White, Lynn C. "Maternal Employment and Anxiety Over Mother Roles," *L. S. U. Journal of Sociology,* 2 1972: 61–81.

Whyte, William Foote. *Human Relations in the Restaurant Industry.* New York: McGraw-Hill, 1948.

———. "The Social Structure of the Restaurant," *American Journal of Sociology,* 54 1949: 302–310.

Winer, B. J. *Statistical Principles and Experimental Design.* New York: McGraw-Hill, 1971.

PART 2
STRUCTURING THE DATA-COLLECTION PROCESS

CHAPTER 5
HYPOTHESES IN SOCIAL RESEARCH

Two necessary features of most social research are the formulation and testing of hypotheses. In this chapter we will examine closely several different kinds of hypotheses, their respective origins, functions, and relation to theories, and various ways in which tests of hypotheses may be made. We will also examine the role of probability theory in hypotheses testing and discuss some of the problems that accompany the interpretation of hypothesis tests.

The researcher is interested in devising practical solutions to all types of social problems.[1] He observes social events and seeks to explain their occurrence by developing theories. Enabling him to determine the adequacy of his theory as an explanatory tool is one important function of the hypothesis.

WHAT IS A HYPOTHESIS?

A hypothesis is a tentative statement about something, the validity of which is usually unknown. For example, to declare that upper-class people have fewer children than lower-class people might be construed as a hypothesis concerning the effect of social class on family behavior. Whether or not it is a hypothesis as opposed to a simple statement of fact depends on whether the declarer *knows* if it is true. If he simply has a hunch that social class influences family behavior, the statement "upper-class people have fewer children than lower-class people" is a hypothetical one. On the other hand, if he has census information that confirms his hunch (ie. data showing clearly that smaller families are associated with upper-class individuals), then the statement becomes a fact, a declaration about the known condition of things. Many facts we have today used to be hypotheses until their validity was determined by some kind of empirical verification.

In social research some likely hypotheses about things might be:

1. Suicide rates vary inversely with social cohesion.
2. Children from broken homes tend to become delinquent.
3. Job satisfaction decreases as working hours increase.
4. Aggression is associated with frustration.
5. Punishment-centered leadership leads to alienation among group members.
6. Crime increases as urban blight increases.
7. The average income in group X is $10,000.
8. Cold, aloof individuals prefer isolation in their job conditions.
9. Children will be more satisfied with *laissez-faire* leadership compared with autocratic leadership.
10. Foster children adopted before age six have fewer adult adjustment problems than foster children adopted after age six.

It is apparent from this list that hypotheses can pertain to virtually anything. There are no restrictions about what can be hypothesized. Hypotheses do not necessarily have to be true, however. The truth of many hypotheses the researcher formulates is most often unknown. *Hypotheses, therefore, are tentative statements about things that the researcher wishes to support or refute.*[2]

TYPES OF HYPOTHESES

There are several different kinds of hypotheses used in social research. The primary types of hypotheses we shall treat in this section are: (1) research hypotheses, (2) null hypotheses, and (3) statistical hypotheses.

RESEARCH HYPOTHESES

Hypotheses derived from the researcher's theory about some social phenomenon are called *research hypotheses* or *working hypotheses.* The social investigator usually believes that his research hypotheses are true or that they are accurate statements about the condition of things he is investigating. He believes that these hypotheses are true to the extent that the theory from which they were derived is adequate. Determining the adequacy of a theory was discussed in the previous chapter.

Because theories are, in one sense, suppositions about the true nature of things and thus regarded as tentative statements about reality until they have been verified to the scientist's satisfaction, the hypotheses derived from theories must also be regarded as tentative suppositions about things until they have been tested. Testing the hypothesis means to subject it to confirmation or disconfirmation. Testing the hypothesis, "the average income expectation of boys in a poverty area is $500 a month" can be done by drawing a sample of boys from a poverty area and asking them questions about their average income expectation. If their average income expectation is at or near $500 a month, the hypothesis is said to be confirmed. If the income expectation of these boys is much higher or much lower than $500, then the hypothesis is not supported, or is said to be disconfirmed. In a subsequent section of this chapter, we will examine some of the conventional procedures followed in tests of hypotheses.

NULL HYPOTHESES

Null hypotheses are, in a sense, the reverse of research hypotheses. They are also statements about the reality of things, except that they serve to *refute or deny what is explicitly indicated in a given research hypothesis.* To continue with the example used above, if the investigator states as his research hypothesis that "the average income expectation of boys in a poverty area is $500," he may also state a null hypothesis that can be used to evaluate the accuracy of his research hypothesis. The null hypothesis would be, "the average income expectation of boys in a poverty area is not $500." If the researcher is able to demonstrate that the income expectation of the boys is at or near $500, then he concludes that the null hypothesis is refuted or regarded as not true. And, logically, we may conclude that if it is not true that "the average income expectation of boys in a poverty area is not $500," then the statement, "the average income expectation of boys in a poverty area is $500" is supported.

In other words, the researcher constructs a situation that contains two contradictory statements, namely, "the average income expectation for boys in a poverty area is (and in the case of the null hypothesis, is not) $500." He words these statements in such a way so that the confirmation of the one is the denial or refutation of the other. Both cannot coexist simultaneously.

Null hypotheses, therefore, *are hypothetical models used to test research hypotheses.* They do not nor were ever intended to exist in reality.

By now you are probably throughly bewildered by these last few paragraphs, and it is expected that you will eventually ask the question, "Why does the social investigator want to bother with so-called 'null hypotheses'?" After all, he has a research hypothesis he believes to be true. Why doesn't he test the hypothesis directly and let it go at that? This question has been asked time and time again by every student confronting null hypotheses for the first time. There are at least three reasons why null hypothesis models are used, none of which may answer this question to your satisfaction. They are:

1. Because a scientist defines his role as being more detached and objective about phenomena compared with the layman, it would appear as though he were not behaving objectively if he attempted to prove true that which he believed to be true initially.   Trying to show the truthfulness of research hypotheses would imply to some, at least, a definite bias toward trying to confirm one's suppositions and possibly ignoring those things that would tend to refute one's beliefs. Null hypotheses assist the researcher, therefore, because such hypotheses are denials of what he believes to be true. If he is able to reject or refute null hypotheses, then the case supporting his research hypotheses is supposedly that much stronger.

2. It "seems" easier to prove something false than to prove it true.   There are those who would argue that it is easier to find fault with something (i.e., an idea, belief, or hypothesis) than to look for those things that would support it. Whatever the relative merits of this argument happen to be, the null hypothesis is believed to be the tool that should act as the true indicator of things until proven otherwise.

3. The third reason is very significant here.   It may be summed up in one word: *convention.* It is conventional in social research to use null hypotheses. Most social scientists utilize null hypotheses in one way or another. It will be shown later that null hypotheses perform specific functions in relation to probability theory and tests of research hypotheses.

4. A fourth reason involves probability theory. Under a probability theoretical model, hypotheses have a likelihood of being either true or false. Null hypotheses are particularly useful in such theoretical models. The null hypothesis is an expression of one alternative outcome of a social observation. The probability model specifies that the null hypothesis may be either true or false but not both simultaneously. Another alternative hypothesis is the research hypothesis discussed earlier. This hypothesis also has a probability of being either true or false. Thus, the null hypothesis logically specifies a hypothetical social condition that may or may not be true, and that may be subject to statistical verification or refutation. Neither the research hypothesis nor the null hypothesis is absolutely true or absolutely false under any given test of it. Both probabilities (being either true or false) coexist for each type of hypothesis *always*.

STATISTICAL HYPOTHESES

Statistical hypotheses are statements about statistical populations that, on the basis of information obtained from observed data, one seeks to support or refute (Winter, 1962). The statistical population may refer to either people or things. It is generally the case in the test of statistical hypotheses that observations about people or things are reduced in some way to numerical quantities, and decisions are made about these quantities. For example, suppose we are concerned about age differences between two groups of people. We hypothesize that one group is older than the other. To test the research hypothesis, "Group A is older than Group B," we might first establish a null hypothesis that would be "Group A and Group B do not differ in age, or Group B is older than Group A."

To subject these hypotheses to empirical test, we must reduce the variables used in them to measurable quantities. We obtain information pertaining to age from each person in each group. We average the ages of members of both groups and determine whether or not there is a difference between the average age of members of Group A and the average age of members of Group B. In effect, we have transformed our research hypothesis and corresponding null hypothesis into a statistical hypothesis that now may be evaluated by numerical means. (It should be noted that it is not always possible to quantify our research and null hypotheses about things. Statistical hypotheses are restricted in their application, therefore. These applications and restrictions will be discussed subsequently.)

A statistical hypothesis concerning the difference in average ages between Groups A and B can be represented symbolically. Suppose we use $\bar{X}_1$ (read: X bar sub one) to stand for the mean or average age for Group A or the first group. The subscripts for each $\bar{X}$ denote to which group the $\bar{X}$ applies. The symbolic representation of our statistical hypothesis would be:

$$H_0 : \bar{X}_1 = \bar{X}_2$$
$$H_1 : \bar{X}_1 \neq \bar{X}_2$$

H_0 denotes the null hypothesis which says that the mean age for the first group is the same as the mean age for the second group. H_1 denotes the research hypothesis which says that the mean age for the first group is not equal to the mean age for the second group. H_0's typically stand for *null hypotheses,* whereas H_1's usually stand for *research hypotheses.* (Notation systems may vary from textbook to textbook, however.)

Notice that the research hypothesis symbolically described above does not say that Group A is older than Group B. All that is said is that the groups differ regarding average age. Accordingly, the null hypothesis states that the groups do not differ regarding average age. If we were to test the research hypothesis *"Group A is older than Group B,"* we would have to portray this hypothesis differently symbolically. We would want to represent both H_0 and H_1 as follows:

$$H_0 : \bar{X}_1 \leq \bar{X}_2$$
$$H_1 : \bar{X}_1 > \bar{X}_2$$

The symbol, $>$, means "greater than," and the symbol, $\leq$, means "equal to or less than." Therefore, the hypotheses H_0 and H_1 read respectively, "The average age of Group 1 is equal to or less than the average age of Group 2," and "The average age of Group 1 is greater than the average age of Group 2." Subsequently, if we were to test the null hypothesis and find that it was not true that the average age of Group A is equal to or less than the average age of Group B, then we would conclude that Group A, the first group, must be older. Carefully inspect these hypotheses to see if you would arrive at the same conclusion. Had we tested the null hypothesis "Group A is the same as Group B regarding age," and furthermore, had we rejected the null hypothesis as a result of that test, we could have concluded only that Group A is *different from* Group B regarding age. We would have no way of determining which group was older than the other from the way the hypothesis is worded. It is important, then, how the researcher originally sets up the null hypothesis model in accordance with the specific research hypothesis he wishes to test.

Statistical hypotheses are usually established to delineate: (1) differences between two or more groups regarding some trait or collection of characteristics that they possess, (2) association between two or more variables within one group or between several groups, and (3) point estimates of sample or population characteristics.

Statistical Hypotheses of Difference

A hypothesis of a difference between one group and another might pertain to average age as discussed in a previous example. Two groups may be exposed to two different teaching methods for the same material, and the researcher wishes to evaluate which teaching method is best for aiding knowledge retention by the respective classes of students. Five groups of workers may be exposed to different types of supervision, and the investigator wants to determine whether a particular supervisory behavior is better than the others at stimulating the employees to produce more. In each of these cases, the investigator begins with a research hypothesis about the differences he expects to find between two or more groups regarding some characteristic or characteristics they possess. The resulting statistical hypotheses geared to symbolically portray the research hypotheses are subjected to statistical *tests of significance of difference.* (The notion of "significance" of a particular observed difference between one group and another has been mentioned. It will be explained more fully later in the chapter. For the time being, we shall simply concentrate on differentiating between various types of statistical hypotheses and illustrating their unique functions.)

An example of a statistical hypothesis of difference between two groups is the following:

$$H_0 : \overline{X}_1 = \overline{X}_2$$
$$H_1 : \overline{X}_1 \neq \overline{X}_2$$

The null hypothesis (symbolically portrayed as H_0) says that the mean of Group 1 ($\overline{X}_1$) is the same as the mean of Group 2 ($\overline{X}_2$). The alternative hypothesis (symbolically portrayed as H_1) says that the means of the two groups are not equal to one another.

Statistical Hypotheses of Association

Hypotheses of association specify whether one variable is related or associated with another in some predictable manner. Hypotheses of association may also pertain to relationships between more than two variables. The social investigator may wish to determine the association existing between delinquency and socioeconomic status. Or he may wish to examine the degree of association existing between success in graduate school and a person's scores on the Graduate Record Examination, Miller Analogies Test, and the ACT. In the first instance, he has a simple two-variable association problem. In the second, he is dealing with four variables and their covariation or the extent to which they are all related to one another.

Association between two or more variables is represented by degree, and the magnitude of association between any pair of variables can extend only from −1.00 to +1.00. A coefficient of association of ±1.00 means perfect association between two or more variables. If a worker gets $1.50 for every unit of product he produces each day over a previously determined standard, we say that there is a perfect association between the bonus and productivity. In this instance, the perfect association between bonus and productivity would be characterized by +1.00. Suppose the worker loses esteem and prestige in his work group the more he produces. The other workers may feel that he is showing them up and making them appear to be lazy in the eyes of higher level supervisors. The relationship between productivity and prestige in the group in this case may be −1.00, or a perfect negative association. The more he produces, the less esteem he has in the eyes of other group members. The first instance of association would be a perfect *positive* association; the second instance would be indicative of a perfect *negative* association. Where one variable increases (decreases) whereas the other increases (decreases), we say that a positive association is obtained. Figure 5-1 illustrates graphically a positive association between two variables. If one variable changes in the opposite direction to the other (i.e., one variable increases [decreases] while the other decreases [increases]), we say that a *negative* or *inverse* association is obtained. Figure 5-2 illustrates a negative association between two variables.

Sometimes variables vary together (in the same direction) for a time, and then the relation changes or reverses itself, and one variable moves in the opposite direction to the other. Such an association is called *curvilinear*. Figure 5-3 illustrates a curvilinear relation between variables. Statistical texts cover such variations in association in more detail, and the reader is encouraged to refer to one of several texts cited at the end of this chapter as a supplement to the discussion here.

The symbolic representation of statistical hypotheses of association is provided by the following example:

$$H_0 : r_{xy} = 0$$
$$H_1 : r_{xy} \neq 0$$

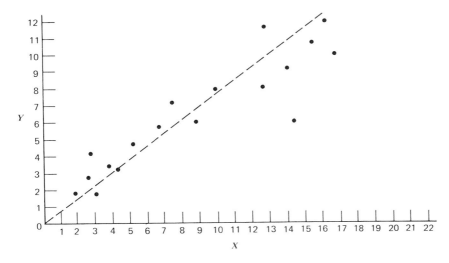

Figure 5-1.   A positive association between variables.

The null hypothesis states that the relation between variables X and Y is equal to zero, whereas the alternative research hypothesis says that the relation between X and Y is not equal to zero. Any departure from zero, therefore, is indicative of the degree of association between variables. The greater the departure from zero, the greater the association. The sign, + or −, depicts the nature of the association between variables. It is generally conventional to describe both the degree and the nature of association existing between any combination of phenomena.

Statistical Hypotheses of Point Estimation

Hypotheses of point estimation are designed to evaluate a researcher's guess as to the value of some characteristic of a sample of individuals or a population. He may estimate (based on previous information) that the average yearly income for a specified population is $10,000. His hypothesized income estimate is then compared with the actual average income of the sample he selects. The adequacy of his estimate is evaluated by such a comparison and by use of the hypothesis of point estimation. (Some statisticians regard point estimate hypotheses as hypotheses of difference also. This is because the researcher ultimately evaluates the *difference* between some hypothesized value and an observed value for a single sample.)

The symbolic representation of a hypothesis of point estimation is

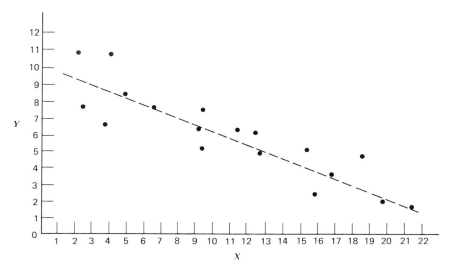

Figure 5-2.   A negative association between variables.

the following:

$$H_0 : \bar{X} = 75$$
$$H_1 : \bar{X} \neq 75$$

The null hypothesis says that the mean (of some sample characteristic) is equal to 75, whereas the research hypothesis says that the mean is not equal to 75.

SUMMARY OF TYPES OF HYPOTHESES

To summarize briefly and to provide some meaningful association between each of the general types of hypotheses, there are three classifications of hypotheses that are important to the social scientist. These are research hypotheses, null hypotheses, and statistical hypotheses. As a result of one's theoretical formulations, research hypotheses are derived. Null hypotheses are established in accordance with research hypotheses. Null hypotheses are hypothetical models established so that research hypotheses can be tested. Numerical expressions of null hypotheses and of the alternative research hypotheses are called statistical hypotheses. Statistical hypotheses are those ultimately subjected to some sort of empirical test. On the basis of one's observations and the test of the statistical hypothesis, a conclusion is reached about the corresponding null hypothesis which, in turn, enables the researcher to support or refute the research hypothesis derived from the theory. Table 5-1 illustrates this relationship.

Hypotheses are composed of variables. A hypothesis may contain one variable, two variables or *k* variables. One-and two-variable hypotheses may be called *simple hypotheses,* whereas those containing more than two, or *k* variables, are called *complex hypotheses.* Hypotheses containing more than two variables are usually more difficult to test than those more simply constructed. This is due, in part, to the fact that the interrelatedness of more than two variables acting simultaneously is more difficult to assess quantitatively and theoretically.

FUNCTIONS OF HYPOTHESES

Theories are relatively elaborate tools used to explain and predict events. The social scientist develops a theory to account for some social phenomenon, and then he devises a means whereby the theory can be tested or subjected to verification or refutation. Seldom does the researcher test the theory directly. Most of the time he conducts tests of hypotheses that have been generated and derived from that

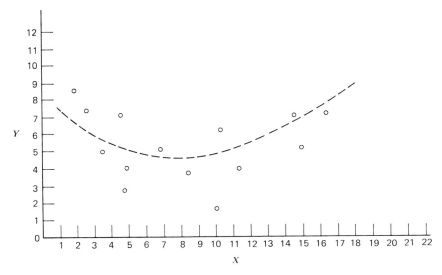

Figure 5-3.   A curvilinear relation between variables.

Table 5-1. The Relation between Research, Null, and Statistical Hypotheses

H_1	H_0	H_1 and H_0
RESEARCH HYPOTHESIS	NULL HYPOTHESIS	STATISTICAL HYPOTHESIS (Symbolically expressed)
Two groups differ according to age.	*Two groups are the same regarding age.*	$H_0:\ \bar{X}_1 = \bar{X}_2$
(Derived from theory)	(Based on research hypothesis)	$H_1:\ \bar{X}_1 \neq \bar{X}_2$
		If the conclusion is to *reject* H_0, H_1 is supported. We conclude that the null hypothesis is not true based on what we have observed and that the research hypothesis is supported.

theory. If the hypotheses "test out" as the researcher has specified, or if his empirical observations are in accordance with what has been stated in the hypotheses, we say that his theory is supported in part. It usually takes many tests of different hypotheses from the same theory to demonstrate its predictive value and its adequacy as a tool of explanation for some event or sequence of events. A major function of hypotheses, therefore, is *to make it possible to test theories.* In this regard, an alternative definition of an hypothesis is *a statement of theory in testable form.* All statements of theory in *testable form* are called *hypotheses.*

It is likely, however, that some hypotheses are not associated with any particular theory. It could be that as a result of some hypothesis, a theory will eventually be constructed. Consequently, another function of hypotheses is *to suggest theories that may account for some event.* Although it is more often the case that research proceeds from theories to hypotheses, occasionally the reverse is true. The social investigator may have some idea about why a given phenomenon occurs, and he hypothesizes a number of things that relate to it. He judges that some hypotheses have greater potential than others for explaining the event, and as a result, he may construct a logical system of propositions, assumptions, and definitions linking his explanation to the event. In other words, he devises a theory. Working from the hypothesis back to the theory is not necessarily poor methodology. Eventually, the investigator is going to have to subject the resulting theory to empirical test to determine its adequacy. The predictive value of the theory can be assessed at that time.

Hypotheses also perform a descriptive function. Each time a hypothesis is tested empirically, it tells us something about the phenomenon it is associated with. If the hypothesis is supported, then our information about the phenomenon increases. Even if the hypothesis is refuted, the test tells us something about the phenomenon we did not know before. Even the inventor who discovers 600 ways of doing something wrong learns something as a result of this experience. The accumulation of information as a result of hypothesis testing reduces the amount of ignorance we may have about why a social event occurs a given way.

For the social scientist, the main functions performed by hypotheses are:

1. *to test theories*
2. *to suggest theories*
3. *to describe social phenomena.*

Hypotheses also have important secondary functions. As a result of testing certain hypotheses, social policy may be formulated in communities, penal institutions may be redesigned and revamped, teaching methods may be altered or improved, solutions to various kinds of social problems may be suggested and implemented, delinquents and criminal offenders may be treated differently, and supervisory practices may be changed in factories and businesses. Testing hypotheses refutes certain "common sense" notions about human behavior, raises questions about the explanations we presently use to account for things, and most generally alters our orientation toward our environment to one degree or another. All hypotheses have to do with our knowledge of things, and, as this knowledge changes, we change also.

WHERE DO HYPOTHESES COME FROM?

Scanning several professional journals will expose any student to a wide variety of studies, each with its array of hypotheses and theory. People often ask, "Where do those hypotheses come from?" Quite simply, hypotheses come from our thoughts about things. Hypotheses are generated in graduate student "bull sessions," conversations and discussions between student and professor, from random observations and reflections on life as a person goes to and from work or contemplates in his easy chair at home, and of course, they are deduced from theory. Because of the diverse circumstances under which hypotheses are formulated, it stands to reason that there will be a wide variation in the quality of hypotheses. Also, there is variety associated with the standards social scientists employ in determining whether a hypothesis is good or bad, useful or not useful, and so on. It is possible, for example, that two different researchers working independently can derive the same hypothesis from a common theory, but they may word it differently and/or they may select different circumstances to conduct the empirical test of it. Both may be dissatisfied with the other's statement of the same hypothesis. The evaluation of hypotheses is quite often a relative matter, therefore. What one social scientist regards as a good hypothesis may not be regarded similarly by another social scientist. We do not want to convey the impression that social science advances purely on the whims and personal preferences of members of the professions. What is important to understand here is that there are flexibility and latitude that enable the social investigator to design the study the way he wishes and to word the hypotheses and specify the empirical test of them somewhat in accordance with his personal standards. And although personal standards of social scientists vary, there are conventional procedures that are nevertheless established as guidelines. So in spite of the personal variation in methodological inquiry, there is a high degree of uniformity with respect to the application of these guidelines. Table 5-2 shows the relation between events, theories, and hypotheses and graphically summarizes much of what has been discussed here. Table 5-2 illustrates a simplified view of the relation between events to be explained, the explanation generated to account for them, the theory and subsequent hypotheses that subject the theory to support or refutation, and the resulting hypothesis test. The E_i's each reflect a particular frame of reference or way of looking at a problem or the event.

HYPOTHESIS FORMULATION: GOOD, BETTER, AND BEST

The goodness or badness of any given hypothesis is dependent on the relative circumstances of the theory from which it was derived. For one type of study, Hypothesis A may be suitable, while for another type of study, Hypothesis A may be inadequate. One way of evaluating hypotheses generally is in terms of *the amount of information they provide about phenomena.* Consider the example of a simple association between two variables, Y and X.[3] Notice that each successive hypothesis form below provides an increasing amount of information about the nature of the association between Y and X.

  A. Y and X are associated. (or, There is an association between Y and X.)
  B. Y is related to X. (or, Y is dependent on X.)
  C.   As X increases, Y decreases. (or, Increases in values of X appear to effect reductions in values of Y.)

Notice that in Hypothesis A above, a simple statement of association between Y and X is provided. Nothing is indicated about the association that would allow the social researcher to determine which variable, Y or X, would tend to cause the other variable to change in value. (Of course, assuming that the hypothesis was derived from a particular theory, it could be determined which variable was causing the other to change in value by inspecting the propositional relations within that theory.) An exploratory study might use such wording of a hypothesis if little was known about the population being studied. Before a more explicit hypothesis could be tested, the researcher

Table 5-2. The Relation between Theories, Hypotheses, and Events

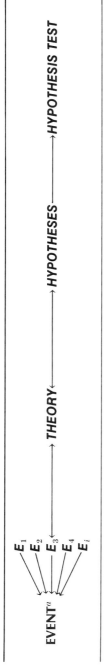

EVENT[a] ⟶ THEORY ⟵ HYPOTHESES ⟶ HYPOTHESIS TEST

EVENT[a]	THEORY	HYPOTHESES	HYPOTHESIS TEST
Some observable behavioral situation in reality that requires explanation.	Consists of a series of logical relations between things. Acts as the formalization of explanation. Couches E_i (explanation) into a model of both *explanation* and *prediction*. Is the tool that links the event logically to the explanation of it.	Statements of theory in testable form. Derived from the theoretical model and subjected to empirical test in some suitable situation.	Supports or refutes theory for which it was derived. The test of any hypothesis neither "proves" nor "disproves" the theory, however.
E_i = Alternative explanations to account for event.	A model that helps to establish cause-effect relations or predictable linkages between things.		
	Each theory deals with a specific E_i.		

[a] The word, EVENT, is used instead of the word, PROBLEM. The idea of "problem" connotes things that serve to confuse the beginning student. There is a tendency to equate PROBLEM with "social problems," and of course, not all events falling within the interest of social scientists and requiring some kind of explanation are social problems. Consequently, the term, EVENT, is preferred.

would want to determine if any association at all existed between the two variables, Y and X.

Hypothesis B is also a simple statement of association between Y and X, but this time it may be inferred that values of Y are in some way contingent upon the condition of the X variable. This additional information gives us some idea as to which variable has the greater influence over the other. Such hypothesis wordings are suggestive of previous investigations of the population being studied currently.

Hypothesis C is the most specific of the three. Not only does it say that Y and X are related and that Y is dependent on X for its value, but it also reveals something more about the nature of the association between the two variables. It says that as one variable (X) changes in value, the other variable (Y) changes in value in a specified *direction*. In other words, Hypothesis A is least informative about the relation between Y and X, whereas Hypothesis C is the most informative about this association. Each hypothesis form becomes increasingly specific about the nature of association between the two variables, Y and X. Of course, an even more informative form of this hypothesis could specify *how much* one variable would change as a result of specified changes in the other variable.

Which hypothesis is best? This is a difficult question to answer. Again, we must turn to the objectives of the research one conducts. If little is known about Y and X, hypothesis A may be suitable. The researcher may simply be interested in determining, in an exploratory fashion, if an association can be established between the two variables. On the other hand, if the association between X and Y has been investigated previously, the researcher may wish to know more about the nature of this association. Therefore, he uses a research design that is more experimental than the first to determine which variable has the greater strength to predict the other. In this case, either hypothesis B or C would be useful.

TESTING HYPOTHESES

Testing hypotheses means *subjecting them to some sort of empirical scrutiny to determine if they are supported or refuted by what the researcher observes.* Testing hypotheses means that the researcher will need to do a number of things. Some of these prerequisites to hypothesis testing are:

   1. **A real social situation is needed that will suffice as a reasonable testing ground for the hypothesis.**[1]   If the hypothesis concerns mana-

gerial behavior, it will be necessary for the investigator to study some real organization or organizations where managerial behavior can be taken into account empirically.

Identifying and securing a testing ground for one's hypotheses is not always an easy thing. There are permissions to secure from organizational officials as well as (in many instances) the permissions of the people being studied. If the social researcher is interested in testing some hypothesis about delinquency, he may encounter difficulty getting a sample of delinquents from a given community. Not only will he have difficulty getting permission to study them, but he may have to work out special arrangements with the courts, police officials, parents of delinquents, and school leaders, to mention a few.

This particular prerequisite is frequently spoken of as "getting access to data that will enable the investigator to verify or refute his hypotheses." Once a given social setting is selected, the relevant data in that situation must be obtained to make the hypothesis test a valid one.

2. The investigator should make sure that his hypotheses are testable. This means that he should limit his investigations to empirical phenomena or events that can be taken into account through the senses. The variables used in the hypotheses tested should be amenable to measurement of some kind. If they are not subject to measurement, the resulting test of the hypothesis will be relatively meaningless, if, in fact, it is capable of being tested at all. (In the next chapter, the problem of measuring variables will be discussed in detail. For the time being, it is sufficient to know that the terms used in the hypotheses one tests must be a part of the empirical world. This is a fundamental requirement whenever the scientific method is employed in studying what is and why.)

Terms that cannot be taken into account empirically render the hypothesis *irrefutable* and *untestable*. How can a scientist reject a hypothesis containing variables that he cannot experience in some empirical form? For example, if a researcher were to hypothesize "*evil spirits cause delinquency*," he can neither support nor refute this statement by using conventional scientific methods. He obviously has empirical tools to determine the incidence of delinquent or nondelinquent behavior, but by what empirical means is he able to assess meaningfully the influence or impact of "evil spirits" on delinquent behavior? Unless there are empirical means of evaluating the impact of nonempirical phenomena on particular variables, the researcher cannot validly subject the hypothesis to a true scientific test.

To illustrate this problem with another example, Von Hentig (1947)

wrote that "accelerated motor innervation" was responsible for crimi-
nality among western outlaws, and that it tended to be identified by
the presence of red body hair. Since many redheads are law-abiding,
it follows that the color of one's hair has little or nothing to do with
whether or not he has accelerated motor innervation. Unless Von
Hentig could devise a method whereby we could empirically assess
the existence of and degree to which individuals possess accelerated
motor innervation, his explanation of deviation has little or no predictive utility, and hypotheses employing this variable cannot be tested.
Perhaps the biologist or biochemist could provide some empirical
means of evaluating this phenomenon in individuals, but at this point,
at least, the social scientist cannot do much with the term. (Of course,
it is possible that terms that are presently undefinable empirically
might, at some later date, become amenable to the senses through the
discovery of new means of measuring such phenomena. This always
exists as a possibility.)

Suppose the social researcher has complied with these two prerequisites. He has obtained a social setting that will allow for a
reasonable test of his hypotheses, and he uses variables amenable to
some means of measurement. Next, he collects data pertaining to his
hypotheses and tabulates or records what he has found. What are the
bases upon which he concludes that his hypotheses are supported or
refuted? What would prevent two researchers working independently
from arriving at quite different conclusions pertaining to the identical
information studied? To avoid or at least reduce the amount of subjectivity that exists when social scientists interpret what they have
found, several rules are spelled out in advance of the test of
hypotheses. These are called *decision rules,* and they usually specify
the conditions under which the researcher will decide to refute or
support the hypotheses he is testing. It may be argued, of course, that
the researcher has the opportunity to be quite subjective here as well.
Why not set up decision rules that will bias one's results and increase
the likelihood of supporting hypotheses believed to be true by the
investigator? Although there is nothing to prevent a social researcher
from doing this, there are certain moral and professional considerations that exert a strong influence on him. He usually abides by those
rules that have achieved some degree of consensus among his
colleagues in the profession. He is, in a sense, bound by *convention* to
establish decision rules that provide the most objective assessment of
the hypotheses to be tested. If he strays too far from these conventional guidelines, his colleagues usually are able to spot such un-
conventional practices and subsequently, this person's research efforts
are viewed as unprofessional or of little consequence.

The decision rules usually established in advance of hypothesis tests pertain to (1) the level of significance, and (2) the specification of a sampling distribution. Before we discuss these decision rules, it will be helpful to talk about probability theory and its unique role in tests of hypotheses. It is essential to have a general idea of the usefulness of probability theory to understand better what is meant by the two decision rules noted above.

Probability in social research concerns *the likelihood that one's observations or results are expected or unexpected.* If we were to flip a coin 50 times, we would expect that we would get 25 heads and 25 tails. This assumes that the coin is not biased. A biased coin, however, would reflect a greater proportion of either heads or tails compared with an unbiased one. When a distribution of observations is observed (i.e., the results of 50 coin flips), does the distribution differ from what would be expected? Determining what is expected is based on the possible outcomes associated with our observations. In the flip of a coin, the possible outcomes are limited to two: heads or tails. (Coins landing on their edges are excluded as unlikely events in this case). We say that the likelihood or probability of getting a head is 50 per cent or 0.50, and the likelihood of getting a tail is also 50 per cent or 0.50. Getting either a head or a tail in any given coin flip is equal to the sum of the independent probabilities of the two events, or 0.50 +0.50 = 1.00. In other words, there is no doubt that whenever we flip the coin, we will get either a head or a tail. It is 100 per cent likely, or 1.00.

When we flip the coin 50 times and observe 23 heads and 27 tails, we must decide whether the coin is biased in favor of tails, or whether the difference is not a significant departure from what would be expected by chance. Our chance expectation regarding 50 coin flips would be 25 heads and 25 tails with an absolutely unbiased coin. Consider the following possible outcomes of 50 coin flips:

HEADS	TAILS	HEADS	TAILS
25	25	25	25
24	26	26	24
23	27	27	23
22	28	28	22
21	29	29	21
20	30	30	20
19	31	31	19
18	32	32	18

At what point do we decide to regard some outcome as significantly different from what we would expect according to probability? Who decides when and where to draw the line and conclude that all more radical outcomes are significantly different from the 25–25 split expected? Do we say that a 23–27 split is the limit, or should the 22–28 split be that point at which we should draw the line?

Similar questions are asked pertaining to observations made of social events (i.e., outcomes on tests, differences between group characteristics, correlation coefficients, and the like). Fortunately, we are able to employ the decision rules to assist us in determining where lines should be drawn concerning the significance of any given set of observations. These decision rules work directly in conjunction with probability.

USING DECISION RULES

When a difference between two groups is observed regarding some trait they mutually possess, such as age, sex, or years of education, at what point do we conclude that the difference is a significant one? We are usually going to observe differences between various people regarding commonly held characteristics, but how do we decide that the differences mean anything of importance to us? If we examine age differences between two groups, how do we judge these differences? What may be a significant difference to one researcher may not be considered as such by another investigator. In order that we may introduce greater objectivity into our interpretations of observations, we establish decision rules. To state a level of significance is to state a decision rule. How do levels of significance operate to enable us to make decisions about our observations?

There are always two possibilities regarding any given hypothesis. The hypothesis is either true or false. It cannot be both true and false simultaneously. This holds for null hypotheses and statistical hypotheses as well as for research hypotheses. If we reject a statistical hypothesis and it is true and should not be rejected, we have committed an error. Also, if the hypothesis is false and should be rejected but we decide not to reject it, we have committed another type of error as well. These errors are referred to as Type I (rejecting a true hypothesis) and Type II (failing to reject a false hypothesis), and are designated by probability values of Alpha and Beta. Alpha error is Type I error and Beta error is Type II error. Table 5-3 demonstrates the relation of Type I and Type II errors more clearly.

Of course, the social researcher would like to eliminate both types of error in the decisions he makes regarding tests of hypotheses. At no time, however, can he eliminate either type of error. He can take steps to minimize both types of error, however.

Table 5-3.   Type I and Type II Error

		Hypothesis is:	
		True	**False**
Decision is to:	Reject Hypothesis	Type I Error (Alpha, α)	Correct decision
	Fail to Reject Hypothesis	Correct decision	Type II Error (Beta, β)

Type I error lies under the direct control of the researcher. Type II error is only indirectly controlled by him. Changing one type of error will always cause a change in the other type, however. If one is minimized, the other is increased, or if one is increased, the other will generally be decreased. There is not a one-to-one relation between both types of error, though. For instance, such things as the size of one's sample act to influence Type II error in addition to the influence exerted by Type I error.

The level of significance as one of the researcher's decision rules is the amount of Type I error the investigator is willing to permit in testing his hypotheses. Although any probability level can be selected as the amount of Type I error permitted, conventionally used levels of significance are 0.10, 0.05, and 0.01. If the researcher states in advance of the hypothesis test that he has decided to use the 0.05 level of significance (allowing only 5 per cent probability for Type I error), and if later he makes a decision to reject some hypothesis he is testing at that level of significance, then there is a 5 per cent chance that he has made the wrong decision in rejecting the hypothesis, that it is possibly true and should not be rejected. If he uses the 0.10 level of significance and if he rejects a hypothesis at that level, then there is a 10 per cent chance he is wrong in making the decision, and so on.

To familiarize the reader with tests of hypotheses in various forms utilizing different levels of significance, the following illustrations are provided:

1. $H_0: \bar{X} = 50$
     $H_1: \bar{X} \neq 50$
     $\alpha = 0.05$

HYPOTHESIS SAYS: H_0, the null hypothesis, is that the mean of some group or collection of elements is 50, whereas H_1, the alternative research hypothesis, is that the mean is not equal to 50. We are making the hypothesis test at the 0.05 level of significance.

DECISION: (HYPOTHETICAL) The decision is to reject H_0 in support of H_1, according to our observations.

INTERPRETATION: We conclude that $\bar{X} \neq 50$. According to probability, five times in 100 we could be wrong in rejecting H_0 possibly a true hypothesis—(see Table 5-3) that $\bar{X}$ is really 50.

2. $H_0: r_{xy} \leq 0$
   $H_1: r_{xy} > 0$
   $\alpha = .01$

HYPOTHESIS SAYS: H_0, the null hypothesis, is that the relationship (r) between X and Y variables (subscripts x and y denote what r is representative of) is equal to or less than 0, whereas H_1, the alternative research hypothesis, says that r is greater than 0, implying that there is a direct or positive association between variables X and Y. We are making the test of the hypothesis at the 0.01 level of significance.

DECISION: (HYPOTHETICAL) Our decision, based on our observations, is not to reject H_0. We have failed to support H_1 by failing to reject H_0.

INTERPRETATION: We interpret this decision as meaning that there is no positive association between X and Y. This conclusion is made at the 0.01 level of significance.

Levels of significance, therefore, assist us to be more objective about our observations and the interpretations of them. When we establish certain decision rules in advance of the test of our hypotheses, there remains little room for subjective manipulation of the findings we observe. (It should be noted that null hypothesis formulation is *entirely* dependent on the way the research hypothesis is formulated. Null hypotheses should be stated in such a way and symbolized so that if they are rejected in a subsequent test, the specific research hypothesis is supported clearly and directly.)

Specifying the sampling distribution is another important decision rule that precedes tests of hypotheses. Suppose we collect a sample of 100 people from a larger population of 10,000. Furthermore, suppose we compute a mean representing the average height of the sample we have drawn. We now have a *sample statistic,* or an observation for a sample—the average height. Let us replace this sample in its original population and draw another 100 elements from that universe. Let's continue to compute a mean for the average height of the new sample we have drawn. Suppose we continue this until we have obtained all possible *different* samples that could be drawn theoretically. If we computed means representing the average height for all possible samples of size 100 from the population of 10,000 and arranged these means into an array from smallest to largest, we would then have a *sampling distribution of sample means*. (The possible number of samples that can be drawn from any given population, with replacement, is N^n, where N = the population size, and n = the sample size. In our example, the possible number of samples of size 100 that could be drawn from a population of 10,000 would be $(10,000)^{100}$.)

Continue to suppose that each time we drew a sample and computed a mean for it, we used that particular mean as an educated guess or estimate of the mean height of the entire population. It follows that each time we had a new sample and computed a mean for it, the new mean would differ from the previously computed sample mean. In fact, most of the sample means would differ from one another to some noticeable degree. Each mean would be closer to or farther away from the true population mean than the others. Some would be good estimates (closer to the population mean); others would be poor estimates (farther from the population mean). Because we have no way of determining the true population mean without getting the entire universe of elements, each sample estimate is as good as another. If the samples vary in size (number of elements), however, the larger sample sizes generally make the better estimates of true population values. This statement holds only when the selection process for the inclusion of elements is a random one. (Chapter 8 discusses various sampling procedures to insure randomness.) Therefore, if our selection process for the samples was random, that is, if we made it possible for each element to have an equal and an independent chance of being drawn each time a new sample was selected from the population, we would say that each sample mean would represent a reasonable guess of the true population mean. Statisticians call this reasonable guess an *estimate* of the population value or parameter. (Parameters are population characteristics whereas statistics are characteristics of samples.) And if we had several sample means, the *average* of these means would be the best estimate of the population value.

Statisticians can demonstrate that the true population mean, average height for 10,000 people, for example, will fall within a specified distance from the sample mean computed for any given sample, according to some probability. In fact, the mean of all possible sample means computed for samples of a given size is the *true population mean.* The mean of the sampling distribution of the means and the population mean are identical. Because sampling distributions of various statistics are *theoretical* distributions and seldom seen by any researcher, we will say that for any given mean computed from a sample we have obtained, there is a likelihood or probability that the true population mean is close to that value.

The main thing to be drawn from this discussion is that when statistical hypotheses are tested, sampling distributions of particular statistics are used. They are probability distributions, and accordingly, probability statements can be made about the accuracy with which sample statistics reflect population values of which they are estimates. The level of significance is used to give the probability statement greater meaning. Rather than say that there is some probability that two groups differ regarding some characteristic, we can now say that the groups differ at the 0.05 (0.10, 0.02, 0.001) level of significance. Bear in mind that there is always the likelihood or probability that we are in *error* in drawing that conclusion. (The complexities of deriving sampling distributions and their accompanying characteristics will not be presented in this volume. It is suggested that the reader refer to a statistics textbook that will explain these procedures in greater detail. The primary function of the present discussion is to familiarize the beginning social researcher with some of the fundamentals of hypothesis testing and to briefly acquaint him with some of the statistical operations in such tests. The role of probability theory should be recognized as extremely important, particularly during that part of the investigator's research dealing with theory verification.)

The researcher is in a more strategic position regarding hypothesis tests when he sets up decision rules pertaining to levels of significance and the specification of the sampling distribution of the statistic he determines. He can assess more objectively the particular observations he makes. And he is in the position to know from a probability standpoint, at least, how much error is involved in any given decision to reject or fail to reject some hypothesis.

INTERPRETING THE RESULTS OF TESTS OF HYPOTHESES: SOME IMPORTANT CONSIDERATIONS AND NOTES ON THEORY VERIFICATION

Suppose a researcher has complied with most of the conventions regarding tests of hypotheses. He has constructed a theory to account for a given event and has logically deduced hypotheses from the theory. Subsequently, he tests the hypotheses and makes decisions regarding the outcomes of such tests at a conventional probability level. The researcher will observe one of three possible outcomes on the basis of the information he has collected:

1. All of the hypotheses tested are supported.
2. None of the hypotheses tested is supported.
3. Some of the hypotheses tested are supported and some are not supported.

The neophyte researcher will probably make the following kinds of interpretations based on each of the three outcomes noted above.

Outcome 1: If he observed that all of the hypotheses tested are supported, he will most likely conclude that his theory is valid or is at least strengthened considerably by this particular outcome.

Outcome 2: If he notices that none of the hypotheses tested is supported, he will probably conclude that his theory is not valid or is inadequate in some respect.

Outcome 3: The most perplexing of situations is where some of the hypotheses are supported and some are not supported by the data one has collected. The researcher is often unable to determine what sort of interpretation should be made here. Sometimes he simply states that a part of his theory is supported and other portions of it are not supported by what he has found. He usually declares that further study is necessary to determine with greater assurance that such and such variables are related meaningfully to the event predicted.

Each of these interpretations of the different outcomes of hypothesis tests is legitimate to a degree. But it is not enough to make a blanket generalization of support or refutation of a theory based on such tests. Making the right kinds of interpretations of hypothesis tests is a complex procedure. In this section, we will identify and discuss some of the more important considerations that must be taken into account before a meaningful interpretation of a hypothesis test can be made. It is extremely important to keep in mind that, *regardless of the outcome of any given test of hypotheses* (i.e., Outcome 1, 2, or 3 above), the researcher should raise questions concerning each of the following potential problem areas: theory, sampling, measurement, data collection, statistics, and participant involvement. Raising such questions will help the researcher to:

1. improve the quality and meaning of the interpretation of any hypothesis test;

2.   evaluate the relative importance of a given hypothesis test for theory building;

3.   determine the degree to which the study supports the work of others; and

4.   determine the reliability of the explanation of the event that is either implicitly or explicitly stated by the hypothesis.

THEORETICAL CONSIDERATIONS

Whether the hypotheses are supported or not supported, the researcher is obligated to improve continually on the theory he uses. The modification and reformulation of various elements in the theory should enhance the internal consistency and predictive utility of it. Asking questions repeatedly that concern the general adequacy of the theory may focus attention on certain theoretical weaknesses such as poor conceptualization of variables. The researcher should subject his theory to continuous reexamination and reassessment, regardless of how good he thinks it is.

Some of the questions that should be raised center around the following:

1.   The general adequacy of the theory

2.   The degree of control over antecedent and intervening variables

3.   The adequacy of hypothesis formulation

4.   The degree of consistency in the theoretical and substantive literature

5.   The number of hypotheses supported and the number not supported by the findings.

THE GENERAL ADEQUACY OF THE THEORY

Does the theory allow for the derivation of testable hypotheses? Is the theory too broad or too narrow, given the nature of the phenomena it attempts to explain? An inspection of the postulates, assumptions, and propositions that make up the theory will provide the researcher with an impression of the rationality and completeness of it. Do the elements of the theory fit together logically? Are the phenomena used in the theory a part of the empirical world and amenable to scientific inquiry? Is the theory clearly presented, and are there precisely defined interrelationships between each of its parts?

Because theories are causal models in part, to what extent is it clearly demonstrated that certain phenomena cause others to occur? What is the likelihood that an alternative theoretical scheme could account for the same event with comparable predictability? Under the circumstances, does the theory include all logically relevant factors in the grasp of the social investigator? Does the theory reflect a meaningful combination of these factors in the best possible arrangement?

THE DEGREE OF CONTROL OVER ANTECEDENT AND INTERVENING VARIABLES

Has the theory taken into account certain antecedent conditions that would logically affect the outcome of the event? To what extent has the theory controlled for the possible influence of such factors? Also, are intervening variables accounted for in the theoretical scheme? How is the researcher able to detect the influence of such factors on his theoretical formulations? To what extent can he effectively separate the impact of spurious variables from the causal relation between the event and the variables that significantly influence its occurrence? This is generally accomplished only through the careful construction of his theory and the strategic inclusion of provisions that function to eliminate systematically the potential sources of spuriousness. This is perhaps the most difficult part of the theory construction process. (See Chapter 3 for a discussion of theory construction.)

THE ADEQUACY OF HYPOTHESIS FORMULATION

Are the hypotheses stated correctly in terms of their logical derivation from the theory? Or do they contain terms that have not been fully defined and/or treated in the theoretical scheme? One common problem encountered by social researchers is testing hypotheses that contain terms not treated adequately in the theory. If the hypotheses to be tested are systematically derived from the body of theory one constructs, this problem will not exist. But occasionally, terms occur in hypotheses that the researcher *implicitly* included in the theory. The correct procedure would be to make the inclusion of these terms in the theory *explicit*. This would help to ensure that the theory has made adequate provisions for these terms and their subsequent hypothesized relation to the event predicted.

Sometimes the hypotheses may not be phrased or stated in accordance with the logical interrelatedness of variables in the theoretical scheme. It could be, for example, that a variable in a hypothesis is treated as *independent,* whereas in the theory it was treated exclusively as a *dependent* variable. It is always necessary for the researcher to specify clearly which variables are to be treated as independent and which ones are to be used as dependent, and to follow through the hypothesis tests using these terms as consistently as possible.

On occasion, the social investigator will test a hypothesis in such a way that it will be inappropriate for supporting or refuting the theory from which it was derived. A hypothesis is tested, but the theory supported is not necessarily the one the investigator started with. The researcher should carefully examine each hypothesis to see that it is consistent with the order of terms and variables used in his theory.

THE DEGREE OF CONSISTENCY IN THE THEORETICAL AND SUBSTANTIVE LITERATURE

Assessing the importance of a given hypothesis test and the meaning we should attach to it should be influenced by the degree of consistency in previous studies that pertain to the present one. Obviously, if no other studies have been done that relate directly or indirectly to our present research, we have no alternative but to be very conservative in our interpretation of the significance of whatever we find. Our research work is viewed as a "pioneering effort," and as such, it requires that we confirm our conclusions by observing outcomes of subsequent related studies. Repetition of the study, or "replication research" as it is sometimes called, is about the only way we have of arriving at a reliable evaluation of our theories.

A particularly difficult situation we are confronted by at times concerns inconsistent findings in the literature. For example, in industrial sociological research, it is often reported that the type of supervision influences worker job satisfaction. But there are inconsistencies pertaining to the specific nature of the influence type of supervision exerts. Some studies show that close supervision gives rise to low job satisfaction, whereas other studies show that general supervision also gives rise to low job satisfaction. The researcher is in a dilemma. If he were to study job satisfaction and supervision, his findings would support one of the competing conclusions. Of course, he would try to identify differences in the studies pertaining to the definition of terms. Each study defines the same phenomenon (i.e., job satisfaction and/or supervision) differently. This fact alone could be responsible for the inconsistencies in findings. In any event, inconsistencies in research findings relating to the same topic are perplexing to any researcher. Such situations make it extremely difficult to argue clearly that the researcher's findings are conclusive. Rather, a simple statement of support for one position or the other is in order.

When findings from several studies are relatively consistent with one another, and when the investigator continues to support such findings with his own, his argument for the viability of his theory is strengthened considerably. And when the researcher's findings are in direct contradiction to what appears to be a general trend in the literature, there is some question as to whether the hypothesis supported was a "chance" finding (the more likely alternative in this case) or whether it reflects the better theoretical position. Again, repeated study of the same phenomenon on different samples of elements will generally be sufficient to assess the accuracy of the original hypothesis test.

THE NUMBER OF HYPOTHESES SUPPORTED AND THE NUMBER NOT SUPPORTED BY THE FINDINGS

As has been argued previously, it cannot be ascertained whether a theory is supported or refuted by merely counting the number of hypotheses supported and weighing them against the number not supported by one's research findings. It is purely arbitrary as to how many hypotheses a researcher will test in any study. Generally, it is assumed that all hypotheses tested in a given study have been derived from the same theory. Each hypothesis concerns a different part of that theory, however. Showing that some hypotheses test out and others do not test out may only be indicative of a theory with both strong and weak parts. Or it may mean nothing at all. Ideally, the situation most researchers prefer is when all of their hypotheses test out as predicted. This would constitute the most clear case for supporting the theory. Seldom is this seen in actual practice, however.

And so we are left with the more frequent outcome of partial support for our theoretical position. One way of resolving this problem is *to assess the relative importance of each hypothesis tested.* Some may be more central to the theory and hence, more important than the others. Perhaps some sort of hierarchy of hypothesis importance could be formulated. The researcher would be more concerned with those major hypotheses most closely related to the theory he is using. He could argue that if the hypotheses supported tend to be those of greatest importance to the theory whereas those hypotheses not supported tend to be somewhat removed from the theoretical mainstream of things, then his theory would have somewhat greater value as a predictive instrument. But keep in mind that such a ranking of the theoretical importance of hypotheses could backfire, and the researcher might find that the most important hypotheses were not supported by his findings, whereas the least important hypotheses were supported.

SAMPLING CONSIDERATIONS

Interpreting the results of hypothesis tests involves some evaluation of the sampling plan chosen to obtain the original information. Questions should be raised concerning: (1) sample representativeness, and (2) the adequacy of the sample in relation to the problem studied.

SAMPLE REPRESENTATIVENESS

Is the sample representative of the population being studied, or is it a biased sample? Using a biased sample to test a hypothesis could give the researcher misleading results. Testing a hypothesis concerning racial segregation on a sample of segregationists rather than including individuals reflecting various types of integration-segregation philosophies would be an example of how a researcher might obtain a result that would not be typical of the population as a whole. Using some type of probability sampling plan and/or drawing a sample of considerable size would help to overcome sample bias and cast the test of the hypothesis in a somewhat different light.

THE ADEQUACY OF THE SAMPLE IN RELATION TO THE PROBLEM STUDIED

Sometimes the investigator will obtain a sample of elements that has little relation to the problem he is investigating. For example, he may administer a questionnaire to a classroom of college students regarding their perceptions of wardens' attitudes toward prisoner punishment. Most of the students will have had no experience whatsoever with wardens' attitudes. Their perceptions would be guesses at best. If the researcher were to conclude later that wardens' attitudes toward prisoner punishment are of a particular nature based on the impressions and perceptions of a small sample of college students, his hypotheses concerning wardens' attitudes would be seriously impugned. Therefore, the social investigator should make every effort to ensure that the sample he selects is adequate in terms of having information relating directly to the problem he is investigating. This means he should ask wardens about wardens' attitudes, workers who are supervised about the type of supervision they receive, and so on. This will enhance the reliability of responses provided by elements in the sample and the generalizability of the findings will be strengthened.

MEASUREMENT CONSIDERATIONS

Because hypotheses contain variables that must be operationally defined or measured by some means, it is quite important to assess the *quality* of measures employed in any given hypothesis test. Whether or not any specific hypothesis is supported rests in part on the measures of phenomena that make up the hypothesis. The researcher should raise questions concerning the adequacy and appropriateness of the operational definitions of terms from the standpoints of (1) the validity of the measures used to represent variables in hypotheses, and (2) the reliability of the measures. (An extended discussion of the validity and reliability of measuring instruments is presented in Chapter 7.)

THE VALIDITY OF THE MEASURES USED TO REPRESENT VARIABLES IN HYPOTHESES

A measure of something has validity if it measures what we say it measures. Obviously, if measures used for terms in hypotheses are not valid, then the subsequent tests of hypotheses containing those terms are equally invalid. In other words, the researcher does not know what he is testing. If the validity of a measure or of several measures is seriously questioned, then the interpretation of the test of the hypotheses should be made even more conservatively.

It is difficult to assess the degree of validity of measures of variables. Demonstrating the validity of a measure often rests on logic alone. If it is reasonable and apparent that the measure we have devised is appropriate for the phenomenon we wish to take into account, then we argue that the measure is probably a valid one. The problem is, of course, that *several* definitions can have a high degree of validity and yet yield different results regarding hypothesis test outcomes. Continuing with an example used previously, suppose we were to measure degree of job satisfaction by asking a person how satisfied he is with his income. Assume, also, that we ask another person in the same company his satisfaction with his working hours. Assume that a third individual is asked how satisfied he is with his job content. Each of these individuals answers the question according to some *Strongly Agree–Strongly Disagree* Likert response pattern, the responses are weighted and summed, and the researcher defines the resulting scores as the degree of job satisfaction for each person. Basically, each person may have the same feeling toward the general job, yet when asked about specific job aspects, each individual may respond quite differently. Such differences in definitions could seriously affect the outcome of tests of hypotheses.

This problem illustrates that the replication of theories and repetitive tests of the same hypotheses do not always follow a standard pattern. A researcher often conducts what he believes to be a replication of previous research, but somewhere along the line, some of the definitions of terms change. Any change in definition of terms affects the research replication to a degree. Significant changes in the conceptualization of terms and the operationalization of them will undermine the value of the study as a replication of previous research. It is not a true replication if previous procedures are not followed precisely. The matter of validity, therefore, raises at least two questions that have relevance to the social researcher:

1.   To what extent do the measures of certain phenomena reflect their true degree for any given individual or group?

2.   To what extent is a particular measure of an individual or group property consistent with other definitions used in previous studies?

THE RELIABILITY OF MEASURES OF VARIABLES USED IN HYPOTHESES

Reliability of a measure refers to the extent that the measure of some individual or group property consistently reflects that property. An intelligence measure is said to be reliable if it gives a consistent indication of the degree of that phenomenon for any individual. Say a person receives an intelligence score of 125 the first time he is tested. Then, if after a two week period (or some other reasonable interim), he receives the same intelligence score of 125, this is regarded as evidence of the reliability of our measure of intelligence.

It is expected that most individuals will change their attitudes toward things over time, and we will want to take into account the extent of certain attitudinal changes of relevance to our research. We will want to employ a measure we can rely on to give us a consistent appraisal of how one feels about things. If a person changes his attitude (Attitude X) from one time period to the next, we want a measure of Attitude X that will reflect the change accurately. Simply observing changes in scores for a person from one time period to the next may or nay not be meaningful. The measure may not be reliable, hence score changes will mean relatively little. When our measuring instrument is reliable, then score changes have greater meaning, and we are able to delineate cause-effect relations between phenomena more easily. Score changes using a reliable measuring instrument are generally interpreted to be the result of some independent variable that we have identified theoretically.

In effect, what can be said about tests of hypotheses is influenced significantly by the validity and reliability of measuring instruments employed to take certain variables into account. If our measures of things lack validity and/or reliability, our conclusions are subject to question. We are not sure of what we have measured, and furthermore, we may not be measuring the phenomena consistently.

DATA COLLECTION PROCEDURES

Another factor that could seriously affect the interpretation of our findings is the nature of our data collection procedures. What means were employed to collect our data initially? From what source did we obtain our information about the phenomenon under investigation? The questions pertaining to data collection procedures center around the following: (1) the use of observation, personal interviews, and/or questionnaires, and (2) the reliability of secondary sources.

OBSERVATION, PERSONAL INTERVIEWS, AND/OR QUESTIONNAIRES

If data were obtained through observation of individuals, personal interviews with them, or by self-administered questionnaires, there are questions we must ask about the reliability of the observer and/or interviewer, and of the questionnaire itself. The most common problem regarding observation and interviewing is the personal bias of the observer and/or interviewer. The observer may misinterpret what he sees, or he may fail to see something that is important to the group he is observing. The interviewer may misinterpret or misrecord what he hears in an interview. Also, it is likely that the observer will influence the individuals he is observing. The fact that a person is being watched may cause him to alter his natural behavior to a degree. This is known as *reactivity* on the part of the respondent. In the event that a person does not know he is being watched, then much emphasis is placed on the ability of the observer to record accurately what he sees and to make reliable and meaningful interpretations of it.

In the interviewer situation, the respondent is often prone to give answers he believes the interviewer wants to hear. This is typically labeled as *social desirability* and is generally present as a significant factor in all interviewer-respondent situations. The degree to which social desirability operates to affect respondent answers will affect accordingly the reliability of the data one collects and the meaning of subsequent hypothesis tests.

When questionnaires are used, it is possible that choices provided the respondent for different questions are not realistic ones in terms of the respondent's personal experience. Certain questions are often omitted that should have been included. The way in which questions or statements are phrased can affect the respondent's interpretation of what he is being asked, and accordingly, the answers he provides. (Observation, interviewing and questionnaire construction and administration are treated separately and more extensively in certain chapters to follow.)

THE RELIABILITY OF SECONDARY SOURCES

We must also question the reliability of any secondary source material used to obtain information for one's research. Secondary source material includes such things as speeches, autobiographies, historical records, newspaper accounts of events, general articles, magazines, court records, vital statistical compilations, and monographs of various kinds. When material is gathered from such sources and is subsequently used in the test of hypotheses, several problems are apparent.

First, and perhaps most important, is the fact that the data obtained from such secondary resources was not necessarily collected originally for the investigator's immediate purposes. The researcher will need to make inferences about the source from which the data are gathered, and he will probably have to shape the data to conform to the requirements of his own research. It could be that some information may simply not be available to the investigator through the use of secondary sources. Consequently, he may be led either to reformulate his theory and hypotheses or select other data sources.

Second, there are potential pitfalls in using secondary data arising from the bias of the individuals who originally collected the information. When newspaper accounts of events are used to test hypotheses about some contemporary phenomenon, the accounts are nothing more than the impressions of the newspaper writers. The same questions raised in the previous section regarding the bias of the interviewer and observer can also be raised here concerning the objectivity of the original data gatherer.

It has been said that the research one conducts is no better than the data he collects. If this is true, then the social investigator must strive to collect data that are as reliable as possible, and he must take into account in his interpretation of findings those things about his data collection procedures that would seriously affect the meaning and significance of any hypothesis test.

STATISTICAL CONSIDERATIONS

The major factors pertaining to statistical problems in one's research concern: (1) the choice of statistical techniques in data analysis, and (2) the level of significance used.

THE CHOICE OF STATISTICAL TECHNIQUES IN DATA ANALYSIS

Tests of hypotheses generally, though not always, include particular statistical tests. Because there are many kinds of statistical procedures available for testing hypotheses, it is important that the researcher select those tests most appropriate for the particular data he has obtained. He makes his selection of statistical test largely on the basis of its specific function and the assumptions underlying it. If he is able to meet the assumptions of a particular statistical test with the data he has, and if the test is suitable from the standpoint of the questions he would like to answer, then his selection is a good one. On the other hand, if his choice of a statistical test is faulty (i.e., he selects a test that is not suitable for the problem at hand or he fails to meet the assumptions that underlie the procedure he has chosen with the data he has), then the resulting hypothesis test lacks a degree of validity. The researcher's interpretation of his results will be distorted accordingly. The social investigator must delineate clearly the kinds of questions he would like to answer in his research, and then, methodically and logically, he must take steps to select the most suitable statistical test in terms of the technique's functions and underlying assumptions.

THE LEVEL OF SIGNIFICANCE USED[5]

The test of any hypothesis with a statistical technique involves establishing a significance level. The level of significance selected serves as an objective standard and assists the researcher in making a decision about the significance of what he has found.

Commonly used significance levels are 0.05 and 0.01. Referring to our previous discussion of levels of significance and reviewing briefly, when the researcher is able to reject a null hypothesis at the 0.05 level, we say that five times in 100 he could be rejecting a true hypothesis. The level of significance defines the probability of making a Type I error or rejecting an hypothesis when, in fact, it should not be rejected. Supporting or failing to support a given hypothesis, in terms of probability, depends on the level of significance chosen. If the researcher selects levels of significance that are too low (i.e., 0.20, 0.30 or 0.50), then he makes it somewhat easier to reject null hypotheses and support his research hypotheses. But note that as *the level of significance is lowered from 0.05 to 0.20, the chances now become 20 in 100 that the hypothesis rejected is a true one.* There is considerable Type I error present in this hypothesis test. This means that the research supported under such a statistical test and at the 0.20 level of significance is of comparatively little value in the long run. If the 0.50 level of significance were used and a null hypothesis subsequently rejected at that level, this would be commensurate with saying that the chances are 50–50 that the hypothesis supported is true. Such odds are not significant at all.

A level of significance should be chosen that offers a fair appraisal of the hypothesis being tested. It should be rigorous enough that Type I error is minimized, but not so rigorous that Type II error is increased appreciably. Type II error is the probability of failing to reject a hypothesis when it is false and should be rejected. The conventional levels of significance, 0.05 and 0.01, are frequently accepted as reasonable in hypothesis tests, although under certain circumstances other levels of significance are chosen. (Selecting less conventional significance levels is done on the basis of sample size and type of sampling procedure, in part. Most statistical textbooks have discussions of how to choose levels of significance based on these factors.)

PARTICIPANT INVOLVEMENT AS A CONSIDERATION

A problem area that receives comparatively little attention has to do with the nature of participant involvement in the research activity. When human subjects are used in a given study, they are observed, interviewed, or in some way questioned concerning the information they have which the researcher wants. It is suggested that the way in which a respondent becomes involved in a research project will affect the kinds of reponses he gives.

It has been shown, for example, that individuals are more likely to respond willingly when there are immediate and apparent rewards that accrue to them as a result of their participation in some activity. When the appeal is altruistic in nature, implying that someone other than the respondent will benefit from his participation, the respondent is less likely to involve himself willingly.

The relationship between researcher and respondent may be characterized as a *power relation*. The researcher is interested in obtaining the compliance of the respondent. He wants the respondent to answer certain questions, to allow himself to be observed in a social situation, or to perform some other behavior relating to the researcher's project. How the researcher enlists the cooperation of the respondent will affect the nature of respondent involvement subsequently.

Etzioni (1965) suggests a typology of compliance relations that allows for the prediction of type of involvement following as the result of the use of differential kinds of power. (Although this typology was originally used to characterize relations in formal organization power hierarchies, it will be adapted here as a means of illustrating respondent involvement accompanying manipulation by a social investigator.) In Etzioni's typology, the following kinds of involvement are said to logically accompany compliance behavior precipitated by power of reward, coercion, and legitimacy. In the actual model illustrated in Table 5-4 remunerative, coercive and normative compliance are used. A person who complies with someone else because of perceived remunerative power would most often calculate the advantages and rewards of such compliance behavior and would manifest calculative involvement. Accordingly, a person complying

Table 5-4. Etzioni's Typology of Compliance Relations

		Type of Involvement		
		Calculative	**Alienative**	**Moral**
Type of compliance	Renumerative	X		
	Coercive		X	
	Normative			X

because of perceived coercion would probably reflect a type of alienative involvement. And a person who complies because he believes it is normal (or legitimate, proper, or right) does so probably because of moral involvement.

Probably the most desirable type of involvement from respondents from the researcher's point of view would be moral involvement. Certainly such involvement would enhance the reliability of the respondent's answers to questions asked by the social researcher. (This will be dealt with shortly.) The next most desirable involvement might be calculative, where there is some indication that the respondent will answer somewhat reliably because of the rewards offered for complying with researcher requests. The least desirable type of involvement would be alienative. It is this type of involvement that readily encourages resistance to researcher requests and poses other types of difficulties that directly and/or indirectly affect the performance (and consequently, the reliability) of the respondent.

One important implication of this typology for the social researcher and his subsequent use of human subjects is that the type of involvement elicited from the respondent will depend on the approach or power-type the researcher selects to obtain compliance. A research design that fails to make provision to include respondents in ways that will minimize the coercive aspects of their involvement will have to reckon with the likelihood that the reliability of their responses will be questionable. Obtaining the compliance of individuals through any form of coercion seems to be the most likely circumstance that will affect respondent reliability.

Because the reliability of any person's response is based on several things, it is difficult to say what the precise effect of coercion will be. It is well known that the level of education of the respondent, his age, sex, socioeconomic status, occupation, ethnic identity, and ability to read and understand the intent of the questions he is asked will collectively exert an effect on the quality of responses he gives. Misspelled words and omitted pages on questionnaires, awkward phrasings of questions, unreal or irrelevant questions and the like all contribute to affect the respondent's answers as well. Reliability, therefore, is a fairly complex characteristic that is difficult to evaluate precisely. When the element of coercion is added, it is believed that the reliability of responses is further affected. To what extent and in what ways will coercion affect the reliability of the respondent's answers? Some suggested effects are the following:

1. The respondent may not identify with the questions he is asked;

thus, he follows the line of least resistance and gives the most con-venient and not necessarily the most accurate and complete answers. Checking randomly any response in a fixed-response type of ques-tionnaire is an example of possible unreliability as a result of the alie-nation he might experience.

2.   Alienative involvement may predispose the respondent to lie by purposely choosing those responses or giving those answers he does not believe to be true of him. This is perhaps the most likely be-havioral alternative a respondent will select. This is because it offers the greatest opportunity to retaliate, to get even for the supposed coercion to participate.

3.   Another effect of alienative involvement is to cloud the person's judgment in responding so that even if he mildly wishes to tell the truth and respond accurately, he is latently affected by the coercion implicit in the interview or questionnaire administration.

The primary purpose for presenting each of these factors at this time is to illustrate that the meaningfulness of the test of any hypothesis or set of hypotheses is contingent upon many things. It should now be apparent that theory verification is a complex procedure. There are many places where the researcher can make mistakes and/or exercise poor judgment. Each step of the research process is an important one, and there are few places where shortcuts are warranted.

Research replication has been emphasized at various points throughout this discussion. Through the replication of research we are able to determine the degree to which *chance* operates as a primary factor in affecting outcomes of hypothesis tests.

SOME QUESTIONS FOR REVIEW

1.   Differentiate between null hypotheses and research hypotheses. What are some functions of statistical hypotheses?

2.   Write the symbolic expression of null hypotheses for the following research hypotheses:

    a. $H_1: r_{xy} = 0$
    b. $H_1: r_{xy} \quad 0$
    c. $H_1: \bar{X}_1 \neq \bar{X}_2$
    d. $H_1: \bar{X} \geq 75$

3.   What are some functions of hypotheses in general? What is the relation between theories and hypotheses?

4. What are some of the criteria that must be met before hypotheses can be tested meaningfully? What is the importance of having empirical variables?

5. Differentiate between Type I error and Type II error in tests of hypotheses. What are decision rules and how do they relate to hypothesis tests?

6. What is meant by a negative association? What is a positive association? What is a curvilinear association? Give some examples of each from practical experience.

7. What can a researcher say about his study when none of the hypotheses he tests is supported? What can be say about his research when some hypotheses test out and some do not?

8. What is the role of theory in interpreting the results of statistical tests?

9. What is meant by the following terms: reactivity, social desirability, reliability, and validity?

10. How should the way in which a respondent involves himself in a researcher's study influence his response to interviews? Explain.

NOTES

1. The term *problem* used here refers to any social event needing a satisfactory explanation. Any unanswered question might also be considered a problem.
2. Some scholars define hypotheses as proposed solutions to problems (Doby, 1967), propositions that can be tested to determine their validity (Goode and Hatt, 1952), or statements of relation between two or more variables (Kerlinger, 1965; and Denzin, 1970).
3. Conventional treatment of hypothetical variables defines the independent variable as X and the dependent variable as Y.
4. Sometimes artificially contrived testing grounds are used, such as pure experiments in laboratory settings. These are used frequently particularly if a researcher's objectives include completeness of experimentation. (See Chapter 4.)
5. Levels of significance are employed only when the researcher meets certain requirements with the sample he is studying. First, he must have a random sample drawn from a population known by him. He must also use inferential statistical techniques to

properly generalize to the larger population. Third, his data must meet certain levels of measurement requirements such as the interval level. These requirements often limit the generalizability of one's information because the researcher is unable to satisfy all of them.

BIBLIOGRAPHY

Denzin, Norman K. *The Research Act: A Theoretical Introduction to Sociological Methods.* Chicago: Aldine, 1970.

DiRenzo, Gordon J. *Concepts, Theory and Explanation in the Behavioral Sciences.* New York: Random House, 1966.

Doby, John T. *An Introduction to Social Research.* New York: Appleton-Century-Crofts, 1967.

Etzioni, Amitai. *A Comparative Analysis of Complex Organizations.* New York: Free Press, 1961.

Goode, William J., and Paul K. Hatt. *Methods in Social Research.* New York: McGraw-Hill, 1952.

Kerlinger, Fred N. *Foundations of Behavioral Research: Educational and Psychological Inquiry.* New York: Holt, Rinehart, and Winston, 1965.

Lastrucci, Carlo L. *The Scientific Approach: Basic Principles of the Scientific Method.* Cambridge, Mass.: Schenkman, 1963.

Stephens, William N. *Hypotheses and Evidence.* New York: Thomas Y. Crowell, 1968.

Von Hentig, Hans. "Redhead and Outlaw," *Journal of Criminal Law and Criminology* 38: 6–10 (1947).

Winer, B. J. *Statistical Principles in Experimental Design.* New York: McGraw-Hill, 1962.

CHAPTER 6
SOME FUNDAMENTALS OF THE MEASUREMENT OF SOCIAL AND SOCIAL PSYCHOLOGICAL VARIABLES

This chapter deals with one of the most important phases of the research process—the measurement of social and/or social psychological variables. All social research involves measurement of one sort or another. There has been increased interest in measurement in the social sciences during the past 25 years (Bonjean, Hill, and McLemore, 1967). Several thousand measuring instruments have been devised during the period 1955–1970, and there are indications that measures of social variables are continuing to multiply.

Our major objectives are the following:

1. To show the relation of measurement to the total research process. We have stressed repeatedly the notion that research consists of a series of stages carefully calculated and designed to provide answers to social questions. Inasmuch as the quality of research generally is no better than the weakest stage of that process, it is necessary that we examine the fundamental role of measurement as one of the most vital stages. To that end we will demonstrate the importance of measurement and some of the functions it performs in the process of social inquiry.

2. To outline the fundamental procedures in the measurement process. This involves the question of how measures of social phenomena are obtained. We will delineate methods used by social scientists to bring social variables into some kind of empirical perspective.

3. To review some of the more important methods of measuring social phenomena. We will examine some of the popular scaling methods (e.g., Likert, Thurstone, and Guttman) and illustrate the relevance of each for particular research purposes. The weaknesses and strengths of each of these methods will be discussed, together with some recommendations for their functional application in social research.

4. To portray some of the major theoretical and substantive issues of measurement in social science. This objective stresses the variety of professional opinion regarding the measurement of social variables in general. To what extent is it legitimate to assume (1) that social phenomena exist, (2) that social phenomena exert a causal influence on social behavior, (3) that methods of measurement can accurately reflect the degree of any given social or psychological property for a specific group or individual, and (4) that particular social variables can have demonstrable causal relationships to social behaviors experimentally?

MEASUREMENT DEFINED

What is measurement? Several definitions have been provided in the methodological literature. Stevens (1951) defines measurement as the assignment of numerals to objects, events, or persons, according to rules. Cohen and Nagel (1934) defines measurement as the correlation with numbers of entities that are not numbers. In addition, a definition of measurement has been given by DiRenzo (1966): "Measurement refers to the procedures by which empirical observations are made in order to represent symbolically the phenomena and the conceptualizations that are to be explained."

Most other definitions of measurement offer little in the way of extending the general meaning of the term, but for the most part they are various versions of those definitions provided above. The definition of measurement we will use here consists of an integration of each of these above definitions. Retaining the essential elements of each, we suggest that measurement is *the assignment of numbers to nominal social and/or psychological properties of individuals and/or groups according to rules, and the correlating of these numbers with these properties symbolically.* As an alternative to the above definition, measurement may be defined as *the assignment of numbers to, and the symbolic correlation of the numbers, with nominal social and/or psychological properties of individuals and/or groups.* For our purposes this definition places measurement squarely within a social context, and this is particularly relevant for the discussion of social variables to follow.

WHY DO WE NEED TO MEASURE SOCIAL PHENOMENA? A PRELIMINARY STATEMENT

The measurement of social phenomena is a fundamental prerequisite to most social research. It is important to measure social phenomena for a number of reasons. In the general case, when the researcher develops an explanation for social problems or events, he constructs a theory that acts as a *linking* tool. The theory links the event to the explanation of it. Although causal relations between phenomena are difficult to delineate, particularly in the social sciences, it is a tacit assumption that theories function as *causal models* for the most part. Theories are usually tested empirically by subjecting hypotheses derived from them to some kind of verification, frequently statistical.

Consider the following hypothetical illustration as an example. Suppose we were to theorize about the causes of delinquent behavior and conclude that boys who are deficient in the trait *ego strength* (a social psychological component of personality) will tend to become delinquent more frequently than boys with a greater degree of this social psychological factor (Barron, 1963). We would develop our rationale into a formal theoretical scheme where ego strength would be related systematically to delinquent behavior in a causal fashion.

One part of the verification process would consist of determining from police records the boys who would constitute our sample of delinquents. Also, we could generate a crude index of delinquency simply by paying attention to the frequency and intensity of delinquent behaviors that are a part of each boy's record. Such classifications are fairly easy to construct. We could match those boys with another group of boys randomly selected from the community who have no police records and are therefore designated as *nondelinquent* (Selltiz, et al., 1959). To ensure comparable samples of delinquents and nondelinquents, the groups could be matched according to several salient characteristics such as age, sex, years of education, socioeconomic background, occupation of parents, and others. Such matching would decrease the possibility of certain variables interfering with observed differences between the two groups of delinquents and nondelinquents. For example, if we failed to match according to socioeconomic status, this factor might contaminate the study to such an extent as to mislead us to conclude that ego strength was a significant factor when in fact socioeconomic status was the more important variable.

But how would we go about assessing the social psychological variable, ego strength? How do we determine, for any given number of boys, delinquent or nondelinquent, that certain ones have more or less of this trait than the others? If we could not quantify this variable, ego strength, in some way, it would be very difficult to test hypotheses that include it. We must be able to take ego strength into account empirically. We must be able to say with some degree of assurance that boys vary according to this characteristic, and furthermore, we should specify the degree to which each boy possesses this variable. Only then will we be able to satisfactorily subject our hypotheses about ego strength in relation to delinquent behavior to some reasonable verification. *One of the most important reasons for measuring social phenomena, therefore, is to allow the researcher the opportunity of using these phenomena in hypotheses to determine the effects of these variables on others.* In the following discussion, additional functions of measurement will be delineated, and it will become increasingly apparent that the measurement phase of social research is a crucial one.

FUNCTIONS OF MEASUREMENT

There are several functions of measurement in the process of social research. Some of the more important ones are: (1) to describe social and psychological phenomena empirically, (2) to render data amenable to some kind of statistical manipulation and treatment, (3) to assist in the testing of hypotheses and theories, and (4) to enable the researcher to differentiate between objects or people according to the degree of certain properties they possess. None of these functions is necessarily mutually exclusive of the rest. All functions listed above have logical relevance for each of the others.

THE DESCRIPTION OF SOCIAL AND PSYCHOLOGICAL PHENOMENA

In descriptive study designs the primary objective of the researcher is to describe the social setting and the participants in that setting in detail. The anthropologist in New Zealand, for example, is interested in describing various behaviors and customs of the Maori people, a collection of tribes indigenous to that part of the world (Mead, 1928; Benedict, 1934). It is important for the researcher studying small groups to be able to describe what is going on in the group, who is saying what to whom, how often, and to depict the nature of interaction as vividly as possible (Hare, Borgatta, and Bales, 1965).

One implication of the accurate description of social settings and the people in them is that hypotheses may subsequently be formulated about various behaviors in those settings and subjected to some kind of empirical test. The researcher, therefore, sets out to classify and categorize the cultural patterns and behaviors he observes. Assisting him in the classification process are various kinds of measuring devices. These devices may consist of questionnaires, fixed responses to questions in interviews, and impressionistic categorization by the researcher himself. Once he has described what he has observed, he is in a more strategic position to hypothesize things about the people he is studying. He has become informed about what to study and has perhaps focused on those methods that would be most appropriate for investigating a certain culture.

On the basis of the particular *statistics* (characteristics of the people he observes) he compiles, he may be led to believe any number of things about the culture and the people. Some of these statistics may be the sex ratio, average age at which people marry, their average height, size of dwelling units and overall community size, the modal behavior patterns (which behaviors are engaged in most frequently by a majority of the tribe or group), and the religious and ethnic composition.

RENDERING DATA AMENABLE TO SOME KIND OF STATISTICAL TREATMENT

Another function of the measurement of social and psychological variables is to bring the phenomena into a form that can be manipulated statistically. In data analysis the social investigator must "make sense" out of the information he has collected from various sources and respondents. He may have data consisting of interviews, responses to questionnaires, or notes he has taken while observing a group of individuals interacting.

Suppose an observer is paying attention to workmen in a small informal work group. The men are assembling radio parts along a large table. Each man passes some completed work to another man where additional operations are performed on the product being manufactured. The men chat informally about things. The topics may be job-related or non-job-related. The men take a lunch break, and some stay at the work place and eat lunch with others from their own work room whereas some of the men join with other workers in related work areas and eat elsewhere. During the day the observer gives the men a questionnaire to complete containing questions about certain social and psychological behaviors. Questions ask about job satisfaction, satisfaction with pay, working hours, type of job performed, the monotony of the task, age, sex, years of education, salary level, length of time on the job, and the like. At the end of the day, the observer has compiled a good bit of information about the men in the work room. What does he do with it now?

His next step is to *analyze* the data. This means that he must classify the data into specific information categories and attempt to explain what is going on in the particular work setting and why. He is interested in assigning numbers to the information he has, or in other words, *he wants to quantify the variables under study.*

The assignment of numbers to information sounds simple enough at first, but in reality the measurement of social and psychological variables is somewhat involved. The observer wants to quantify his information because the statistical procedures he proposes to use require that data be portrayed numerically for easy manipulation mathematically.

There is a wide variety of statistical techniques the researcher uses for the analysis of his data, provided that he meets certain assumptions required by most of them (Champion, 1970). One of the assumptions underlying statistical tests is that the data be amenable to quantification of some sort. The assignment of numbers to his social and psychological phenomena will make it possible for the researcher to put the information on IBM cards or in some other convenient paper form so that he can use machines to sort and classify the information rapidly. Because most statistical techniques require that data be reduced to numerical form, the data analysis phase of the research process will be facilitated greatly owing to the reduction of the data to such quantities.

ASSISTING IN THE TESTING OF HYPOTHESES AND THEORIES

An important objective of the research process usually is to test theories through tests of hypotheses derived from them. Theories are devised to explain and predict social and/or psychological phenomena (e.g., why do we have high delinquency and other forms of deviance, why are there high divorce rates, why do we have urban blight, what social factors relate to high productivity in a factory, what causes high anxiety, low morale, high job satisfaction, and so on?).

The researcher derives hypotheses from these theories and subjects them to some kind of empirical test. He selects a social setting that is consistent with the theory (i.e., if the theory concerns delinquency, he samples delinquents from a given community) and provides an adequate testing ground for it. He defines his variables nominally and proceeds to quantify them so that they can be manipulated statistically. Once data are in numerical form, hypotheses can be tested more easily. In the general case, if a hypothesis concerns the relation between two variables, X and Y, and is of the form,

$$\text{as } X \text{ increases, } Y \text{ decreases,}$$

then the researcher merely observes whether or not decreases in Y do indeed accompany increases in variable X. Of course, statistical techniques exist to portray the nature or direction and degree to which two or more variables are related to one another. These statistical techniques also involve probability theory (discussed briefly in Chapter 5), which enables the researcher to assign some probability value to the accuracy of his conclusions about the truth or falsity of the hypothesis statements he tests (in each situational instance).

When hypotheses are supported in social research, this means that the theories from which they were derived (most hypotheses are derived from some theory, either explicitly or implicitly) are also *supported*, at least tentatively. Supporting a theory is tantamount to endorsing the explanation provided for why certain events occur as they do. And, accordingly, this places us in a better position for unraveling the mysteries surrounding the origin of many social phenomena.

ENABLING THE RESEARCHER TO DIFFERENTIATE BETWEEN THE OBJECTS HE STUDIES ACCORDING TO THE PROPERTIES THEY POSSESS

One of the primary functions of measurement is to allow us to make distinctions between objects (or people) according to certain properties they mutually possess. Suppose we are looking at several tables in a large room. We might wish to determine which table is the longest. To do this, we must pay attention to the *length* property of each table. A tape measure or ruler enables us to take this property into account. These are so-called *standards of measurement* that help to identify consistently the length property of many objects in terms of inches or feet. By observing different measures for each table, we can easily determine which table is longest.

Suppose we wish to determine which of several people weighs the most? A way of answering this question is to have each person stand on some scales that will give different values of the *weight* property for each person. After each person has weighed himself, we can easily determine which of the persons weighs the most by paying attention to the largest numerical quantity. In this case, we pay attention to only one of the many properties that characterize the individual, namely, his weight.

Suffice it to say that for any object or person there are several qualities or properties we may be interested in measuring or taking into account empirically. In the case of a table, for instance, various properties we may be interested in measuring or taking into account empirically may be hardness, weight, length, shape, height, mass, type of wood, color of wood, and so on. The wood craftsman could go on indefinitely pointing out other properties of tables to us. By the same token, the individual has an infinite number of characteristics including age, sex, years of education, socioeconomic status, I.Q., race, ethnic background, membership in particular organizations, clubs or groups, hair color, eye color, height, weight, general shape, and a host of other variables identified as social and/or attitudinal (e.g., anxiety level, thick-skinned or insensitive, warm, sociable, effeminate, aloof and cold, degree of satisfaction of work group, and prejudice).

In the social sciences we frequently confront problems that ask whether several groups differ from one another. Do men perform better than women on college entrance examinations? Do older workers stay on the job longer than younger workers? Do work groups vary according to their joint productivity? Do boys reared in one type of home environment (fatherless) become delinquent more frequently than boys reared in another type of home environment (both parents present)? Do blacks differ from whites regarding different types of crime and the amount of deviant behavior? Sometimes the questions we ask are confined to a single group. What is the group like in terms of certain salient social and psychological characteristics?

To deal with all these questions and others like them, it is necessary that we first measure the variables we plan to use in our descriptions of a group or several groups. If we fail to measure the variables, we will have no way of including them meaningfully in our research activity. Measurement of our variables, then, will enable us to classify individuals or objects according to their possession of particular properties. Therefore, *measurement performs a classificatory function.*

MEASUREMENT AND LEVELS OF MEASUREMENT

Most social research involves the measurement of variables. Some common variables assigned numerical values are age, sex, years of education, socioeconomic status, job satisfaction, supervisory style, criminal behavior, employee productivity, and all types of social attitudes. Specifically, suppose we were to assign numerical values to worker productivity in an industrial setting. We observe the following hypothetical distribution of *productivity scores* (units of product) for five of the workmen:

Work Group	Productivity
Worker 1	15
Worker 2	19
Worker 3	12
Worker 4	10
Worker 5	25

It is apparent from these worker productivity scores that worker #5 has produced more units of product compared with the other workmen. It is also apparent that the workers *vary* according to productivity, our hypothetical variable. In this particular work situation, the measurement of productivity might be considered as a fairly easy task. We simply count the units of product produced by each workman and sum them.

Although some social variables are equally easy to ascertain and measure, others are further removed from our empirical world. How easily can we measure differences between workers, for example, according to their degree of *job satisfaction*? Job satisfaction might also be labeled as a *variable quantity.* And it is unlikely that all workmen will have the same level or degree of satisfaction with their jobs. How do we measure this variable if we choose to study it in our social research?

Considering another fairly elusive variable, how do we measure *race prejudice*? What do we pay attention to? What do we count and sum, if counting and summing are integral parts of measurement of all social phenomena? At this point, it is apparent that the social scientist's work becomes increasingly involved, apart from the theoretical framework he must develop and the people from whom he must obtain information. If he elects to include *any* social variable or *any* psychological variable in his research, he must make provisions for bringing each of these variables into the empirical realm. In other words, *he must devise some means of measuring these phenomena.*

Using the example of the work group above, suppose the researcher notes that a certain number of men are Protestant and the rest are Catholic. He decides, quite arbitrarily, to assign the number 1 to each Protestant, and a 2 to all Catholics in his sample. He has just defined the variable, *religion,* and two subclasses on the religion variable, namely, Protestant and Catholic. A 1 stands for all members of the first subclass on the religion variable, Protestant, and a 2 stands for all members of the second subclass on the religion variable, Catholic. It is evident that other subclasses may be created as needed (e.g., Jewish, Moslem, and so on), but for purposes of his research, it is necessary only to define the two subclasses noted above (since no other religions are represented among his sample apart from Protestant and Catholic). Suppose further that he identifies age by recording the actual ages of the workmen. Do the numbers he has assigned to the subclasses on the religion variable mean the same thing as the numbers he has assigned to values on the age variable subclasses (i.e., young, middle-aged, old, or thirty-five, forty-one, twenty-two, fifty-six, sixty-two, and so on)?

Consider that while we can say that a person who is forty years of age is older, in fact, twenty years older than a person who is twenty years of age, we cannot say that a person who is assigned (by virtue of his religious classification) a 1 on the religion variable is more than or less than (in some respect) a person who scores a 2 on the religion variable. This would be the equivalent of saying that a Protestant is higher (or lower) in the religious spectrum than Catholics and/or Jews. The illogic of such an interpretation is obvious.

This example illustrates clearly the fact that there are basic differences between numbers in terms of the variables they represent. Numbers have different meanings depending on their particular use in the research process.

Traditionally, numbers have four different kinds of interpretations, depending on the level of measurement assumed. These levels of measurement are: (1) nominal, (2) ordinal, (3) interval, and (4) ratio (Stevens, 1951).

To test many hypotheses in social research, the variables used in the hypotheses must be brought into the empirical world in some way. Some variables are more directly a part of the empirical world than are others. For example, tangible objects (e.g., chair, table, book) are directly perceived by the individual, but it is more difficult to "see" many so-called intangibles (e.g., attitudes, the psyche, and the like). The quantification of all social variables involves the assignment of numbers to such phenomena. Because the phenomena in the social and psychological world vary in the degree of their visibility and attachment to the empirical world directly, it makes sense to consider the numbers assigned to such phenomena in terms of *degree* as well. Accordingly, there exist the four measurement levels listed above.

In terms of "high" and "low" relation between these measurement levels, they are ordinarily considered in the following hierarchy:

RATIO (HIGHEST)
INTERVAL
ORDINAL
NOMINAL (LOWEST)

One reason a distinction is made in this fashion is that the more "higher-level" data (meaning that a ratio or interval level of measurement is said to underlie his data rather than an ordinal or nominal one) the researcher has, the greater is the variety of permissible mathematical operations that may be performed with the data. Also, when he analyzes data statistically, more sophisticated statistical procedures accompany the higher measurement levels. This means that generally the researcher can do more things and make more types of analyses with his data if they are of the higher levels of measurement.

Depending on how any variable is defined and subsequently measured by the researcher, it may be labeled as a nominal variable, an ordinal variable, an interval variable, or a ratio variable. Variables are not necessarily intrinsically nominal, ordinal, interval, or ratio. The researcher must examine the methods used to measure the phenomenon to determine precisely what kind of measurement level underlies it.

THE NOMINAL LEVEL OF MEASUREMENT

The most simple measurement level is the nominal level. This level involves the classification or categorization of variables into several nominal subclasses. For example, the variable, *sex*, has two nominal

subclasses: male and female. Accordingly, religion has an almost infinite number of subclasses, among which are included Protestant,
Catholic, and Jewish.

Numbers used at this level of measurement perform only a classificatory function. A 1 is different from a 2 and a 5 is different from a 6
and so on. No attempt is made to manipulate the numbers
mathematically other than to note how many of a given number exist.
There are five 1s, ten 2s, eight 3s, etc. Most mathematical operations
are not permissible with data of the nominal level. We cannot add 1s
and 2s in the following manner:

$$1 + 2 = 3.$$

A 1 plus a 2 does not equal 3 in this instance. This would be the
equivalent of saying that a Protestant plus a Catholic equals a Jew.
Variables of the nominal level of measurement are religious affiliation,
race, ethnic background, school affiliation, political affiliation, and the
like.

THE ORDINAL LEVEL OF MEASUREMENT

A higher level of measurement (in relation to the nominal level) is the
ordinal level. Numbers used at this level of measurement not only
allow the investigator to define differences between variable subclasses (a 1 is different from a 2), but also to determine *greater than* or
less than relationships between numbers. A 2 is not only different
from a 1, but it is in a higher or lower position relative to a 1.
Therefore, numbers used on an ordinal scale define relative positions
of variable subclassifications. For example, the North-Hatt Occupational Index (1947) has numbers ranging from 100 to 0 and is designed
to identify ordinal differences between occupational classifications.
Each occupation is assigned a particular value relative to the others
(e.g., 15, 90, 85, 50, and so on), and it can be determined readily that
one occupation is higher or lower than another on the occupational
vertical continuum. Some occupations have a higher position on the
continuum than the rest. A Supreme Court justice may have a 93,
whereas a shoeshiner may have a 6. When numbers are used according to some ordinal scale, there is no attempt to say that an equal
distance will be found between all numbers. We cannot say that the
same distance exists between 10 and 20 as exists between 20 and 30.
We can only conclude that one number is in a different position and
in a particular direction in relation to another number. Consider the
illustration in Figure 6-1. The values 5, 10, 11, and 20 are placed in such

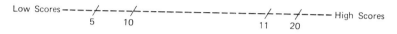

Low Scores — High Scores
5   10   11   20

Figure 6-1. An ordinal continuum.

a way as to show that only the position of values is relevant. We never say how much more or how much less one value is from another. Consider the space between 10 and 11 and then compare it with the distance between 11 and 20. This should convey the meaning of ordinality quite clearly.

Variables frequently observed as conforming to the ordinal scale or level of measurement are social class, social distance, prestige rankings or ratings of universities and business organizations, and many attitudinal phenomena. Within the ordinal level, it is generally impossible to determine precisely how far one score is from another. There is no standard distance between units along a horizontal continuum measured according to an ordinal scale.

THE INTERVAL AND RATIO LEVELS OF MEASUREMENT

When data are of the interval level of measurement and numbers have been assigned to them, there is an equal spacing between units along some interval continuum. The interval level of measurement has all the properties of the preceding levels of measurement discussed (i.e., nominal and ordinal), and in addition, it has equal spacing between intervals. On a continuum of values ranging from high to low, an equal distance between units will be found. For example, examine the continuum in Figure 6-2. The values along this continuum are an equal distance from one another. A 1 is the same distance from a 2 as a 2 is from a 3, and so on. Fahrenheit temperature is an example of an interval variable. Ten degrees is five degrees more than 5 degrees. One disadvantage of the interval level of measurement, however, is that it does not have an absolute zero. Consequently, it is not possible to make *ratio statements* concerning variables. A 2 is not twice as much as a 1. It is only one unit more than a 1. Twenty degrees is not twice as hot as 10 degrees. With an absolute zero, ratio statements can be made. Income is an example of a ratio variable (one that is measured according a ratio level of measurement) having an absolute zero. A person with $10 has twice as much as a person with $5.

Most statistical techniques require *no more than* the interval level of measurement for manipulation of variables. The major difference

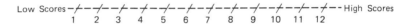

Figure 6-2.   An interval continuum.

between the interval and ratio levels of measurement is the absolute zero distinction. For most purposes in social science, though, data of the ratio level are treated as if they were at least interval (which they are).

These measurement levels are important to the social scientist because they allow him to differentiate between the data he analyzes. Accordingly, such differentiation dictates a particular set of statistical procedures and techniques of analysis that are permissible under certain scientific and mathematical rules. The researcher complies with these rules by matching appropriate analysis techniques with the data he has. As a result, he decreases the possibility of making misleading interpretations from his data, and he makes a more valid contribution to science by his research activity.

CONCEPTS AND CONSTRUCTS

Before any theory can be tested, the terms in that theory must be defined clearly. In addition, they must be linked in some meaningful way with the empirical world. This means that the terms used must be amenable to some kind of measurement or quantification. Terms not amenable to measurement are of little value to the theorist or to the practitioner. In the same sense, to deal with questions that lie outside the realm of empirical reality would be fruitless activity for the social scientist. For example, to try to answer the question, "where does God live?" would be outside the domain of the social scientist because the scientific method is simply not designed to handle such a question. (Of course, science can be used to study *attitudes and opinions* of people as to where God lives.)

Freud's notion of the id, ego, and superego are also examples of terms that are difficult to define empirically (Strachey, 1959). In fact, this is one of the most important reasons why social scientists reflect such disagreement when it comes to assessing the importance of Freud's psychoanalytic theory. It is quite difficult either to support or refute his ideas when they cannot be tested readily in the empirical world.

Theories, therefore, are made up of an interrelated set of ideas. For a theory to be tested, the terms used in the theory must be measurable. What is the nature of the terms used in social science? One way of looking at the terminology of social science is to make a distinction between terms that are *concepts* and terms that are *constructs.*

CONCEPTS ARE TERMS THAT HAVE DIRECT EMPIRICAL REFERENTS[1]

This means that when we enunciate the word, we can point to an object the term represents. In other words, there is something in empirical reality that we say the term stands for. For example, when we say "book," we can point to numerous objects the word represents. We can also examine the properties of books such as length, weight, thickness, color, type of print, subject matter, and the like. When we say "chalk," we can point to many objects the word represents. Other examples of concepts would be table, chair, typewriter, pencil, window, and so on. Each one of these terms has direct empirical referents, or things we can point to in our world of empirical reality that the term stands for.

Such terms are most amenable to measurement of some kind. Other conceptual variables might be race, religious affiliation, nationality, and political party. Although these terms are less a part of our empirical reality than a chair or table (i.e., we are more prone to respond to our *definition*—Democrat, Republican, Catholic, or athiest—of someone rather than specific observable characteristics what do we pay attention to when we *see* a Democrat?), they are nevertheless a part of the empirical world and can be taken into account readily in our theories.

CONSTRUCTS ARE TERMS THAT HAVE NO DIRECT EMPIRICAL REFERENTS

When we enunciate terms that are not directly part of our empirical world, we label these terms as constructs. Some examples of constructs are anxiety, faith, intelligence, social class, and prestige. Figure 6-3 illustrates graphically the distinction between concepts and constructs being made here. What does one look at when he sees *anxiety*? To what does one pay attention when he looks at *prestige*? There are no directly observable phenomena for which the words *anxiety* and *prestige* stand entirely. Yet, it is a fact that virtually all of

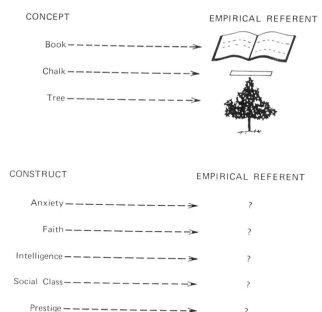

Figure 6-3.   An illustration of the distinctions between concepts and constructs.

the so-called attitudes people manifest are not directly a part of the empirical world. But social scientists use these terms quite freely in explaining and predicting social phenomena and personal behaviors.

Much of the terminology of the social scientist is constructual in nature. Therefore, it is imperative that if the social scientist is going to employ such terminology meaningfully in theories, he must devise a means of rendering this terminology to a measurable quantity. In other words, he must supply a set of attributes to constructs to bring them closer to the empirical world. He must bring them more into a measurable form similar to concepts that already have relatively convenient and direct empirical referents.

NOMINAL AND OPERATIONAL DEFINITIONS

The explication of theory involves the use of nominal definitions extensively. *Nominal definitions of terms are those definitions frequently found in the usual desk dictionary.* Terms are often defined nominally by giving other words that are synonomous with them. This establishes a merry-go-round or circularity of terms that is disturbing to the social scientist because the terms are seldom defined in such a uniform fashion as to provide one, and only one, meaning that can be measured consistently by independent social investigators. Webster's (1964) dictionary defines anxiety (p. 66) as a state of being uneasy, apprehensive, or worried about what may happen; misgiving; a thought or thing that causes this; an eager and often slightly worried desire. If we look up the word, misgiving, we find (p. 941) that it means a disturbed feeling of fear, doubt, apprehension. When we look up the word, apprehension (p. 71), we find that it means foreboding, fear, dread. And when we look up the word, fear (p. 530), we find that it means to be uneasy, anxious, or doubtful, to expect with misgiving. And when we look up the word, uneasy (p. 1588), we find that it means disturbed by anxiety or apprehension. In other words, when we seek to tie down empirically a particular word such as anxiety, we eventually wind up where we started—with the same word, anxiety.

Nominal definitions of things suffice at the outset for linking ideas to one another logically. In fact, most theories that are verbalized consist of a logical set of statements using nominally defined terms. The statements are connected on the basis of how the terms used in them are defined nominally. This permits the researcher the opportunity of constructing a theory based purely on logical interrelationships between terms without ever tying them into the empirical world.

To test the theory, the terms that are nominally defined must eventually be brought into the empirical realm. This generally involves the measurement process or the assignment of numbers to varying degrees of personal and/or social properties. Social properties refers to the process of reducing nominal definitions to an empirical form or to measurable quantities such as operationalization. The operational definition is the result of operationalization. Operational definitions are quantifications of nominal definitions. Some researchers define operationalization as the process of reducing a construct to the level of a concept. Another way of looking at an operational definition is one that assigns meaning to a construct or a variable by specifying the activities or "operations" necessary to measure the construct or variable (Kerlinger, 1965, p. 34).

An example of an operational definition of anxiety, for instance, would be anxiety is what an anxiety test measures. The anxiety test (or measure) consists of agreement or disagreement (depending on the wording of the statement) with several statements that are logically derived properties of anxious individuals (psychoneurotic patients in a mental hospital or other similar situation diagnosed by competent physicians and psychiatrists as *anxious*). Persons who agree with more of these statements than someone else are said to be and are defined as *more anxious* than these other persons. The operationalization of anxiety in this instance consists of specifying several statements that are properties of individuals (psychological, social, and/or biological characteristics). Taylor's (1953) Manifest Anxiety Scale is an illustration of what is done here. Portions of this questionnaire are reproduced in Table 6-1. The items in Table 6-1 refer to properties of individuals at the psychological, social, and biological levels. These characteristics are supposedly correlates of the property, *anxiety*. More accurately, these characteristics are *behavioral correlates of anxiety*, logically derived and defined by the researcher. And, logically, a person manifesting more (or fewer) of these behavioral correlates than someone else is assumed to be more anxious (or less anxious) than the other person.

Table 6-1. Some Items From the Taylor Manifest Anxiety Scale[a]

The following items are answered by respondents with either "True" or "False" answers. In parentheses are the anxiety-prone responses.

I am often sick to my stomach.   (True)
I am about as nervous as other people.   (False)
I blush as often as others.   (False)
I have diarrhea once a month or more.   (True)
When embarrassed, I often break out in a sweat, which is very annoying. (True)
Often my bowels don't move for several days at a time.   (True)
At times I lose sleep over worry.   (True)
I often dream about things I don't like to tell other people.   (True)
My feelings are hurt easier than most people.   (True)

Source: These items are part of 50 items Janet Taylor extracted from the Minnesota Multiphasic Personality Inventory (MMPI) (1941) and utilized to measure anxiety level. Her research is reported in the *Journal of Abnormal Social Psychology*, 48:285–290, 1953. One point is given for each anxiety response, and therefore the range of scores is from 0 to 50, depending on the number of anxiety responses given by any particular subject. The raw scores are then used in conjunction with other measuring instruments in diagnostic and therapeutic capacities.

An important objective of the researcher is to construct a measure that will enable him to compare individuals with one another relative to certain attitudinal properties they possess. A solution to this problem is the operational definition of an attitudinal phenomenon. This kind of definition takes the form of a set of statements in Table 6-1.[2] Agreement or disagreement with each statement will be indicative of a subject's possession of an attitude (in this instance, anxiety) to varying degrees. Persons receiving larger scores (more agreements) than other persons are assumed to be located at a different position on the attitude scale ranging from high to low.

VARIOUS METHODS OF MEASUREMENT

The measurement of social and psychological variables may be accomplished by applying several popular methods devised by researchers. In this section we will consider in detail the following methods: (1) Likert or "summated rating" methods, (2) Thurstone or "equal appearing interval" measures, and (3) Guttman measures. These methods refer to various types of scaling. *Scaling* is the process of developing a measurement standard whereby individuals may be compared relative to one another regarding the properties they possess. At the end of the discussion of each scaling method mentioned above, some advantages, disadvantages, and applications of these methods will be presented. In addition, several less popular methods of measurement (with special applications) will be discussed briefly in a concluding section of this chapter.

The researcher may measure social phenomena according to varying degrees of precision. He may be interested in simply classifying his information into two or three categories. For example, if he is investigating the influence of political party affiliation on voting behavior toward a particular bond issue, he may easily sort the subjects into a few discrete categories: Democrat, Republican, and American Independent. (Other categories may be added as needed to include all respondents in any given study, e.g., Socialist, Communist, and so on).

Next, he may sort each of these subclasses on the political affiliation variable into whether the person is for or against the bond issue. The data are then *cross-tabulated,* as is shown in Table 6-2. Plotting information into a table such as Table 6-2 allows the investigator to infer things about the relation between two variables (political affiliation and opinion on particular bond issues). The information in Table 6-2 represents a cross-tabulation of two nominally defined variables. Sub-

Table 6-2.   Political Affiliation and Opinion toward Bond Issue

		Republican	Democrat	American Independent
Bond Issue	For	35	22	15
	Against	10	25	50
		$N_1 = 45$	$N_2 = 47$	$N_3 = 65$

jects are classified according to two nominal variables, and the categories are cross-tabulated with one another. Subsequently, statistical tests may be applied to the information distribution in the table to determine whether there is a significant relation between the two variables. This procedure is closely related to hypothesis testing. This discussion is elaborated in Chapter 5.

In effect, the researcher has obtained measures for each individual in his study on the political affiliation dimension and the opinion toward the bond issue dimension. These are considered measures even though they are only *countables* or amenable to classification. Classification is primarily the measurement method appropriate for the nominal level. For higher levels of measurement, variables may not only be classified, but they may be given greater degrees of precision in terms of ordinality or intervalness. Thus, the distinction is made conventionally between so-called *countables* or *classifiables, rankables,* and *measurables* (Peatman, 1963). Typically, a researcher has countable information that corresponds to the nominal level of measurement, rankable information that corresponds to the ordinal level of measurement, and measurable information that corresponds to the interval or ratio levels of measurement.

Few social scientists take the time to distinguish between rankable and measurable, however. Most of them assume that the data they have are countable or measurable, and all researchers ultimately regard all data they collect as measurable, even though very crude measurement or very refined measurement is applied.

LIKERT MEASUREMENT

Rensis Likert (1932) was instrumental in developing the *method of summated ratings* as a means of differentiating between subjects according to their possession of varying degrees of some ordinal characteristic, typically attitudinal in nature. It has become conventional to refer to such a measurement method as a *Likert-type measure*. The Likert measurement method is by far the most popular of all measurement methods presently used in social research. Some reasons for its popularity include the ease with which it may be applied in actual research situations, and the simplicity of interpretation of Likert measures following data collection.

We are able to identify Likert-type measurement by paying attention to the construction of questionnaires geared to measure ordinal phenomena such as attitudes. Subjects are provided a list of statements with which they may agree or disagree to varying degrees of intensity. For example, the following statements are indicative of typical Likert-type items and response patterns:

A Measure of Ethnic Discrimination

1.   *Members of ethnic category X should be excluded from this country.*

| Strongly Agree | Agree | Undecided, Probably Agree | Undecided, Probably Disagree | Disagree | Strongly Disagree |

2.   *Members of ethnic category X should be allowed to vote in national elections.*

| Strongly Agree | Agree | Undecided, Probably Agree | Undecided, Probably Disagree | Disagree | Strongly Disagree |

3.   *Members of ethnic category X should not be permitted to attend schools of the dominant ethnic category Y.*

| Strongly Agree | Agree | Undecided, Probably Agree | Undecided, Probably Disagree | Disagree | Strongly Disagree |

Notice that these items purportedly are designed to measure a person's degree of discrimination toward ethnic group *X*. In the actual case, there are usually many more statements (perhaps from ten to fifty) comprising the researcher's measure of phenomenon *X* (ethnic discrimination, in this case).[3]

The researcher assigns weights to each of the responses as individual measures of the intensity with which a person reacts to any given statement. The responses given to all statements are then summed (hence, the term *summated rating*) and compared with one another as total scores varying along some continuum of ethnic discrimination from high to low. Let's take a closer look at how the researcher applies Likert measurement in a hypothetical research situation.

Suppose an investigator wishes to examine the influence of some attitude on behavior. He provides a nominal definition of the attitude in question together with a logical rationale for why a specific behavior should be linked with it. This is saying, essentially, that individuals who possess attitude *X* will manifest behavior *X'*, hence, the general predictive model,

$$\text{Attitude } X \longrightarrow \text{Behavior } X'$$

His next step is to provide attitude *X* with an operational definition. He must be able to distinguish between individuals possessing differing amounts of attitude *X*. If he defines the attitude as being the degree of response various subjects give to a series of statements that have been derived from the universe of attitude *X*, he then must derive several statements consistent with this definition. (The problem of whether or not he is measuring what he thinks he is measuring and how consistently he is measuring it will be discussed in Chapter 7, Validity and Reliability in Variable Conceptualization.)

To illustrate the application of Likert measurement, we will assume that several statements have already been derived that have a high likelihood of coming from the universe of attitude *X*. The logic is that agreement or disagreement with each of these statements constitutes possession of either a high or a low degree of attitude *X*. For example, if I were to say "agree" to the statement, "I like my job," this response would be indicative of my job satisfaction. If I were to say "disagree" to the same statement, however, this would be evidence of a lack of job satisfaction or perhaps low job satisfaction, or even job dissatisfaction. An impression is formed of my attitude toward my job based on my agreement or disagreement with statements concerning my work. This type of assessment process can be repeated to cover virtually every attitude imaginable.

The summated rating feature of Likert measurement is designed to evaluate the *intensity* with which an attitude is expressed. Again, the logic is that individuals who possess some attitude more strongly than others will occupy a different position along the attitudinal continuum from high to low. Individuals at different positions along the continuum may be expected to behave differently from one another under certain social conditions. The researcher expects to predict behavioral differences precisely because of the fact that individuals occupy different positions on some attitudinal dimension or dimensions related to the behavior in question. (We will not enter into a discussion of the soundness of linking particular behaviors to specific attitudes. In the present example, we are assuming that the statements are from the attitudinal universe we wish to measure.)

The intensity of a given attitude is determined in part by weighting the responses a person gives to each statement. *Weighting* is the process of assigning numerical values to each response to a statement.

For example, the statement, "I like my job" has the following response pattern:

Strongly Agree	Agree	Undecided, Probably Agree	Undecided, Probably Disagree	Disagree	Strongly Disagree
6	5	4	3	2	1

The response, "strongly agree," receives a numerical weight of 6, "strongly disagree" receives the weight of 1, and so on. Logically, the larger the score, the more the person likes his job, and the lower the score, the less the person likes his job.

Suppose the same statement were to be reworded negatively, such as, "I do not like my job." In this case, we might consider reversing the weights and applying them to the item response pattern as follows:

Strongly Agree	Agree	Undecided, Probably Agree	Undecided, Probably Disagree	Disagree	Strongly Disagree
1	2	3	4	5	6

Persons who like their jobs should logically disagree with the statement, "I do not like my job." Persons who dislike their jobs will probably agree with the statement. Again, the lower the score, the more likely it is that the person likes his particular job.

If we were to ask 100 people to respond to this statement, we would have 100 responses ranging from 1 to 6. Many people would be tied (received the same score) who answered "strongly agree," many people would be tied who answered "disagree," and so on. Do individuals who answer "strongly agree" to the same statement necessarily feel the same way about their jobs? Chances are that they do not. It is unlikely that one statement such as this will tap fully the sentiments people manifest toward their work. Perhaps if the measuring instrument were more precise, we might be able to distinguish between degrees of job satisfaction between people. This focuses squarely on the reason why several statements are used in summated rating procedures—for the purpose of achieving greater precision. In any random group of people, we can assume that any trait or characteristic individually possessed by group members is not necessarily held by all members to an identical degree. It is unlikely that all employees of a given company are equally satisfied with their jobs. It is unlikely that all residents of a given state are of the same attitude or opinion toward "right to work" laws. It is unlikely that in any group of people, all group members have the same degree of ethnic prejudice. To differentiate people from one another according to varying amounts of some attitudinal property each possesses, a Likert-type measure may be applied, consisting of several statements with gradated responses ranging from "strongly agree" to "strongly disagree." (The range is determined by taking the largest score minus the smallest score plus 1).

Suppose we were to weight the responses to ten statements from 1 to 6. The most points a person could receive for any response would be 6. The least number of points per statement would be 1. Therefore, the maximum number of points received for the entire set of statements would be $10 \times 6 = 60$. The least number of points would be $10 \times 1 = 10$. By expanding the number of statements from one to ten, we have increased the range of response from 1 to 6 = 6 to 10 to 60 = 51 or, from 6 to 51. Maintaining the same response pattern (based on a 1, 2, 3, 4, 5, 6 point spread), by increasing the number of statements to 20 we would have a range of 20 ($20 \times 1 = 20$) to 120 ($20 \times 6 = 120$) or 120 − $20 \times 1 = 101$ possible different total responses (i.e., 20, 21, 22, 23, . . . 118, 119 and 120).

By increasing the range of scores of any given measure, the researcher can increase the precision of the measuring instrument by decreasing the likelihood of tied scores.

Perhaps the most crude form a measuring instrument may assume is the simple "yes-no" response. It is easy to see the lack of precision that obtains when a researcher asks a question relating to whether the respondent is prejudiced toward specific racial categories:

"Are you prejudiced toward racial category X?   Yes __   No __

Asking this question of 100 people will obviously split the group into a dichotomy, those who say "yes" and those who say "no." Are all the people responding "yes" equally prejudiced? Not likely. Do those who say "no" feel the same way among one another as well? Again, not likely. The Likert or summated rating measure will help to differentiate intensities of attitudinal expression. This is one of its chief advantages.

If we asked the same people to agree or disagree with ten statements, and if we maintained a six-point response pattern, we would then be able to spread responses over a 51 point range from 10 to 60. This would introduce greater precision in assessing the prejudice attribute by leaving fewer ties.

Forms of Response

The Likert measure is not limited to agree-disagree response patterns. Any response pattern that is gradated (very strongly, very weak, increasing, decreasing, very positively, very negatively, more, less, and so on) may be adapted to fit the Likert pattern. The most common response pattern consists of agree-disagree, however.

There is very little uniformity relating to the number of response categories, and there is no uniformity regarding the number of statements for any given attitudinal measure. Decisions as to how many statements and the number and nature of response patterns the statements will have are made arbitrarily by the researcher. Of course, the researcher must allow the size of the group to which the measure will be administered to influence the length (number of statements) and the content of the measure. If he intends to administer the questionnaire to thousands of people, then he will want a degree of precision that will require more statements and perhaps more extensive responses than if he were to administer the set of statements to a small group.

The Number of Responses Per Question

Typical response patterns are the following (the agree-disagree format will be used although other formats can be adapted to fit the number pattern):

RESPONSE PATTERN
NUMBER
1. *Agree, Undecided, Disagree*
2. *Strongly Agree, Agree, Undecided, Disagree, and Strongly Disagree.*
3. *Strongly Agree, Agree, Undecided, but Probably Agree, Undecided, but Probably Disagree, Disagree, and Strongly Disagree.*
4. *Low . . . . Medium . . . . High*

Notice that the first three types of response patterns contain fixed responses. The fourth pattern contains a continuum of response where the respondent is permitted to place a check mark anywhere along the continuum that is consistent with the direction and the intensity of his attitude.

Response patterns Nos. 1 and 2 contain a category labeled "undecided." Respondents who select this category supposedly have no opinion (also included as an alternative in some Likert-type formats) on the statement expressed. Alternative response pattern No. 3 stretches the response range to six selections, obligating the respondent to commit himself to one side of the continuum or the other. *"Undecided, but probably agree"* and *"undecided, but probably disagree"* responses are designed to force a choice to either side of the continuum. When a person responds as "undecided" or "no opinion," the researcher cannot justify placing the person on either side of the continuum if, subsequently, he decides to dichotomize the group of respondents on that particular attitudinal dimension. There is little, if anything, that can be done with the "undecideds" in data analysis. The researcher is mainly interested in those who have an opinion one way or another. (Some investigators focus specifically on the characteristics of those who say "no opinion" to statements in questionnaire administrations.) Of course, if a choice is forced when, in fact, the person really has no opinion, it is easy to see how the researcher can end up with data that are questionable in terms of their theoretical and substantive import. No hard and fast rules exist for deciding whether to include an "undecided" category or whether there should be a forced-choice alternative. The researcher makes the final decision in the construction of his questionnaire based on the nature of the intended audience of respondents, their educational level, their familiarity with the information requested in the questionnaire, and a number of other equally relevant factors. Chapter 11 on questionnaire construction will discuss these factors more extensively.

The Meaning of Scores Derived from Likert Measures

A raw score based on summated ratings to a series of statements means relatively little by itself. Raw attitudinal scores are of the greatest value when they are used relative to other scores from other respondents on the same instrument in a comparative sense. If the range of response to an attitudinal questionnaire is 15 to 75 and we know that a person X has a score of 50, this is meaningful to the social scientist to the extent that he can predict what persons who have scores of 50 will do under certain social situations. Often, however, the score of 50 is compared with another person's score, and the behavioral differences between the two persons are equated with differences on the attitudinal measure. The process of equating attitudes expressed with observed behavior is common but occasionally misleading. It has been demonstrated that under certain conditions, persons express attitudes inconsistent with their subsequent behaviors (LaPiere, 1934).

Suppose two individuals were to react to the same measuring instrument, a questionnaire designed to measure attitude X. One person receives a score of 50, the other person a score of 25. The persons are later observed to behave differently under a particular social situation logically related to the attitudes expressed by them. Perhaps the dimension measured by the instrument is the degree to which a person wishes to join social groups. "Joining behavior" (the actual number of groups a person is a part of) is then compared with the attitudes expressed toward joining behavior (the social needs of companionship and camaraderie). We infer from the score of 50 that the person has high needs to join groups. The person with a score of 25 has relatively low needs to join groups. If our observations confirm this, we have established a small link between attitudes and behavior.

Consider the significance of this process when we have the scores of two hundred individuals measured according to the same phenomenon. Observe the information in Table 6-3. Table 6-3 reveals that all the low joiners (as indicated by their scores on the measure) are members of two or fewer groups, whereas high joiners (as revealed by their questionnaire scores) are members of three or more groups. These figures support the notion that the measure we have developed does indeed measure joiner behavior. Note the inclusion of the word *support* in this last statement. Observations of social events such as the information in Table 6-3 serve to provide *empirical support* and not necessarily *absolute proof* of the relation between attitudes and behavior.

Raw scores, therefore, are useful in comparison with the scores of other individuals on the same measure. In summary, people who are

Table 6-3. The Relation Between Joining Attitudes and Joining Behavior

		Attitude		Totals
		High Joiner	Low Joiner	
Number of Groups to which Person Belongs as Member	2 or Fewer	0	100	100
	3 or More	100	0	100
Totals:		$N_1 = 100$	$N_2 = 100$	$N_T = 200$

located at various positions along the attitudinal continuum (presumed measured by the measuring instrument) are regarded as possessing some trait or attribute to different degrees. Generally, there is a logical link between the attitude measured and some behavior manifested by in reality some subject or subjects.

Advantages of Likert Measurement

Some of the major advantages of summated rating measurement are as follows.

Likert scales are easy to construct and interpret. Because the researcher combines his professional experience with logic to derive items from an abstract theoretical universe of some trait, it is not too difficult to construct a questionnaire as a measure. The researcher is at liberty to word the statements he derives in any manner he chooses, provided that he adheres to a logical standard of continuity between the trait measured and the items selected to measure it. Scoring is easy as well. Statements may be worded positively or negatively, and numerical weights can be assigned to any common Likert response format. It is a simple matter to sum the responses to individual statements and derive a total score that may be compared with other scores on the same instrument. The larger (or smaller) the score, the more (or less) the subject possesses some attribute (an inference based on logic).

Likert scaling is the most common measurement format. Likert summated rating measures are most frequently used in social research. The ease of application and simplicity of interpretation are factors that increase the popularity of this measurement form. It has become conventional to apply summated rating measures in research designs that explore social psychological phenomena.

Likert scaling is flexible. The flexibility of summated rating scales is unparallelled by any other measurement technique. The researcher is at liberty to include as many or as few items in his measure as he chooses. Response patterns are equally subject to manipulation by the investigator. Because each item is presumed to count equally in the measure of some phenomenon, increasing the number of statements will increase the ability of the instrument to reveal differences in the trait measured between individuals as group size increases.

Summated rating measures lend themselves to ordinal measurement. Numerous ordinal level statistical techniques exist for assessing variations and patterns in social and psychological phenomena (Siegel, 1956; Freeman, 1965). Some researchers erroneously apply interval level statistical techniques to data based on summated ratings. Certain mathematical operations are not permissible unless a particular level of measurement is obtained. Averaging of scores or determining mean ($\bar{X}$) values are not permissible functions using data based on summated ratings. Yet, because of convention, many researchers commonly treat summated rating ordinal data as though they were of the interval level (a level permitting computation of means and averaging. There are several arguments favoring a variety of positions on this issue (Champion, 1968; Morris, 1968; Labovitz, 1967; Labovitz, 1968).

Likert scales are similar to other forms of attitude measurement such as Thurstone scaling and Guttman scales (Kerlinger, 1965).

Weaknesses of Likert Measurement

The major weaknesses or disadvantages of summated rating measures are as follows:

There is no consistent meaning that can be attached to the raw scores derived by such measurement.   There is little that can be said about a raw score by itself. Raw scores vary according to the number of questions and the extensiveness of response patterns used. This adds to the inconsistency of things as well. Summated rating measures are primarily useful when they allow comparisons to be made between individuals.

It is assumed that each item in a measure has identical weight in relation to every other item. This is not necessarily a valid assumption.   Certain statements compared with other statements may have greater meaning to a subject. Different individuals may possess a given attitude to the same degree, yet they may respond differently to the items on the measure. It is difficult, if not impossible, to ensure that each item counts the same as every other item.

Persons receiving the same score on a measure do not necessarily possess the trait (presumed measured by the instrument) to the same degree.   This means that our measure is never as precise as it could be. Raw scores are crude estimates at best.

The validity of summated ratings is questionable.   Because the process of deducing items from an abstract universe of traits is a logical one, the possibility always exists that some items may be wrongly included in the measuring instrument at any given time. How do we know that we are measuring what we say we are measuring? The validity of our measures (a topic discussed in detail in Chapter 7) is generally determined by comparing score results with manifest behaviors of subjects in predicted situations. This is not an infallible process.

Applications of Summated Rating Measures

The primary application of Likert measures is in attitude measurement. Summated rating measures have been applied (in extension form) to measuring socioeconomic status, intelligence, interests, and special skills.

THURSTONE SCALING METHOD

A second type of measuring technique is Thurstone equal-appearing interval scaling (Thurstone and Chave, 1929). This technique differs from the Likert summated ratings method by supplying each statement with a specific scale value standing for the intensity of the statement, instead of deriving a total score for a subject based on his responses to several statements with gradated response categories. Consider the two statements below that are included in a hypothetical measure of race prejudice:

A.   I would consider living next door to members of race X.
B.   I would consider marrying a member of race X.

Both statements concern a subject's degree of social distance in relation to members of race X. Persons who agree with statement B above will almost certainly agree with statement A. Persons agreeing with statement A will not necessarily agree with statement B, however. The two statements differ in terms of the *intensity of sentiment* toward race X. The Thurstone method seeks to affix a numerical value or weight to each statement in terms of the intensity it expresses pertaining to some attitude—race prejudice, in this instance. This task is accomplished through the use of judges.

The researcher constructs several statements, usually (according to Thurstone) about 100. The statements are logically related to the attitude in question. At least 25[4] judges are asked to sort the statements into seven[5] categories ranging from high to low intensity.

The weight of each statement is based on the average of the categories into which it has been sorted by N judges. For example, suppose a statement has been placed into the following categories by 25 judges:

STATEMENT A:

Category	Number of Judges Placing Item in Category	Category Multiplied by Number of Judges
1	5	5
2	2	4
3	6	18
4	8	32
5	3	15
6	0	0
7	1	7
Totals:	25	81

The average value of the statement is the average of the categories into which the statement has been placed (weighted according to the frequency with each statement is located within any category), or

$$\bar{X} \text{ (Mean)} = 81/25 = 3.2.$$

The weight of Statement A is equal to 3.2.

After all items have been sorted and assigned a numerical weight, it is possible to select approximately 20 of these for use in the final questionnaire. The 20 statements should be selected on the basis of gradated weights from high to low. Some statements will have weights in the 6 to 7 range; others will have weights in the 1 to 2 range. The researcher should include items that represent all degrees of the attitude from high to low. Twenty statements and their respective weights are shown as a general model below:

Statement	Weight	Statement	Weight
1	6.8	11	3.9
2	6.2	12	3.4
3	5.9	13	3.2
4	5.6	14	2.8
5	5.2	15	2.7
6	5.0	16	2.2
7	4.8	17	1.9
8	4.6	18	1.8
9	4.2	19	1.6
10	4.1	20	1.2

The next step is to ask a number of respondents to select two or three statements from the list of 20 that best reflect their sentiments toward the psychological object in question. Individuals will presumably select those statements that are close together according to item intensity. For example, a respondent who chooses item 1 as being closest to his views will likely select item 2 or item 3 as alternative choices. These items are within the area of his original selection. It would be unlikely that he would select item 1 and item 20 as representative of his sentiments, however. According to the weights, these items represent basically different points of view. In any event, the median weight of the items selected by the respondents (the mean is frequently used as well) is used to portray their positions along the attitudinal continuum underlying our measure of it. For example, if respondents were to select items 1, 5, and 6 as best representative of their sentiments, we would either average the weights of each of these items or take the median of them to portray their positions along the continuum of intensity. Both computations are shown below:

Item	Weight
1	6.8
2	5.2
3	5.0
Total:	17.0

$$\bar{X} \text{ (Mean)} = 17/3 = 5.7$$

The median would be the central value, or 5.2. Both values could be used to represent where the persons lie along the attitudinal continuum.

Individual scores may be compared with other scores to determine differences in the degree or intensity of the attitude expressed. Thurstone believed that the weight assigned each scale item is a better way (compared with Likert scaling) of assessing attitudinal variations among people and plotting their differences along some attitudinal continuum. One assumption he made was that the resultant weights enable the researcher to approximate the interval level of measurement with his data. He used the term *equal-appearing intervals* in support of this assumption. Many investigators question the legitimacy of such an assumption and argue that even though judges are used in the classification of items, the level of measurement approximated by the Thurstone method is ordinal at best.

To briefly review the Thurstone equal-appearing interval technique of scaling items, judges sort items into either seven, nine, or 11 categories, and weights are subsequently assigned designate positions on an attitudinal continuum from high to low. Depending on the *direc-

tion of the weight (i.e., a large numerical value as a weight may indicate possession of the attitude to a high degree, whereas a small numerical weight will be indicative of the presence of the attitude to a low degree), a person's attitudinal position may be determined readily. The actual range of response will vary from 1 (the smallest possible average of judges' ratings under the condition that all judges rate the item identically) to 7, 9, or 11 (i.e., the largest averages depending on whether 7, 9, or 11 categories are used in the original rating of statements). In reality, however, judges seldom agree completely, and therefore, the weights assigned statements are expressed such as 3.8, 2.2, 8.1, 10.3, and so on. If seven categories are used, the attitudinal continuum would look something like this:

Low 1-------2-------3-------4-------5-------6-------7 High

Once judges have rated all items, a representative selection of items covering all positions along the attitudinal continuum are included in a final questionnaire (usually 20 to 30 items). The subject is asked to agree with two or three statements (sometimes he is asked to pick the five most representative statements reflecting his sentiments). The statements he selects are averaged to determine his score and position along the attitudinal continuum in relation to others.

Advantages of Thurstone Scales

Some of the major advantages of Thurstone scaling are as follows:

Thurstone derived scales enable the researcher to differentiate between large numbers of people regarding their attitudinal positions. When item weights are averaged, a greater variety of attitudinal positions is revealed when compared with Likert-type scale values. This would seemingly have the advantage of making it possible to render finer distinctions between people according to the attitudes they possess.

Another argument in favor of using Thurstone derived scales is the fact that judges—usually professional persons—have achieved a high degree of agreement on the items used, and hence, they perform a screening function by eliminating the "bad" items that evidence little or no agreement. The researcher applies the scale with increased confidence that the items he uses have a greater claim to reliability than would be the case if he were to construct a Likert-type questionnaire by himself.

Some Disadvantages of Thurstone Scaling

Some of the more important disadvantages of Thurstone scaling are as follows.

Thurstone scales are time consuming to construct. The investigator must solicit judges who must take the time to sort numerous items. Then he must determine scale values for each item based on the ratings of the judges. Finally, he must average scores of respondents to place them on the attitudinal continuum relative to one another. And we have not even included the time and effort of the researcher who must select the items to include in the questionnaire in its final form. Some researchers contend that if not very many judges are used, and if items to be sorted are limited to 100 or fewer, the time involved in constructing a Thurstone scale is no more than that devoted to constructing a Likert scale (Edwards and Kenney, 1946).

It is possible to derive identical scores based on widely divergent attitudinal views. Suppose a person were to select items with respective weights of 2, 4, and 6 as representative of his attitudinal position. His mean score would be 4. Another person may have three scale items with weights of 3, 4, and 5 for the same mean score of 4. Although both persons would be placed on the attitudinal continuum at the same point, there would be some question whether the persons really hold the attitude to the same degree. The fact that a greater variation in score values resulted from the first subject compared with the second would place the validity of the items in question.

There is no way of controlling the influence of a judge's bias in item sorting. This could possibly result in the inclusion of items that are not truly representative of fixed positions on the attitudinal continuum. Some research indicates that this is extremely unlikely, however, particularly if judges are asked to make impartial judgments regardless of their personal feelings toward the psychological object in question. It has been demonstrated repeatedly that even when judges holding diverse views sort numerous items, there is relatively high agreement among their judgments.

In reality, Thurstone scale values are no better at predicting behavior than Likert-based measures. Because Likert measures are considerably less difficult to construct and score, the logical preference would be to use this procedure over Thurstone-derived methods.

Application of Thurstone Scaling

The primary application value of Thurstone scaling is in attitude measurement.

SCALOGRAM ANALYSIS

A third major scaling method is called *scalogram analysis* or cumulative scaling (more popularly called *Guttman scaling*). Guttman (1944) has devised a method of scaling which allows researchers to determine whether the statements used in their measures of some attitudinal trait are in fact *unidimensional* (i.e., whether each item measures the same dimension of the same phenomenon). Edwards (1957, p. 172) defines a unidimensional scale in the following passage:

> In the case of attitude statements, we might say that this means that a person with a more favorable attitude score than another person must also be just as favorable or more favorable in his response to every statement in the set than the other person. When responses to a set of attitude statements meet this requirement, the set of statements is said to constitute a *unidimensional scale* (emphasis his).

It will be recalled that Likert and Thurstone scales contain items associated with the attitude in question but do not necessarily have to comprise a unidimensional scale. For example, there is no way of easily ascertaining which items in a Likert questionnaire are the most intense, nor is there any guarantee that only one dimension is represented. Items included in a Likert questionnaire measuring attitude toward job satisfaction might be concerned with pay, working hours, informal group members or associations, type of supervision, quality or challenge of work and the like. It is possible for many employees to arrive at the same score on the job satisfaction dimension and yet react differently to the above factors, which are all related in one way or another to job satisfaction. One person may dislike his pay, working hours, and type of supervision, but he may simultaneously like the challenge of the work and his informal work group. Someone else may dislike his informal work group and working hours, but he may like the type of supervision he receives and the pay. Both men may turn up an identical job satisfaction score based on their differential response to various *dimensions* of the variable, job satisfaction.

The Thurstone scaling method is not unidimensional, either. There is no attention given to isolating a single dimension. The researcher is primarily interested in the intensity of the statement and whether a subject agrees or disagrees with it.

In view of the fact that the Likert and Thurstone techniques of scaling allow us to place individuals somewhere along an attitudinal continuum of intensity from high to low, relative to one another, the Guttman scaling technique does not necessarily perform the same function. Edwards (1957, p. 172) notes that:

> . . . scalogram analysis can perhaps be most accurately described as a procedure for evaluating sets of statements or existing scales to determine whether or not they meet the requirements of a particular kind of scale. Scalogram analysis is not a method for constructing or developing an attitude scale, although it has been referred to as such by other writers.

In this particular case, Guttman scaling is designed to determine the unidimensionality of an attitude scale.

Guttman (1947) has devised the Cornell Technique of scalogram analysis, which will be illustrated shortly. Before discussing the procedural aspects of the technique, we need to review briefly an earlier discussion of attitudes and attitudinal universes. It will be recalled that attitudes are believed to be reflected in the reactions subjects give to statements involving behavioral choices as alternatives. The researcher derives numerous statements from the abstract universe of the attitude in question and includes these in a questionnaire as a potential measure of the attitude. Likert and Thurstone scaling procedures are used to determine where a person may be placed along the attitudinal continuum. The Guttman Cornell Technique can be used to determine whether a single dimension is being measured by these sets of statements or whether several dimensions are being represented. The question Guttman proposes to answer with his technique is whether the set of statements is unidimensional or multidimensional.

Table 6-4, illustrating the application of the Cornell Technique, uses five statements of varying intensity that are assumed to form a unidimensional scale for 15 individuals. The table contains five statements, each with agree-disagree response categories placed below it. Fifteen individuals are listed in the left-hand column and their responses (i.e., agree or disagree) are shown in the body of the table. The statements are arranged from most intense to least intense from left to right. Individuals who agree with statement 1 (the most intense statement) will predictably agree with statements 2, 3, 4, and 5. Individuals who agree with statement 2 will also agree with statements 3, 4, and 5, but they

Table 6-4. An Illustration of the Guttman Cornell Technique[a]

Individual	Statement 1		Statement 2		Statement 3		Statement 4		Statement 5		Score
	A	D	A	D	A	D	A	D	A	D	
1	x		x		x		x		x		5
2	x		x		x		x		x		5
3		x	x		x		x		x		4
4		x	x	a	x		x		x		4
5		x		x	x		x		x		3
6		x		x	x	a	x		x		3
7		x		x		x	x		x		2
8		x		x		x	x	a	x		2
9		x		x		x		x	x		1
10		x		x		x		x	x		1
11		x		x		x		x	x		1
12		x		x		x		x	x	a	1
13		x		x		x		x		x	0
14		x		x		x		x		x	0
15		x		x		x		x		x	0

[a] The horizontal lines (dashes) in the body of the table are defined as "cutting points" for each statement.

will not necessarily agree with statement 1. A person's score is determined by counting the number of agree responses to the five statements. Scores for each of the 15 individuals are shown in the right most column of the table.

Notice that individual 1 has agreed with all five statements. His score is 5. Individual 2 has responded identically. These individuals have the largest scores. Individual 3 has responded "disagree" to item 1, but he has agreed with the other four statements. His score is therefore 4. Person 4 has responded identically to individual 3. Ideally, persons who receive a score of 5 on this particular set of items have responded positively (agree) with all five statements. Persons who receive a score of 4 have responded negatively (disagree) with item 1 but positively with the remaining items. Persons who receive the score of 3 have responded negatively (disagree) to the first two items (1 and 2) and positively (agree) with the remaining three items (3, 4, and 5). Persons who receive a score of 1 have responded favorably to the least intense item, i.e., item 5, but they have responded negatively (disagree) with the first four items, 1, 2, 3, and 4.

When items form a perfect scale and vary in a gradated fashion in intensity as items 1, 2, 3, 4, and 5 in Table 6-4, Guttman calls the resulting scale a perfectly reproducible one. This means that a person's response pattern to all items in a set can be perfectly reproduced simply by knowing a person's total score on the scale. This is an impossible task to accomplish for either the Likert or Thurstone methods.

There are few perfect scales in existence, however. Most scales contain inconsistencies in response or *errors,* as they are most frequently labeled. An error can be illustrated by the response pattern shown in Table 6-5. Both persons in the example shown in Table 6-5 have scale scores of 4, but errors are present for each of them. Person 1 has responded favorably to statements 1 and 2, disagreed with statement 3, and accepted or agreed with statements 4 and 5. (This example presumes that the items are arranged in order of most intense to least intense). The disagreement with statement 3 constitutes an error and suggests the possibility that the scale is nonunidimensional. Person 2 has responded favorably to items 1 and 3, 4, and 5, but negatively to item 2. This, too, is an error.

An error-free situation (assuming that the statements form a unidimensional scale and are arranged from most to least intensity would be similar to that shown in Table 6-6. In each case, the person's response pattern is perfectly predictable or reproducible from a knowledge of his total score. No errors are apparent. When the number of errors is excessive, however, the scale is said to be nonre-

Table 6-5.   A Scalogramatic Presentation of Errors

Individual	Statements[a]					Score
	(Most intense)			(Least intense)		
	1	2	3	4	5	
1	+	+	⊖ [b]	+	+	4
2	+	⊖ [b]	+	+	+	4

[a] A plus equals acceptance or agreement with statement; a minus equals rejection or disagreement with statement.
[b] Circled responses indicate errors.

Table 6-6. An Error-free Scalogramatic Presentation

	Statement					
	(Most intense)			(Least intense)		
Individual	1	2	3	4	5	Score
1	+	+	+	+	+	5
2	−	+	+	+	+	4
3	−	−	+	+	+	3
4	−	−	−	+	+	2
5	−	−	−	−	+	1

producible. Guttman originally defined a reproducible scale as one where the *coefficient of reproducibility* was 0.90 or higher. The coefficient of reproducibility is simply determined by the following formula:

$$\text{Coefficient of reproducibility} = 1 - \frac{\text{Number of errors}}{\text{Number of responses}}$$

where:

Number of responses = Number of people times the number of statements.

For example, if we were to observe the distribution of responses in Table 6-7, we would have a coefficient of reproducibility of:

$$\text{Coefficient of Reproducibility} = 1 - \frac{3}{(10)(5)}$$
$$= 1 - 3/50$$
$$= 1 - .06 = .94.$$

The coefficient of reproducibility would be 0.94 in this case. In this instance, the item responses are said to be reproducible and therefore unidimensional. The few errors that exist are inconsistencies in a person's response pattern. Person 2 responded favorably to item 1, but he responded negatively to item 2, supposedly a less intense item. When the number of errors lowers the coefficient of reproducibility below 0.90, the scale item responses are said to be nonreproducible.

Table 6-7. An Error Illustration of Scalogram Analysis

Individual	Statements[a]					Score
	(Most intense)			(Least intense)		
	1	2	3	4	5	
1	+	+	+	+	+	5
2	+	⊖	+	+	+	4
3	−	+	+	+	+	4
4	−	+	+	+	+	4
5	−	−	+	+	+	3
6	−	−	+	+	+	3
7	−	⊕	−	−	+	2
8	−	−	−	+	+	2
9	−	−	−	+	⊖	1
10	−	−	−	−	+	1
Errors[b]	0	2	0	0	1	

[a] A plus equals acceptance or agreement; a minus equals rejection or disagreement.
[b] Circled responses indicate errors.

In this event, the items should not be used in an attitudinal investigation when the researcher wants to assume unidimensionality.

Guttman originally recommended that a maximum of 10 to 12 statements be selected and administered to not less than 100 persons. These statements were to be selected from what the researcher believed to be the universe of items measuring attitude X. (See Chapter 7 for an extended discussion of the meaning of an attitudinal universe). Through the application of his scaling technique, certain items were designated as scalable and therefore included in a subsequent measure of attitude X, whereas other items were designated as nonscalable and not included.

Advantages of Guttman Scales

Some of the major advantages of Guttman scales are as follows.

Guttman scaling demonstrates unidimensionality of items in an attitudinal measure. Compared with the Thurstone and Likert scaling methods, which do not perform this function, determining scale unidimensionality is a definite advantage.

Assuming a scalable set of items used in an attitudinal measure, the researcher is in a good position to identify inconsistencies in responses of subjects and possible untruthful replies. This feature could be of significance in increasing the researcher's confidence in the quality of information provided by his respondents.

Guttman's procedure is relatively easy to use when applied to small numbers of items. When the number of items exceeds 12, however, the technique becomes cumbersome and tedious.

A person's response pattern can be reproduced with a knowledge of his total score on the scale. Likert or Thurstone techniques cannot do this.

Disadvantages of Guttman Scales

Some of the more important disadvantages of Guttman scaling are as follows.

The Guttman scaling technique fails to provide as extensive an attitudinal continuum as the Likert and/or Thurstone methods. If a scaling method such as the Guttman scale were employed with several hundred subjects, there would be an excessive number of tied scores. In this event, the researcher would have to restrict his application of statistical methods to those that permit large numbers of ties. These methods are frequently not the best in terms of their explanatory value.

The Guttman technique is most easily applicable to situations where the researcher has few items with dichotomous responses. Although the technique is potentially applicable to statements having more than two responses, it becomes quite cumbersome and difficult to apply. Because many researchers are interested in making more precise distinctions between individuals according to their possession of specific attitudinal characteristics, limiting response categories of statements to agree-disagree would have to be considered a major disadvantage.

If the researcher were to use a large number of items, more than 12, and if his sample were quite large, in excess of 100, the scoring and error determination associated with scalogram analysis would be extremely awkward to employ. Through the effective use of computers in recent years, however, this phase of applying scalogram analysis has been made increasingly simple.

Applications of Guttman Scaling

The primary application of Guttman scaling lies in the area of attitude measurement and the determination of unidimensionality of attitudinal scales. This particular form of cumulative scaling can also be used in opinion studies of a political, economic, or social nature. It may also be employed in conjunction with Likert or Thurstone scaling procedures to encompass a wide variety of attitude measurement alternatives. A thorough discussion of these extended applications is reported in Edwards (1957) and in Lindzey (1954).

THE SEMANTIC DIFFERENTIAL

The scaling methods discussed thus far in this section are the most frequently used to assess attitudes in social research. Other techniques of attitude measurement exist, although none has the degree of general applicability as the Likert, Thurstone, and/or Guttman scaling methods. For example, Osgood, Suci and Tannenbaum (1957) have devised a measure of the meaning of psychological, social, and/or physical objects to a subject. They call their measure the *semantic differential.*

The semantic differential consists of a series of bipolar characteristics such as hot-cold, popular-unpopular, witty-dull, and the like. According to Osgood, Suci, and Tannenbaum, these characteristics should represent three basic dimensions of the person's attitude toward the object: (1) *potency,* the strength or physical attraction of the object, (2) *evaluation,* the favorableness or unfavorableness of the object, and (3) *activity,* the degree of movement of the object. A list of fifty pairs of terms (called *scales*) were developed and arranged on a continuum such as:

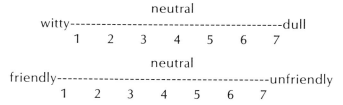

Persons responding to the semantic differential are asked to place a check mark on each of the continua which describes a particular object according to their perceptions. The marks can be scored easily.

Social researchers may apply the semantic differential (made up of terms to suit their particular needs and not necessarily following those patterned by Osgood and his associates) in a variety of ways. They may be interested in determining the strength of a political candidate among a group of voters, or they may measure the credibility gap that exists between what the candidate says he stands for and what the people think he stands for. The semantic differential can be used for personality assessment as well. The subject is asked to identify those characteristics that portray him as he would like to be. Then he is asked to specify those traits that are characteristic of how he sees himself in reality. The potential discrepancy may be enlightening to clinical psychologists and others studying personality development and change.

The researcher is not obligated to include the three dimensions of potency, evaluation, and activity, although for maximum effectiveness of the semantic differential, it is recommended.

The semantic differential may also be used to characterize the nature of interpersonal relations in organizations. This information may be invaluable to investigators who are interested in explaining various aspects of the organizational social milieu.[6]

The primary usefulness of the semantic differential is to assess the subject's perception of the attractiveness of social or personal objects from several dimensions. This assessment, in turn, can lead to the delineation of reasons for behaviors in relation to those objects, to the extent that attitudes and behaviors coincide in reality.

SOME MEASUREMENT ISSUES

The measurement of social attitudes and related social psychological phenomena has been a steadily developing process. It has not been without its critics (DeFleur and Westie, 1958; Tarter, 1969). Some of the major criticisms leveled against social scientists concerned with measuring social and psychological variables are:

1. Most social and psychological variables cannot be directly observed, and therefore, they do not belong to the empirical world. as such, they are not legitimately within the scientific domain.

2. Even if social and psychological variables are capable of being measured or brought into the empirical realm in some fashion, how can the researcher possibly untangle the complex interrelationships between variables as they act on individual and group behavior?

3. When several different measures of the same attitudinal phenomenon are applied to the same group of subjects, they often

reflect widely different values. With such discrepancies between measures purportedly measuring the same thing, which measure is the best, if any?

4. Because the measurement of attitudinal variables often involves the cooperation and involvement of subjects, how can the researcher be sure that the respondents are telling him the truth?

5. A philosophical question is whether or not the subject is capable of revealing to anyone, even to *himself,* how he really feels about psychological objects in his life-space? Although the question is probably a rhetorical one, it acts as a general caution to the researcher to view his findings with some degree of skepticism.

6. Persons are known to respond differently to the same question under different social circumstances. How do we know, for example, that a person has a certain degree of attitude X when he expresses it on paper in a self-administered questionnaire or reveals it orally to an interviewer (Selltiz, et al., 1959)?

7. There is frequently a significant discrepancy between what a person says he will do and what he actually does in a social situation. It is unlikely that attitude measures reflect true behavior at all (DeFleur and Westie, 1958; LaPiere, 1934).

8. The quantification of social and psychological phenomena such as attitudes through the process of operationalization removes from the phenomena much of the original meaning conveyed by the terms as they are used in theory. A term that has been reconstituted in a hypothesis in operational form probably leads to an unreliable hypothesis test. A logical relation between phenomena theoretically does not necessarily mean that any kind of relationship will obtain between the same phenomena operationally defined in hypotheses.

These criticisms focus on the general adequacy of sociology as a science from the standpoint of a researcher's inability to measure, control, and interpret the social variables at his disposal. The controversy is well documented (Lundberg, 1942; Blumer, 1931, 1940). There is also the question concerning what an investigator has once he has measured it.

The rationale for measuring social and/or psychological variables is that the existence of such phenomena may be inferred from observing subject reactions to various types of situations, hypothetical or real. Individuals who react with greater intensity compared with other subjects are defined by their more intense reaction as possessing the phenomenon to a greater degree. If social scientists were unable to make such an assumption, they would be equally unable to investigate systematically social behavior in virtually every scientific sense.

The question is whether attitudes or any other social and/or psychological phenomena for that matter can be brought into the empirical world by existing social scientific methods. Most social scientists believe that individuals in group interaction or in isolation exhibit personal and social traits or characteristics capable of being measured. They realize that the problems of measuring attitudinal phenomena, for example, are difficult and complex but not necessarily impossible to solve. It is significant to note that couched within the context of the prevailing weaknesses of the social measurement process lies the investigator's awareness of many of the strengths and limitations accompanying his acquisition of information about the social world. It is often more important to know what may or may not be said about social behavior on the basis of collected information. Scientific knowledge at the social level, not unlike scientific knowledge at the physical and natural levels, accumulates slowly. Scientists in general are trained to regard the products of their research as tentative.

Before generalizations can be made about the real world, a significant amount of information should be compiled pertaining to it. And then, at best, the scientist makes statements about the real world conservatively. The tentative nature of science is probably a good thing, particularly when we consider the wide variation in research strategies accruing between investigators even in the same academic field. The point is that researchers understand the basic limitations of various measurement methods upon which much of their work is based. As a result, much effort is directly channeled toward overcoming these limitations and improving research strategies. At the same time, the researcher has few unrealistic ideas about the quality of information he has collected.

The fact that certain properties of objects (e.g., attitudes) cannot be observed directly does not necessarily disqualify them from being studied scientifically. Atoms cannot be seen directly, yet their effects on objects can be determined readily. Similarly, attitudinal phenomena may be brought into the empirical realm through several inferential steps. So long as the social scientist is aware that attitudes are inferred from behaviors rather than exactly determined, he is usually on safe ground.

Measures of attitudinal phenomena and other related variables at the individual and social levels are regarded by the social researcher as indicators of potential behavior. One definition of attitude is *a tendency to act in a given way* (Green, 1954). The fact that a person holds an attitude to a particular degree (as measured by the instrument in whatever form) does not necessarily mean that he will behave in a manner consistent with the expressed attitude, but the possession of specific personality characteristics logically increases the propensity for a subject to behave predictably. Naturally, behavioral predictions cannot be made precisely with a knowledge of only one variable. Man's behavior alone or in groups is a function of many variables acting conjointly, only one of which may be the variable under investigation.

The sociologist searches for many variables believed to be linked logically to specific behaviors man exhibits. It is easy to identify relationships between one specific attitude and one specific behavior. Consequently, most social scientists spend their time examining a limited number of variables that potentially interact with certain behaviors they wish to predict. More complex variable interactions (perhaps more realistic) are handled by computer.

As a means of explaining the logic of the social scientist, consider that behavior of an individual or group at the social level is totally unpredictable until we determine which variables appear to cause it to occur. (Causation is inferred on the basis of an observed association between two or more variables. The occurrence of an association between variables is a necessary but not a sufficient condition to establish causality links between variables, however. See Chapter 3, for a more detailed explanation). The investigator increases the predictability of behavior by explaining the variation of it. He *reduces the unexplained variation of behavior* by identifying variables that appear to be related to the behavior under investigation. This is a slow process but a necessary step toward understanding human behavior at the social level.

One goal of the social scientist is to delineate patterns of social behavior. Once patterns are established, prediction and understanding are enhanced. The quest for social patterns leads first toward the identification of variables and second toward the development of theoretical schemes to handle the interrelation between variables and behavior to be predicted. Measurement of these variables used in theory is a vital and a fundamental step toward the identification and delineating of such patterns.

When several researchers work independently to measure the same variable, it is too often assumed that they are tapping the same attitudinal universe. When the findings of several studies are compared regarding relationships between the same phenomena, it is expected that a high degree of consistency will be found between them. In reality, there are numerous factors that exist to account for subsequent inconsistencies in the literature. The samples selected for each study may be quite different as well as the social situations under which the measures were administered. Different dimensions of the same phenomenon may account for inconsistencies as well.

It is naive to assume that the findings relating to a common topic in any field will yield perfect consensus all the time. Of course, the crudeness of the instrumentation will no doubt increase the occurrence of inconsistencies in the findings of several related studies. Inconsistencies in the literature are slowly reduced and eliminated as a result of social investigators' persistence in replicating research and accumulating more information. And instruments that purportedly measure the same phenomenon but reflect wide differences when applied to a common sample of subjects are continually refined, revised, and improved as a means of increasing their predictive utility. Some measures are retained and others are discarded as they are increasingly used in experimental research situations. The extent of improvement in instrumentation will help to test theories more adequately and to move our present knowledge of social behavior to new plateaus.

When the researcher elects to solicit information from random subjects, there is always the possibility that the resultant data will be biased to a degree. Bias comes from a variety of sources. The researcher may evidence bias in nature of his questions and the way he asks them of selected respondents. There may be a gap of misunderstanding between the researcher and the subject relating to the meaning assigned questions and the responses to the questions. The researcher may wish to convey one thing by asking a particular question, and the respondent may understand something entirely different. The response does not always mean what the researcher thinks it means.

It has been illustrated in an earlier chapter that under certain conditions of coercion and stress, subjects may deliberately provide the researcher with false information as a means of retaliating against him. Surely this possibility always exists regarding the precision and general adequacy of attitudinal measures. Problems of misinterpretation, researcher bias, and respondent untruths and distortions are usually reduced and sometimes eliminated by maintaining proper rapport between subject and researcher. The assurance of anonymity and the treatment of subject responses as privileged communication (similar to client-attorney interaction) will frequently alleviate bias and distortion. The maintenance of a nonthreatening social setting within which information is requested will contribute to greater cooperation on the part of the target subjects. Some measuring instruments have built-in mechanisms to determine the probability that the respondent is lying or supplying false or inconsistent information about himself (Levitt, 1967). Usually the mechanism consists of a consistency factor that checks responses to similar questions or statements in the instrument. A high degree of inconsistency in response makes the information questionable and exposes it as probably unreliable. Inconsistency also exists because people generally tend to give socially desirable responses. *Social desirability is the act of responding to statements according to what the respondent considers socially desirable and not necessarily true of him.* Levitt (1967) states that:

> . . . inventories which measure attitudes and beliefs are more susceptible to response sets than those which deal with emotional states. In the measurement of anxiety, or of any other undesirable phenomenon, response set is of less consequence than is the effect of social desirability. People want to think of themselves as possessing socially desirable motives, feelings, and behavior patterns. They tend to deny, either deliberately or without actual awareness, their socially undesirable qualities. Many people might very well respond "false" to the item, "I sometimes feel like killing somebody," no matter how they really felt.

Researchers seldom accept information from a single source as the final word on any social observation. In other words, the questionnaire as a measuring instrument may be used as a part of a particular research design. As another part of it, the investigator may employ participant observation and interviewing to collect information about the same phenomenon. Later, he collates the information obtained by the various data collection methods as a means of increasing the validity of the explanation of the social phenomenon he will later provide. This method is known as *triangulation* (Denzin, 1970), and it is increasingly utilized to verify one's observations of social acts.

Perhaps the most significant problem generated by the measurement of social phenomena occurs in the testing of theory. When an event is observed, a theory is usually devised to account for the event. The theoretical explanation of the event is based on specific predictor variables. These variables are logically associated with the predicted event that is eventually measured. When a term is operationalized or reduced to a numerical quantity for the purpose of manipulating it more easily statistically, and allowing researchers to observe more precisely whether covariation exists between the two or more variables, the meaning of the term is changed. The degree to which the meaning is changed will affect the meaning of the hypothesis test in a corresponding manner. In essence, it is likely that the researcher may end up testing hypotheses made up of operationally defined terms but terms having little or no meaningful relation to the theory from which the hypotheses were derived. This problem could have serious implications for any research that utilizes operational definitions of social phenomena. Conceivably, over 90 per cent of all social research could be affected. An illustration of the general problem is provided in Figure 6-4. Notice in Figure 6-4 that the term or terms used in the original theory are operationally defined to enable the researcher to render the hypotheses derived from the theory as testable. A testable hypothesis is usually, though not always, one containing terms that are empirically based and measurable.

Little chance exists at present to eliminate this problem, but the investigator is equipped to operate systematically and objectively in the construction and design of his measures of social phenomena. Every effort should be made to maximize the likelihood that the measures are valid and reliable. Validity determines what the instrument measures, and reliability determines the degree of measurement consistency. Chapter 7 will discuss the problems of instrument validity

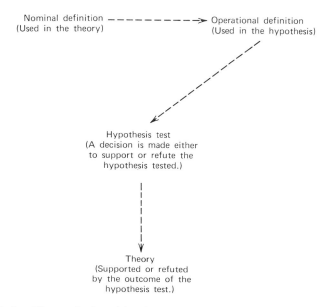

Nominal definition — — — — — — — — —→ Operational definition
(Used in the theory)   (Used in the hypothesis)

Hypothesis test
(A decision is made either
to support or refute the
hypothesis tested.)

Theory
(Supported or refuted
by the outcome of the
hypothesis test.)

Figure 6-4. The relationship between nominal definitions, operational definitions, tests of hypotheses, and theory verification.

and reliability in detail along with the methods of satisfying these measurement requirements.

SOME QUESTIONS FOR REVIEW

1.   What is measurement? Differentiate between nominal, ordinal, interval, and ratio scales. Give two examples of each by using variables from common experience.

2.   What are some important functions of measurement for the social scientist? Discuss.

3.   Differentiate between concepts and constructs. How do concepts and constructs relate to theory? Discuss briefly.

4.   Discuss some of the weaknesses of Guttman scaling contrasted with Likert-type scaling. What sorts of limitations are associated with Likert-type scaling? Discuss.

5.   Under what conditions would the following scales be useful:

   a.   Likert
   b.   Guttman
   c.   Thurstone

Which attitudinal measurement form do you prefer? Why?

6.   What is meant by a unidimensional scale? Is there any particular advantage in having a unidimensional scale compared with having a multidimensional one? Why or why not? Discuss.

7.   What is the "semantic differential?" What kinds of functions does it perform?

8.   Identify four key issues in measurement. Discuss each and indicate in your own words what you believe to be the more probable issues to be resolved in the near future. Why have you selected these? Defend in your own words the choice of issues indicated above.

NOTES

1.   See Carlo L. Lastrucci, *The Scientific Approach: Basic Principles of the Scientific Method,* (Cambridge, Mass.: Schenkman Publishing Co., 1963), pp. 76–81, for an extended discussion of the distinction between concepts and constructs.

2. Not all measuring instruments consist of sets of statements with which one agrees or disagrees. In psychology, for example, other types of measuring instruments include Rorschach Ink Blots, Thematic Apperception tests, word association tests, and dream interpretation. In early sociology, Emile Durkheim (1951) used one's membership in a particular religious faith or marital status as indicators or measures of social cohesion. In content analysis (discussed in Chapter 12) measures are formed by paying attention to the amount of emphasis given a topic in a political speech or cartoon (Berelson, 1952). In ethnomethodology researchers refer to *accretion measures* (observation of accumulations of cigarette butts in a maternity waiting room to denote anxiety of expectant fathers) and *erosion measures* (the tiles in front of particular exhibits at museums to denote those exhibits most popular with the public) (Garfinkel, 1967).

3. This figure is neither a minimum nor a maximum specification or standard. The researcher develops his Likert-type instrument partially on the basis of the audience to which it will be directed.

4. The number of judges can vary. The researcher should employ at least 15 judges and probably many more. No qualifications exist for determining the best judges, although our recommendation would be to select professional persons (professors in social science departments) or students majoring in social science courses to make the judgments. The primary reason for making this recommendation is that these persons usually have more experience with social measurement and can use their skills and expertise to render the better classification of items compared with persons outside the social science area.

5. The number of categories into which the items are to be sorted may be any number, although Thurstone originally recommended either seven, nine, or 11 categories. Maintaining an odd number of categories ensures the existence of a neutral classification for possible neutral statements.

6. A good discussion of some of the major methodological issues of the semantic differential is found in David R. Heise's article, "Some Methodological Issues in Semantic Differential Research," *Psychological Bulletin,* 72 (1969): 406–22.

BIBLIOGRAPHY

Barron, Frank. *Creativity and Psychological Health.* Princeton, N.J.: Van Nostrand, 1963.

Benedict, Ruth. *Patterns of Culture.* Boston: Houghton Mifflin, 1934.

Berelson, Bernard. *Content Analysis in Communication Research.* Glencoe, Ill.: The Free Press, 1952.

Blumer, Herbert. "Science Without Concepts." *American Journal of Sociology,* 36 (1931): 515–533.

―――. "The Problem of the Concept in Social Psychology," *American Journal of Sociology,* 45 (1940): 707–719.

Bonjean, Charles M., Richard J. Hill, and S. Dale McLemore. *Sociological Measurement: An Inventory of Scales and Indices.* San Francisco: Chandler Publishing Company, 1967.

Champion, Dean J. *Basic Statistics for Social Research.* San Francisco: Chandler Publishing Company, 1970.

―――. "Some Observations on Measurement and Statistics: Comment," *Social Forces,* 46 (1968): 541.

Cohen, Morris R. and Ernest Nagel. *An Introduction to Logic and Scientific Method.* New York: Harcourt, Brace, 1934.

DeFleur, Melvin L. and Frank R. Westie. "Verbal Attitudes and the Salience of Attitudes," *American Sociological Review,* 23 (1958): 667–673.

DiRenzo, Gordon J. (ed.) *Concepts, Theory, and Explanation in the Behavioral Sciences.* New York: Random House, 1966.

Denzin, Norman K. *The Research Act: A Theoretical Introduction to Sociological Methods.* Chicago: Aldine, 1970.

Durkheim, Émile. *Suicide.* (Translated by George Simpson). Glencoe, Ill.: The Free Press, 1951.

Edwards, A. L. *The Social Desirability Variable in Personality Assessment Research.* New York: Dryden, 1957.

―――, and K. C. Kenney. "A Comparison of the Thurstone and Likert Techniques of Attitude Scale Construction," *Journal of Applied Psychology,* 30 (1946): 72–83.

Freeman, Linton C. *Elementary Applied Statistics: For Students in Behavioral Science.* New York: Wiley, 1965.

Garfinkel, Harold. *Studies in Ethnomethodology.* Englewood Cliffs, N.J.: Prentice-Hall, 1967.

Green, Bert F. "Attitude Measurement." In Gardner Lindzey's (editor) *Handbook of Social Psychology.* Reading, Mass.: Addison-Wesley, 1954, pp. 335–369.

Guttman, L. "A Basis for Scaling Qualitative Data." *American Sociological Review."* 9 (1944): 139–150.

―――. "The Cornell Technique for Scale and Intensity Analysis," *Educational Psychological Measurement,* 7 (1947): 247–279.

Hare, A. Paul, Edgar F. Borgatta, and Robert F. Bales. (editors) *Small*

Groups: Studies in Social Interaction. New York: Alfred A. Knopf, 1965.

Kerlinger, Fred N. *Foundations of Behavioral Research.* New York: Holt, Rinehart, and Winston, 1965.

Labovitz, Sanford. "Some Observations on Measurement and Statistics," *Social Forces* 46 (1967): 151–160.

———. "Reply to Champion and Morris," *Social Forces,* 46 (1968): 543–544.

LaPiere, R. T. "Attitudes vs. Actions." *Social Forces,* 14 (1934): 230–237.

Levitt, Eugene E. *The Psychology of Anxiety.* New York: Bobbs-Merrill Co., 1967.

Likert, R. "A Technique for the Measurement of Attitudes," *Arch. Psychol.,* 1932, No. 140.

Lindzey, Gardner (ed.) *Handbook of Social Psychology.* Reading, Mass.: Addison-Wesley, 1954.

Lundberg, George A. "The Operational Definition in the Social Sciences," *American Journal of Sociology,* 47 (1942): 727–745.

Mead, Margaret. *Coming of Age in Samoa.* New York: Morrow, 1928.

Morris, Raymond. "Some Observations on Measurement and Statistics: Further Comment," *Social Forces,* 46 (1968): 541–542.

Osgood, C. E., G. J. Suci, and P. H. Tannenbaum. *The Measurement of Meaning.* Urbana: Univ. of Illinois Press, 1957.

Peatman, John G. *Introduction to Applied Statistics.* New York: Harper and Row, 1963.

Selltiz, Claire, Marie Jahoda, Morton Deutsch, and Stuart W. Cook. *Research Methods in Social Relations.* New York: Holt, Rinehart, and Winston, 1959.

Siegel, Sidney. *Nonparametric Statistics for the Behavioral Sciences.* New York: McGraw-Hill, 1956.

Stevens, S. S. "Mathematics, Measurement, and Psychophysics." In S. S. Stevens (editor) *Handbook of Experimental Psychology.* New York: Wiley, 1951, pp. 1–49.

Strachey, J. (ed.) *The Standard Edition of the Complete Psychological Works of Sigmund Freud.* London: Hogarth, 1959.

Tarter, Donald E. "Toward Prediction of Attitude-Action Discrepancy," *Social Forces,* 47 (1969): 398–405.

Taylor, Janet A. "A Personality Scale of Manifest Anxiety," *Journal of Abnormal Social Psychology,* 48 (1953): 285–290.

Thurstone, L. L. and E. J. Chave. *The Measurement of Attitude.* Chicago: Univ. of Chicago Press, 1929.

Webster's New World Dictionary of the American Language. New York: The World Publishing Company, 1964.

CHAPTER 7
VALIDITY AND RELIABILITY IN VARIABLE CONCEPTUALIZATION

It is apparent that there are many ways of measuring social phenomena empirically (Abell, 1969). One of the more common measuring instruments is the *questionnaire*. (Chapter 11 will discuss questionnaires in detail). The researcher extracts from some abstract universe of characteristics a number of items that presumably reflect the trait to be measured. He arranges the items into some type of questionnaire and elicits responses from a sample of individuals. These responses are assumed and interpreted to be reflections of the degree to which these individuals possess the traits measured by the instrument (usually a questionnaire).

Measuring instruments have at least two important properties of interest to social scientists—(1) validity and (2) reliability. In this chapter we will examine closely the validity and reliability of measuring instruments, outlining how each of these properties is determined for any given measure, and how each is affected by various factors and conditions. In this section we focus specifically on questions of validity and reliability and how they pertain to self-administered question-naires.[1]

VALIDITY

One of the first questions a researcher asks about any measuring instrument he devises and/or uses is: "Does the instrument measure what it is supposed to measure?" For example, does the measuring device reveal the true degree of some trait or characteristic a person presumably possesses? This question focuses on a very important measure characteristic, namely, the *validity* of the measure (Renner, 1962). *The validity of a measuring instrument is defined as the property of a measure that allows the researcher to say that the instrument measures what he says it measures* (Selltiz, et al., 1959; Allport, 1937).[2]

A test is said to be valid when it measures what we say it measures. If we say that some test measures trait *X*, then our measuring instrument is valid to the extent that it truly measures trait *X*. If our measuring instrument measures some other trait instead of trait *X*, it is said not to be a valid measure of trait *X*, but it may be a valid measure of some other trait instead.

Most measuring instruments are manmade. Men arrive at some kind of agreement as to what something measures, and this measure suffices as a standard to serve them. In early periods of the world, some primitive cultures used the distance from the tip of the thumb to the first thumb joint as a measurement standard in the absence of more refined instruments. Various kinds of things could be purchased according to so many thumb-lengths. However, it soon became evident that certain people were getting more and some were getting less simply because of the random variation or lack of uniformity in thumb lengths from person to person. More objective measures were employed subsequently to determine amounts of products. Rulers and various kinds of weights are common standards of measurement used today. Rulers measure feet, inches, meters and millimeters: weights measure pounds, ounces, and grams.

Using these kinds of measuring instruments leaves little room for dispute among most people. They have agreed that certain measuring instruments will be used to take into account various properties of objects such as length and weight. We say that a ruler is a valid measure of feet *to the extent that it is patterned after some commonly agreed upon standard that has been determined to measure feet. If the ruler* is constructed of wood and if the wood gets wet, there is the possibility that due to shrinkage of the instrument, the measure will not accurately reflect feet as it did previously. It may, in fact, measure some other length that we have not agreed that it should measure.

The fact is that *all* our measuring instruments, without exception, are vulnerable to contamination by some source either outside (external) or inside (internal) the instrument itself. The validity of measuring instruments, therefore, is said to be a variable property.

English and English (1958) state that:

> . . . there is no such thing as validity. Nor is there absolute validity. We (always) determine the *degree* of validity. And the validity index has no meaning apart from the particular operations by which it is determined. Some measures of things have high validity, others have moderate or low validity, and some have no validity at all.

To determine the validity of rulers and weights as measures of things, we can compare these instruments with other instruments accepted as standards. If the rulers and weights correspond to the accepted standard measures, then we conclude that our measuring instruments are valid. In social science, however, it is somewhat difficult to establish the validity of many types of measuring instruments. The phenomena to be measured are often nonempirical phenomena such as attitudes, prestige, or power. Because many types of attitudes are said to be important in predicting human behavior at various levels (i.e., individual, small group, or large social aggregate), it is necessary for social scientists to devise measures of these attitudes so that their usefulness as predictors may be assessed empirically.

Once a measure has been devised for a particular attitude, there is usually no objective standard to which the present instrument can be compared. How does the social scientist determine whether the measuring instrument is valid? How does he know that the instrument measures what he says it measures? For example, suppose an employment counselor uses a measuring instrument such as a questionnaire that is said to be a measure of employee adaptability to the job. In the course of several interviews with some prospective job applicants, he administers the measure to each of them and derives several scores of employee adaptability. Should he hire those with a particular score or higher and not hire those who fail to achieve at or above this same score? How does he determine that the measure of employee adaptability is what it purports to be? Again, this raises the question of the validity of the measuring instrument, and to answer it adequately, we must examine validity from a number of different dimensions.

Before commencing our discussion of various types of validity, we need to give some consideration to the relation between items included on a paper-pencil questionnaire measure and the so-called universe of traits that measure the phenomenon. The universe of items may contain an infinite number of questions, statements, social, psychological, and/or biological behaviors which, to one degree or another, are indicative of the trait X. This universe exists only as an *abstraction*. An infinite universe of characteristics exists for all traits nominally defined currently and for all of those presently undefined and unknown. Consider the illustration in Figure 7-1. The researcher extracts items from this abstract universe almost wholly arbitrarily, although logic is an integral feature of this method. Of course, because the researcher has absolutely no way of proving that the items he extracts are indeed from the universe he wishes to measure, he is in a relatively difficult position to demonstrate that his measure is valid for measuring trait X. The main arguments he cites that support the validity of his measure are founded entirely on logic and/or statistical support.

TYPES OF VALIDITY

In the discussion to follow, when we refer to various types of validity, we mean that each type denotes a different way of interpreting the degree to which a test measures what we say it measures. The validity

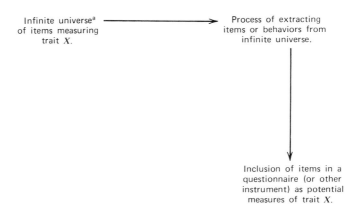

Figure 7-1.   **An illustration of the process of extracting items from an abstract infinite universe of traits measuring phenomenon X.**

of a measure may be defined from several different perspectives (e.g., content, concurrent or predictive, and construct) (Downie and Heath, 1965, pp. 222–227).

There are at least three different types of validity: (1) content, (2) concurrent or predictive, and (3) construct.[3] Each of these will be treated in the discussion to follow, and examples will be provided to reflect the major differences between each type.

Generally, the validity of a test rests on two important factors: (1) logic, and (2) statistical proof. Measuring instruments are defined as having validity through the application of logic and/or statistical procedures. Each of the three types of validity noted above uses either logic, statistical verification, or both as means of defining the degree of validity of any measuring instrument.

CONTENT VALIDITY

Content validity or face validity is exclusively a *logical* type of validity that any given measuring instrument may have. In the construction of a verbal or quantitative test such as the Graduate Record Examination it is important that the test have content validity. This is the same as saying that it is essential that items should be included on the test that reflect the abilities and achievements of the persons taking the test or their personal experience and professional background. If the examination were to emphasize a rather narrow treatment of mathematical skills rather than cover a broad spectrum of mathematical items (i.e., if the emphasis were on trigonometry rather than algebra, calculus, and/or simple arithmetic), the content validity of the measuring instrument as an index of general mathematical knowledge would be called into question. Specifically, we would challenge the test as a valid measure of general quantitative aptitude. And accordingly, if the verbal portion of the Graduate Record Examination emphasized only grammatical rules exclusive of reading comprehension and word understanding, we would seriously question whether it was a valid measure or indicator of one's verbal aptitude as that is generally understood and defined.

Therefore, for any given test or measuring instrument to have content validity, the researcher must endeavor to ensure that the instrument contains a logical sampling of items from the so-called universe of items that presumably reflects the characteristic to be measured and correspond with it in some consistent fashion.

In the classroom students have been heard to rationalize poor performances on examinations because professors supposedly selected test items from textbook chapters or from lectures that he failed to emphasize as important in class. The student lament is "I knew all the material he didn't ask on the examination." These statements are direct criticisms of the examination's content validity as a measuring instrument. The professor is interested in measuring the degree of comprehension of course material on the part of students, and consequently, he devises examinations as indicators or measures of this comprehension. If an examination has content validity, the professor has included items that pertain to representative aspects of the course material covered in class as opposed to his emphasis on obscure material that students might otherwise overlook.

Content validity is based on the logical inclusion of a sampling (presumably a representative sampling) of items taken from the universe of items that measure the trait in question.

The only way content validity can be demonstrated is by examining the test or instrument items and comparing them with the universe of items that *could theoretically be included, if known.* The researcher judges, on the basis of the items that make up the instrument, whether the test or instrument is valid according to its representative content.

Content validity may also be applied to attitudinal measures. The researcher assumes his attitude measuring instrument has content validity when an examination of the items he has included reveals that they are logically relevant and consistent with the trait presumably measured. For example, suppose we examine the measuring instrument (shown in Table 7-1) in the form of a set of questions designed to measure job satisfaction of employees in the work setting. Table 7-1 shows a hypothetical index of job satisfaction. For each item included in the index of job satisfaction shown in Table 7-1, the respondent is to select one of five responses following each item (i.e., strongly agree, agree, undecided, disagree, or strongly disagree). In the table the responses have been excluded. On the face of the instrument, an inspection of the items reveals that the questionnaire pertains to job satisfaction and not to some other variable such as type of supervision. We may say that the instrument has face validity or content validity. Of course, there is an infinite number of items that could be used to measure the variable, job satisfaction. Obviously, this accounts in part for the existence of many such indicators of this variable. In fact, no two measuring instruments developed thus far are exactly alike. All the instruments may measure the phenomenon adequately, but this is not likely because many measures are designed for special application

Table 7-1. A Hypothetical Index of Job Satisfaction

Each of the following items has the following response pattern respondents must select from: "strongly agree," "agree," "undecided, probably agree," "undecided, probably disagree," "disagree," and "strongly disagree."

1. I would recommend this organization to my friends as a good place to work.
2. I would like to continue my present work arrangement for an indefinite period.
3. There are many things about my job that I do not like.
4. My work is challenging and interesting.
5. If I had the opportunity, I would leave this job to work in another company doing entirely different things.
6. My work assignments are boring and repetitious.
7. It would take a sizable change in pay to get me to move from my present work assignment and work with another company.
8. I don't get along well with the persons with whom I work.
9. There are many things that should be changed on my job to make it more interesting for me.
10. I like my job more than most of my work associates like theirs.

in specific settings (e.g., banks, space centers, communities, petroleum refineries, steel mills, automobile manufacturing plants, and so on). To administer them outside their intended social setting may decrease the validity associated with the measure.

Some Problems Associated with Content Validity

One of the important problems associated with content validity is that it is subjectively determined. Because content validity rests on the subjective professional judgment of the researcher to a large extent, what one person regards as high content validity may be regarded by another as low content validity. Consider the divergent views of both teacher and student toward the same examination. The teacher may feel strongly that the test has high content validity, but the student may take issue with this belief for what he feels to be good reasons.

Content validity depends on the quality of judgment of the researcher. Whoever devises the measuring instrument must be careful to include as much as possible a representative set of items that will measure the particular trait, whether it be verbal or quantitative aptitude, degree of anxiety, or socioeconomic level.

Another problem concerns the reality of defining the universe of items from which the measuring instrument will be drawn. The universe of items may consist of all facts included in specific chapters of some textbook students have been assigned. Or the universe of items may consist of all biological, social, and/or psychological features of anxiety. How does one go about identifying all these features? For all practical purposes, anxiety has an infinite number of physiological, psychological, and/or social factors that can be extracted and potentially included on an anxiety measure. Again, the judgment of the researcher assists him in drawing a representative set of items that measures the trait.

It is difficult to argue that a test does not have content validity primarily because there is usually some resemblance of items in the test to the trait presumably measuring it. Few measuring instruments, if any, are perfectly valid indicators of social and psychological traits. The general content validity of any test rests to a great extent on the skill and judgment of the constructor of the test. If poor judgment has been exercised (a factor that always exists as a possibility), then the test or measure will likely have low content validity or no validity at all.

PREDICTIVE AND CONCURRENT VALIDITY

Perhaps the most useful types of validity are predictive validity and concurrent validity. *Predictive validity* is based on the measured association between what a test predicts behavior will be and the subsequent behavior exhibited by an individual or group (Magnusson, 1967). For example, if we obtain from a group of people attitudinal scores presumably reflecting the degree of discrimination toward minority group members (written expressions of what each person would do if placed in a situation requiring interaction with minority peoples), the relationship between the scores on the measuring instrument and the subsequent behavior of these same subjects in the real interaction situation with minority people will provide us with evidence of the predictive validity of the measure. If a subject's score is indicative of discriminatory behavior toward minorities, and if the subject exhibits discriminatory behavior toward a minority group member, this is evidence that the test is measuring what we say it measures.

Suppose we devise a test to measure male chauvinism among

personnel officers of several companies and we find that some officers possess male chauvinistic attitudes to a high degree and others possess such characteristics to a low degree. A comparison of the subsequent hiring practices of each officer and his chauvinism score may provide evidence of the validity of the measure. If the officers possessing the trait to a high degree later have a hiring record revealing sex discrimination against women, and furthermore, if the officers having the trait to a low degree subsequently do not exhibit sex discrimination in their hiring, the measure of male chauvinism is said to have predictive validity.

Predictive validity is identified by the simple correlation of behavior predicted by a measure with behavior subsequently exhibited or expressed. A high correlation or relationship between the prediction and the result means that the measure appears to have predictive validity. Various statistics textbooks contain statistical formulas for computing numerical association coefficients between scores on a measuring instrument and actual behavior observed (which may be measured by specifying simply "behavior present" or behavior absent") (Champion, 1970; Blalock, 1972).

A variation of predictive validity is *concurrent validity*. Concurrent validity differs from predictive validity in that the scores of predictive behavior are obtained simultaneously with the exhibited behavior. For example, suppose we obtain measures of manual dexterity and work efficiency from workmen operating drill presses in a factory. At the same time, supervisors provide us with productivity records for each workman. A comparison of the work productivity records with the dexterity and efficiency scores will indicate whether our measures are valid from the standpoint of concurrent validity. Again, the numerical relationship or high association between productivity (observed behavior) and dexterity and efficiency (predictive behavior) will be evidence of the validity of our measures. Consider the hypothetical data in Table 7-2. Table 7-2 shows the relation between productivity level and dexterity-efficiency scores for 20 workmen in Factory X. Observe particularly those instances where high productivity levels accompany high dexterity-efficiency scores. Although this is visual evidence of the validity of our measure of dexterity-efficiency, a statistical procedure may be used to portray the degree of association between the two sets of scores numerically.

Our statistical results should reveal that a high association exists between the productivity levels observed and the dexterity-efficiency scores of these workmen. We would conclude as a result that our measure has a high degree of concurrent validity.

Table 7-2. The Relation Between Productivity Level and Dexterity-Efficiency Scores for Twenty Workmen in Factory X (Hypothetical Scores)

Workman	Concurrent Measures	
	Dexterity-Efficiency[a] Scores	Productivity Level[b]
1	45	20
2	42	18
3	40	18
4	38	17
5	36	15
6	36	16
7	36	15
8	34	12
9	34	13
10	34	12
11	33	11
12	32	10
13	32	11
14	31	10
15	30	10
16	30	9
17	26	6
18	25	7
19	24	5
20	23	3

[a] The larger the score, the higher the dexterity-efficiency.

[b] The larger the score, the higher the productivity level.

Some Problems Associated with Predictive and Concurrent Validity

One of the major problems underlying predictive and concurrent validity is that simply observing a numerical association between a test score and some actual individual or group behavior is no guarantee that the measuring instrument is a valid indicator of the trait we have nominally defined. It could be, for example, that our measure is really a valid indicator of something else closely associated with the phenomenon under investigation. Therefore, we are led to suspect that our instrument is a valid measure of what we say it is, when in fact it may be a measure of something else. This problem always exists, of course, whenever attitudinal measures are constructed. There is no way of ever being sure that we are measuring what we say we are measuring. However, we consider as *evidence* of the potential validity of the instrument the relationship between the predicted and the observed behavior in question. This should serve as a caution. The researcher must always be aware of the potential limitations of his measuring instruments. He should not be unusually confident that he is measuring what he says he is measuring even when a high degree of correspondence exists between the predictive behavior and the observed behavior.

Another problem closely associated with the problem discussed above concerns the researcher's interpretation of exhibited behaviors by a respondent as representing the predictive behavior. Some attitudinal measures are so abstract that several different kinds of interpretations of given behavior patterns could be possible according to a variety of social researchers who define the situation. Again, the judgment of the researcher is a crucial element in determining the degree of predictive validity that exists.

CONSTRUCT VALIDITY

The third basic form of validity is called *construct validity*. Construct validity is useful for measuring traits for which external criteria are not available, such as latent aggressiveness (Magnusson, 1967; Cronbach and Meehl, 1955). Construct validity is generally determined through the application of *factor analysis* to a measuring instrument. Factor analysis is a statistical technique designed to determine the basic components of a measure (Blalock, 1970, pp. 97–102). For example, if we were to factor analyze a measure of role clarity, we might find that the variable consists of three predominant factors—close supervisory behavior, seniority, and group cohesiveness. Several measuring instruments developed in the area of psychology have used factor analysis to demonstrate that several distinct dimensions of personality are being assessed. Cattell's 16 Personality Factor Inventory (1950), developed and published by the Institute for Personality and Abilities Testing, has been shown to "factor" into 16 separate dimensions of personality. The Minnesota Multiphasic Personality Inventory (1943, 1945) has likewise been factored into a variety of personality components. (Because factor analysis is beyond the scope of this text with respect to the mathematical procedures that accompany it, it will not be possible to discuss this type of validation in detail. The reader is encouraged to consult more advanced sources if such a technique is to be meaningfully applied.)

Some Criticisms of Construct Validity

Construct validity can be used to demonstrate whether or not a measuring instrument is in fact measuring a particular phenomenon. If a measure is supposed to reflect only one dimension, and if factor analysis shows that more than one dimension is being included by the instrument, this raises the serious question of the instrument's validity, at least as it concerns the extent to which the instrument acts as a measure of the phenomenon under investigation.

One problem of construct validity is that it requires a rather sophisticated statistical background on the part of the researcher. By comparison, predictive and/or concurrent validity would be considerably easier to apply.

Because construct validity pertains almost exclusively to traits that are not directly observable, there is a greater risk that the instrument is measuring some phenomenon similar to the one under investigation. Compared to predictive validity, for instance, there is no direct opportunity to correlate actual behaviors with test scores as a means of demonstrating the construct validity of the instrument.

CONTENT, PREDICTIVE AND/OR CONCURRENT, AND CONSTRUCT VALIDITY COMPARED

Because each of the three types of validity discussed above functions in a different capacity, it is difficult to make a blanket generalization as to which is the best to use under any circumstances. Depending on the particular interests and objectives of the researcher, each type may provide him with advantages the others do not offer. For example, if the researcher must work in a narrow time span and has little or no time to utilize statistical techniques as a means of checking the validity of his measures, he may find content validity useful to apply. On the other hand, if he has direct access to the sample under investigation and can observe their behaviors for a prolonged period, predictive validity would be a likely choice. Concurrent validity would be useful if the researcher were able to gain access to the sample for only a brief period, say, just long enough to administer a questionnaire to a group of employees. Each of the three types of validity is summarized briefly below, including a listing of some of their respective advantages and disadvantages:

CONTENT VALIDITY

Some advantages of content validity are:

Content validity is directly applicable without using statistical procedures, may be observed and inferred based upon question content, and it is easy to apply and is not time consuming.

Some disadvantages are:

Content validity relies heavily on subjective interpretation and judgment of the individual researcher. There is too much likelihood for error and/or mistakes in judgment. It is not directly subject to statistical verification. It seems to rest entirely on perceptions of the researcher. Also, there is no way of demonstrating the degree of correspondence between the traits measured and the items reflecting the traits. Finally, content validity is possibly the least reliable method of establishing validity of a test.

PREDICTIVE VALIDITY

Some advantages of predictive validity are:

Predictive validity can demonstrate the numerical association between predictive behavior and observed behavior. This technique actually involves prediction, whereas the other measures of validity do not. It is the most reliable method for determining validity under most circumstances. It is easy to apply, but it requires some elementary statistical knowledge.

Some disadvantages are:

Predictive validity does not prove that the instrument measures the trait absolutely. It serves only as evidence of the validity of it. The use of statistical computations may provide a slight disadvantage to persons with limited statistical experience. However, predictive validity takes longer to determine compared with content validity.

CONCURRENT VALIDITY

Some advantages of concurrent validity are:

Concurrent validity requires elementary facility with correlational methods to compute the degree of association between predictive behavior and observed behavior. It is not necessary to examine respondent behaviors for a prolonged time period. It is much faster to apply compared with predictive validity.

A disadvantage is that concurrent validity may not be as reliable a method for establishing validity compared with predictive validity inasmuch as the prediction element is lacking. This is not a serious disadvantage, however.

CONSTRUCT VALIDITY

Some advantages of construct validity are:

Construct validity measures the validity of latent attitudinal instruments. It enables the researcher to determine the components of an attitude as portrayed by the instrument. It uses statistical analysis to justify the validity of the measure. This provides a numerical strength particularly in comparison with content validity.

Some disadvantages are:

A serious disadvantage is that construct validity utilizes statistical procedures that frequently exceed the scope of the average researcher's abilities. It does not necessarily improve the quality of the decision of the researcher to determine the validity of any given instrument compared with the predictive validity procedure.

RELIABILITY

Another important test property is reliability. The reliability of a measuring instrument is defined as *the ability of the instrument to measure consistently the phenomenon it is designed to measure* (Selltiz, et al., 1959).[1] Reliability, therefore, refers to *test consistency.*

A practical example illustrating the usefulness of the reliability of a test may be provided in before-after study designs. The before-after study design is geared to assess the impact of an experimental variable(s) on a dependent variable(s) between two time periods. (See Chapter 4 for a discussion of major types of study designs.) The researcher selects a social setting in which a change is anticipated, and he observes the behavior of several individuals in the setting both before and after the change has occurred. He compares the individuals between the two time periods to determine whether a change in behavior has occurred. If any significant change in behavior is apparent and observable, he considers as an alternative explanation of the change the introduction of the experimental variable between the two time periods. Of course, in addition to the experimental variable, other factors may account for behavioral changes of individuals from one time period to the next. The problem of distinguishing between variables and the differential effects they have on factors will be considered later in this chapter. For the present, we focus on behavioral changes that occur as the possible result of the experimental variable.

First, the researcher theorizes that when individuals are exposed to a particular stimulus or stimuli, predictable changes will occur along specific behavioral dimensions. A comparison of individual behavior both before and after the introduction of the stimulus (experimental variable) should either confirm or refute the theory of the impact of the experimental variable on behavior. If a significant and predicted change in behavior is noted, this is generally interpreted as support for the theory. If no change in behavior occurs, the investigator considers this as evidence for the refutation of his theory, at least in this one instance.

To tap specific behaviors of individuals, potential measures of these behaviors are developed and appear in several forms. The questionnaire is one major form of attitudinal measurement. Several statements are usually prepared that resemble the trait or traits under investigation. The respondent is asked to agree or disagree with specific statements or is obligated to say which statements are true of him.[5]

On the basis of the respondent's overt reaction to these statements, the researcher infers things about the extent to which the respondent possesses some attitude or attitudes. The possession of particular attitudes is potentially indicative of behaviors corresponding to those attitudes, although some research reveals important contradictions in the attitude-behavior relationship.[6]

WHY IS IT IMPORTANT TO HAVE RELIABLE MEASURING INSTRUMENTS?

It is important to have reliable measuring instruments for at least two reasons: (1) reliability is a prerequisite for the validity of a test, and (2) the researcher wants to be able to determine the effect of one variable on another. A reliable measuring instrument will assist him in drawing conclusions about the causal relationship of the two variables.

RELIABILITY AS A PREREQUISITE FOR TEST VALIDITY

For the validity of a measuring instrument to be supported, it must be demonstrably reliable. Any measuring instrument that does not reflect some attribute consistently has little chance of being considered a valid measure of that attribute. For example, suppose a person has conservative political views. A measure of conservatism would be regarded as unreliable if, after repeated measures on the same individual, widely different scores were reported. (This assumes, of course, that other variables did not intervene to affect the score results.)

If it can be reasonably ascertained that the individual is relatively uninfluenced by extraneous variables that are a part of his environment from one test administration to the next (i.e., his day-to-day behavior and social encounters are regular and patterned between repeated test administrations), then the chances for a measure to be considered unreliable are greatly increased if significant score differences are observed.

The reliability of a measuring instrument is seldom, if ever, determined by examining responses of a single individual to that measure. Most often, evidence of the reliability (or unreliability) of a measuring instrument is gathered from large aggregates of individuals who bear some similarity to the population for which the measure is intended. For example, if a researcher intends to study physicians in a particular city, he will want to pretest his questionnaire on an independent sample of physicians elsewhere to determine if the questionnaire can be improved in any respect. Pretesting the questionnaire on any other occupational or professional group (e.g., lawyers, construction workers, and so forth) will not necessarily represent a good pretest of the instrument. Any information different occupational groups provide the researcher regarding the improvement of the questionnaire intended for physicians will be wholly speculative and probably of little value. But other physicians can be quite critical of questions directed toward other target groups of physicians. Their suggestions about the improvement of the questionnaire or other measures employed by the researcher should be taken seriously.

RELIABILITY AS AN ESSENTIAL GAUGE OF CAUSALITY

Scores on a reliable measuring instrument will fluctuate only in response to some independent factor or condition causally associated with it directly or indirectly. Caution should be exercised in interpreting apparent relationships between two or more variables as causal relationships. The discussion of spuriousness in Chapter 3 should be reviewed to familiarize the student with the proper or conventional interpretation of any observed association.

If the researcher observes a change in a person's score on some attitudinal dimension from one time period (t_1) to the next (t_2), he wants to be able to say that this is empirical evidence of the potential effect of one variable on the other. Ideally, 100 or more subjects should be used to determine the degree of reliability associated with any attitudinal measure. In reality, however, the researcher sometimes (1) obtains a reliability estimate based on an extremely small sample of accessible elements dissimilar to the target population, or (2) neglects to get a reliability estimate at all.

Generally, if a factor X is introduced between two time periods, then theoretically certain changes in specific attitudinal dimensions (which relate meaningfully to factor X) should occur. For example, in some police departments in the United States, films dealing with human relations skills are shown to units of patrolmen to enhance their interaction with the public. If patrolmen manifest poor human relations skills in dealing with the public prior to seeing the film, but they are much improved in this respect after the film is shown, then this is considered as tacit support for the assumption that the film helped to account for the change. This does not necessarily *prove* that the film caused the change, but it is nevertheless *strong support* for this contention. t_1 and t_2 respectively are time 1 and time 2, usually a period of from two to four weeks in a pretest-posttest situation. No standard period has been defined experimentally. The length of time between measures is the option of the researcher. An illustration of the before-after design where a change in score is observed is provided in Figure 7-2. Notice that a change in score on factor Y from time 1 (t_1) to time 2 (t_2) may be at least partially explained by the introduction of factor X as an experimental or intervening variable. This does not prove that factor X and factor Y are related, but it does constitute support for this assumption.

Another simple illustration of the importance of test reliability in action is the case of the two-variable association in a before-after study conducted by Champion and Dager (1967). These researchers were concerned with assessing employee adaptability to operational changes in work requirements elicited by a new computer system introduced into a bank setting. Measures of employee behaviors and attitudes were devised and administered to employees both before and after the installation of computer equipment in the bank environment. One measure used was *depersonalization,* defined as the perceived amount of control an employee exerts over the quality and quantity of his work. Such a phenomenon touches on worker perceptions of importance, job repetitiveness, and perceived autonomy in task performance and completion.

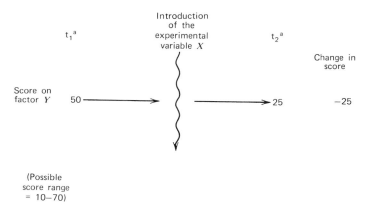

Figure 7-2.   The effect of an experimental variable on factor Y.

Champion and Dager argued that automation constitutes a depersonalizing experience for employees because it subsumes much of their previous work into one continuous electronic operation. It eliminates certain tasks and greatly simplifies others. It reduces much of the meaning of work from the life of employees, and it curtails the necessity for employees to interact with one another on the job to complete their work. These researchers hypothesized that employees would become increasingly depersonalized by increased automation in the bank setting. They set out to measure changes in employee depersonalization by comparing responses to this variable from one time period to the next (before and after the introduction of automation). If the measure of depersonalization were reliable, then a significant increase in depersonalization scores for these employees could be interpreted as possibly the result of the introduction of automation. (Again, other interpretations are possible, but the most apparent change taking place in the work lives of these employees to account for the changes in scores was the changeover to automatic data processing or increased automation, the experimental variable.) The changes in depersonalization scores are evidence of and support for the notion that automation increases employee depersonalization.

How did Champion and Dager know that observed changes in depersonalization scores from one time period to the next were due to changes in the depersonalization of employees, and not due to a chance fluctuation in scores (the latter alternative always existing as a possibility in any evaluation of test reliability under any condition)?

One indication of the reliability of the measure of depersonalization devised by these researchers was a pretest of the instrument.[7] Champion and Dager gave the depersonalization questionnaire to a sample of employees of another bank in the area prior to giving it to the employees in the final study. The bank selected for the pretest of the measuring instruments (other measures were included besides depersonalization) was not currently undergoing internal change of any kind. The employees had been with the bank for several years, and there was absolutely no reason to suspect that their feelings collectively would vary significantly from one day to the next. Under conditions such as these it was reasoned that a test-retest of the questionnaire over a two-to-four-week period in the stable bank setting would reveal little or no change in measure scores, because there would be no significant stimuli interfering with the work attitudes of the employees in that setting. (This assumes, of course, that the instruments were reliable to begin with.)

In reality, Champion and Dager noted little change in test scores in the stable bank environment from one time period to the next, and they concluded that this was evidence of the reliability of the measuring instruments. To support the reliability of the measures for use in the target population, these researchers administered the questionnaire to the final group of bank employees about two months prior to the changeover to automation. Four weeks later, or about a month prior to the changeover, they again administered the questionnaire to the group. This procedure was the same as that followed in the pretest situation in the stable bank setting. Results of the test from one time period to the next were compared and revealed little or no differences in responses. Subsequently, the same questionnaire was administered a third time to the experimental group about three months after the changeover to automation. This time, changes in scores on the questionnaire were noted. Thus, the simple method of test-retest of the measures in the population to be studied prior to the change strengthened the significance of subsequent score changes observed after automation had been introduced.[8]

METHODS USED TO DEMONSTRATE THE RELIABILITY OF MEASURES

Several methods exist for determining the reliability of a measuring instrument. These methods may be divided into two categories: (1) external consistency procedures, and (2) internal consistency procedures.

External Consistency Procedures

External consistency procedures utilize cumulative test results against themselves as a means of verifying the reliability of the measure. Test results for a group of people are compared in two different time periods, or two sets of results from equivalent, but different, tests are compared. Two major methods of determining the reliability of a test by external consistency are: (1) test-retest, and (2) parallel forms of the same test.

Test-Retest: The method of test-retest is probably the most common technique used by researchers for establishing the reliability of a measuring instrument. To determine the reliability of a measure using the test-retest procedure, an attitudinal measuring instrument (or an instrument that measures any other social and/or psychological phenomenon) is administered to a sample of individuals at a given point in time (t_1). After a given interval of time elapses, the instrument is again administered to the same sample of individuals. The two sets of test results are correlated, and the resulting correlation coefficient is a measure of the degree of reliability of the attitudinal measure.

A reliable measure will reflect the characteristic to the same degree over two different time periods where no intervening variables can interfere significantly with test scores. A high correlation or similarity between the two sets of scores for the same individuals is considered support for the reliability of the measure (again assuming that nothing has intervened between the two test administrations to affect the scores). Then, if the researcher wishes to use the measure in an experimental situation later to determine whether some experimental variable will modify certain attitudes, he can use his measuring instrument that has been pretested or checked for its degree of reliability. When scores on some measured characteristic are observed to change after the introduction of an experimental variable, the investigator is increasingly confident that the change was due, at least in part, to the experimental variable rather than to some random factor operating in the situation.[9]

The test-retest reliability method is useful only in stable social situations where it is unlikely that the environment will change significantly from one test administration to the next (particularly over relatively short time periods such as a few months).

Ideally, for a measuring instrument to be demonstrably reliable, the researcher expects a situation similar to that shown in Table 7-3. In this table scores are shown for 10 individuals in a test-retest situation with

Table 7-3. Scores for Ten Individuals on Measure of Attitude A

Individual	t_1		t_2	Difference in scores $t_1 - t_2$
1	45	Experimental	45	0
2	35	variable	35	0
3	27	absent	27	0
4	50		50	0
5	46		46	0
6	31		31	0
7	29		29	0
8	30		30	0
9	41		41	0
10	45		45	0
1	45	Experimental	20	−15
2	35	variable	18	−17
3	27	present	22	− 5
4	50		31	−19
5	46		40	− 6
6	31		22	− 9
7	29		26	− 3
8	30		29	− 1
9	41		40	− 1
10	45		38	− 7

" In reality researchers do not expect that their instruments will be perfectly reliable. This example illustrates what they would like to achieve. It is more realistic to expect minor score differences, however. The measure may still be regarded as reliable in any event.

no intervening variable occurring between the two test administrations. There are no differences between scores comparing both time periods. The lower half of Table 7-3 illustrates score changes from one time period to the next. The researcher wants the measure to be reliable so that any observed score differences following the introduction of the experimental variable can tentatively be attributable to it. Score differences from one time period to the next should reflect actual differences in the trait being measured rather than the result of some chance fluctuation of an unreliable instrument.

Some of the major advantages of the test-retest method of determining reliability are as follows.

Test-retest can permit the instrument to be compared directly with itself. An instrument that performs unreliably in a test-retest situation may require some kind of item-by-item analysis to determine which items discriminate between individuals possessing varying amounts of the trait under investigation and which items do not discriminate. By removing the items that do not discriminate, the reliability of the measure is generally increased. (An item-by-item check of a measuring instrument used in social science involves an inspection for internal consistency. In the following section, two internal consistency measures will be discussed in detail.)

Test-retest most directly reveals the continuity of the measure from one time period to the next. It is easiest to use in an external reliability check compared to other methods designed for the same purpose.

Test-retest is quick to apply and easy to evaluate. An inspection of test scores from two time periods prior to the introduction of an experimental variable will assist the researcher significantly in evaluating the results of his investigations.

This method offers the greatest degree of control over extraneous factors that would otherwise operate to contaminate the measure.

Some disadvantages of the test-retest follow.

One of the most significant criticisms leveled against the test-retest reliability method is that individuals often are able to recall how they responded to the measuring instrument in the original time period. In an effort to be consistent with their original response, they will often go to great lengths to replicate their first reactions. The bias resulting from such efforts is quite apparent. To the extent that the ability of the subject to recall his previous responses to the instrument will affect his responses in the second instance, the researcher may falsely attribute reliability to his measuring instrument when it is not deserved. Unfortunately, there is little we can do to overcome the effects of memory and recall by subjects on the way they respond to questionnaire items when the same test is used.

One method of partially dealing with this problem is to expand the time interval between the two test administrations. This has the effect of making it more difficult for individuals to remember their original responses. But at the same time, natural changes in attitudes could occur as a result of maturational factors entirely unrelated to the social setting under investigation. A reasonable test-retest time interval is conventionally regarded as being from two to four weeks. There is no definite time period established in the literature, however, and this option rests primarily with the researcher.

As stated earlier, there is no prescribed time period that should prevail between the two test administrations. Because of the wide variation in time periods used by many researchers, it is impossible at present to effectively evaluate the influence of the time factor on before-after test administrations.

The test-retest method of determining test reliability is not foolproof. All attempts to verify the reliability of a measuring instrument should be regarded with caution, particularly to the extent that the instrument is applied to a variety of target groups. It is wise to understand the implications of these kinds of test weaknesses.

It is extremely difficult for the researcher to recognize the impact of extraneous variables on any sample of individuals participating in a test-retest reliability check. A high correlation between test results over two time periods is not sufficient to guarantee the reliability of the instrument absolutely. A test may erroneously be regarded as reliable as a result of chance fluctuations of scores. For this reason alone the researcher should continually subject his measures of attitudinal phenomena to empirical scrutiny for each sample he studies.

When a researcher reenters a social situation for the purpose of administering a measuring instrument a second time, he must expect that his first visit was, in a sense, an intervening variable that must be considered. Some researchers have noted that managers of businesses have become quite defensive after an initial exposure to the tools of the social scientist. A questionnaire delving into employee attitudes of job satisfaction, role clarity, and the like often generates concerns and questions among employees who otherwise would not regard these things as important. As a result in some instances staff interpersonal relations become strained, some employees quit, some strike for better fringe benefits and environmental conditions, and others engage higher-ups in conversations about how unfairly they are treated. It must be concluded that a questionnaire is an educating medium for many people in social settings. Reentering the setting for a retest of the original instrument may be quite different compared to the first questionnaire administration-interview experience.

Parallel Forms of the Same Test: A second major external reliability check is the use of parallel forms of the same test. When a researcher uses parallel forms of the same test, he devises *two* measuring instruments that include different items but which purportedly measure the same phenomenon equally. Cattell's (1950) 16 Personality Factor Inventory mentioned earlier is an instrument using parallel forms (A and B in this instance). Form A and Form B of Cattell's personality inventory measure the same phenomena equally. In this case, if a test-retest is desirable to ascertain the impact of an experimental variable, form A of the test may be given in time 1, and form B may be administered in time 2. This overcomes the effects of memory and recall as factors that influence and bias response in the test-retest of the same instrument discussed above. Because different items are used, there is no way for the respondent to recall specific responses given in the first test administration.

Some major advantages of parallel forms are as follows.

Perhaps the chief advantage of this reliability method is that respondents are unable to affect the test results through recall in a test-retest situation. The fact that different tests are used in each instance increases the likelihood that score differences observed from one time period to the next are the result of some experimental variable rather than the function of bias through recall.

The fact that recall of former responses cannot affect significantly the responses a subject gives to an alternative form of the same test should mean logically that using parallel forms of the same test would be an improvement in reliability over test-retest using the same instrument.

The conventional waiting period between the two test administrations is not necessary to gauge a test reliability. One form of the test may be administered on one day and another form of the test administered the next day (possibly during the same day). Where a high correspondence in response exists, the case for the reliability of the instrument is strengthened.

Some disadvantages of using parallel forms of the same test are as follows.

An important disadvantage of using parallel forms of the same test to determine the reliability of subject responses is that two tests must be constructed instead of one. All the problems of measuring social and/or psychological phenomena are compounded by having to construct two instruments. Now, the researcher must deal not only with intratest reliability, but he must also assess comparatively the different reliabilities of both measures. The additional time and effort spent in developing two equivalent measures of the same phenomenon is certainly a disadvantage.

Equivalence of tests is difficult to establish. Observing a simple correlation between two tests purportedly measuring the same phenomenon does not automatically allow the researcher to conclude that the tests measure the same thing. It could be, for example, that both tests correlate highly with each other, but in fact they measure different phenomena. One test measures factor X, the other measures factor Y. Both factors X and Y are theoretically related, but they refer to basically different things. The fact that they correlate does not mean that they are necessarily valid indicators of the nominally defined variable, conceivably variable Z. Or factor Y may be a valid and reliable measure of some variable, whereas factor X is reliable but not necessarily valid as an indicator of it (implying that it is a valid indicator of some other factor closely related to it).

Up to now we have considered two external methods for determining the reliability of an attitudinal measure by using the test against itself in the test-retest instance, or by using parallel forms of the same test under two different test administrations. In the next section, two methods will be discussed that help to increase the reliability of the test indirectly by effecting improvements in the consistency of the test internally.

INTERNAL CONSISTENCY MEASURES OF RELIABILITY

Another way to attack the problem of reliability of measuring instruments is to examine the internal consistency of items used in the measure. Items that measure the same phenomenon should logically cling together in some consistent pattern. A person who likes his job will not give responses that reflect that he dislikes his job. The argument is *that persons with particular traits will respond predictably to items affected by those traits.*

Suppose we construct a measure of some attitude and include 20 items in our instrument. These 20 items are statements with Likert-type agree-disagree response patterns. Ten of the items are positively worded, whereas the other 10 statements are negatively worded. Persons who have the attitude to either a high degree or a low degree should respond to all 20 items consistently, *provided that each of these items has been extracted from the same universe.* Examining the internal consistency of the instrument enables the researcher to determine which items are not consistent with the test in measuring the phenomenon under investigation. The object is to remove the inconsistent items and improve the internal consistency of the test. An internally consistent test increases the chances of the test being reliable. Determining the internal consistency of a measuring instrument can be accomplished by using: (1) the split-half technique, and (2) an item discrimination analysis.

The Split-half Technique

The split-half technique is designed to correlate one half of the test items with the other half of them. For example, if an attitudinal measure consists of 30 items, a suitable procedure for establishing the internal consistency of the test would be to divide the items into two equal parts and correlate each part with the other. Some researchers recommend numbering the items from 1 to N, and then correlating the odd-numbered items with the even-numbered ones. The higher the correlation, the more internally consistent the measure.

There are no conventional standards currently existing specifying how to interpret coefficients thus derived. One rule of thumb might be to regard a correlation of 0.90 or higher as being indicative of high internal consistency and of the probable reliability of the instrument. The Kuder-Richardson 20 test is designed to be used for split-half internal consistency reliability assessments.[10]

Some advantages of the split-half method are as follows.

The split-half method of establishing the reliability of a test pits one half of the test against the other half of it. It will reflect inconsistencies fairly clearly by applying one of several correlational techniques discussed in more advanced sources. More specific item analysis procedures may then be applied to modify and improve the reliability of the instrument and enhance its value as a research tool.

Another advantage of the split-half method is that it is a straightforward means of verifying the internal consistency of a measure. It is easy to interpret, and with some degree of statistical sophistication, the researcher may apply it readily. Computer programs are available at many computer centers that can do this fairly rapidly for the researcher.

A disadvantage of the split-half method is that *split-half reliability verification does not pinpoint specific problem items.* It simply allows the researcher to conclude that the test does not correlate with itself internally and that the problem must be corrected by some means before the measure can be used profitably in a social setting.

Item Discrimination Analysis

The second method of approaching the reliability of a test internally is through *item analysis.* For example, let us assume that a researcher has administered an attitudinal instrument to 100 people. Further assume that the instrument contains 10 items, each having a six-response Likert-type pattern of attitudinal intensity (i.e., strongly agree, agree, undecided, probably agree, undecided, probably disagree, disagree, and strongly disagree). If we weight each response per item according to a 1, 2, 3, 4, 5, and 6 intensity pattern (or, 6, 5, 4, 3, 2, and 1 in the case of negatively worded items), it would be possible for a person to obtain a maximum high score of $10 \times 6 = 60$. This would be the number of items times the largest weight for a single item. Because 6 is the largest weight in each case there are 10 items, a person could obtain a large score of 60. The smallest score anyone could receive, assuming the respondent answered all statements, would be 10 × 1 = 10, or the number of statements (10) times 1, the smallest weight for a single item. The range of response of attitudinal intensity, therefore, would be from 10 (low intensity) to 60 (high intensity).

Logically, a person with a large score would tend to respond to each item in such a way that the weight assigned his particular response would be either a 4, 5, or 6. A person with a small total score would probably give responses to each item that would be weighted with a 1, 2, or 3. Sometimes, people who consistently give responses weighted with a 4, 5, or 6 respond to a particular item with either a 1, 2, or 3. The same is true of individuals who consistently provide responses weighted with a 1, 2, or 3. Sometimes, a response to a particular item in the set of items will have a weight of 4, 5, or 6. These deviations in response patterns are labeled *inconsistencies*. If there are too many inconsistencies in any given set of item responses, the inconsistent items may become suspect. An inconsistent item may not be from the same universe as the other items. Possibly it should be excluded to improve the internal consistency of the test and thereby improve its reliability. To illustrate an obviously inconsistent item according to response patterns, consider the information in Table 7-4. This table contains the response patterns of 12 research participants to 10 items in a questionnaire designed to measure variable X. The body of the

Table 7-4. An Example of Item Discrimination Analysis

Item	Subject #											
	1	2	3	4	5	6	7	8	9	10	11	12
1	6	1	3	2	5	1	6	4	1	4	1	6
2	5	1	2	1	5	1	6	4	1	4	1	6
3	6	2	2	1	5	2	6	4	1	5	2	5
4	6	1	3	1	4	2	6	4	1	4	2	6
5	2	5	6	4	2	4	2	2	5	2	4	3
6	6	2	1	1	5	2	6	4	1	3	2	5
7	6	1	2	2	6	2	5	4	2	5	1	6
8	5	1	3	3	5	2	5	4	3	5	2	4
9	5	1	3	1	5	2	6	4	1	6	2	5
10	6	1	2	1	5	1	6	4	3	6	2	4

table consists of weights assigned to each item. Each column consists of the response pattern of an individual to all 10 items in the question-naire. Note the consistency of subject 1 to all items except item 5. Note also the consistency of subject 2 (the opposite response pattern indicating low attitudinal intensity) to all items except 5. Subject 3 is equally consistent in his response to all items except 5 as well. When certain items stand out from the rest as being inconsistent, this is considered as evidence to challenge not only the reliability of the item but also its validity. If the item were to be discarded and total at-titudinal scores refigured on the basis of the new item arrangement and composition, the resulting score would be considered a more re-liable estimate of the person's attitude X.

Another way of spotting inconsistent items is to deal with the *dis-criminatory power* of each item and reject those items that fail to dis-criminate between individuals possessing the attitudinal trait to a high and a low degree respectively. This method is as follows. We would first obtain responses from N individuals and rank them according to their total score on a measuring instrument from high (largest score) to low (smallest score). We would then divide the total scores into the upper and lower quartiles. The upper quartile would contain the up-per 25 per cent of the largest scores in the distribution, and the lower quartile would contain the lower 25 per cent of the smallest scores. Those individuals with scores in the center of the distribution (the middle 50 per cent) are excluded from further consideration accord-ing to this particular internal consistency procedure. The argument fa-voring their exclusion is that if an item discriminates, it is most obser-vable in the case of extreme attitudinal intensity scores.

We now have two groups of respondents representing both extremes of attitudinal intensity. As an example, consider the hypothetical data in Table 7-5. Taking one item on the measure at a time, we construct a table identifying the response weights of all indi-viduals in the upper and lower quartiles. In Table 7-5, all responses to item 1 (the first item on the questionnaire) have been recorded for subjects in both the upper and lower quartiles. In this particular instance, note that the weights of persons in the upper quartile (those individuals with the largest total scores on the test) are considerably larger collectively compared with the weights shown for the subjects in the lowest quartile. This is what we would logically expect of an item that discriminates between individuals possessing varying degrees of some attitudinal characteristic.

On the basis of the total score a person receives on a set of at-titudinal items, we infer that his response for each item should be

Table 7-5. An Illustration of Item Discrimination Analysis for a Single Item

The Responses of Upper and Lower Quartiles to Item 1	
$N_1 = 10$ Upper Quartile	$N_2 = 10$ Lower Quartile
6	1
5	3
4	2
5	3
4	4
5	3
6	4
6	1
5	2
5	1
Sum of item scores = 51	Sum of item scores = 24
$\bar{X}_1 = 5.1$	$\bar{X}_2 = 2.4$

consistent with his total response. Therefore, persons identified as belonging to the upper quartile should have consistently larger weights assigned their responses to each item in the questionnaire, and those who belong to the lower quartile on the basis of their total score should have consistently smaller weights assigned each item. In the case illustrated in Table 7-5, item 1 (any item taken from a set of items in the questionnaire) appears to discriminate. We must verify this statement further, however.

The next step is to determine the average weight for item 1 among the subjects of the upper and lower quartiles. Averaging the weights of both groups, we have an $\bar{X}_1$ (the average score for the upper quartile on item 1) = 5.1. The $\bar{X}_2$ value (the average score for the lowest quartile on item 1) = 2.4. A visual inspection of the difference between the means of both groups would reveal that the item appears to discriminate between those who possess the trait to a high degree and those who possess it to a low degree.

We continue our item analysis by selecting item 2, recording the response weights for all individuals in the upper and lower quartiles, determining the average response for both groups, and so on. Finally, we would generate a table containing the means and mean differences of the upper and lower quartiles of subjects for all 10 questionnaire items as is shown in Table 7-6.

In Table 7-6 the column to the far right contains mean differences between average weights of the upper and lower quartiles of respondents based on total scores to a measure of attitude X. Notice that items 1, 4, 5, 7, 8, and 9 appear to discriminate between the two groups to varying degrees. These averages are consistent with what we would predict them to be. Note also that items 2, 3, and 6 do not discriminate at all. In fact, item 6 contradicts slightly the way the average weights should logically be arranged in relation to one another. (Predictably, averages for each item among the upper quartile of respondents should be larger compared to averages of item weights for members of the lower quartile.) Finally, observe that item 10 discriminates but does so *in reverse!*

There are several reasons why the item fails to discriminate as predicted. First, it could be a poor item and should not be grouped with the rest. It does not measure the phenomenon under investigation. Second, it may be that the researchers assigned the wrong weights to that particular statement. They must double-check the statement and the response pattern assigned to it before throwing it out altogether. It can be observed that if response weights have been assigned inappropriately to that item, then a correction will reinstate the item as a discriminating one. The function of item discrimination analysis is to improve the reliability of a test by eliminating those items inconsistent with the rest.

Table 7-6.   A Comparison of the Upper and Lower Quartiles

Item	Upper Quartile $\bar{X}_1$	Lower Quartile $\bar{X}_2$	Mean Difference $\bar{X}_1 - \bar{X}_2$
1	5.1	2.4	+2.7
2	4.6	4.5	+0.1
3	3.3	3.3	0.0
4	5.5	3.1	+2.4
5	4.8	1.8	+3.0
6	3.9	4.1	−0.2
7	5.0	4.0	+1.0
8	4.8	2.5	+2.3
9	4.9	2.8	+2.1
10	1.3	5.4	−4.1

If a researcher were to use item discrimination analysis, it would be advisable to begin by including a large number of items, at least in excess of 20. When item analysis is completed, several of the statements will be eliminated from the list because of their inability to discriminate between those individuals possessing variable amounts of the attitudinal property under investigation. As a result of eliminating items, the range of response that is possible to achieve is narrowed. Considering the above response pattern of 1, 2, 3, 4, 5, and 6, a 20-item questionnaire will yield a total response range of from 20 to 120. Decreasing the number of items to 10 will narrow the range of response to 10 to 60. Decisions to eliminate items are based in part on the following considerations:

1. The degree to which the item discriminates.
2. The number of individuals to whom the instrument is directed.
3. The degree to which precision is desired by the researcher in his attempt to measure the attitudinal phenomenon.

If a researcher rejects too many items, this increases the likelihood of a larger number of tied scores among respondents. This narrows the latitude of flexibility in the data analysis stage and will affect tabular construction and significantly limit statistical treatment. On the other hand, if he retains too many items, the chances increase of including items that discriminate poorly.

Choices as to which items should be retained and which ones excluded are almost always arbitrarily made by the researcher. Again, no specific conventional guidelines exist for making these kinds of decisions. Some researchers have advocated conducting a test of significance of difference between two means as a way of introducing probability theory into their decision to accept or reject specific attitudinal statements. In Table 7-6, items 1, 4, 5, 8, and 9 would probably be included in a final form of a measure of factor X. The others would either be excluded entirely or modified and reexamined within another subject situation. The decision to include specific items from Table 7-6 in this case was based on a mean difference of 2.00 or larger in the predicted direction. This was purely arbitrary.

When the final items are chosen, it is possible to rescore the entire sample according to the remaining items. The results for all persons involved should be more reliable than before item analysis was done. At least the internal consistency of the test was improved significantly, and to that extent, the reliability of the measure was improved.

A question may arise concerning why the middle 50 per cent of subjects were not considered in the item analysis. The reason these individuals were not included is that the persons associated with the extreme attitude intensities in either direction are more likely to manifest or reveal those items which best discriminate in the long run. Individuals with scores in the middle ranges are more likely to have response weights of 3 or 4. It would not be very profitable to include them in the item analysis, inasmuch as the effects of discriminating items would be greatly obscured.

Some advantages of item discrimination analysis are as follows.

Discrimination analysis assists the researcher to eliminate more objectively and directly those items inconsistent with the rest. This is perhaps the best method for spotting inconsistent, and hence, unusable items.

This method of internal reliability can increase significantly the internal consistency of any measuring instrument. This will strengthen the argument that the measure is valid as well as reliable.

Some disadvantages of item discrimination analysis include:

Because the choice and elimination of items is almost wholly arbitrary, this somewhat lessens the value of item discrimination analysis. This limitation is not very serious, however, particularly when we consider the increased objectivity in spotting bad items.

It is always possible that the items eliminated from the original list in an item analysis procedure may, in fact, be the best items for measuring the trait under investigation. This is difficult to accept, but it must be considered as a remote possibility nevertheless. It is possible that by chance the researcher may have collected a group of predominantly bad items instead of a group of predominantly good ones. Item analysis will reveal which items are the best (in terms of the greatest number that cling together consistently) in this remote instance. (Goodness and badness of particular items is determined by how well the statement functions as a valid indicator of the trait under investigation.)

If the difference between means test is employed (frequently called the "t" test), it is likely that several assumptions underlying the appropriate application of this statistical technique will not be met with the data the researcher has. The problems here would be of a statistical theoretical nature and certainly worth considering when the validity of the measuring instrument is at stake.

SOME GENERAL RELATIONSHIPS BETWEEN VALIDITY AND RELIABILITY

Throughout this chapter we have alluded to the fact that validity and reliability as test properties are interrelated to a significant degree. To make more explicit the interrelatedness of these factors, the following four general relationships may be defined.

A TEST THAT IS VALID IS ALWAYS RELIABLE

What this statement means is that if a test measures what we say it measures, then by definition it must be reliable. The major difficulty is to determine the degree to which validity exists when taking into account some social and/or psychological phenomenon. It is apparent that validity is difficult, if not impossible, to determine in an absolute sense. But to the extent that we know that a test measures what is has been constructed to measure, the test will always be a reliable indicator of that variable as well.

A TEST THAT IS NOT VALID MAY OR MAY NOT BE RELIABLE

This says simply that if we construct a test to measure variable X, it may be that the test in reality measures variable Y instead. In this case, it would be possible to have a test which is *not* a valid measure of variable X, but nevertheless it *is* a valid measure of variable Y. If the measure is a valid measure of something, then it has to be reliable as well. In essence, what we are saying is that we do not know what we are measuring, but it is significant (from the standpoint of its consistency in reflecting the unknown trait). Remember that test validity is based upon what the test is *supposed* to measure. It may not be a valid measure of one variable, but it can be considered to be a valid measure of another closely related to it.

A TEST THAT IS RELIABLE MAY OR MAY NOT BE VALID

This is similar to the second statement above. It says that a test can be demonstrably reliable, but we do not know for sure if it is valid as a measure of a specific individual or group property. In all likelihood, the test is a measure of *something,* but it does not necessarily have to be a valid measure of what we say it is.

A TEST THAT IS NOT RELIABLE IS NEVER VALID

Because a necessary condition of validity is reliability, an unreliable measuring instrument cannot have validity for measuring anything. It would seem that the more important of the two test properties is reliability. Reliability is a necessary prerequisite for validity, but validity has little or nothing to do with the reliability of a test. Reliability is more directly demonstrated statistically and/or logically, whereas validity is more frequently inferred by a comparison of predicted and/or observed behaviors.

This discussion is not intended to imply that we should ignore the validity of a test altogether. Rather, it merely points out that reliability is easier to measure and demonstrate than validity. It is extremely important that any social and/or psychological measuring instrument be *both* valid and reliable. We should make every effort to maximize these factors in any test administration.

In the following section we will examine various kinds of factors that can influence adversely the validity and reliability of measures.

FACTORS THAT AFFECT VALIDITY AND RELIABILITY

Thus far we have examined validity and reliability in considerable detail and have outlined several ways by which each of these test characteristics can be determined. In this section we will focus on various factors and conditions that affect significantly the validity and reliability of measures.

We do not intend to develop an exhaustive list of factors in this regard. Instead, we will attempt to highlight some of the more important kinds of things that must be taken into account as possibly altering the usefulness of measuring instruments as predictive devices. These factors may be grouped under several headings: (1) the test and its contents, (2) environmental factors, (3) personal factors, and (4) researcher interpretations.

THE TEST AND ITS CONTENTS

Whenever the validity and reliability of a test are evaluated, the first aspect to be critically scrutinized is the list of items included in the test. Are the items valid? Have they been drawn from the universe of traits and characteristics that measure the phenomenon under investigation? If the researcher has been careless and included items from a universe other than the one consistent with the trait designated in his theoretical scheme, the validity of the test will be seriously affected. Apart from the logical and theoretical connection between the items included in the measure and the trait to be measured, other aspects of the test emerge as crucial as well. Some of these factors are:

The Length of the Test

A long test will sometimes cause the respondent to give answers based on convenience rather than the way he really feels. A long test may become boring, and the subject checks any answer he sees to complete the test quickly. The investigator should make a point of checking carefully responses given on longer tests to see that a set response has not been given (Cronbach, 1946, pp. 475–94). One example of a set response is when the subject answers all items in the test (which has Likert-type responses of "strongly agree" through "strongly disagree") the same way (i.e., he answers "strongly agree" to all responses, regardless of whether the answers to some items are inconsistent with the answers to other items reflecting the same nature and direction of attitudinal intensity). Obviously, if there are two items in a job satisfaction questionnaire such as "I like my job" and "I do not like my job," and if the person answers "strongly agree" to both items, this is strong evidence of a set response.

It is apparent that the subject was responding in the most convenient way just to "get it over with." Response sets such as this render the questionnaire unusable. Of course, the researcher should always double-check questionnaires of any length to make sure that a set response has been given. But the longer the questionnaire, the more likely that a set response will occur.

The Cultural Date of the Test

A test employing words or phrases not used conventionally becomes increasingly unreliable and hence, not a valid indicator of the trait in question (Noelle-Neumann, 1970). Using terms such as "ice box" to refer to "refrigerators" may create a misunderstanding between the meaning intended by the statement (defined by the researcher) and the way it is understood by the subject. The cultural currency of the test or the degree to which it is up to date will be an important factor in assessing the validity and reliability of any attitudinal measure.

Open-end vs. Fixed-response Questions

Tests that utilize open-end questions (questions that have responses requiring the subject to write out an answer himself in the space provided in the questionnaire, or questions in interviews that require the subject to verbalize an extended reply) place a strong emphasis on the ability of the respondent to express himself (Noelle-Neumann, 1970). The educational sophistication of the person becomes an important variable here. Because the type of response provided to open-end questions determines the degree of intensity of some attitude possessed by the subject, it is clear that the ability to express oneself may seem to reflect differences in attitudes held by people of varying educational levels when actually there are none.

Mechanical Factors

Under the heading of mechanical factors might be grouped such factors as the type of printing used in a self-administered questionnaire, misspelled words, illegible words, missing pages, poorly phrased items, and the like. All these things can cause misunderstanding that will affect the validity and reliability of the test. The same is true of a face-to-face interview. If the researcher leaves certain statements out of his list of questions or uses alternative words at random, the information he obtains becomes less reliable. Ideally, the same administration conditions should prevail for each respondent. This uniformity minimizes the possibility of errors due to differences in the way various subjects are approached by the investigator.

Environmental Factors

The environmental conditions under which the test is administered must also be regarded as important in assessing the validity and reliability of a test (Pelz, 1959). The following environmental factors are particularly important in this regard:

Face-to-face interviews vs. self-administered questionnaires. Varying the degree of anonymity or confidentiality under which the test is completed may generate score differences for the same person under various test administration conditions (Andreason, 1970). Persons sometimes report feelings about things to an interviewer face-to-face that are quite different from those feelings they would reveal in a more confidential self-administered questionnaire requesting the same information (Boruch, 1971, pp. 308–11; Pearlin, 1961).

The clarity of instructions for completing the test. If the investigator fails to clarify the procedure for subjects to follow in taking a test (or responding in an interview or completing a questionnaire), there is a good chance that the subjects will provide misleading information unintentionally.

Personal Factors

Some of the more important personal characteristics of the respondent which will affect test validity and reliability are:

Socioeconomic status of respondents. Occupation, educational level, income, and ethnic background are the primary components of socioeconomic status. We have shown in an earlier section of this chapter that these factors may operate to cause variations in test performance or attitudinal intensity scores. The researcher should attempt to gear his measuring instruments to closely approximate the socioeconomic level of the audience he studies. The cultural aspects of any measuring instrument will limit the generalizability and utility of it to particular social aggregates.

Age, sex and maturity level. Like socioeconomic status, age and sex are important considerations in any test administration. Closely associated with age and sex are differences in maturity levels. The maturity level of the intended target of social research will affect the manner in which the researcher is accepted and the degree of cooperation and interest demonstrated by the subjects.

Ethnic background. Although we have listed ethnic background as a part of socioeconomic status above, it is worthwhile noting that ethnic background can account for misunderstanding pertaining to word usage in questionnaire items. Different words mean different things to people of different ethnic backgrounds as well as to people of different socioeconomic status (Osgood, 1965).

In testing and measurement social scientists are increasingly moving toward the development of culture-free measures. They are learning more and more to appreciate the fact that tests have built-in cultural biases that affect significantly the interpretations that can be made of test results for varying ethnic audiences.

Memory or recall. The ability of a subject to recall earlier responses on a before-after test administration may elicit responses consistent with earlier ones, regardless of whether or not the respondent's beliefs are the same in both time periods. Parallel forms of the same test are used frequently to overcome the effects of memory or recall in test-retest situations, particularly if the span of time between the two administrations is short (i.e., less than two weeks) (Selltiz, et al., 1959).

Social desirability. Many questionnaires have social desirability measures incorporated in them to ascertain the effect of this important variable on a subject's overall response pattern. Social desirability, or responding in accordance with what the subject believes to be a desirable set of traits rather than what might be true of him (i.e., undesirable characteristics) is a frequent test contaminator (Edwards, 1957). In fact, some researchers have gone so far as to say that any given attitudinal measure is, in reality, an indication of what the person regards as socially desirable rather than what is actually true of him. Certainly we cannot disregard the potential impact of social desirability on subject responses that in turn could affect both the validity and the reliability of our measures (Larsen, 1958).

Researcher Interpretation

Finally, an important consideration in assessing test validity and reliability is the kind of interpretation made of results by the researcher. Under this heading are the following:

Coding procedure. The researcher is at liberty to code his obtained information virtually any way he wishes. The validity and reliability of a test hinge in part on the coding pattern followed by the investigator. Although this opportunity varies considerably from study to study, it is possible for a researcher to code his information in such a way as to increase the chances of supporting a particular theoretical explanation of a social event under investigation. Objectivity in coding should be maximized. If possible, the researcher should consult with other investigators to obtain their opinion of the coding procedure he has selected. This will not guarantee that the coding procedure he chooses will be the best one, nor will it ensure the validity and reliability of it, but the researcher will have at least decreased the possibility that his own values have biased the way in which the findings are interpreted.

Interpretation of raw scores. Raw scores on any attitudinal measure are seldom meaningful apart from their comparison with other scores on the same instrument. When a researcher extracts a raw score from a list of them and attempts spontaneous interpretation of it, he runs the risk of assigning a meaning to the score that is quite different from the practical meaning it has in relation to the other scores in a comparative sense. Single-score interpretations should be regarded conservatively and tentatively in accordance with appropriate scientific behavior.

SUMMARY

This chapter has sought to acquaint the reader with two important test properties—validity and reliability. The measurement phase of social research is a very important one. Quite apart from the necessity of having a good theory as a sound scientific base, the researcher must be able to demonstrate that there is a high likelihood that his concepts (or constructs, as the case may be) are measured reliably and have validity consistent with the theory under investigation (so far as validity can be determined).

This chapter and the preceding one have been designed to familiarize the student with some of the basic problems of measuring social and/or psychological phenomena. Among the things these chapters have illustrated repeatedly is that measurement is a complex process. The researcher is never in the position of being absolutely sure he is measuring what he says he is measuring. Although this aspect of his inquiry is somewhat dissatisfying, it nevertheless encourages him to be conservative in his interpretation of social phenomena and tentative in the conclusions he draws about observed sociological associations.

NOTES

1. Validity and reliability are terms that are not only meaningful for questionnaires as measuring instruments, but they may also pertain to such things as appropriateness of a given study design for a specific problem area, the adequacy of observational data collection techniques (e.g., participant, nonparticipant), the adequacy of interviews and all secondary source material, and to the generalizability of study findings to other populations and social situations (i.e., external validity) (Campbell and Stanley, 1963, pp. 5–6). Various uses of these terms will be noted in following sections dealing with specific topic areas.

2. Some researchers believe that it is more important to ask, "What is it that *this* test measures?" rather than "To what extent does the test measure what it purports to measure?" (Tyler, 1963, p. 29).

3. Some researchers distinguish between concurrent and predictive validity as two separate types (Downie and Heath, 1965). This would mean that four types of validity exist according to some defining systems. In this chapter we will treat concurrent and predictive validity as subtypes within the same category sometimes referred to as "pragmatic validity" (Selltiz, et al., 1959).

4. Allport (1937, p. 453) states as an alternative, "the reliability of any instrument is defined as 'prediction of itself alone.' If the instrument does not measure something with some degree of regularity, it is worthless and lacks cohesion. The scale should agree with itself."

5. Sometimes the respondent is asked to interpret hypothetical situations (e.g., if you were chairman of the board of some company, what do you think you would do, or how do you think you would feel if this or that happened in your presence?), and on the basis of what the person says he *thinks he would do,* an *inference* is made by the researcher about the attitudes possessed by the respondent. Also, thematic apperception tests are administered, particularly in clinical psychological experimentation, and the person is asked to interpret such things as Rorschach ink blots or stick figures, or he is asked to tell a story about a picture he sees. On the basis of the story he tells or the interpretation he makes of things, the psychologist draws inferences about the person's attitudinal configuration as a potential explanation for such things as neuroses or psychoses the person may have.

   Although the ultimate contribution of such techniques of personality and individual assessment is presently unknown, there is some evidence to indicate that these methods have been useful in providing clues or insights about why people behave as they do. Such methods are usually employed in conjunction with other behavioral indicators such as observations of real behaviors in the natural setting, or with interviews and questionnaires, and other secondary source material such as letters and autobiographies.

6. LaPiere's classic study of the discrepancy between attitudes and behavior is a significant case in point. An oriental couple visited a number of establishments throughout the United States, including several hotels, motels, and restaurants. Several months later, these same establishments were contacted and the owners were asked whether or not they serve or accommodate oriental people. The overwhelming response was "no." Since these individuals *had* been served without incident, a strong case was made for arguing that actions do not always follow attitudes expressed.

7. Pretesting of measuring instruments, particularly those in questionnaire form, is done frequently in social research. Such procedure is comparable to test-driving new automobiles to determine if there are any significant defects in workmanship prior to marketing them before the general public. Accordingly, if there are questions that are difficult to understand, ambiguous phrasings of items, excluded items, or inappropriate or obscure items, these can either be modified or omitted as means of im-

proving the questionnaire before it is administered to the target population.

8. A two to four week interval between repeated test administrations is usually considered time enough to allow respondents to forget how they responded initially. Sometimes, if respondents can remember how they responded in the first questionnaire administration, they want to appear to be consistent in front of the researcher, even though significant changes in their feelings and attitudes have occurred. They will try their best to replicate their original responses. This strain for consistency acts as a biasing factor in interpreting measure results. To overcome the potential bias of such a situation, researchers sometimes devise parallel forms of the same test, using different items to measure the same attitudinal phenomenon. This will be discussed in a later section of this chapter dealing with various ways to measure test reliability.

9. It is usually considered good practice to double-check the reliability of measures within the sample studied. Some researchers rely too heavily on reliability estimates taken from other groups in a pretest pilot situation, and they assume that if their measure is reliable for one group, then it should also be reliable for another. This is not necessarily true. Although previous tests of reliability of measures lend support to its usefulness as a reliable measure in the present instance, the fact is that the final target group of subjects constitutes a new group. Sometimes, reliability of a measure varies from one sample to another to a significant degree, and it is therefore strongly recommended that the measures should be checked for reliability each time they are used in new sample situations. There is nothing more discouraging than to learn that a test is unreliable for a particular audience the researcher has studied. Findings based on unreliable measures are not entirely valid, and in many instances, they are considered to be utterly worthless.

10. An excellent source that includes step-by-step statistical procedures for applying the Kuder-Richardson 20 reliability formula is David Magnusson, *Test Theory*, Addison-Wesley Publishing Company, Reading, Mass., 1967. It also includes a rather detailed and sophisticated discussion of other types of reliability methods of a statistical nature.

QUESTIONS AND SUGGESTED PROBLEMS

1. Construct a short questionnaire of approximately 20 statements geared to measure some attitudinal phenomenon of your choice (and different from those used as examples or suggested in this and the previous chapter). Administer the questionnaire to 30 students and test each item's discriminatory power through item-discrimination analysis. Discuss the implications of your findings in class.

2. Briefly compare the advantages and limitations of using external vs. internal reliability checks. Which methods of reliability check are most useful? Why?

3. Why is reliability easier to determine than the validity of a test? Discuss the relative importance of each of these traits in terms of their theoretical value.

4. Write a short essay on the importance and influence of social desirability as it pertains to attitudinal test scores. Is it possible to determine fully the impact of social desirability on attitudinal measures? Why or why not? How would you go about lessening the effects of this variable on any measure you construct?

5. Evaluate briefly the following types of validity in terms of their functional utility in measurement: (1) content validity, (2) concurrent validity, and (3) predictive validity.

6. Write a short essay on the factors that affect the validity and reliability of a test from the standpoint of the test content itself.

7. How can the researcher influence the scores of subjects on attitudinal measures? Explain.

8. What are some major differences between measuring instruments in the social sciences and those developed in the physical sciences? Explain.

9. Why is it necessary for the social scientist to retain a degree of conservatism in interpreting research findings in the light of validity and reliability procedures that have been established conventionally? Discuss.

10. Discuss the validity and reliability of tests designed for different ethnic groups. Is it necessary for a researcher to construct a different test for different socioeconomic aggregates in the same sense that

tests are constructed for different ethnic groups? What are some of the ethical considerations and decisions social scientists must make in the construction and administration of tests?

BIBLIOGRAPHY

Abell, Peter. "Measurement in Sociology: Measurement, Structure, and Sociological Theory," *Sociology* 3 (1969): 397–416.

Andreason, Alan R. "Personalizing Mailed Questionnaires Correspondence," *Public Opinion Quarterly* 34 (1970): 273–288.

Blalock, Hubert M., Jr. *Social Statistics.* New York: McGraw-Hill, 1972.

Boruch, Robert F. "Assuring Confidentiality of Responses in Social Research: A Note on Strategies," *American Sociologist* 6 (1971): 308–11.

Campbell, Donald T., and Julian C. Stanley. *Experimental and Quasi-experimental Designs for Research.* Chicago: Rand-McNally, 1963.

Cattell, Raymond B. *The 16 P.F. Test.* Champaign, Ill.: Institute for Personality and Abilities Testing, 1950.

Champion, Dean J. *Basic Statistics for Social Research.* San Francisco: Chandler, 1970.

———, and Edward Z. Dager. "Some Impacts of Office Automation upon Status, Role Change, and Depersonalization," *Sociological Quarterly* 8 (1967): 71–84.

Cronbach, L. "Response Sets and Test Validity," *Educational Psychological Measurement* 6 (1946): 475–94.

Downie, N. M., and R. W. Heath. *Basic Statistical Methods.* New York: Harper and Row, 1965.

Edwards, A. L. *The Social Desirability Variable in Personality Assessment Research.* New York: Dryden, 1957.

Larsen, William R. "Social Desirability as a Latent Variable in Medical Questionnaire Responses," *Pacific Sociological Review* 1 (1958): 30–33.

Magnusson, David. *Test Theory.* Reading, Mass.: Addison-Wesley, 1967.

Noelle-Neumann, Elizabeth. "Wanted: Rules for Wording Structured Questionnaires," *Public Opinion Quarterly* 34 (1970): 191–198.

Osgood, Charles. "Cross Cultural Comparability in Attitude Measurement via Multilingual Semantic Differentials." In *Current Studies in Psychology* edited by I. D. Steiner and M. Fishbein. New York: Holt, Rinehart, and Winston, 1965.

Pearlin, Leonard R. "The Appeals of Anonymity in Questionnaire Response," *Public Opinion Quarterly* 25 (1961): 640–647.

Pelz, Donald C. "The Influence of Anonymity on Expressed Attitudes," *Human Organization* 18 (1959): 88–91.

Renner, K. E. "Must All Tests be Valid?" *American Psychologist,* 17 (1962): 507–8.

Selltiz, Claire, Marie Jahoda, Morton Deutsch, and Stuart W. Cook. *Research Methods in Social Relations.* New York: Holt, Rinehart, and Winston, 1959.

Tyler, Leona E. *Tests and Measurements.* Englewood Cliffs, N.J.: Prentice-Hall, 1963.

CHAPTER 8
SAMPLING METHODS*

When a research plan specifies the inclusion of people, the investigator may decide (1) to study the entire population of *elements* (people or things), or (2) to study only a portion of elements taken from the larger portion or population of them. A portion of elements taken from the larger population of them is called a *sample*. The process of drawing those elements from the larger population or universe is called *sampling*.

There are many types of sampling. In this chapter a variety of sam-

* Certain parts of this chapter require some elementary facility with statistical procedures. It is therefore advisable that the student review some appropriate social science statistics text or take a short course in statistical methods in order to better understand what is being discussed. Portions of this chapter requiring this facility will refer the reader to the Notes section. For the most part, however, the chapter objective can be achieved without a statistical review.

pling plans will be discussed. A sampling plan specifies (a) how elements will be drawn from the larger or "parent" population, and (b) how many elements will be drawn.

THE NATURE OF SAMPLING PLANS

Most sampling plans can be categorized according to whether they are (a) *probability* or (b) *nonprobability*[1] (*Blalock, 1960*).

PROBABILITY SAMPLING PLANS

Probability sampling plans are those that specify the probability or likelihood of the inclusion of each element. Ideally and technically, probability sampling plans require that the researcher satisfy the following conditions:

1.   The size of the parent population or universe from which the sample will be obtained must be known.
2.   The desired sample size must be specified.[2]
3.   Each element or group of elements must have an equal chance of being included in the subsequent sample.

For example, if the investigator knows that the population he is studying contains 100 elements, and furthermore, if he knows that all elements are accessible and may be included in a subsequent sample, then we say that each element in that population has an equal chance of being included, or each element in the population of 100 has 1/100th of a chance of being selected. Similarly, if the population is 10,000 and if the same conditions hold concerning our knowledge of the elements and their accessibility, then each element in that population of 10,000 has 1/10,000th of a chance of being drawn.

In reality, however, researchers are not always able to know for sure that conditions (1) and (3) will be satisfied. Sometimes the population studied is so large as to be considered infinite and unknowable for all practical purposes. The population of the United States is so large and changes so rapidly (thousands of people die and many others are born every second) that it is quite impossible for any research organization, particularly a single investigator, to identify *all* elements at any given point in time and to ensure that each element will have an equal opportunity of being included in a subsequent sample.

A positive feature of probability sampling plans is that the resultant samples are considered *representative*, and hence, *generalizable* to the same and to similar populations from which they were drawn. The investigator is able to specify *how closely* his sample and its characteristics (sample statistics) portray or are representative of the parent population and its characteristics (population parameters). He infers things about the population by studying the characteristics of elements taken from it in accordance with some specified probability sampling plan. Statisticians label particular statistical methods as *inferential* when they perform the function of allowing the investigator to infer things about the population by examining the sample characteristics.

Because the researcher has only a portion of the entire population of elements, a certain amount of sampling error exists. *Sampling error* has to do with the degree to which the sample characteristics approximate the characteristics of the population. The smaller the sample, the greater the sampling error. Also, the larger the sample, the smaller the sampling error. This holds true generally, however, only when a probability sampling plan is used.

For example, suppose we were to examine all Boy Scouts in the state of Nevada. Furthermore, suppose that the average age of all Boy Scouts in Nevada was 14.1 years. Let us assume that we have obtained a sample of Boy Scouts from Nevada and that we have determined the average age of the sample of Boy Scouts to be 13.9 years. It is obvious that 13.9 years does not equal 14.1 years, but we say that 13.9 is an estimate of 14.1. According to certain laws of probability, we conclude that our particular estimate of Boy Scout ages for the state of Nevada, 13.9 years, is near the true population value, 14.1 years. Of course, had we obtained the entire population of Boy Scouts for the state, there would be no sample, and hence, no sampling error. Some sampling error always exists when we do not have complete observations for all elements in a given population. By virtue of the fact that some elements in the population are excluded from the sample we happen to draw, a certain amount of sampling error exists. Using a probability sampling plan will enable us to calculate fairly accurately how much error exists with respect to estimating the true population characteristic by paying attention to the particular sample characteristic.

Commonly used probability sampling plans to be discussed in this chapter include (1) simple random sampling, (2) proportionate stratified random sampling, (3) disproportionate stratified random sampling, and (4) area or "cluster" sampling.

NONPROBABILITY SAMPLING PLANS

Nonprobability sampling plans are those that provide no basis for estimating how closely the sample characteristics approximate the parameters of the population from which the sample was obtained. In fact, the investigator is generally unable to identify the parent population at all. Hence, the generalizability of samples drawn in accordance with some nonprobability sampling plan is severely limited.

It is meaningless even to discuss sampling error associated with such samples inasmuch as nonprobability sampling plans are not designed to perform inferential functions. On occasion, however, there are special situations when the investigator employs certain aspects of probability sampling together with a nonprobability sampling plan. Perhaps some elements are included randomly whereas others are not. For example, in a study of academic discipline and faculty religiosity, Lehman and Shriver (1968) used a stratified systematic sampling method to obtain 99 faculty respondents at a southeastern state university. Although not generally recognized as a probability sampling method, systematic sampling used in conjunction with stratified sampling rendered what Lehman and Shriver concluded to be a "sample which was considered representative of the target population" (p. 174). It is the judgment of the investigator to determine whether or not certain rules apply pertaining to probability and inference, and ultimately what he can and cannot say about the population based on the particular sample he draws. Certainly it can be argued that the generalizability of the sample is improved by the inclusion of some elements randomly. But to what degree the sample can be designated as a *probability sample* is a matter of judgment. In any event, social researchers using some nonprobability sampling plan are usually not interested or intent on generalizing a great deal in view of what they find. Those who do intend to generalize should caution their readers about the limitations inherent in the sample selected.

The nonprobability sampling plans to be covered in this chapter include (1) systematic sampling, (2) quota sampling, (3) accidental sampling, (4) judgmental or purposive sampling, (5) snowball sampling, (6) saturation sampling and (7) dense sampling (Coleman, 1958–1959; Selltiz, et al. 1967).

THE DECISION TO SAMPLE

In the process of formulating the research design, the investigator must determine whether or not to use some kind of sampling plan. If he plans to study people, he may elect to study a particular population of them or only a portion or sample of elements taken from the larger population or universe. In making this decision he usually considers at least three important factors:

1. The size of the population.
2. The cost of obtaining the elements.
3. The convenience and accessibility of the elements.

THE SIZE OF THE POPULATION

If the population to be studied is relatively small, say, less than 500 elements, the investigator may decide not to sample at all, but rather, to study the entire population.[2] If the researcher conducts a case study of a single bank or business, his population of elements may consist of 100 employees, in which case he decides to study them all. This task is easily manageable, and sampling does not become a meaningful consideration here.

However, if the population to be studied is quite large, sampling becomes a more feasible alternative to studying the entire universe of elements. For example, if an investigator is studying interfaith marriage in California for the past 10-year period, his population of interfaith marriages may be 100,000. In this case, the size of the parent population of interfaith marriages makes it a very unwieldy task to study the entire number.

Generally, it can be said that as the population of elements to be studied becomes larger, sampling becomes increasingly important. It should be evident, however, that size is a relative matter. What one researcher regards as a large population may be regarded by another as a small one, and vice versa. No precise guidelines currently exist for differentiating large from small populations.

THE COST OF OBTAINING THE ELEMENTS

Deciding whether or not to sample also depends on how much money the researcher has budgeted for the research project. In the example of interfaith marriages in California for the past 10 years, it is no doubt true that the researcher would like to study all the marriages, but because he has only $50 to $100 budgeted for his study, he is forced to be content with a sample of interfaith marriages instead, perhaps a few hundred. The proposed cost of a research project often requires that the researcher do things that fall somewhat short of what he would want to do ideally.

THE CONVENIENCE AND ACCESSIBILITY OF THE ELEMENTS

A third consideration in deciding to sample is: How accessible are the elements in the population specified? Significantly assisting Émile

Durkheim in his classic study of suicide were certain relatives who held high governmental positions (Durkheim, 1951). These governmental contacts were able to provide Durkheim with immediate access to French statistical records on suicides. His research efforts were also assisted by several groups of employees in a number of governmental offices. For Durkheim, the convenience of having data made immediately available to him together with a staff of workers for which he bore little or none of the cost made the prospect of studying the population of suicides in French districts considerably more attractive.

Some investigators work in computer centers or have access to facilities and staffs where large amounts of data can be compiled and handled quickly and relatively easily. Some researchers study the organizations they are employed by, or they study organizations very similar to those they have had extensive experience with. In each of these instances, convenience and accessibility have played major roles in determining for the investigator whether to study the entire population of elements or a sample taken from it.

Briefly summarizing, decisions to study entire populations or the samples taken from them are generally based, in part, on the size of the population, the anticipated cost of the study in relation to the budget of the researcher, and the convenience and accessibility associated with obtaining the elements, although other factors are involved in making these decisions. Such factors will be discussed in conjunction with various sampling plans to be treated later in this chapter.

IDEAL VS. REAL SAMPLING CONSIDERATIONS

As a general rule, books such as this present techniques and methods in an ideal fashion. That is, given ideal circumstances, the researcher should do this and that. Some ideal conditions that are presumed to exist are: (1) unlimited funds for one's research, (2) unlimited assistance by way of staffs and consulting support, and (3) an unlimited timetable for research completion. More realistically, however, the researcher works with a limited budget, has little or no part- or full-time assistance, and must work within a restricted timetable. Earlier it was noted how the cost factor could act as a constraint on the investigator, causing him to take a sample of elements that would be more within his means rather than to deal with the entire population, an alternative he could not afford.

Much research takes place in graduate departments of most large universities. Doctoral dissertations and masters' theses are evidence of some of this research. Students involved in such research experiences find that they must complete their doctoral or masters' programs within preestablished time periods imposed by the graduate schools or departments of their respective institutions. The student soon comes to the realization that what is ideally taught in the classroom is very difficult, if not impossible, to achieve in the actual research situation. This conflict between what ideally *should* be done and what realistically *is* done is frequently quite perplexing to many student researchers.

The researcher should make every reasonable effort to be consistent with proper methodological conduct, but he should also understand that periodic departures from the prescribed way of doing things often stem from certain circumstances over which the investigator has little or no control. When he departs from the norm to any great extent, the researcher usually reveals these departures to his readers, and he judges what is found subsequently on its own relative merits. This is one reason why some people regard research methods and their proper application as an art rather than as a series of mechanical steps in a cut and dried formula.

MAJOR PROBABILITY SAMPLING PLANS

The controlling factor underlying all major probability sampling plans is randomness (Peatman, 1947). *Randomness* refers to the fact that all elements in a given population have an equal and independent chance of being included in a particular sample. Before presenting each of the probability sampling plans in this section, it will be helpful to illustrate, in detail, how random samples are drawn.

HOW TO DRAW RANDOM SAMPLES

Several methods are available to the researcher for obtaining random samples. Before a random sample is selected, the investigator must answer a number of questions that should help him to choose a particular sampling method for his study. These questions are:

1. How large is the parent population?
2. How large a sample does the investigator want to draw from the parent population?

3.   Is it possible to enumerate the population by assigning each element a number, or is the researcher interested in selecting clusters of elements such as specific neighborhoods or geographical areas?

4.   Does the researcher want to stratify the sample in any way, such as dividing it according to age, sex, years of education, race, socioeconomic status, or the like?

We will now consider several ways of obtaining a random sample in the context of the questions raised above.

THE FISHBOWL DRAW

The simplest and most familiar type of sample selection consists of putting numbers on slips of paper or marbles and depositing them in a large container. The numbers identify and stand for specific elements in the population, and presumably the entire population of elements has been numbered and is represented in the bowl. After mixing the numbers thoroughly, the investigator selects one number at a time, blindfolded, until the desired sample size is obtained. This is called a random sample.

A great deal of criticism has been leveled at this type of sample selection, however. Some critics argue that this method is not very sophisticated, and hence some questions can be raised concerning the validity of the sample drawn. The primary argument against this method is simply that better methods exist for obtaining random samples. Such methods include the use of a random numbers table or a computer-determined array of random numbers. These methods are considered less vulnerable to the possible bias of the researcher (i.e., peeking from underneath the blindfold and selecting preferred numbers from the bowl while purposely excluding others).

But suppose we allow the fishbowl method of sample selection. First, such a method presumes that the population we draw from will be somewhat small. Otherwise, it would become an unwieldy task to number tens of thousands of elements and then find a container large enough to hold the numbers. Such a method is easy to employ, but it does suffer these restrictions. Simply put, other methods exist that *are* better.

THE TABLE OF RANDOM NUMBERS

A table of random numbers consists of a continuous row-column sequence of numbers, not appearing in any particular order, and no number appears any more frequently than any other number. When the researcher uses a table of random numbers to select his sample, by definition, the sample drawn is a random one.

Table A-1 of Appendix A is a table of random numbers. Numbers have been grouped to allow for easy access and reading. Other than that, no significance is attached to the divisions of numbers as they appear in the table. To use the random numbers table, the researcher first specifies how many elements are in the population he is studying. He then enumerates them from 1 to N, where N is defined as the total number of elements in the population. Suppose the population consists of 1,000 elements. The researcher numbers all elements from 1 to 1,000. Next, he decides how large a sample he would like. Let us assume that he wants a random sample of size 50.

He enters the random numbers table at any point. He might open the book to any page and, while not looking, place his finger somewhere on the page of random numbers. Where his finger lands is where he will begin. Investigators should be aware that consistent use of a random numbers table will make the book open "automatically" to a given page. The researcher will then use the same numbers as used in previous random draws.

Because his population is of size 1,000, this number contains four digits. Populations of size 300 contain three digits, those of 10,000 contain five digits, those of 1,000,000 contain seven digits, and so forth. He considers groups of four digits in the random numbers table in accordance with the present example. Suppose he decides to start in the upper left-hand corner of the table. The first four digits in the table reading across are 1009. Because there are only 1,000 elements in the population, no element is numbered 1,009. Consequently, he skips this number and moves down the column to the next four digits, 3754. Again, no element in the population is numbered 3,754, and so he systematically moves down the column. The next four digits are 0842. This refers to the person numbered 842. (The first zeroes are ignored.) There is such a person in his population, and so he includes this person as a part of the random sample he is drawing. He continues to move down the column, skipping numbers that are too large and also those numbers that have already been drawn. (The latter event is extremely unlikely, but it does happen occasionally.)

When the researcher reaches the bottom of a column, he may simply move one digit to the right, and start at the top of the column again. Doing this will bring him back to the next four digits at the top of the column, which are 0097. This is person 97 and is included in his sample. The next digits are 7542, 8422, 9019, 2807, and so on. He keeps moving systematically through the table until he has obtained his random sample of 50 different elements. If he prefers, he can skip two, three, or more numbers over each time he changes columns in the table. He can work sideways, diagonally, or any way that is systematic. He must not skip around and pick groups of numbers at will. This undermines the purpose of the random numbers table.

Whether or not the researcher would want to use a random numbers table to draw his sample would again be contingent on how large a population he has. Can it be enumerated? And does he want to stratify it in any way? (Using the random numbers table in sampling plans that stratify elements according to certain dimensions will be explained in discussions of those sampling plans later.)

Advantages of Using Random Numbers Tables

The random numbers table is ideal for obtaining random samples from relatively small populations. When populations are quite large, drawing numbers from the table becomes extremely tedious. Imagine the time it would take to enumerate a population of 25,000 and draw a sample of 2500 elements from it using a random numbers table. (During one academic year, one of the authors had his research methods class of 40 students draw a random sample of 500 students from a university of 23,000. From this experience it was, in our judgment, extremely tedious!)

Another advantage of these tables is that they are immediately accessible to most researchers and are easy to use.

COMPUTER-DETERMINED RANDOM SAMPLING

If the population under investigation is particularly large and if the facilities are available, it would profit the researcher to use a computer system to obtain a random number of elements corresponding to elements in the population. The computer can be programmed or electronically instructed to print out a series of numbers, as many as the researcher desires, that will be defined as a random sample of elements.

No attempt will be made here to discuss the steps in programming computers to render such information. For a nominal fee, any computer center, public or private, will usually assist a researcher in determining numbers to be used in the selection of a random sample.

For populations under 5,000 (remember the question of what is large and what is small), it is generally a toss-up as to which method will be preferred—the random numbers table or the computer. Computer centers are usually in constant use, and there may be a waiting period of up to a week or two before the center can handle the researcher's request. On the other hand, the random numbers table, although involving a bit of tedious work for the researcher and his staff, is immediately accessible, can be used any time, and is free. In the final analysis, the investigator is the judge of which method he will use.

SIMPLE RANDOM SAMPLING

Necessarily included in all probability sampling plans is simple random sampling. This sampling technique assures each element an equal and independent chance of being included in subsequent samples. An equal chance means that each element has the same probability of being included. For example, in a population of 500, each element theoretically has 1/500th of a chance of being included. In a population of 1,000, each element theoretically has 1/1,000th of a chance of being included. Where some elements are purposely excluded from the sample, the resulting sample is not a random one. Sometimes the researcher chooses to exclude certain elements from the sample because of their inaccessibility. Poverty researchers studying moonshine activities in Kentucky and Tennessee often have difficulty interviewing prospective respondents. To avoid risking their lives, they purposely exclude particular people from their samples.

Certain socioeconomic groups are more difficult to enumerate than others as well. Where there is high mobility among a given segment of the population (the poor often migrate from area to area in search of employment and better opportunity), it is difficult for the researcher to obtain a current, accurate listing of all population elements.[3] The greater geographical stability associated with certain socioeconomic status groups makes it more likely that they will be included in the final sample. Sometimes certain elements may not have been identified as a part of the original population, and consequently, they are excluded simply because they are not known to exist.

An independent chance of being included means that the draw of one element will not affect the chances of other elements being included in subsequent draws. Suppose in a population of 500 we were to use a fishbowl draw for determining a random sample. As we remove numbers from the fishbowl or container, fewer numbers remain in the bowl after each draw. Hence, the chances for the remaining elements in the bowl to be drawn theoretically increase. To illustrate, the removal of the first element from the bowl of 500 will leave 499 elements. On the first draw, each element had 1/500th of a chance of being included. All elements remaining in the bowl after the first draw will now have 1/499th of a chance of being included. On the following draws, the elements remaining in the bowl will have, successively, 1/498th of a chance, 1/497th of a chance, and so on.

This sampling procedure is called *sampling without replacement,* which refers to the fact that elements, once drawn, are not replaced in the bowl. When elements *are* returned to the bowl, such sampling methods are designated as *sampling with replacement.* Sampling with replacement guarantees each element an equal and independent chance of being included in each draw. It is apparent, however, that elements previously drawn and replaced in the bowl have a chance of being drawn again. When the original population is quite large, say 5,000 or over, the probability of drawing any element twice or more is quite low. But if an element is drawn again, the common procedure is to ignore the element, put it back in the bowl, and draw again until *n* different elements are obtained in the random sample.

The major difference between sampling without replacement and sampling with replacement has to do with the number of possible samples of size *n* that theoretically could be drawn.

For sampling without replacement, the possible number of samples of size *n* that could be drawn is:

$$\binom{N}{n} = \frac{N!}{(N-n)!n!}$$

where N = the size of the parent population, and
n = the size of the sample

For a population of size 4 and samples of size 2, the number of possible samples that could be drawn would be:[1]

$$\binom{4}{2} = \frac{4!}{(4-2)!2!} = \frac{(4)(3)(2)(1)}{(2)(1)(2)(1)} = 6$$

Six samples of size 2 could be drawn from a population of 4 by using sampling without replacement. If the elements in the population of 4 were labeled A, B, C, and D, respectively, then the six samples of size 2 would be:

AB	BC
AC	BD
AD	CD

For sampling with replacement, the number of possible samples of size *n* that could be drawn from a population of size *n* would be:

$$N^n$$

where N = the size of the population, and
     n = the sample size.

Again, for our example of a population of size 4 and a sample size of 2, the possible number of samples that could be drawn with replacement would be:

$$(4)^2 = 16$$

Sixteen samples of size 2 could be drawn from a population of 4. These samples would be as follows (presuming the same letter identification as in the first example: A, B, C, and D):

AA	BA	CA	DA
AB	BB	CB	DB
AC	BC	CC	DC
AD	BD	CD	DD

The AA, BB, CC, and DD combinations reflect the fact that with sampling with replacement, an element once drawn can be drawn again. From a strictly mathematical standpoint, element combinations such as these are theoretically included. In actual research practice, however, an element once drawn is not included again. It would be absurd to ask a respondent to fill out a questionnaire twice while he is being interviewed. In most cases, researchers use sampling without replacement.

The mechanics of drawing a simple random sample include:

1. Enumerating all elements in the population.
2. Specifying that each element has an equal and independent chance of being included.
3. Drawing numbers by (a) the fishbowl technique, (b) a table of random numbers, (c) a computer-determined array. Alternatives (b) and (c) are generally preferred over (a).

ADVANTAGES OF A SIMPLE RANDOM SAMPLING PLAN

Some advantages of simple random sampling plans include the following:

1. All elements in the population have an equal and independent chance of being included. Theoretically at least the resulting sample will be a representative one. Samples drawn in such a way as to pro-

hibit some elements from being included or to make it more likely for some elements to be included over others (i.e., the interviewer interviews his close friends or relatives instead of the elements he was randomly assigned) are said to be *biased,* and hence, not random or representative of the population from which they were obtained.

2. The method of simple random sampling is used in conjunction with all other probability sampling plans. Therefore, it serves as a foundation upon which all types of random samples are based.

3. Simple random sampling is the easiest to apply of all probability sampling plans. It is the most simple type of random sampling to understand.

4. The researcher does not need to know the true composition of the population beforehand. The simple random sample will theoretically reflect all important segments of the population to one degree or another.

5. The amount of sampling error associated with any given sample drawn can easily be computed.[5] Sampling error is the degree to which sample estimates of population values fail to reflect the true population values. It exists whenever samples are studied instead of entire populations of elements. Sampling error is determined by the formula:

$$s_x = \frac{s}{\sqrt{n-1}}$$

where s = the sample standard deviation[6]
(See pps. 324–325)
and
n = the sample size.

This is also the formula for the standard error of the mean, and it can be illustrated that for random sampling plans, the larger the sample size, n, the smaller the standard error of the mean, $s_{\bar{x}}$, and the smaller the sampling error. This is an important reason why larger samples are preferred over smaller ones.

The standard error of the mean is usually reserved for data of the interval level or better. For situations where ordinal data are used and associated with n observations in a sample, the standard error of the median can be determined, which is:

$$\text{Standard error of the median} = \frac{1.253s}{\sqrt{n-1}}$$

where s = the sample standard deviation, and
n = the sample size.

6.   Because the researcher need not be thoroughly familiar with the population characteristics prior to the selection of the simple random sample, he cannot make possible *classification errors.* Classification errors refer to errors resulting from improper classification of population parameters or characteristics. Suppose an investigator were to devise the classification, race, as one dimension used to obtain elements. It may be that in a subsequent draw of a random sample of elements from various classifications of race, some elements could be wrongly assigned to some racial category. Using simple random sampling as his sampling plan, however, he avoids potential classification errors that might otherwise occur under some other probability sampling plan such as stratified random sampling. Such plans will be discussed shortly.

DISADVANTAGES OF SIMPLE RANDOM SAMPLING

Following are some of the disadvantages associated with simple random sampling.

1.   Simple random sampling plans do not necessarily fully exploit the knowledge the researcher has concerning the population. He may have access to information about the population that could make the resulting sample drawn *more representative* than otherwise would be the case. Representativeness in this instance is in relation to certain specified characteristics of the population such as proportion of males and females, proportion of old and young, proportion of redheads, blondes, and brunettes, and so on.

Perhaps the researcher has access to personal records of students in a high school conselor's office. The records include information that would be of significant value to the investigator's research. But the records show that only a small minority of students possess such information. If the researcher were to use simple random sampling, the sample would be only theoretically representative of the population. And theoretical representativeness is always subject to question, particularly if the researcher knows a great deal about the population he is investigating. Using a simple random sampling plan would not guarantee that a small minority of students would be represented in the sample. If the researcher wanted to ensure the representation of such students, then he must employ some alternative random sampling plan such as stratified random sampling to accomplish this task.

2.   Simple random sampling does not guarantee that certain elements existing in small numbers in the population will be included in

any given sample. This is very similar to the first advantage. Suppose in a population of 500 persons, only 10 have trait X. If the researcher wanted to have some members of the population included in his sample who possess trait X, the chances are very slim that such individuals would be drawn. The class of seniors in a college might be small enough to make it unlikely that any seniors would be included in a simple random sample of college students there.

3. Another disadvantage is revealed by comparing simple random sampling plans with stratified random sampling plans. It is usually the case that there is greater sampling error in a simple random sample of size n compared to a stratified random sample of the same size. This is because sampling error is based in part on the heterogeneity of the sample drawn. Samples that have been stratified or drawn in accordance with the proportional distribution of some important sample characteristic (proportion of males and females, for example) are at least somewhat typical of the population in terms of that characteristic. And more typical samples are usually increasingly accurate estimates of populations from which they were obtained. Therefore, sampling error is a function of both the size of the sample selected and the representativeness of that sample in reference to some set of important population characteristics previously specified.

One conclusion that may be drawn is that the more that is known concerning the characteristics of a given population and the extent to which that knowledge enables the researcher to draw a more representative sample from it, the less will be the sampling error associated with the resulting sample.

SOME SUGGESTED APPLICATIONS OF SIMPLE RANDOM SAMPLING

Simple random sampling is useful for obtaining a probability sample from virtually any source. It may be used in obtaining random samples from city directories, census tracts, geographical divisions of various territories, schools, prisons, communities, businesses and industrial organizations, political districts, and telephone directories, to mention a few. It may also be used for assignment of elements randomly to different experimental conditions in psychological and social psychological experiments. Because all forms of probability sampling must employ simple random sampling at various levels and stages, this sampling form is indispensable.

SOME QUESTIONS ABOUT USING SIMPLE RANDOM SAMPLES

One issue frequently raised about simple random sampling (and all probability sampling, for that matter) is what Kaplan (1964) refers to as the *paradox of sampling.* For the sample to be useful in generalizing to the population from which it was drawn, it must be representative of the population. Because it is impossible to know for sure if the sample is ever fully representative of the population unless the true population distribution and its characteristics are known, a paradox of sampling is found. If the true population distribution and characteristics *are* known, then there is no need for sampling. There is no way except by studying the entire population that the investigator can know that his sample is truly representative of the population from which it is drawn. He evaluates the representativeness of his sample partially on the basis of the size of the sampling error, which is made up of the standard deviation[8] and sample size. The standard deviation is principally affected by how the sample was drawn initially. Simple random sampling, in theory, reduces the amount of sampling error as the sample size increases. And so the paradox is partially resolved by the method of sampling employed by the researcher and by how large the sampling unit (sample size) becomes.

PROPORTIONATE STRATIFIED RANDOM SAMPLING

Whenever the investigator possesses some knowledge concerning the population under study (e.g., he knows the age and sex distribution of all members of the population), he may wish to use a proportionate stratified random sampling plan. Such a plan is useful for obtaining a sample that will have specified characteristics in exact proportion to the way in which those same characteristics are distributed in the population. A simple example will illustrate this type of sampling plan.

Consider a population of students at a small college. The investigator wants to obtain a proportionate stratified random sample of them, stratifying according to year in school. (Whenever the investigator wants to take one characteristic or *k* characteristics into account in his sample, he is said to *stratify according to this one, or to these, k characteristics*). Suppose the students at this college are originally distributed accordingly as is shown in Table 8-1. The researcher decides that he wants a sample of size 100. Stratifying according to year in school and maintaining the same proportionate balance in the sample as occurs in the population will give him the sample composition as

Table 8-1. A Distribution of 1,000 Students According to Year in School

Year	Composition of Population	Proportion of Each Class
Freshmen	$N_1 =$ 400	0.40
Sophomores	$N_2 =$ 300	0.30
Juniors	$N_3 =$ 200	0.20
Seniors	$N_4 =$ 100	0.10
	$N_T =$ 1,000	1.00

shown in Table 8-2. The researcher determines the compositions of the sample taking each proportion of the stratifying characteristic in the population and multiplying it by the desired sample size. For example, to determine how many freshmen should be included in the sample, he multiplies 100, the desired sample size, by 0.40, the proportion of freshmen in the population, or

$$(100)(0.40) = 40.$$

Therefore, he must include 40 freshmen in his sample. This procedure is repeated for each subcategory on the stratifying characteristic, as illustrated below:

$$\text{Freshmen in sample} = (100)(0.40) = 40$$
$$\text{Sophomores in sample} = (100)(0.30) = 30$$
$$\text{Juniors in sample} = (100)(0.20) = 20$$
$$\text{Seniors in sample} = (100)(0.10) = 10$$
$$\Sigma n = 100$$

Table 8-2. A Proportionate Breakdown of a Sample of 100 Students

Year	Composition of Sample	Proportion of Each Class
Freshmen	$n_1 =$ 40	0.40
Sophomores	$n_2 =$ 30	0.30
Juniors	$n_3 =$ 20	0.20
Seniors	$n_4 =$ 10	0.10
	$n_T =$ 100	1.00

Each of the subcategories on the stratifying characteristic is treated as individual "population" totals. The researcher merely uses simple random sampling for drawing the desired number of elements from each subcategory. Because there are 400 freshmen in the first category and the investigator needs 40 freshmen from this category in his sample, he numbers the freshmen from 1 to 400, uses a table of random numbers of other appropriate means, and obtains 40 different elements from this subpopulation. The same procedure is followed for each of the other subcategories. Finally, each of the simple random samples of freshmen, sophomores, juniors, and seniors is combined with the others into the resulting *proportionate stratified random sample* of college students.

More complex proportionate stratified random sampling is illustrated by the example in Table 8-3. In this table the investigator has stratified the original population of 1,700 boys according to delin-

Table 8-3.   A Population Stratified According to Three Characteristics

			Child Delinquent **(First Characteristic)**					
			Yes		*No*			
			Age **(Second Characteristic)**					
Over 13		*Under 13*		*Over 13*		*Under 13*		
			Mother in Home **(Third Characteristic)**					
Yes	*No*	*Yes*	*No*	*Yes*	*No*	*Yes*	*No*	
f^a = 150	250	400	100	150	150	300	200	N = 1700
P^b = 0.09	0.15	0.24	0.06	0.09	0.09	0.18	0.12	= 1.02^c
1	2	3	4	5	6	7	8	
			(Category)					

[a] f = frequencies (elements) in each category.

[b] P = proportion of frequencies (elements) in each category.

[c] The proportion, P, exceeds 1.00 owing to rounding of proportions under each subcategory. Assumes rounding in direction of nearest *even* number.

quency, age and whether the boys have mothers in the home. Category 6 consists of 150 boys who are not delinquent, who are over thirteen, and who do not have mothers at home.

To draw a proportionate stratified random sample from this population we follow the same procedure as was illustrated in the previous example. The researcher determines the proportion of each subcategory to the total population, or, $150/1700 = 0.09$, $250/1700 = 0.15 = 0.24$, and so on. These proportions are illustrated for each of the eight subcategories in Table 8-3.

Next, the researcher determines the desired size of the sample, let's say 200. Because he wants the sample proportionately stratified according to those three characteristics (i.e., delinquency, age, and mother in home), he needs to have elements represented in the sample according to how they are proportionately distributed in the population. He must multiply each proportion by the desired sample size, or

	Category
$(200) (0.09) = 18$	1
$(200) (0.15) = 30$	2
$(200) (0.24) = 48$	3
$(200) (0.06) = 12$	4
$(200) (0.09) = 18$	5
$(200) (0.09) = 18$	6
$(200) (0.18) = 36$	7
$(200) (0.12) = 24$	8

$$N_T = 204 \text{ elements}$$

His sample will consist of 204 elements proportionately stratified according to the three characteristics identified in the original population.[7]

ADVANTAGES OF PROPORTIONATE STRATIFIED RANDOM SAMPLING PLANS

The primary advantages associated with proportionate stratified random sampling plans are:

1. Proportionately stratifying the sample enhances the representativeness of it in relation to the population. The representativeness is strengthened by making certain that those elements that exist in few numbers will be included accordingly. This is not necessarily guaranteed under the simple random sampling plan. It should be

noted, however, that where extremely large samples are drawn, stratifying the sample will make little difference to the representativeness compared with simple random sampling. Obviously, the larger the sample becomes, the more representative it is of the entire population, simply because of sheer numbers. Such is the value of large samples.

2. The resulting sample is actually a better estimate of what the true population characteristics are compared with a simple random sample. This fact derives from the first advantage noted above.

3. Another important advantage is that the sampling error associated with the sample as a population estimator is reduced over that found to occur with a simple random sample of the same size. In this sense, proportionate stratified random samples are more efficient than simple random sampling, where increased efficiency is a function of decreasing the sampling error.

4. This type of sampling plan eliminates the necessity of having to weight the elements according to their original distribution in the population. The weight of any particular value is the frequency of it in the population. And because the sample is proportionately stratified according to several salient characteristics, it is said that the sample is already weighted. Each subsample within the sample we draw is said to be weighted in accordance with the frequency with which it exists proportionately in the parent population.

Suppose we have a sample of 100 elements consisting of 60 males and 40 females. If, in fact, the parent population is distributed in the same manner, (i.e., 60 per cent male and 40 per cent female), and if the sample is randomly drawn, then it is said to be representative of the population and stratified proportionately according to sex. If we were to compute a mean age for the total sample, it would reflect a greater weight from the male representation. In effect, this would amount to summing all persons' ages and dividing by the sample size, 100. This would not be mathematically equivalent to summing males' ages and females' ages separately, dividing each sum by its respective subsample size, summing the resulting means ($\bar{X}$'s) and dividing by 2 (the number of subsamples). Weighted and unweighted computations with some hypothetical data are illustrated in Table 8-4. The weighted average age (taking into account male and female proportionate representation in the sample) is 26, whereas the unweighted average age (treating each mean as though males and females were represented equally) is 25. This is a small difference, but in many cases, averaging means with different N's while not taking into account

Table 8-4. Weighted and Unweighted Average Computations for Some Hypothetical Data.

	Weighted Average Age		Unweighted Average Age
N_i	$\bar{X}_i$	$(N_i\bar{X}_i)$	$\bar{X}_i$
$N_1 = 60$ (Males)	$\bar{X}_1 = 30$	$(60)(30) = 1800$	$\bar{X}_1 = 30$
$N_2 = 40$	$\bar{X}_2 = 20$	$(40)(20) = \;\;800$	$\bar{X}_2 = 20$
		$\Sigma(N_i\bar{X}_i) = 2600$	$\Sigma\bar{X}_i = 50$

$$\frac{(N_i\bar{X}_i)}{N_1 + N_2} = \frac{2600}{60 + 40} = 26 \qquad \frac{\Sigma\bar{X}_i}{2} = \frac{50}{2} = 25$$

those different N's (treating each mean as though it were represented equally) will make a considerable difference and will often result in erroneous and misleading information. The true mean of the sample is 26, and this operation is equivalent to summing all persons' ages and dividing by the total N.

DISADVANTAGES OF PROPORTIONATE STRATIFIED RANDOM SAMPLING

Some of the more important disadvantages of this sampling method are:

1. Proportionate sampling is somewhat more difficult to obtain. It requires that the researcher know something of the composition of the population and distribution of population characteristics prior to the draw of the elements. This is often an unrealistic assumption. Simple random sampling avoids this problem, but it may not provide us with as representative a sample in the long run.

2. This method involves more time to obtain elements from each of several strata. But the reduction of sampling error compared to simple random sampling plans possibly offsets the additional work required to obtain the proportionate stratified random sample.

3. When several strata must be identified, there is always the likeli-

hood that classification errors might result. Classification errors refer to categorizing elements in the population in such a way as to put them into the wrong strata. This may lead to an erroneous interpretation of one's results in the final random sample. The researcher must exercise extreme care in setting up his categories for classification initially, and then he should be very careful that the elements he assigns to various categories really belong there.

RECOMMENDED APPLICATIONS OF THIS SAMPLING FORM

Because of the additional time involved in drawing the sample and the potential difficulties that arise in designing proper classifications of elements, the researcher should apply this sampling plan only when it is essential that specific population characteristics be included. Applications where it might be warranted include school systems where year in school, academic major, age or sex would be important. Military studies might successfully employ this sampling plan where military rank, special assignment and the like would theoretically affect other variables in the research project.

It is possible to stratify according to attitudinal characteristics regarded as important by the researcher. Again, the investigator must know a considerable amount about the population studied. Including southern and northern people in a study of racial prejudice and discrimination could conceivably cover individuals reflecting various attitudinal positions. Because attitudes are even less empirical than age and year in school variables, the investigator runs the risk of misclassification and most of the other pitfalls associated with the reliability and validity of attitudinal measures. (For a discussion of some of the important issues pertaining to reliability and validity, see Chapter 6).

SOME QUESTIONS ABOUT PROPORTIONATE STRATIFIED RANDOM SAMPLING

Perhaps the most important question raised concerning proportionate stratified random sampling plans is: Which variables or characteristics should be stratified? Similarly: Which dimensions are the most significant ones for any given study? There is an infinite number of population characteristics for any collection of elements, and the researcher is often in a dilemma as to which dimensions to stratify. If he stratifies on too many dimensions, he will seriously reduce the size of the subpopulations in each substratum. Consider stratifying on 10 characteristics for a sample of 100. By the time the researcher has completed the stratification of his elements, it is quite likely that some of the categories will have no elements in them, simply because few if any elements will be able to fit specific 10-dimensional categorizations.

Determining how many dimensions to stratify is up to the individual researcher. He uses his theory as a basis for making such decisions in the final analysis. Without employing theory, his decisions for stratifying certain dimensions become almost purely arbitrary.

It has been said that stratified random sampling will reduce sampling error over simple random sampling plans. It is possible, however, for the reverse of this situation to occur. In the event that the investigator selects inappropriate or irrelevant dimensions to stratify in the population, he may actually increase the bias of the resulting sample, thereby increasing the sampling error associated with it. The selection of characteristics to stratify is theoretically based, in part, and to an extent, subjective.

Stratified random sampling plans are usually more costly than simple random sampling plans. A second question concerns the relative costs of both types of plans in relation to the additional information obtained through the stratification of certain dimensions. No hard and fast rules exist for drawing lines as to when to stratify and when not to stratify. But the researcher is guided in terms of how much sampling error is to be risked and the extent to which it is important to guarantee the inclusion of elements manifesting certain traits theoretically relevant to solving the investigator's research problems.

DISPROPORTIONATE STRATIFIED RANDOM SAMPLING:

Disproportionate stratified random sampling involves essentially the same ideas that are associated with proportionate stratified random sampling plans. The basic difference is that the substrata of the resulting sample are not necessarily distributed according to their proportionate weight in the population from which they were drawn. It may be that some substrata are overrepresented while other substrata are underrepresented.

Using socioeconomic status (SES) as an example, suppose the researcher divides a given population into six substrata, using the SES labels of *upper-upper class, lower-upper class, upper-middle class, lower-middle class, upper-lower class,* and *lower-lower class* for each of the substrata. Assume that the following percentage breakdown pertaining to the distribution of elements among the various substrata is observed:

Class	Percentage
Upper-upper class	15%
Lower-upper class	10%
Upper-middle class	20%
Lower-middle class	20%
Upper-lower class	10%
Lower-lower class	25%
Total =	100%

Should the researcher wish to draw a disproportionate stratified random sample from this population, stratified according to SES, he may elect to make his sample consist of six equal parts, each part or ⅙th taken from each of the substrata. This means that if he wants a sample of size 60, then he must draw 10 elements from each of the substrata. One-sixth is equal to 16.67 per cent, and it is therefore apparent that he will undersample from the upper-middle, lower-middle, and lower-lower classes, while at the same time he will oversample from the upper-upper, lower-upper, and upper-lower classes.

Sampling disproportionately means that either (1) the researcher will give equal weight to each of the substrata, or (2) he will give greater weight to some substrata and not enough weight to other substrata in accordance with their disproportionate distribution in the population.

From the example above, we have seen that it is possible to divide the population according to k categories on some variable, then divide the sample equally throughout k categories, or n/k. In the case of SES, the population size was k divided according to k categories. In determining the size of each subsample for each stratum, the researcher merely employed the formula,

$$n/k$$

where n = the sample size, and
   k = the number of categories on the stratified variable.

This gives equal weight to each subclass on the stratified variable, regardless of whether or not the sample distribution and population distribution on that stratified variable were identical.

Another way of sampling disproportionately would be to take a great number of elements from one substratum compared with the proportion of elements drawn from the other substrata. If there are too few elements included in some substratum in the population, the researcher may simply elect to use all elements from that particular substratum. In effect, this is attaching greater weight to some substratum compared with its original contribution in the population distribution. In a study of military attitudes, it may be that there are so few generals in the population of military personnel that the investigator decides to use all generals in his sample, while taking a smaller proportion of other ranks to make up the total composition of it. Using a tabular example, consider the data in Table 8-5. The researcher may decide to use a proportionate stratified random sample stratified according to type of crime. But he notes that only 1 per cent of his population consists of aggravated assault cases. He decides to use all aggravated assault cases in his final sample. His sample becomes a disproportionate one at that point. If his resulting sample size is 100, then by using all 10 aggravated assault cases, he makes their contribution to the sample 10 per cent instead of their original population representation of 1 per cent. In effect, this is giving greater weight to the aggravated assault cases than to the other crime classifications.

Table 8-5. The Distribution of Crimes for Population A

Type of Crime	Frequency	Percentage Represented in Population
Forcible rape	50	5%
Burglary	100	10%
Auto Theft	500	50%
Aggravated assault	10	1%
Larceny	140	14%
Robbery	150	15%
Homicide	50	5%
Totals	$N = 1,000$	100%

ADVANTAGES OF DISPROPORTIONATE STRATIFIED RANDOM SAMPLING

The major advantages of this sampling method are:

1. It is less time consuming compared with proportionate stratified random sampling. The researcher is not necessarily as concerned

about the proportionate representativeness of his resulting sample compared with the proportionate stratified random sampling situation. He does not have to be as careful in drawing specified numbers of elements from each of the substrata he identifies.

2.   Weighting of particular groups of elements is more likely with this sampling form. The investigator is able to give greater weight to certain elements that are not represented as frequently in the population compared with other elements. Weighting is a means of making certain some substrata are more comparable with other substrata, particularly if there is a considerable proportionate difference between various substrata in the original population.

DISADVANTAGES OF DISPROPORTIONATE STRATIFIED RANDOM SAMPLING

The major disadvantages of this sampling method are:

1.   The method does not give each substratum proper representation relative to its distribution throughout the original population. When some substrata are represented more heavily than others, a certain amount of bias enters. The assignment of greater weight to one set of elements in a particular substratum may cause the sample to become more biased, and hence, less representative.

2.   This sampling method requires that the researcher know the composition of the original population. This disadvantage is the same as that for the proportionate stratified sampling case. It is not often likely that the investigator will have a great deal of familiarity with the population he studies. If he conducts a community study of some kind, he may not be fully aware of the SES distribution of elements throughout the community. If he chooses to stratify according to SES, he finds the classification procedure a tedious one compared with the simple random sampling method. The various elements must be identified and judged as belonging to a particular SES stratum.

3.   In close connection with disadvantage 2 above, stratification of any kind implies the possibility of classification errors. It is possible that the researcher may misclassify certain elements (e.g., he may conclude, in stratifying according to six SES strata, that element A belongs to SES stratum 4, when in fact element A belongs in SES stratum 3.) Simple random sampling can overcome the hazards of classification, however, and the resulting sample will become increasingly representative as it becomes larger. Again, stratification of any kind should be done only if the investigator has considerable knowledge about the population he studies and can assume that there will be little likelihood of error in subsequent classification of the elements.

SOME APPLICATIONS

The primary use of disproportionate stratified random sampling in research design is when elements exist few in number among certain substrata within the dimension one stratifies. If there is a strong likelihood that one or more substrata will not be included in a simple random sample of elements (i.e., some substrata exist in so few numbers that it is quite likely that elements from those substrata will not be drawn), then the researcher should take steps to see that elements from those particular substrata will be included. This detracts from the randomness of the draw, however, and to that extent is less a probability sample than before. The researcher exercises his judgment as to whether the particular substratum is important enough so that steps should be taken to ensure that elements from it are included in the subsequent sample.

When the population under investigation can be stratified according to some characteristic with which the investigator has some familiarity, it is usually amenable to disproportionate stratified random sampling. Again, the primary criterion for determining whether the sample should be stratified is the theoretical importance of the stratifying characteristic.

SOME QUESTIONS ABOUT THE APPLICABILITY OF DISPROPORTIONATE STRATIFIED RANDOM SAMPLING

The major questions about proper application of this sampling technique are concerned with: (1) What are the significant dimensions for stratification, and (2) Are the elements that are disproportionately represented in some substrata randomly selected? The theoretical scheme of the investigator is of primary importance in determining whether to stratify. And in addition his theory helps to identify salient dimensions that should be taken into account more precisely. If the investigator is planning to draw a very large sample from the population, there is little to recommend any kind of stratified random sampling plan except the possibility that certain dimensions should be taken into account by virtue of their theoretical importance and relevance to the problem under investigation. If such is not the case, a simple random sampling plan will be a perfectly acceptable alternative that is considerably easier to apply in the long run and just as valid.

AREA OR CLUSTER SAMPLING

Area or cluster sampling as a probability sampling plan has its origin in agriculture. Farming experiments conducted to determine the effect of various kinds of fertilizers and soil conditioners, soil treatments, and a variety of planting methods on crop yield stimulated the application of a sampling technique that would take into account random areas of crops. A specified acreage would be divided into sections according to a number of vertical and horizontal grid lines drawn across the total area. An example of a geographical area divided into sections is shown in Figure 8-1. The different sections could be numbered and selected at random from a random numbers table. In this way, the investigator could control for possible variability in soil quality even within the same geographical area. Once the sample of sections was selected randomly, the researcher could determine crop yield for the combined sample of sections and compare it with crop yield for another sample of sections taken from another area subjected to different soil treatment conditions.

Social science applications of this sampling method have been extensive, particularly in survey designs in field research and demographic and ecological studies. Geographical divisions are made on a

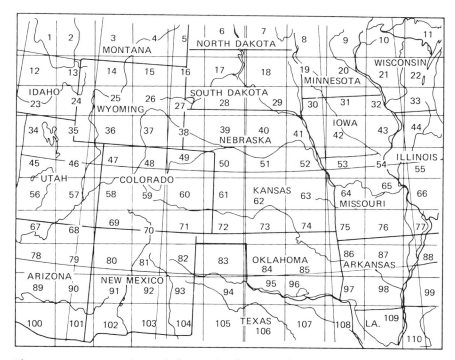

Figure 8-1. A section of the United States showing vertical and horizontal grids or sections. (Each section is numbered from 1 to 110.)

map (of a territory, community, neighborhood, group of city blocks, and so on), the sections are numbered, and a certain number of them are drawn at random and designated as the sample. The investigator proceeds to interview all elements living within a particular section. The section may be a city block, a cluster of homes in a farming region, and the like. Hence, the term *cluster sampling* has been applied to this sampling method.

Suppose the investigator were to study political attitudes of residents in a given state. It would not be feasible to study all persons, not only from the standpoint of the cost involved and the manpower requirements for field interviewing, but also because a sample of state residents would probably give us comparable information. If much of the state is farm area, the prospect of interviewing a random sample of residents would still prove difficult. Interviewers would have to travel great distances between interviews, and the time factor alone would be enough to discourage any sampling plan we have discussed in this section so far. The researcher decides to employ an *area* or *areal sampling plan.*

He divides the state into sections with several horizontal and vertical grid lines. He then numbers each section from 1 to *N*, *N* being equal to the total number of sections. Using a random numbers table, he draws a specified number of sections to constitute the sample he will study. He sends interviewers to study all persons or families living in the sections he has randomly drawn. One section may include five farm families. Another section may include 50 families. All families clustered in a given section are interviewed and included in his final data compilation.

If the sections selected contain an extremely large number of families (one section may have included a block of tenements in downtown New York City), the researcher may draw another random set of sections from the originally drawn sections. He does this by subdividing each original randomly selected section as he did at the outset and then drawing a random number of sections from the first ones. Each time he subdivides sections drawn and samples from them, the samples that result are referred to as second-stage units, third-stage units, fourth-stage units, and so on. Seldom does the researcher continue to sample past the third stage. This process is generally called *multistage sampling.* An example of this sampling method is illustrated in Figure 8-2.

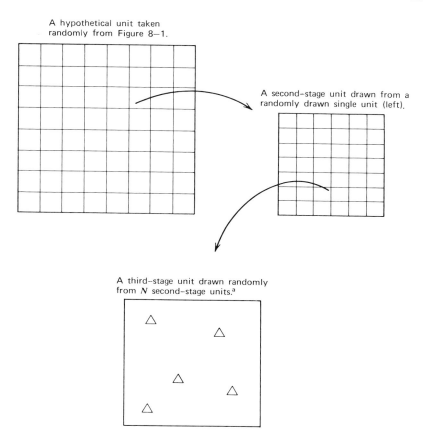

A hypothetical unit taken randomly from Figure 8–1.

A second-stage unit drawn from a randomly drawn single unit (left).

A third-stage unit drawn randomly from *N* second-stage units.[a]

[a] △ = a farm home or other dwelling unit within a third-stage unit.

Figure 8-2. Multistage sampling (cluster or area sampling). △ = a farm house or other dwelling unit within a third-stage unit.

SOME ADVANTAGES OF AREA SAMPLING

The primary advantages of this sampling method are:

1. Area sampling is much easier to apply when large populations are studied or when large geographical areas must be canvassed. It is easier in the sense that the researcher does not need to have predetermined lists of individuals inhabiting a given area. He simply draws a

random number of geographical sections, and then he interviews all residents living within the boundaries of the random section. When all residents have been interviewed from each randomly drawn section, the result is referred to as a probability sample. In this sense, area sampling is easier to apply than simple random sampling or any other variation previously discussed. It should be noted that to obtain the various sections at random, the investigator must use a random numbers table or other comparable method. This procedure introduces the control of randomness.

2.   The cost of area sampling is much less compared with other sampling methods previously discussed. Interviewers can concentrate their efforts in specific regions, and consequently they save time and money by not having to travel great distances to interview specific individuals living at random points in a geographical area.

3.   Another advantage of area sampling is that respondents can be readily substituted for other respondents within the same random section. Clusters of elements are sampled, and not individuals. Otherwise, the matter of substituting elements would be a sensitive one compared with the other random sampling techniques.

4.   If field research crews are located at different places throughout the state, cluster or area sampling facilitates their contacting various elements within a specified area. In this sense, area sampling is more helpful than the other sampling plans.

5.   Another advantage of this sampling is flexibility. In a multistage area sampling design it is possible to employ different forms of sampling in several successive stages. For example, the investigator may draw several sections randomly in the first stage, but he may decide to stratify each of the first-stage units and select sections from certain strata to make up the second-stage units. He may even employ a third type of sampling plan (including a nonprobability sampling plan) in the third and fourth stages. This does raise certain questions about the probability nature of the resulting sample, however. The extent to which the final sample is a random one will, of course, depend on the type of sampling employed at each stage.

6.   A sixth advantage of this sampling method is that it is possible to estimate the characteristics of clusters of elements drawn. Again, this derives from the fact that the sample, consisting of several clusters of elements, is a probability sample and hence is generalizable to other sections from which it was obtained.

SOME DISADVANTAGES OF AREA SAMPLING

The major disadvantages of cluster or area sampling are:

1. There is no way to ensure that each sampling unit included in an area sample will be of equal size. The researcher has little control over the size of each cluster. This variation in the uniformity of cluster sizes could increase the bias of the resulting sample. If the researcher were to interview all adults living in each section he draws randomly, one section may include either no families or one family, whereas another section might be in downtown Chicago. There would be a certain bias resulting from the heavy inclusion of city dwellers.

2. There is greater sampling error associated with area sampling plans. This assumes that sample size remains constant for both area sampling and the other probability sampling plans with which it is compared. Because of this factor, in part, area samples are less efficient than the other probability sampling methods.

3. It is also difficult to ensure that individuals included in one cluster are independent of other randomly drawn clusters. Perhaps an individual is interviewed in one cluster, and the next morning he travels to an area that falls within another randomly selected section. He is interviewed again, this time by a different interviewer. There is little that can be done to prevent this type of thing from happening except to interview all elements throughout all clusters simultaneously. If this were done, the probability of including the same individual several times would be very small.

SOME RECOMMENDED APPLICATIONS

Area sampling serves many functions. Public opinion polls are frequently conducted using an area sampling plan. Surveys of farming regions or areas that are sparsely populated and cover extensive geographical sections are more easily conducted employing this sampling form.

When lists of specific individuals are unobtainable or are inaccessible, area sampling is again recommended. Not being able to identify the elements to be interviewed in any other type of random sampling plan makes it mandatory that area sampling be employed. Area sampling should not necessarily be confined to extremely large geographical regions. This method is frequently applied to city blocks or urban territories. Peatman (1947) refers to applications as *extensive* (where area sampling would be employed for an area on the scale of the United States), and *intensive* (where the scale would be considerably smaller, an example being a city block, neighborhood, or city enumeration district).

Large scale surveys of political and social behavior would also be amenable to area sampling. The sampling method also has an advantage for the researcher on a limited budget. It is much less expensive compared with the other techniques of probability sampling.

SOME QUESTIONS ABOUT AREA SAMPLING

Perhaps the most important question raised concerning area sampling is whether this sampling method conforms to probability sampling plans. This question becomes quite critical when multistage sampling is done using different sampling methods at successive stages. The investigator could use random sampling in deriving a specified number of first-stage units, but he may employ a judgmental sampling procedure (to be discussed in a later section) to obtain successive units in the second and third stages.

The fact that, case for case, area sampling plans are subject to greater sampling error means that the researcher must make a decision as to which plan would result in the greater loss—the increase in sampling error for less money, or the increased expenditure of funds to employ a different sampling method with less sampling error. One criterion for making this decision is what the investigator intends to do with the information once he obtains it.

MAJOR NONPROBABILITY SAMPLING PLANS

Many types of research designs do not require that random samples be drawn. Rather, the investigator may be interested only in obtaining a sufficient number of elements to satisfy limited research objectives. The researcher may wish to test the reliability of some attitudinal measuring instrument he has developed. It is probably not necessary to go to the trouble of obtaining a random sample for this purpose. In this instance, a classroom of students or a haphazard selection of people off the street may be sufficient. Or perhaps the researcher would like to gain a general impression of the characteristics of people in a given neighborhood or other geographical area. Conducting an exploratory study of some kind could also make it unnecessary to have a random sample.

The general objective of nonprobability sampling plans is to gain a rough impression of a collection of elements. Such sampling plans can lay the groundwork for a subsequent, more sophisticated probability sampling form. The possibility exists that when an investigator confronts a particular population for the first time, little information is readily available about it. The simplicity and rapidity of nonprobability sampling enables the investigator to learn about the population to the extent that he will be able to use a more sophisticated sampling plan subsequently. As more becomes known about the characteristics of a particular population, the investigator is in a better position to obtain a proportionate stratified random sample or something comparable to it.

The primary difference between a probability sample and a nonprobability sample is that the former sampling method uses randomness as a primary statistical control, whereas the latter sampling form does not. Therefore, the findings based on probability samples are usually generalizable to similar populations from which the sample was drawn, and the amount of sampling error can be readily determined. It is difficult to determine the amount of sampling error for nonprobability samples, however, and the researcher cannot legitimately generalize his findings to any larger population. This is because the population remains largely unidentified with any or all nonprobability sampling plan variations.

SYSTEMATIC SAMPLING

A sampling plan having certain characteristics of randomness and at the same time possessing some nonprobability traits is a systematic sampling plan. *Systematic sampling* is defined as obtaining a collection of elements by drawing every *n*th person from a predetermined list of them. Drawing every tenth name from the city directory or telephone book is systematic sampling. Standing in front of a store and asking certain questions of every twenty-ninth individual entering the store would also be called systematic sampling, although this particular use of this sampling method is not recommended.

In a study of change orientations among the middle class in a Latin American country, Williamson (1968) used systematic sampling to obtain 229 residents of Bogata, Columbia. In his research, every fifth house was chosen on representative streets of each selected area.

The application of the label "systematic sampling" to samples drawn in this fashion is somewhat misleading. For it is true that all probability sampling plans are *also* systematic sampling methods. Therefore, it often sounds as though systematic sampling ought to be included under the general classification of probability sampling. In reality, it should not.

ADVANTAGES OF SYSTEMATIC SAMPLING

The major advantages of systematic sampling are:

1. Systematic sampling is easy to use. It is much simpler than having to employ a random numbers table in the selection of all elements.

2. Because it is a nonprobability sampling method, mistakes in drawing elements are relatively unimportant. That is, should the investigator miscount and draw the eleventh element from a list instead of the tenth element, his sample will not be seriously affected.

3. Systematic sampling makes it easier to check to see that every nth individual has been included. It is easy to spot mistakes as a result of miscounting.

4. Systematic sampling is a rapid method of obtaining a sample of elements. If the researcher is in a hurry or is working on a limited time schedule, the systematic sampling form eliminates several steps otherwise taken in any probability sampling situation.

DISADVANTAGES OF SYSTEMATIC SAMPLING

The primary disadvantages of systematic sampling are:

1. Systematic sampling ignores all persons between every nth element chosen. Because it excludes certain elements from the resulting sample, it is not a probability sampling form. The initial starting place in a list of elements is usually determined by picking a number from a random numbers table. From this standpoint, the first element selected is a random one, but from there on the successive draws of other elements are fixed. This is why it is said that systematic sampling has characteristics of both probability and nonprobability sampling.

Occasionally the investigator will select a different number from the random numbers table after he draws a certain number of elements. For example, suppose he selects the number 8 from the random numbers table. He uses this number to select every eighth person from a list. After selecting 50 elements by using this number, he draws a different number from the random numbers table, this time 4. Now, he selects every fourth element from the continuing list of elements. He does this until he obtains another 50 elements. Selecting a third number from the random numbers table, he continues from there, until he exhausts the list or obtains the desired number of elements required by his particular research design. The only thing this variation of systematic sampling accomplishes is to increase the number of randomly selected elements by the *quantity* of different numbers used to draw the sample. It is still the case that all elements between every *n*th element are systematically excluded.

2. Another disadvantage depends on whether the list of elements is arranged in some particular order. If the list increases or decreases with respect to some trait (e.g., age, years of education, and so on), a certain amount of bias will be found. More individuals will be drawn systematically from those groups represented most frequently on the list. There will be a systematic increase in the variability of the sample which, by definition, will tend to increase the potential sampling error.

3. Blalock (1972: 514–515) suggests a third disadvantage of systematic sampling. He indicates that if lists of individuals are alphabetized, some bias will result pertaining to overrepresentation or underrepresentation of certain ethnic groups. Names beginning with Mc, for example, will tend to be overrepresented, whereas certain oriental names will be systematically excluded or underrepresented.

4. Because each element does not have an equal chance of being included, the sample obtained is not a random one. For some research designs and specific research objectives, this disadvantage could be an important one. When this form of sampling is employed, however, the investigator is usually aware of its limitations and weaknesses as have been mentioned here.

SOME POSSIBLE APPLICATIONS

There is an infinite number of applications of systematic sampling. Obtaining elements systematically from a list of labor union members, elementary and secondary school students, college and university students and faculty, city directories, telephone directories, membership lists for virtually all types of special interest groups and organizations, employees of companies and businesses, prisoners in penal institutions, neighborhoods and the like are but a few of the many instances where this sampling form may be applied.

SOME QUESTIONS CONCERNING THIS METHOD

Because systematic sampling includes aspects of both probability and nonprobability sampling, it is likely that some controversy exists with respect to what the researcher can say about populations from which he samples. It has been shown that some of the bias in a systematic sample is overcome by using a series of random starts. This procedure was discussed as a part of the first disadvantage noted above. Technically, this procedure does not make the sample a random one according to the definition provided in the beginning of this chapter.

If it is essential that the investigator have a probability sample of some kind to satisfy that part of his research design, then in all likelihood he will select some sampling method that will be more suitable than systematic sampling. Selecting the appropriate sampling form is again contingent upon what the investigator wishes to do with his data.

THE QUOTA SAMPLE

Quota sampling is defined as obtaining a desired number of elements by selecting those most accessible to the researcher and those that possess certain characteristics of interest to him. The researcher may specify to his interviewers that he wants them to interview a given number of individuals who are black, Catholic, and live in a particular neighborhood. In a high school toward the end of the school year, the student newspaper staff may send reporters among students to contact five seniors each, and to determine their opinions about certain school practices. Seniors are spotted and selected because of the senior sweaters they wear on some designated day. The sample obtained is called a *quota sample*.

Quota sampling sometimes is referred to as "the poor man's proportionate stratified sample" because such samples are geared to ensure that specific elements will be included and represented in a subsequent collection of them. In no way should they be equated with proportionate stratified random sampling plans, however, because the element of randomness is totally lacking.

ADVANTAGES OF QUOTA SAMPLING

The primary advantages of quota sampling are:

1.   This sampling method is considerably less costly than most other sampling methods, probability or nonprobability.

2.   Quota samples are satisfactory when quick, crude results will satisfy the research objectives of the investigator.

3.   Using the quota method can also guarantee the inclusion of certain types of people in the sample. Interviewing a specified number of seniors in the high school noted in the illustration above would ensure that these individuals would be represented.

DISADVANTAGES OF QUOTA SAMPLING

Some of the major disadvantages of quota sampling are:

1.   Quota sampling provides too much opportunity for interviewers

to select the most accessible elements, even their friends. The most accessible elements are not necessarily typical of whatever population they were drawn from.

2.   Because there is no true means of establishing randomness as a primary control, the resulting sample certainly is not a probability sample. The findings, therefore, are not generalizable to any significant extent, because it is not known what the population is like from which the sample was obtained.

3.   Should the investigator attempt to classify the elements he selects through quota sampling, he increases the degree of classification error because of the inherent bias he possesses. He bases his classification of respondents on the way they appear to him, and he has no special knowledge concerning the way they *should* be classified. He is, in a sense, completely ignorant of many relevant variables that otherwise might have been used in classifying them, had he used some probability sampling plan at the outset.

4.   Although it is true that the researcher can control to a certain extent one variable (e.g., race or religious affiliation), he is unable to control other variables that may have theoretical significance. This is because he generally does not know a great deal about the population from which he selects his sample.

SOME SELECTED APPLICATIONS

Quota sampling is done primarily because of the convenience and lower cost of collecting information. The quality of the information collected may not be as good as that obtained through some probability sampling method, but it may satisfy some limited research objectives. If the investigator is using a research design that is largely exploratory, then quota sampling may be an efficient means of gaining a quick impression of things so that a more sophisticated sampling plan can be used later with the same population.

Like systematic sampling, quota sampling can be used to obtain elements from membership lists and virtually any other source that lists individuals (city directories, telephone directories, and so on). Compared with systematic sampling, however, quota sampling enables the investigator to introduce a few controls into his research. He is able to select people who appear to possess certain traits, such as race, SES, or some occupational characteristic. There is probably little difference in the variability associated with both types of samples. It is generally expected that systematic sampling and quota sampling will have greater variability than probability sampling forms.

SOME QUESTIONS ABOUT THE APPLICATION OF THIS METHOD

Do the convenience and economy of quota samples justify their use when one considers the limited utility of the resulting sample? This question is difficult to answer, and it is particularly difficult to provide a blanket generalization here. For many types of research objectives a quota sample is sufficient and quite adequate. Whatever answer is provided here must be couched in terms of what the investigator intends to do with the sample he obtains. What is his immediate objective and what kind of sample is required to satisfy his research goal? Before this method can be judged as good or bad, appropriate or inappropriate, we must answer these kinds of questions.

ACCIDENTAL SAMPLES

Accidental samples are identical to quota samples with the following exception. Whereas quota samples attempt to include people possessing apparent social characteristics, accidental samples make no such attempt. The investigator is guided principally by convenience and economy. He does not care about including people with specific traits. He takes what he can find and is content with it. Because this is the most crude sampling method he can employ, he is obviously aware that little or nothing can be generalized from a sample obtained in this manner. He may be interested in getting people's impressions of a questionnaire he is developing. Consequently, he asks his accidental respondents to criticize the questionnaire in terms of wording, length, readability, and so forth.

The wandering reporter on the street stopping particular individuals practices accidental sampling when he asks passersby about certain television programs, commercial products, and the like.

The advantages of this technique are primarily *convenience and economy*. The disadvantages include limited generalizability, much bias (arising from the researcher's interests and subjectivity, but also from obtaining respondents in a business locality or store area that many people do not frequent), and no evidence of a probability sample. Comparing this technique with other sampling methods will certainly suggest other limitations as well.

JUDGMENTAL OR PURPOSIVE SAMPLING

A *purposive sample* is one that has been handpicked by the investigator to fully ensure that specific elements are included. The high degree of selectivity accompanying this technique supposedly guarantees that all relevant strata will be represented in a given research design. Purposive samples are frequently called *judgmental samples* because the investigator exercises his judgment to include elements that are presumed to be typical of a given population about which he seeks information. He believes that by carefully handpicking certain elements, he will obtain information comparable to that derived from a sample selected according to some probability sampling method.

Perhaps the social researcher wishes to select factory workers to include in a study investigating the relationship between labor turnover and job satisfaction. He feels that labor turnover will be particularly high among workers performing a certain type of job that is generally dissatisfying to them. His attention is focused only on those workers from a special section of the plant. He handpicks a number of employees from that section and studies their job satisfaction and propensity to leave the company for another type of employment. Or perhaps an investigator is studying the impact of automation in an insurance company. He carefully selects individuals from the insurance company who are most likely to be affected by the automation change, and studies them. It is important to note that the researcher assumes the representativeness of his sample by virtue of the fact that he handpicks elements presumed to be typical of the population from which they were drawn.

ADVANTAGES OF JUDGMENTAL SAMPLES

1. Judgmental samples do not involve any random selection process. Consequently, they are somewhat less costly and are more readily accessible to the researcher. Convenience is an additional incentive to employ judgmental samples. In one sense, judgmental samples are similar to quota samples but with the additional care in precisely selecting elements that will satisfy the research objectives more adequately.

2. Purposive sampling guarantees that certain elements will be included that are relevant to the research design. Few probability and nonprobability sampling plans are in a position to do this for the investigator.

DISADVANTAGES OF JUDGMENTAL SAMPLES

1. Regardless of how strongly one believes in the typicality of the sample selected, there is still no way to ensure that the sample is truly random or representative in the probability sense. This constitutes a

serious disadvantage to this sampling method, particularly if the re-searcher wants to generalize with it.

2.   Random samples are more efficient for generalizing compared with judgmental samples. In judgmental sampling, too much emphasis is placed on the ability of the investigator to assess which elements are typical and which are not. This is probably better accomplished by the chance selection method achieved by a table of random numbers or computer determination.

3.   This sampling method perhaps requires more extensive in-formation about the population one studies, compared with other random and nonrandom sampling forms. Once the investigator has selected the cases to be included according to his subjective judgment and assessment, he is in no position to argue that th resulting sample is a probability sample. He assumes that any errors arising from his se-lection method will be minimal, but there is no legitimate reason for arguing this position conclusively. The use of a probability sampling method would strengthen one's position about the generalizability and utility of the sample he draws.

4.   One general disadvantage that pertains to all nonprobability sampling plans is that inferential statistics cannot be used legitimately. Underlying all inferential statistical techniques is the assumption of randomness. Unfortunately, neither this technique nor any other nonprobability sampling plan can claim randomness and satisfy this assumption.

SOME APPLICATIONS OF JUDGMENTAL SAMPLES

We have already briefly illustrated the utility of judgmental samples for situations in the workplant and neighborhoods. Political scientists, public opinion analysts, and economists are interested in using this sampling method to say things about voting behavior, opinions toward political candidates and issues, and socioeconomic conditions by examining a handpicked sample of elements presumed typical of a population.

Psychologists might employ this method for selecting individuals possessing certain attitudinal dispositions for psychological experi-ments. It is possible to use this sampling form in conjunction with the many experimental designs that have been developed for psychological studies. Several of these designs employ randomness as an integral feature, even though the participants or elements were originally judgmentally selected. They would be assigned eventually to random treatment conditions of the investigator's experiment. Finally, such a sampling method would be useful if errors in selecting elements were not very serious for the investigator's research objectives.

A QUESTION ABOUT JUDGMENTAL SAMPLES

An important question is whether the judgmental sample is of greater value to the researcher than some probability sampling plan such as proportionate stratified random sampling. Because randomness is not a primary means of control in the selection of the judgmental sample, it cannot be argued effectively that judgmental sampling plans are probability sampling plans. From this standpoint, the question of randomness and probability would appear to be resolved. There are those who contend, however, that judgmental sampling, if appropriately carried out, is equally effective with certain alternative random sampling forms. This is a subjective argument that is vulnerable to the criticisms we have noted above.

SNOWBALL SAMPLING

For special sampling situations when the researcher is interested in obtaining an impression of informal social relations among individuals, snowball sampling may be applied. *Snowball sampling* is defined as having all individuals in a limited group or organization identify their friends and associates, and having their friends identify their friends and associates, until the researcher observes a constellation of friendships converge into some kind of complete social pattern. This sampling technique is basically sociometric. Some selected behavior is usually used as the basis of contact and association (e.g., lawyer friendships, physician contacts, professor associations, and the like). For example, in a study of the diffusion of medical information among physicians, snowball sampling might be employed to determine how physicians come to use certain medical products such as drugs and other supplies (Coleman, et al., 1957). A pattern of diffusion of information is revealed through snowball sampling. It can locate physician cliques through which information about new drugs circulates. Does the physician read about the new drug in a medical journal or hear about it at a medical convention, and if so, whom does he contact among his physician friends regarding it? How does the information spread among physicians in a given community? Snowball sampling can reveal answers to these types of questions.

ADVANTAGES OF SNOWBALL SAMPLING

1.   Snowball sampling is extremely helpful in studying small social organizations such as small businesses and industries. Worker associational patterns can be delineated by this method, and much information can become available about informal group organization and its impact on formal organizational structure. It has already been mentioned that snowball sampling, primarily a sociometric sampling technique, can be useful in tracing the diffusion of information among professionals of various kinds.

2.   Communication patterns can be uncovered in community organization. Community power and decision making can be studied as a further advantage of this sampling method.

3.   Such a method of sampling is amenable to scientific sampling procedures at various stages such as random numbers usage or computer determination.

DISADVANTAGES OF SNOWBALL SAMPLING

1.   Perhaps the major disadvantage is that snowball sampling does not allow the researcher to use probability statistical methods. Elements included as a part of a sample are not randomly drawn. They are dependent on the subjective choices of the originally selected respondents.

2.   When the sample exceeds certain size limits, the technique is difficult to apply. This method has very limited utility beyond the sociometric function. It becomes quite cumbersome when N is large. Imagine trying to plot the interpersonal relationships among 200 or more individuals. The potential element combinations and cliques would be overwhelming!

SOME APPLICATIONS OF SNOWBALL SAMPLING

This technique is applied primarily to relatively small business and industrial organizations, or to situations where it is expected that N will not exceed 100. Of course, the smaller the organization, the easier it becomes to see informal organization patterns as a result of the sociometric selection process. Studies of social change and diffusion of information among specific segments of social organizations find snowball sampling advantageous to employ.

SATURATION SAMPLING AND DENSE SAMPLING

Coleman (1958–1959) describes two sampling methods that require extensive coverage of the population studied. *Saturation sampling* is not really sampling at all, because it is defined as obtaining all elements in a given population having characteristics of interest to the researcher. Studying all lawyers in a small community would also be called saturation sampling.

Dense sampling is somewhere between simple random sampling and saturation sampling. Increasing the sampling fraction[10] to one-half and taking a majority of respondents with specified traits or characteristics of interest to the researcher would be comparable to dense sampling. As Coleman states, "dense sampling is sampling 'densely.'" If there were 800 students at a small college, for example, a dense sample would consist of 400 to 500 students. This is far beyond what would ordinarily be required of a simple random sample or any other type of probability sampling plan. Such probability sampling plans would require only about one tenth of the population or somewhere in the vicinity of 100 to 200 students.

We have used the word "small" to describe the application of this technique to various kinds of populations. This method is most functional with small population sizes. When the population exceeds 1,000 or more, dense sampling or saturation sampling becomes increasingly costly and extremely cumbersome for even the most patient of researchers.

The cost factor is perhaps the most prohibitive regarding applications of these two techniques. The investigator generally determines whether either of these techniques would be feasible to employ by using certain criteria such as:

1. Whether interviewers will be necessary.
2. The limits of the budget for questionnaires, postage, and other paper supplies.
3. The size of the staff.
4. The time requirements for the study.

If interviewers are required, saturation sampling or dense sampling would not be feasible if the original population is quite large, say in excess of 1,000. For smaller populations, the prospects for using interviewers in such situations are more positive. Proper utilization of these techniques is, in the final analysis, contingent upon the needs and resources of the investigator, and his judgment is crucial in such decisions.

SELECTING AN APPROPRIATE SAMPLING PLAN: A BRIEF REVIEW

Up to now we have examined various sampling methods, considering their respective advantages, disadvantages, and some suggested applications. For inferential work (i.e., when the researcher intends to generalize his findings based on sample observations to larger element aggregates), it is mandatory that the researcher select some probability sampling method. On the other hand, if he is interested in quick results and does not particularly care about generalizing his findings to larger populations, some nonprobability sampling method will probably suffice. Briefly reviewing the criteria the researcher should employ to determine whether to use a probability sampling form, we have:

1. The cost of the proposed research. Each sampling plan requires different expenditures of funds to obtain. Anticipating the cost of getting elements for a subsequent sample will enable the investigator to focus more quickly on an appropriate sampling form, given his immediate financial resources.

2. The extent of knowledge about the population to be studied. How much information is available about a given population to be studied will help to determine which sampling method would be most appropriate. Where little or no information is available (i.e., no lists or directories are available from which sample elements can be obtained), it is difficult to apply several of the probability sampling forms. Exploratory studies often utilize nonprobability sampling plans to gain a better impression of the population they are designed to investigate. As more knowledge about the population is made available through exploratory research and investigating agencies, more sophisticated sampling methods become more feasible to use and are recommended.

3. The size of the population. If the population to be studied is quite large (e.g., the United States population), it is likely that some form of cluster or areal sampling would be appropriate. If the population were very small (e.g., 500 students at a small college), several other types of sampling plans could be used without difficulty.

4. The accessibility of the elements. For some research projects, it makes sense to select elements who are immediately accessible to the researcher and who fit the research objectives. One of the authors studied role change in a bank and was granted permission to interview bank employees experiencing a changeover to computer accounting methods during a one-year period (Champion and Dager,

1967). The accessibility of the bank employees was a major consideration in using them for the sample, in addition to the fact that they provided a suitable testing ground for the hypotheses about role change and the effects of computers on people.

At various stages in their careers, social scientists learn that, for many research projects they conduct, one takes advantage of the situation and interviews available respondents. In other words, one takes what he can get and does the best he can with what he has!

5.   The importance of generalizability. How important is it for the researcher to generalize from his sample findings to some larger population? Assessing one's research objectives from the standpoint of generalizability to larger populations will help to decide which sampling form is best under the circumstances. Of course, a research plan designed to perform an inferential function requires a probability sampling method. Beyond that, the researcher is in the position of choosing a sampling method in accordance with his particular preferences and interests.

Other criteria exist such as the size of one's work staff, whether university or research agency facilities are available (e.g., calculators, computers, counter-sorters, keypunch machines, and the like), the time limitations imposed on the completion of the research project, and so on. At the risk of oversimplification, the question of which sampling plan to use is dependent on what the investigator intends to do with his research and the extent of his physical and financial resources.

LARGE SAMPLES AND SMALL ONES: ON DETERMINING SAMPLE SIZE

How large should the sample be? This question can be answered according to a prescribed list of sampling ideals. For most practical research projects, it is often difficult to satisfy these sampling ideals by offering a predetermined set of blanket generalizations covering all aspects of how one should sample. Frequently, the researcher does things differently, apart from the prescribed rule, because he has to. The limitations of money, facilities, and staff are enough to jar any social scientist into the position of doing the best with what he has, even though it is far from what he would want to do ideally.

To begin with, considerable ambiguity exists concerning how many elements a researcher should obtain to conduct his research appropriately. The terms "large" and "small" are very difficult to define precisely. In fact, no agreement exists currently as to how many elements constitute a large sample and how many elements make up a small one. The neophyte researcher is confronted by statements to the effect that the sample size depends on what a person intends to do with his research and what social use he intends to make of it. Unfortunately, such statements do not enable the investigator to solve his sample size problem. However, they do call attention to the fact that the objectives of his research are critical factors that must be considered in his choice of sample size.

Several rules of thumb exist for estimating how large a sample should be. The most common is the *1/10th rule,* for the lack of a better name. The 1/10th rule states that a researcher should try to obtain 1/10th of the population he studies in his sample. But like most rules of thumb in social research and statistical work, there are numerous exceptions. The *n/N* ratio (known as the "sampling fraction") is recommended to be 1/10th, although for populations that are considered infinite for all practical purposes (e.g., the United States population), *n/N* is considerably smaller than 1/10th. This does not present much of a problem, however, for statisticians can easily illustrate that when a probability sample reaches a certain size, such as 1,000, its efficiency for estimating population parameters is not much different compared with probability samples of 10,000 or even 1,000,000. Therefore, the researcher can manage quite well with a sample representing a considerably smaller proportion of the population than 1/10th.

It is also possible that the investigator could get a sample that represents much more of the population than 1/10th. If the population studied consists of 1,000 physicians in a large city, the researcher may easily obtain a sample of 250 or more, provided it is within his means to do so. The larger the sample selected (according to some probability sampling plan), the less sampling error will be associated with it and the more efficient it becomes at estimating population parameters. *Efficiency* is defined as the extent to which the sample statistics reflect the true population parameters. The less efficient the sample, the less the sample statistics portray the true population values. Blalock (1960, p. 157) indicates that "... efficiency is always relative. No estimate can be completely efficient since this would imply no sampling error whatsoever." But increasing the sample size will increase the efficiency of the sample estimate, provided a probability sampling method is used to obtain additional elements.

The researcher is interested in minimizing the cost of whatever he does, in any event. Therefore, even though he can easily obtain more elements than he needs for his study, he should be content with an adequate number. Some researchers fall prey to what we shall refer to here as "the fetish of the large sample." This is the urge to obtain a sample so large that few will question its significance as an efficient estimator of population trends or characteristics. Such behavior of a methodologist is comparable to what Thorstein Veblen has referred to as "conspicuous consumption," or the desire to impress others with material possessions far beyond what is needed normally for daily living requirements. Like the person who has a home much larger than he needs, some researchers manage to obtain samples into the tens or hundreds of thousands, when a much smaller sample size would be more than adequate. The adequacy of samples is determined by their efficiency. More rational methods for determining sample size are available as opposed to drawing a large sample for the sake of a large sample.

Another way of attacking the problem of determining how large the sample should be is to consider the *inferential function* to be performed by the sample itself. (The following discussion involves techniques that require some elementary facility with statistical methods. The procedures included are primarily of reference value and will be of assistance to the researcher once he has obtained the necessary statistical skills. For now, the beginning student is en- couraged to follow through the present example with the objective of general understanding rather than specific mastery of the funda- mentals of techniques presented.) Of course, this limits our solution to probability sampling models exclusively. But there is little practical inferential value associated with nonprobability samples, anyway.

This solution consists of dealing with several unknowns in a formula designed to estimate sample size. Because it is impossible to know what our observed sample characteristics will be in advance of obtain- ing the sample, we must again fall back on our judgment, professional expertise, or whatever else the social scientists wishes to call his experience in practical field problems.

To apply the formula for estimating sample size, we must know the following things:

1.   The level of significance or level of confidence.
2.   The tolerance level that will act as the limit of error we will be willing to permit in the sample size estimate.
3.   Some estimate of the sample standard deviation, $\hat{\sigma}$, a measure of variability or dispersion (how the sample values focus around some central point in a distribution of scores.)

It should be noted that all three points above are *arbitrarily defined* by the researcher himself. Changing the level of significance will change the sample size estimate, as will also be the case by changing either or both of the other two terms in the formula.

The formula is the same as that for estimating confidence intervals in statistical work. We have the formula,

$$\bar{X} \pm (Z)\left(\frac{\hat{\sigma}}{\sqrt{N}}\right)$$

where $\bar{X}$ = some average value (sample mean as an estimate of the population parameter, $\hat{\sigma}$);

Z = standard value associated with the level of significance;

$\hat{\sigma}$ = estimated population standard deviation; and

N = the sample size (*to be estimated*).

Because we wish to know N, we must make a decision about the values of the other terms in the formula. The $\bar{X}$ value is unimportant at this point; because we are interested only in the degree of precision we shall have to estimate this value. Suppose this $\bar{X}$ stands for the average age of some sample. Assume that we want our estimate of the age of the population from which the sample is obtained to be accurate to within 0.5 years, according to probability. This means that part of our formula will contain the value, 0.5. This is

$$0.5 = (Z)\left(\frac{\hat{\sigma}}{\sqrt{N}}\right)$$

because we are willing to allow $\bar{X} \pm 0.5$ as our tolerance limit. If we use the 0.01 level of significance or level of confidence, this will define our Z value to be 2.58,[*] so that our formula becomes

$$0.5 = (2.58)\left(\frac{\hat{\sigma}}{\sqrt{N}}\right).$$

We may now solve for N, which is:

$$\frac{(2.58)(1.8)}{0.5} = \sqrt{N}$$

$$= 9 \qquad = \sqrt{N}$$

$$N = (9)^2 = 81$$
$$N = 81$$

According to this estimate, our N should be 81.

This formula is subject to several weaknesses. As has been noted previously, all values of the formula terms have been determined arbitrarily or estimated by the researcher. Also, once a sample N has been determined, there is no guarantee that the estimated values (i.e., $\hat{\sigma}$, the tolerance level, or the level of significance) are necessarily the best values for the particular situation. Considerable significance is attached to the investigator's experience and ability to know which values and levels to use under any given set of conditions. Finally, suppose a sample size of 5,000 was required, as defined by the formula above. This may be impractical, given the financial and personnel resources of the researcher. He may be obligated to take a sample of fewer elements and sacrifice some sampling error and precision.

In the final analysis, the researcher must consider the type of study he wishes to conduct in order to properly determine the size of the sample he should draw. If he elects to do a case study (e.g., *a study of a bank or some company*), then he will want his sample to consist of all employees in the bank or company. If the researcher is studying large populations, such as whole cities or national aggregates, he is obligated to take a much smaller proportion of the whole collection of elements. At this point, how many elements will make up the final sample is entirely dependent on the extent of his facilities and resources, what he intends to say about the population, and how much time he has. For one researcher, a sample of 5,000 will do, whereas another researcher may obtain a sample of 50,000.

Remember that the significance of any piece of research does not rest on the size of the sample alone, but rather on the quality of the theory and the care taken in the development and implementation of an appropriate research design. A study utilizing a sample of 50 can be just as effective or more effective than a study where 10,000 elements are used, particularly when the researcher has carefully delineated several connecting links between his small sample and its characteristics and previous research on the subject. The significance of large N's in social research is undermined whenever the study is weak in theoretical development.

Briefly summarizing some of the pros and cons relative to sample size,

1. Small samples are practical from the financial standpoint. They do not cost as much to obtain as larger ones. At the same time, however, there is greater sampling error associated with them, reducing the precision of sample estimates of population parameters.

2. Large samples are more cumbersome to manipulate and work with compared with smaller ones. In many instances, they involve

more work to analyze, but typically they have greater generalizability, provided that they are drawn in accordance with some type of probability sampling plan. There is less sampling error associated with larger samples.

3.   The theoretical significance of small samples should not be underestimated. Small samples are significant when viewed as specific tests of theories and when they are linked to previous research. The adequacy of the theory gives small samples greater value by placing them in a larger theoretical perspective rather than in fragmented and isolated situations.

4.   When the nature of the study is inferential, it helps to have as large a portion of the population as possible within one's means but not necessarily larger than one tenth of it, particularly if the size of the population is excessive or infinite. Many studies are conducted within populations of size 1,000 or less. In this event, the researcher may be able to conveniently obtain 250 elements, which would be a reasonable sample size. Although he could get by with 100 elements or even fewer, the greater number of elements will probably affect significantly the generalizability of the results. In addition, if he is interested in applying some stratified random sampling plan, the larger number of elements will help to guard against ending up with too few elements in specific substrata on the stratifying variables. But for the researcher who must decide to sample 100,000 elements or 150,000 of them, the greater sample size in this instance would be immaterial, except from the standpoint of the cost of obtaining each additional element. The increase in information and the slight decrease in sampling error would not be nearly enough to justify the increased expenditure of funds.

5.   Another factor that affects sample size in a subtle fashion is the editorial policy of the professional journals. When journals receive manuscripts for publication at the rate of 1,200 or more a year and can accept only about one tenth of them, the articles must be screened according to certain qualitative criteria. One criterion implicitly included in article evaluations is sample size. Although little systematic information is currently available about the relationship between sample sizes in studies and their subsequent acceptance in a professional journal, some publications have the informal reputation of preferring large N's. This is particularly true of those journals based in academic institutions with strong survey research interests, although many journals seem to favor those studies where sample sizes are particularly large. Suffice it to say that although many articles are

published where N's are small, a prospective article contribution can enhance his chances of getting the article published by studying large N's. The social scientist, therefore, leans toward studies of large samples partially as a result of these real or imagined article selection policies.

One potential implication of this large N emphasis is to discredit or play down the value of studies where small N's are used. Standards of what is acceptable and what is not are frequently derived from the most immediate source—the journals. In the long run, it is perhaps more healthy for a discipline to encompass studies favoring a variety of sample sizes. But the fetish of the large sample is still with us.

POTENTIAL SOURCES OF NONREPRESENTATIVENESS IN PROBABILITY SAMPLING

The fact that a probability sampling plan is used to select elements initially does not entitle the researcher to conclude that the resulting sample is representative of the population from which it was drawn. Drawing a sample and then obtaining cooperation from the selected elements are two different things. For example, suppose that in a given study using a mailed questionnaire, 3,000 elements are randomly selected from a city directory. On the average, we should expect that about 30 per cent of the elements will respond to the questionnaire and return it. This means that if our study conforms to other studies in this regard, we should end up with about 900 elements. Seldom is anything done about the 2,100 people who do not respond. Are they necessarily typical of the population from which they were drawn? What about the characteristics of the 2,100 nonrespondents? Obviously the two portions of our initial sample, the 900 and the 2,100, differ on at least one dimension—one group returns questionnaires (at least this questionnaire) whereas the other aggregate does not return them (at least this time). Nevertheless, there remains an unanswered question pertaining to the nonrespondents. What are they like and how would their responses have altered the conclusions drawn about the population compared with the 900 who did respond?

Nonresponse in any type of sampling plan serves to increase the bias present in the resulting sample. All samples, regardless of how they were originally obtained, contain a degree of bias, simply because not all elements of the population were included.

Sometimes researchers followup initial element contacts with letters and personal visits to increase response. But these contacts provide second and third stimuli to otherwise nonresponding respondents. Those elements obtained after a second or even a third contact or followup should be treated separately from those responding initially until it can be established whether each of the groups of respondents does not differ from one another in particularly crucial characteristics. One reason for doing this is to guard against the possible inclusion of people (second stimulus respondents) who might purposely lie to the researcher, a possible consequence of feeling pressured to participate in the research project. By the same token, there is nothing to prevent initial respondents from lying, either. These are just a few of the hazards confronting the social investigator.

Nonrepresentativeness may be introduced by other means as well. Incomplete or inaccurate listings of elements in city directories or other community records could lead the researcher to contact the wrong people or not to contact them at all. Using the telephone directory to obtain elements would definitely introduce a social class bias inasmuch as many lower income families do not have telephones because they cannot afford them. And at the rate at which people are subscribing for telephone service in many cities, it is unlikely that even a truly random sample of elements from the most recent telephone directory would be representative of people in the community *with telephones*, simply because the newest listings have not been included in the current directory. And we have not even mentioned those who prefer to have unlisted numbers!

Earlier in this chapter we discussed representativeness in terms of specific characteristics of the population we were examining. A sample is representative of a population in one respect (e.g., age and sex distribution), but not in another (e.g., income or SES level). Various types of stratified random sampling plans, therefore, are geared to compensate for the problems of representativeness associated with simple random samples. If some elements in the population exist in few numbers, it is unlikely that these elements will be included in a subsequent sample. With stratified random sampling plans, however, some of these elements would be guaranteed inclusion. Such is the way of reckoning with a lack of representativeness of specified characteristics in any given sample selection. But no sample is ever fully representative of the population from which it was drawn. One crude measure of representativeness is sampling error, and we know that *some* degree of sampling error always exists in every sample drawn.

POTENTATES AND INACCESSIBLE ELEMENTS

Obtaining a truly random sample is often complicated by the presence of potentates and/or inaccessible elements. *Potentates* are defined as people who require special permission to contact or interview them. For example, this definition might apply to very powerful people in government or industry, where the researcher must first confront a line of secretaries and other barriers before gaining access to the designated potentate, or it can pertain to small children where parental or school permission is usually required.

For researchers studying the effects of particular teaching methods on student learning, the most crucial factor is obtaining the cooperation of both the school and the parents of students involved in the proposed research activity. School systems as well as other institutional elements in our society have become increasingly concerned about the use of human subjects in social research. Researchers find it more difficult each year to obtain information from people about their behavior. This increased resistance to becoming involved in social research is probably attributable, in part, to one or more of a few social researchers who create poor impressions before the public in the process of social inquiry. Perhaps a researcher promises to keep confidential information that has been provided by a group of workers. But somehow, through a breach of trust or carelessness, the researcher permits information leaks that often prove embarrassing to some of the persons interviewed. Imagine the potential implications of a plant manager becoming aware of some candid remarks made about his supervisory qualities by some of his immediate subordinates, particularly if the remarks were somewhat negative and given in confidence to an interviewer. This sort of thing has happened too often for people simply to pass it off as a rare occurrence. They are suspicious of social researchers for what they regard as good reasons, and in many instances, their suspicions are well founded.

For whatever reasons are given, the fact is that human beings are increasingly sensitive to being observed, and many resent any invasion of privacy. Therefore, the social scientist often falls short of achieving his ideal goal of a truly random sample of elements from a larger population. Some people simply refuse to be included in the sample, whereas others are inaccessible for different reasons. They might be out of town temporarily, or they may have moved out of the city or country, died, or become mentally incapacitated.

Because of the inaccessibility of many elements, random samples are difficult to obtain. In survey research, reaching half of a random sample of elements means that the other half has not been included. What is the resulting sample? Is it still considered a random one? Many investigators argue that it is but that it reflects a greater degree of bias and lacks representativeness *to the extent that other randomly drawn elements were excluded.* Certainly the researcher must be increasingly aware of this bias factor, particularly when it comes to interpreting the results of his study. Again, we are confronted by a situation where the real results do not match up with the ideal objectives. The final sample seldom resembles fully the ideal random sample selected at the outset. To the extent that this occurs, the investigator should interpret his results more conservatively and tentatively.

THE CAPTIVE AUDIENCE

At the other extreme is the situation involving the captive audience. The *captive audience* is defined as a group of people who are, in a sense, forced to become involved in a given research activity by virtue of their obligatory position in some social situation. Inmates of prisons or students in a classroom offer good examples of captive audiences.

In the development of doctoral dissertations and master's theses, graduate students who are involved in teaching at their respective institutions will frequently turn to the most accessible N they can find—the students in their classes. And there is evidence to indicate that professors engage in the same behavior for their own research. Students are subjected to questionnaires prepared by graduate students or are asked to conform to research demands of their friends or teachers. Although it is true that many students simply regard this involvement as a part of their classroom routine, others find the experience annoying. Because of the nature of the questionnaire they are asked to complete, students sometimes become offended and embarrassed; but it is very difficult for them to withdraw from the classroom scene or to refuse to comply with the researcher during the research activity. Not only does group pressure operate to induce the student to conform, but the professor often makes the student think that the research is a part of the student's experience in the course. In some courses, such as research methods or techniques, this is no doubt true; but in many others, there is little relation between the course substance and being questioned or interviewed. Some social scientists complain that what we have generated with our preoccupation with accessible classroom populations is, in reality, the develop-

ment of a sociology of students rather than descriptions of more normally distributed nonstudent aggregates.

One implication of using captive audiences in social research is to
induce such participants to retaliate in some way. Persons who find
that they are being manipulated or forced to comply with a researcher
may lie, purposely distort their answers to a questionnaire, or give any
answer that seems most convenient (e.g., checking all of the "strongly
agree" responses in a Likert-type of questionnaire to hurry through and
get it over with). In Chapter 5 it was shown that the nature of
respondent involvement in a researcher's study could be instrumental
in affecting the quality of answers provided to questions, oral or written.

To reduce the problem of resistance to research participation, the
investigator should make an effort to offer participation alternatives to
potential respondents. Allowing a respondent to make a choice to
participate or not participate will no doubt decrease the size of one's
sample, yet the researcher can be fairly well assured that those individuals responding ultimately will be least likely to distort their
responses as a result of being forced into research involvement.

DOUBLE SAMPLING

From time to time the researcher will engage in the practice of double
sampling. *Double sampling* is defined as drawing a sample of elements
from another sample of them. For example, suppose the investigator
were to conduct a study calling for a cross section of community
residents reflecting several socioeconomic levels. He draws a stratified
random sample and sends each respondent a questionnaire through
the mail. He obtains a 36 per cent response from his initial mailing.
From the 35 per cent who respond he draws another sample. This time
he sends interviewers to each of these person's homes for the purpose
of obtaining more in-depth information concerning their responses to
the initial questionnaire. Later, he assumes that the in-depth responses
are representative of the persons who responded at the outset and
he probably assumes that the entire aggregate of respondents is
representative of the whole community.

The investigator is making several mistakes at this point. First, he has
failed to deal with the 65 per cent of his initial sample who did not
respond. What are the nonrespondents like and how do they differ
from those who did respond? After all, he could be examining a very
biased segment of the population from which he sampled.

To what extent was the initial sample a representative one? If it was obtained through the application of a stratified random sampling procedure, were the salient variables for stratifying taken into account fully? At the outset, the researcher is placing a great deal of confidence in the representativeness of his sampling plan and the sample he obtained. Is this justified under the present circumstances?

A third problem concerns the respondents who have been sampled again. If the initial respondents reflected much bias compared with the real distribution of characteristics of the total population, then the in-depth interviews of these same elements would do nothing more but to magnify the bias that already exists.

For double sampling to be an effective part of a research design, the investigator should make sure that the sampling plan followed from the very beginning will maximize the representativeness of the elements drawn subsequently. One factor that will help to determine whether double sampling is appropriate is the response rate to the questionnaire or interview. If the response is low (i.e., less than half of the elements respond to the mailed questionnaire), double sampling may compound the problem of the lack of representativeness. Remember that a reasonable portion of the original population is required for a sample that is randomly drawn to be regarded as potentially representative. The fewer elements included, the less representative the sample becomes. Where attrition occurs in a random sample (owing to nonresponse, inaccessible elements, and the like), its randomness and hence, its representativeness, are jeopardized seriously.

Double sampling can provide important insights into the responses people give to a questionnaire. Double sampling functions here as a reliability check by exploring opinions and attitudes of individuals in a more in-depth fashion. A simple comparison of their followup responses (obtained through the double sampling procedure) and their first answers to a questionnaire will enable the researcher to estimate the reliability of response for the entire sample he collects. If the researcher chooses to double sample at some stage of his data collection procedure, it is recommended that he assess critically the way in which the sample is representative. This will give him a better vantage point from which to judge the appropriateness of the double sampling he contemplates.

SOME QUESTIONS FOR REVIEW

1. Differentiate between probability and nonprobability samples. Review their functions and limitations.

2.   What are some major considerations in deciding to sample? Why would we want to sample in social research?

3.   If your school has a computer center, contact the center personnel in charge and discuss with them the procedures for programming the computer to provide you with a specified quantity of random numbers. Discuss with them various ways computers can assist researchers with their sampling.

4.   What are some of the primary advantages of judgmental or purposive samples? Do you think they are as good as probability samples designed to perform similar functions? Why or why not?

5.   Some researchers identify systematic sampling as a probability sampling form. In this text, we have chosen to label it as a nonprobability sampling procedure. Discuss some of the pros and cons for treating systematic sampling as a probability sampling form.

6.   Under what conditions would it be appropriate for the researcher to use cluster or area sampling? What are some of the advantages of cluster sampling compared with simple random sampling?

7.   Why is the determination of sample size a problem? Discuss various aspects of the sample size issue with your instructor.

8.   Snowball sampling is used frequently to assess interpersonal patterns of formal organizations. What are some other applications you can think of beyond those discussed in the text? Are there grounds for arguing that snowball sampling could be considered a type of probability sampling method? Why or why not? (Couch your answer in the context of criteria for a probability sample.)

9.   What is the primary control factor in probability sampling plans? Why is it important that this factor be present?

10.   What does it mean for a sample to be "representative"? Discuss the problem of representativeness and the ratio of sample size to population size.

11.   What are some ways by which sample size can be determined? What are some criteria for assessing the practical size of a sample?

12.   Discuss some of the implications of potentates, captive audiences, and inaccessible elements on the reliability of the sample selected. How is the generalizability of the sample affected by each of these factors?

NOTES

1. Some sampling plans incorporate aspects of both probability and nonprobability, which makes them difficult to assess in terms of their generalizability. For example, see the discussion of area samples on pages 293 to 298.

2. How large the sample should be will be discussed toward the end of this chapter.

3. In an independent study carried out by one of the authors, it was found that when 2,700 questionnaires were sent to respondents in three Tennessee cities (Knoxville, Nashville, and Chattanooga) where respondents had been selected randomly from city directories less than one year old, approximately 500 were returned as undeliverable because the potential respondents had moved (Champion and Sear, 1969).

4. The use of factorials in statistical work is frequently encountered. Factorials are calculated rather easily. For example:

$$5! = (5)\ (4)\ (3)\ (2)\ (1)$$
$$3! = (3)\ (2)\ (1)$$

And in the general case,

$$N! = (N)\ (N - 1)\ (N - 2)\ \ldots\ (1)$$

5. Various levels of measurement are treated in Chapter 6. Refer back to this discussion once you have read the levels of measurement discussion.

6. The standard deviation is a statistical term and refers to a measure of the way in which scores from individuals on some characteristic fluctuate around a central value, such as the "average score." Suppose we have two groups distributed around the same value of age.

Group 1: 20 21 22 23 24 25 26 27 28 29 30

Group 2:   0   5 10 15 20 25 30 35 40 45 50

Both groups have the same average age (hypothetically), but Group 1 is more closely distributed around the central value compared with Group 2. The standard deviation is a measure of how the scores are spread around the central point in a distribution. The larger the standard deviation, the more widely distributed the scores will tend to be about the central value or "average score." The smaller the standard deviation, the more closely distributed the scores will be. The reader is referred to any good statistics textbook where he may see various applications of standard deviations in research work as well as learn the computational procedure involved.

7. The discrepancy between his original desired sample size, 200, and the resulting size of 204 is due to rounding error in computing proportions of each subpopulation to the total population. It is not important.

8. 2.58 was obtained from the Table of Areas Under the Normal Curve, Table A.2, Appendix A, which corresponds to the 0.01 level of significance when used in conjunction with confidence levels.

BIBLIOGRAPHY

Blalock, Hubert M., Jr. *Social Statistics.* New York: McGraw-Hill, 1960.

―――. *Social Statistics.* (2nd Edition) New York: McGraw-Hill, 1972.

Champion, Dean J. *Basic Statistics for Social Research.* Scranton, Pa.: Chandler Publishing Company, 1970.

―――, and Edward Z. Dager. "Some Impacts of Office Automation upon Status, Role Change, and Depersonalization," *Sociological Quarterly* (1967): 71–84.

―――, and Alan M. Sear. "Questionnaire Response Rate: A Methodological Analysis," *Social Forces* 47 (1969): 335–39.

Cochran, William G. *Sampling Techniques.* New York: John Wiley, 1963.

Coleman, James S.; E. Katz; and H. M. Menzel. "Diffusion of Innovation among Physicians." *Sociometry* 20 (1957): 253–270.

―――. "Relational Analysis: The Study of Social Organizations with Survey Methods," *Human Organization* 17 (1958–59): 28–36.

Conway, Freda. *Sampling: An Introduction for Social Scientists.* London: George Allen and Unwin, 1967.

Doby, John T. *An Introduction to Social Research.* New York: Appleton-Century-Crofts, 1967.

Downie, N. M., and R. W. Heath. *Basic Statistical Methods.* 2d ed. New York: Harper and Row, 1965.

Durkheim, Émile. *Suicide: A Study in Sociology* (Translated by George Simpson). New York: Free Press, 1951.

Edwards, Allen L. *Statistical Methods.* 2d ed. New York: Holt, Rinehart, and Winston, 1967.

Goode, William J., and Paul K. Hatt. *Methods in Social Research.* New York: McGraw-Hill, 1952.

Kaplan, Abraham. *The Conduct of Inquiry: Methodology for Behavioral Science.* Francisco: Chandler, 1964.

Kaufmann, Felix. *Methodology of the Social Sciences.* New York: Humanities Press, 1958.

Kish, Leslie. *Survey Sampling.* New York: Free Press, 1965.

Lehman, Edward C., Jr., and Donald W. Shriver, Jr. "Academic Discipline as Predictive of Faculty Religiosity," *Social Forces* 47 (1968): 171–182.

Monroe, John, and A. L. Finkner. *Handbook of Area Sampling.* Philadelphia: Chilton, 1959.

Peatman, John G. *Descriptive and Sampling Statistics.* New York: Harper and Brothers, 1947.

Selltiz, Claire, et al. *Research Methods in Social Relations.* New York: Holt, Rinehart, and Winston, 1967.

Slonim, Morris. *Sampling: A Quick, Reliable Guide to Practical Statistics.* New York: Simon and Schuster, 1960.

Williamson, Robert C. "Social Class and Orientation to Change: Some Relevant Variables in a Bogota Sample," *Social Forces* 46, (1968): 317–28.

Yates, Frank. *Sampling Methods for Censuses and Surveys.* New York: Hafner, 1960.

Young, Pauline V., and Calvin F. Schmid. *Scientific Social Surveys and Research.* Cliffs, N.J., Prentice-Hall, Inc., 1966.

PART 3
FORMS OF DATA COLLECTION

CHAPTER 9
OBSERVATION

As important as interviews and questionnaires are as data-gathering devices, there are certain types of problems for which they are not entirely satisfactory. When it is important to see behavior in its natural settings, to grasp the dynamic, situation-based features of conduct, some form of observation becomes essential as the primary method of acquiring information.

Observation is like other instruments of social science data collection in that it demands mastering certain skills if it is to be used effectively. And, like other methods, certain of the skills required of investigators in observational studies are unique to that form of investigation. Whether it is being employed alone or with other methods, the technique of observation can best be understood by discussing its several related aspects. This chapter will focus on the following topics:

1. The nature of observation.
2. Major purposes of observation.

3. Some major types of observation.
4. Factors affecting the choice of observational methods.
5. Problems related to the design and execution of observational studies.

THE NATURE OF OBSERVATION

In the broadest sense, researchers are constantly observing persons' conduct. Whether handing out questionnaires and watching people fill them out and listening to remarks made about various items, noticing certain expressions of respondents in an interview or catching comments made as an aside to the interview context, or scrutinizing the behavior of individuals serving as subjects in experimental settings, investigators are not insensitive to the various ways people behave in the research settings in which they find themselves. Indeed, one of the marks of any experienced investigator is the sensitivity to the setting or locale of the study. Knowing what to expect in advance comes largely from having been there before, regardless of the type of study being conducted. All serious investigators have some first-hand, on-the-scenes contact with the study they are directing.

To appreciate the distinctiveness of observation, it is necessary to draw a line between observations made as a casual by-product of investigations and observations used as fundamentally a data-gathering tool. By observation in this narrower sense is meant watching and listening to other persons' behavior over time without manipulating or controlling it and recording findings in ways that permit some degree of analytical interpretation.

Observation, when properly conducted, is characterized by the following:

1. It captures the natural social context in which persons' behavior occurs.

2. It grasps the significant events and/or occurrences that affect social relations of the participants.

3. It determines what constitutes reality from the standpoint of the world view, philosophy, or outlook of the observed.

4. It identifies regularities and recurrences in social life by comparing and contrasting data obtained in one study with those obtained in studies of other natural settings.

These characteristic features of observation serve to set it apart from the casual, sporadic, and more or less spontaneous observations made by researchers in the course of conducting investigations. They also point up a salient distinction between observational research and experimental social research. In the latter, observations are made as the result of deliberate construction and manipulation of the social context. Observation as it is used here, however, seeks to preserve the natural form of social behavior with no effort at manipulation.

A moment's reflection about the major features of observation suggests that there are some important ways in which it is unique as a data-gathering method. More so than with other methods, the investigator must take whatever steps are necessary to maintain the naturalness of the social behavior being observed. Several avenues for accomplishing this are available, as will be seen momentarily. And whereas significance is used in connection with many other methods to measure the frequency with which things occur, in observational research it assumes a different meaning. That which is seen as being significant by an observer may occur only once or occasionally. Those things, regardless of how frequently they are found, that decidedly affect the social fabric as it is being woven by the participants are counted as being significant.

Finally, because observation is by its nature designed to depict reality as the observed construct it, translating the findings to the context of scientifically useful information is not always an easy task (Wiseman, 1970, pp. 280–83). The skills needed to accurately portray the world from the perspective of others are demanding enough. To these must be added those that enable findings to be generalized in scientifically acceptable ways. All the problems related to validity, reliability, and the representativeness of the data are encountered as often in observation as when other methods are used. They simply have to be resolved somewhat differently.

The novice, drawn to the method of observation out of some fear of statistics or a desire to avoid tedious work, should be deterred after an examination of the nature of observation. Data collected with all scientific tools, observation included, must eventually cast their lot with "facts" gathered by other means before the canons of scientific acceptability. This means that an enormous amount of attention must be paid by observers to the codification and classification of materials to make them scientifically useful. Ultimately there is no way to avoid the demanding, intricate work of data collection and interpretation.

MAJOR PURPOSES OF OBSERVATION

In our introductory comments, we alluded to the fact that investigators are frequently interested in exposing situationally based dimensions of behavior. A major purpose of observation is to capture human conduct as it actually happens, to permit us to view behavior in process. How people respond in an interview or on a questionnaire does little more than tell us how they felt at a particular moment in time. We get a static, snapshot comprehension of their activity. How they behave in actual situations, sometimes modifying their views, sometimes contradicting themselves, but always swayed at least in part by the situation in which they are behaving, is missed. By recording information on how individuals actually go about the business of behaving in a social way relative to one another, observation seeks to address the dynamic nature of behavior.

A second major purpose of observation is to provide more graphic descriptions of social life then can be acquired in other ways.[1] In this connection, it is often used along with other data to lend a certain quality of life or reality to an investigator's overall research findings. There is a surprising number of areas of social conduct for which we have few, if any, thorough descriptions. What, for example, do delinquents do to get into trouble? How do they go about stealing cars, vandalizing, taking drugs, and so on? And what are the specific events and interactions surrounding our decisions to behave or not to behave in other ways? How does a person actually go about learning to be a doctor? or professor? or clergyman? or politician? Clearly, much is taken for granted by social scientists regarding the details of day-to-day living. The descriptive base from which to proceed to other scientific objectives, such as explanation and prediction, is quite frequently provided only by observation.

Yet another objective of observation is exploration. There are many instances when little is known about a topic. By being on the scene, investigators are more likely to obtain some sense of direction with respect to the things that are important. Issues that might otherwise be overlooked are examined more carefully. There is a tendency to want to look beyond what is already known about a subject, to examine the possibility that there might be alternative directions for research, that more important variables have been overlooked, or certain methodological errors made that can be corrected. Observation affords investigators the chance to come to grips with the research setting and these types of problems.

Then, too, there are situations in which the literature is abundant, but it has simply not addressed all the pertinent theoretical questions. In such circumstances, observation encourages new directions for social research by obtaining important information from which to build more rigorous instruments of data collection. To achieve these various objectives, it is important to recognize that there are several types of observation that can be utilized by social science researchers. In the next section we will discuss some of these major types of observation.

SOME TYPES OF OBSERVATION

Observation usually includes any one of a number of activities in a broad spectrum of possibilities. It is a method that, by its very nature, must be suited to the particular needs of the investigator, the exigencies of the problem at hand, and the overall objective of the study. To meet the needs of the bulk of their research problems, social scientists have developed several general types of observational methods. Differentiations can be made in several ways.

One way of differentiating among types has already received some comment, that is, to draw distinctions on the basis of the ability of observational data to generate scientifically useful information. Reiss (1971, p. 4), for example, makes a distinction between systematic and unsystematic observation. Concerning systematic observation, he states:

> By systematic observation, I mean only that observation and re-cording are done according to explicit procedures which permit replication and that rules are followed which permit the use of the logic of scientific inference.

Essentially, this is the same approach that was taken in establishing our definition of observation at the outset of this chapter.

Observational procedures can also be classified in terms of the role played by the investigator. There are two major types: (1) participant observation and (2) nonparticipant observation.

PARTICIPANT OBSERVATION

In this type of procedure, the investigator is a part of the natural set-ting in which the observations are being made. The procedure may develop in one of several ways. An investigator may already be a member of a particular group or organization and decide to observe it in one or more ways. Or an investigator may join a group for the express purpose of observing it in some way. Regardless of how the investigator comes to be a part of the landscape, active participation is an integral feature of the researcher's conduct.

It is fairly easy to see both the strengths and weaknesses of this type of observation. To the extent that the interest of the investigator is in preserving the natural social setting in which the study occurs, participant observation is highly desirable as a method. There are no questions about why this person is present, no altering of the natural course of the conduct of the participant, and no concern for what is and is not being observed. But here lies the greatest weakness of participant observation. The investigator is not always explicit in delineating the reasons why information was or was not recorded. It might very well be that the investigator cannot articulate such specifics, so deep is his involvement in the ongoing activity. In not being able to specify the procedures for gathering information, the investigator runs the risk of placing the possibility of replication of the research findings in serious jeopardy. In addition, to the extent that an observer acting as a participant is unable to carefully articulate the precise manner of observation, it may be difficult to move from the presentation of observational data to its validity. Participant observation suffers from a failure to be precise about the procedures for data accumulation. There is, as Reiss suggests, less attention to the precision than to the discovery.

Other problems plague this type of observation as well. Not everyone is willing or able to invest the time and, where the topic under scrutiny is illegal or negatively valued, risk to achieve the development of data in such ways. Not only are the problems of entry great, but there are simply some researchers who choose not to gather data in this manner.

NONPARTICIPANT OBSERVATION

Less demanding for the investigator insofar as role behavior is concerned is nonparticipant observation. This is a procedure in which the investigator observes the behavior of others in a natural setting but is not an actual participant in the behavior being examined. Some contend that this places those being observed in an awkward position and that their conduct will not be as natural as it would otherwise. Others, however, take the view that after the nonparticipant observer has been around for a little while, less and less attention is paid to his presence. Certainly, skill is required in being able to blend in with the surroundings and record observations in an unnoticed manner. So far as is known now, there is little argument with the fact that intervention in the actual social context creates some problems. There is no evidence, however, that the presence of the nonparticipant observer will have any detrimental effect on the behavior under study.

Nonparticipant observation can be very useful in that some planning can take place with respect to the choice of settings to observe, the representativeness of the data, the problems associated with the presence of the investigator, and so on. More thought can go into the development of explanatory schemes or specific research questions for probing. The specific details associated with recording data can be carefully charted and some decisions reached about which observations to include and which to ignore.

Placed in sharp relief against these attractive features of nonparticipant observation is one crucial shortcoming, and that is that nonparticipant observation does not capture the natural context of social life the way participant observation does. The setting may achieve a degree of naturalness after the participants become accustomed to the presence of the investigator. But it is "new" in its nature, having been formulated by the participants to adjust to the new conditions brought about by the very presence of the investigator. Just how significant this transformation is has not been determined. It is, unfortunately, a problem about which there is more conjecture and speculation than hard evidence.

Whether a researcher is interested in observing as a participant or as a nonparticipant, a further important consideration must be dealt with, having to do with the matter of whether one is going to observe in a disguised manner or in an open manner. Quite aside from the ethical questions, there are very important points to be made in favor of each type of observational choice depending on several factors related to the type of problem under scrutiny, the investigator, and the observed. For example, if the researcher is female, young, and is interested in observing the behavior of relatively older male alcoholics, the question of whether she is going to go as a disguised observer or whether she is going to hire other people to do the observing becomes a very relevant question. These and similar kinds of issues need to be carefully taken into account by anyone considering these types of observation as appropriate scientific tools. Because so much mention has been made of factors that affect the decision to select observation as the primary method of data collection, it is important to examine these in some detail. At the same time, some of the ways in which social researchers have dealt with difficult problems in relatively simple and frequently innovative ways will be considered.

FACTORS AFFECTING THE CHOICE OF OBSERVATION

Investigators are heavily influenced by numerous factors when selecting observation as a method of data collection. At least three sets of factors can be identified. These include factors related to the (1) problem itself, (2) the investigator's skills and characteristics, and (3) characteristics of the observed.

THE PROBLEM

Certain types of problems necessitate that data be gathered on the actual activities of people as they go about their day-to-day living. Such problems are simply not amenable to study in other ways. Explorations of the daily life styles of deviants of various sorts, of groups that cannot communicate by means of other research methods, and secret groups and organizations are examples of types of problems requiring observation. As with interviewing, a method to be taken up later, observation is especially suited to what might be called "microsocial" as opposed to "macrosocial" questions.

In addition, some theoretical frames of reference are more apt to focus on a range of questions requiring these types of data for their resolution. Ethnomethodology, phenomenology, and interactionism are prominent among those orientations in which observation holds a central place as a method.

Some facets of social life, as these perspectives underscore, cannot be comprehended in any other fashion. Just as politicians must sometimes "press the flesh" to grasp the mood of the electorate, social scientists must "get out among them" and see how people naturally behave. What is more important, they must learn to convey this natural context to the larger community of scientific scholars without distortion.

INVESTIGATOR SKILLS AND CHARACTERISTICS

Some social scientists are very uncomfortable in observational contexts. Some can quickly and with a minimum of difficulty grasp the scientific utility of their observations of behavior in the process of its actually occurring. Others are more at ease studying tables and charts and printouts of computer runs. No one really knows what it is that contributes to these idiosyncratic proclivities among social scientists or whether they occur in any systematic, predictable pattern. All that is known is that they seem to exist and serve to influence in subtle ways the selection of observation as a research tool.

None of this should be taken as meaning that observational methods should be used by only a select group of social scientists. No indeed! Investigators can be trained to observe just as they can be trained to interview, administer questionnaires, or scientifically analyze documents prepared by others for nonscientific purposes.

Skills required to observe effectively rest on an appreciation of the impact of certain aggregate characteristics of observers such as age, sex, and race on the context of the investigation. Adjustments have to be made for such characteristics. It is not that possessing some of these characteristics precludes the use of observational methods.

The fact that these or similar characteristics might provide an incongruent contrast to the naturalness of the setting of the observations means only one of two things: Either others must do the observing or the investigator must some how disguise these contradictory qualities. To the extent that an observer can pass as someone else with relative ease, there is no need to have someone else do the interviewing. Wiseman (1970, p. 276–77), in her study of skid row alcoholics, indicates how she accomplished her task:

> Observational data gathering was both participant and nonparticipant. Care was taken that a time sampling was made of a given setting that obtained frequency of phenomena at different times of the day and week.
>
> On Skid Row, observations were made both by myself in the company of a paid "guide," and by paid male observers. My observations were confined to those activities in which a woman can take part on the Row without causing undue comment—walking around during the day, sitting in bars, eating in cafeterias, cafes, and shopping in grocery stores.
>
> Four male observers walked the streets of Skid Row with the men at night, stood talking to them on the street, drank in taverns with them, and met them at the bus returning from jail. These observations were spread in time through one year. Findings were further supplemented by published observations of the Skid Row area by other researchers.
>
> On Skid Row, I passed as a woman friend of a presumed resident there, as a woman looking for a lost boy friend, and as a woman who had returned to the area after some absence and was looking for a bartender friend. In Christian Missionary prayer meeting and in free soup lines, I merely joined the men and few women recipients. At the various screening sessions held at stations on the loop, agents of social control were kind enough to allow me to sit in and pass as a secretary who was taking medical notes.
>
> In the Jail and the State Mental Hospital, no attempt to pass was made for two different reasons: in an all-male world like the Jail, it would be virtually impossible; in a calmly coeducational and research-oriented environment like the State Hospital, it seemed un-

necessary. The first night at the Hospital, when I was introduced to the men in one of the alcoholic wards, they gallantly included me in a late night party based on food raided from the kitchen. From then on they treated me as one of the family.

However, while there were a great many scenes I could observe, it became apparent that as a woman, or as a researcher, access was denied to some areas of the loop. Especially acute problems were presented by the County Jail and the Christian Missionaries (in addition to Skid Row at night where a woman attracts attention no matter how innocuously she is dressed).

For these three areas, as well as a fourth (the courts) where time was at a premium, observers were hired. In jail, at the Christian Missionaries, and on Skid Row they were participant observers, unknown to their subjects as researchers. Recruiting observers for the Jail posed several problems. Obviously, I could not ask someone to commit a crime so as to be sentenced to the County Jail. On the other hand, there was a need for someone who could participate unnoticed in prisoner activities. The decision was to recruit within the jail. Young men who were not in jail for alcoholism were selected. There were four observers in all. These men were not used simultaneously, but two were observing and recording for three weeks and then two others working for the same period of time approximately six months later—some time after the first two had been released. In this way it was hoped that collusion between observers would be prevented.

Special note should be taken of the way in which Wiseman was able to combine participant and nonparticipant observation, utilize various mechanisms for passing, and engage the services of paid observers when her aggregate characteristics did not permit her access to the subjects of her study.

CHARACTERISTICS OF THE OBSERVED

Any time research is undertaken that stresses the need for interaction between investigators and the investigated, those characteristics of the subjects that may have some bearing on the data-gathering process must be enumerated as carefully as possible. In using observational methods, as in interviewing, the status of the observed vis-à-vis the observer is a major factor in determining whether observation will be feasible as a method of data collection.

A key element in this regard is the ability of the observed to forbid observation of their conduct. In effect, observation becomes less likely as the observed are more capable of exercising their right to privacy. Naturally, the reverse also holds true: The possibility of using the techniques of observation increases as the ability of the observed to control their privacy decreases. Several factors influence this capability. Among the numerous possibilities, five will be singled out for comment. These are (1) occupational, (2) economic, (3) political, (4) subcultural, and (5) normative factors.

Occupational Factors

By and large, occupational factors refer to the ability to bring either bureaucratic or professional support to bear on a desire not to have actions directly observed. When permission has to be obtained from appropriate authorities, the choice of observation may have to be abandoned for more administratively acceptable data-collection procedures. Studies such as the one by Reiss (1971) of police activities illustrate how investigators can go about contending with bureaucratic pressures.

In instances where professional considerations are invoked as reasons for not permitting observation, somewhat different problems arise. Doctors and lawyers, for example, are intent on maintaining the sanctity and confidentiality of their relations with patients and clients respectively. That doesn't mean that there are facets of being a professional which cannot be observed. Becker's (1961) study of medical students is an example of the use of the observational method in concert with other techniques to more fully comprehend the factors involved in the training of doctors.

Economic Factors

One way relative freedom from the intrusion of social science observation can be achieved is to be in a position to afford privacy financially. This may come about because of the economic ability of the observed or it may occur as a by-product of the researcher's own relatively meager financial resources.

It is, to put it simply, cheaper to observe groups that are visible because of their economically disadvantaged position relative to the well-to-do. Their economic vulnerability serves to make them more accessible. What questions this poses for the ultimate generalizability of observational data have not been adequately explored.

Political Factors

Individuals have certain rights to privacy which are guaranteed them by the law, at least in our own society. Being a social researcher does not carry with it an automatic license to encroach on these freedoms. Research which has been in direct conflict with the law has been known to be terminated (Ruebhausen and Brim, 1965). That means that those who are going to be observed must either *volunteer* to be studied or be in a position where their privacy is, as suggested earlier, *vulnerable,* or have their activities observed surrepticiously by *disguised observation.*

Subcultural Factors

Variations in the extent to which members of certain segments of a population closely identify with one another on the basis of some ethnic, occupational, kinship, or other cultural factor can be of considerable importance in decisions regarding the appropriateness of observation. Whether it should be used at all and, if so, what types should predominate in gathering data frequently depend on these factors. Closely knit ethnic groups, deviant groups such as snake worshippers, people in communes, people living in small towns, delinquent gangs, mountain folk, and so on are all alike in one respect: Their cohesiveness enables them to accept or reject at will the carefully trained eye of the observer. As the cohesiveness of groups diminishes and they become more and more open and less identifiable as subcultures, observation becomes somewhat easier in the sense that it does not test the ingenuity of the observer nearly so much.

Normative Factors

Finally, there are important variations in the general normative standards (at least in a society like our own with a democratic type political order) with respect to what is considered private. Stinchcombe (1963), for example, points to the fact that privacy is a variable phenomenon from the standpoint of its institutionalization. Certain sectors of our daily lives are regarded by us as being more private than others. Observational methods applied to a problem that is a deeply ingrained, institutionalized, private feature of social existence is bound to be met with great opposition. Researchers can, for example, talk to people about their sex lives and perhaps obtain answers to questionnaire items about such activities. Watching them engage in sexual relations is, however, beyond the pale of all but the most authoritative of researchers, such as Masters and Johnson (1970).

In sum, factors that affect the use of observation as a data-collection device are to be viewed as variations for which there must be advanced calculation. Their importance may be such as to render observation less suitable than other methods. But where data are sought of the sorts that can be provided only by observation, they constitute reasonable criteria for selecting types of observation discriminately. Furthermore, they enable researchers to anticipate beforehand the kinds of obstacles that must be overcome in designing observational research.

DESIGNING OBSERVATIONAL STUDIES

Some who are experienced in the use of observation point out that one of its most vulnerable aspects as a research tool is the lack of a well-established, coherent, methodological protocol for its utilization. Observers are, as Wiseman (1970, pp. 269–70) notes, "often forced to develop strategies for uncovering the author's views that have little precedent and are difficult to test for validity and reliability."

For those just being introduced to observation, it is appropriate to at least specify the sorts of procedures that must be undertaken by one engaging in this type of data gathering. In so doing, two goals ought to be accomplished. First, the procedures should offset the emphasis on the uniqueness of observation as a research device that permeates much social scientific thinking about it. Second, the procedures ought to provide a context for more systematic data collection. Although certainly not the only way, one way of realizing these objectives is to go about observing in the same manner as is used when conducting projects employing other methods. In the pages that follow we will attempt, in the context of the general outline for research designs provided in Chapter 4, to indicate the specific types of concerns that confront those engaging in observation.

1. INTRODUCTION

Even though observation is, in most senses of the word, *current*, the place of observations in some historical context cannot be ignored. The behavior in question does not begin, nor will it end, with the observations made by social scientists. It is important to locate the observations in a broader temporal setting. In that way, the investigator's interest in studying the topic can be brought to the front. Whether it is the study of skid-row alcoholics, slum dwellers, policemen, dope addicts, or whomever, an appreciation of the historical continuity of the subject matter, the current social context and its participants, and the interests of the investigator in all of these at this point in time is a suitable starting point for observational studies.

2. STATEMENT OF OBJECTIVES

Observational studies usually are stated along the lines of their descriptive or explanatory objectives. One of the major problems of many of them is that they are either too restricted in their descriptive content or too exploratory in nature. To be productive of scientifically useful data, observations must do what other studies undertake, that is, to specify the variables being studied as explicitly as possible. Of course, observation is often used to examine more general *conceptual* interests in the hope of being able to more explicitly identify variables for subsequent research. In those types of studies, the concepts being explored must be as articulately defined as possible. Seldom does observation permit refined statements of relations between or among variables in terms of some linear, curvilinear, or power function dimension. At the very least, there ought to be a specifically delineated *question* for study which provides some central focus in the investigator's thinking.

One of the major reasons for having a clear-cut view of what the study is to accomplish is to be able to link it to other information. In that way it will have more potential scientific utility. A second reason is to be able to concentrate on the task at hand once the observations actually begin. As McCall and Simmons (1969, p. 73) caution, "once in the field, the participant observer is typically somewhat overwhelmed by data, the meaning of which is not always immediately apparent and therefore must be mulled over." To have to mull over why one is there in the first place and what the study is about would be disastrous!

Yet another reason for having a firm grasp of the study objective is to be able to respond easily and directly to inquiries into the nature of the project from those being observed. When people begin to ask, "Why are you here?" "What do you hope to gain from all of this?" "How long do you intend to be around here?" "Do you intend to talk to everybody here?" "Are you going to observe everything that goes on?" and so on, answers must be as quick and forthright as possible. Some tactics for accomplishing this will be presented later.

3. LITERATURE REVIEW

Reviewing the literature is an integral feature of any research project. But because literature is no substitute for getting out into the field and actually observing, many would-be observers are prone to ignore much that could conceivably make their task both more efficient and theoretically pertinent than it is without a careful review of literature.

In addition to searching the theoretical and methodological materials associated with the immediate project, investigators engaging in observation should make a special effort to seek out descriptive information that will provide them with some knowledge of the setting and people being observed. As pointed out in Chapter 1, such information can be of considerable value in legitimizing the credentials of the investigator.

4. THEORETICAL CONCEPTS AND ORIENTATIONS

Because one of the major purposes of observation is to obtain definitions of the situation as the people being observed view the world around them and to see the actual kinds of behavior they are engaging in, it is extremely important for researchers to have a firm grasp of the relevant theoretical concepts and orientations to which they wish to relate the world view of the observed. To help in internalizing as thoroughly as possible the conceptual framework from which the study is being conducted, the following steps should be taken by observers:

First, delimit the immediate conceptual interests of the theoretical perspective being used insofar as those concepts pertain to the problem under investigation.

Second, outline the types of observations that will represent or serve as "indicators" of the concepts.

Third, plot in either written form or diagrammatically various ways in which the concepts or variables are related to one another. In that way, logical connections among the theoretical interests being examined can be more explicitly delineated.

Finally, make explicit whatever known assumptions exist about the subject from the investigator's perspective. By preparing such a list, some very important and perhaps unrecognized aspects of the investigator's own preexisting views about the world view of the observed may be brought to the front and effectively eliminated from the study. It is especially important to correct those types of assumptions considered evaluative on the part of investigators.

5. HYPOTHESES

Normally the objectives sought by researchers engaging in observation are such that the formulation and testing of hypotheses in the usual sense is not of central importance. That does not diminish the overall relevance of theoretical concerns in these types of studies, however. It is just that investigators, when relying on observations, go about the business of testing theories in a somewhat different way. By having familiarized themselves with relevant theoretical positions, observers assume the task of depicting natural social settings as accurately as possible and comparing these observations with the known theoretical views about them. More important than testing hypotheses, then, are problems related to portraying the natural context of social behavior in such a way that theories can be assessed in the light of these observational findings.

6. METHODOLOGY

Decisions about how to actually carry out observations revolve around several basic dimensions of the study. In many respects, the decisions are like those that have to be made in any type of project, because the operations necessary to obtain scientifically relevant data through observation are basically similar in all studies. So long as the ultimate objectives of research are related to the accumulation of scientific facts, the operations will invariably follow a certain logic.[2] Because they constitute the core elements of this logic of inquiry, questions about validity, reliability, and representativeness eventually have to be addressed in specifying operational procedures for observers.

Tactics for conducting observations have not received a great deal of attention by social scientists. Especially lacking in the literature are strictly methodological studies designed to compare, contrast, and refine various methods of obtaining data by observation and to assess the relative quality of the data generated by them. Consequently, investigators usually have no demonstrated grounds for making many of their decisions. Sustained attention to these issues is sorely needed.

Still, a sufficient amount of literature exists to pinpoint some of the major operational procedures that require decisions (Becker and Geer, 1960; Hammond, 1964; Vidich, 1955; Vidich, Bensman, and Stein, 1964; Whyte, 1955). Becker and Geer (as quoted in Wiseman, 1970, p. 271) divide these operations into three broad categories:

1. Select and define problems, concepts, and indices.
2. Check on the frequency and distribution of phenomena.
3. Incorporate individual findings into a model of the organization under study.

These categories are not sufficient to chart the way for the person just beginning to do work as an observer. Consequently, the ensuing discussion will center about more specific methodological procedures that must be entertained by those interested in engaging in observation. Following somewhat the outline suggested in Chapter 4 in connection with outlining the methodology section of a research proposal, we can order the discussion by posing several specific questions. First, where are the observations taking place? Second, from whom is information being obtained? Third, what types of data are being collected? Fourth, how are the data being collected?

WHERE ARE THE OBSERVATIONS TAKING PLACE?

This amounts to, if one follows the format suggested in Chapter 4, identifying the characteristics of the groups being observed and determining which elements or aspects of their conduct are going to be observed. With respect to population characteristics one set of questions to obtain information about has to do with locating the groups *spatially* and *temporally*. Where does the behavior being observed occur? In one place? Several places? Are there similar settings elsewhere? Or is this the only place where such activity can be found? What is the time period during which the observations occur? What are the boundaries of the population being investigated? Another set of questions deals with age, sex, ethnic, occupational and other features that are part of the inherited social context and that may in some way affect the type of world view that populations being observed display.

Since not everything about the populations under scrutiny is being observed, those features that are need to be explicitly delineated. In the initial stages of observation, investigators try to find out what it is that will lead them to an understanding of the social behavior being observed (Wiseman, 1970, p. 272). Zeldich (in McCall and Simmons, 1969) suggests that there are two very practical criteria to be employed in deciding how to proceed toward this goal: (1) informational adequacy, and (2) efficiency. By raising these issues early, observers can get to the task at hand much more rapidly and systematically than if they are not anticipated.

FROM WHOM IS INFORMATION BEING OBTAINED?

Observers must make decisions about the *number* of observations to be made. It is frequently not possible for an investigator to observe everything of interest in the study. Under these conditions, a decision has to be made concerning whether to rely on fewer observations or use some other method, such as informants, to provide information based on their observation and knowledge of the behavior in question. When analyzing complex settings it is difficult not to rely on informants as observer's observers (Zeldich, in McCall and Simmons, 1969).

Another problem is the manner of selecting the observed. Procedures for sampling have already been discussed in Chapter 8. It need only be added here that the choice of sampling techniques is dictated by the problem being studied. For example, if special information is needed that can be obtained only through very selective observations, randomization would not be a correct procedure. If, on the other hand, one were attempting to obtain a representative view of the activities of a variety of people in, say, a given neighborhood or a slum area, random observations might be more appropriate.

In designing observation studies care must be taken to plan in advance for these problems. The fact that no established protocol exists to aid in the selection of one procedure over another does not shield investigators from making sure that a way has been found in their study to handle such operations.

WHAT TYPES OF DATA ARE BEING COLLECTED?

Investigators very often find that the data that need to be collected to accomplish the objectives of observational studies necessitate the use of more than one type of observation along with certain other data-collection devices. In a sense, observation is a very delicate and specialized technique and many of the types of information needed to bolster the observations made by investigators have to be obtained through other means. Almost invariably, for example, researchers do not stop with nonverbal observations of the conduct of others. At some point and in some fashion there is an effort to discuss with the others various aspects of their conduct. As a result, it is frequently the case that researchers will incorporate some form of interviewing such as unstructured interviewing in the study design.[3] One of the central strengths of observation is that it permits an investigator to use a variety of research techniques with relative ease. Consequently, those interested in observing must have a working familiarity with a variety of other types of data collection procedures.

In addition to selecting the types of methods that will be used, investigators have to determine whether they are interested in the frequency with which various events occur, whether they are concerned about the significant events that shape the context of situations in a given way, or what. It is only when these types of decisions have been made that it is possible to know which type of data one is interested in obtaining.

What is important from the standpoint of observational research is that a composite of information be gathered that delineates the world as the actors who participate in it perceive their activities.

HOW ARE DATA BEING COLLECTED?

Two immediate problems confront investigators doing an observation study. Unless they are resolved satisfactorily the entire study can be jeopardized. First, there is the problem of how to gain entry into the setting or settings where the observations are to take place. Second, there is the problem of how to maintain accurate and useful records.

Entering the Setting

Approaching those from whom information is to be obtained in a proper manner is an important phase of any research project. When the research involves direct interpersonal relations between investigators and subjects, it becomes particularly crucial. Although each situation will pose unique problems, some basic guidelines can be followed. Dean, Eichhorn, and Dean (in McCall and Simmons, 1969) make several suggestions in this connection. They contend that access to research settings can be facilitated by, first of all, establishing contacts with those in positions of highest authority and working down. In contexts where there is more than one dimension of authority, make contacts with those at the top of each hierarchy. Examples of situations such as this would occur where one was observing activities in a bureaucratic setting such as a university or a large industrial plant where there is both a managerial and a union hierarchy or academic personnel and nonacademic personnel.

Second, it is necessary to have an adequate explanation for why the research is being conducted. It probably would be beneficial to prepare several possible statements and select the most appropriate one. Although there are no firm rules for this selection process, Dean, Eichhorn, and Dean indicate that the statements made by investigators must in no way imply that the conduct observed is being *evaluated*. Rather, researchers should stress their interest in *understanding* or *comprehending*.

Related to this is a third point. Observers who misrepresent themselves or their research objectives are opening themselves up for potentially grave difficulties. Honesty in establishing contact can avoid unanticipated pitfalls later on in the study. According to these authors, gaining acceptance in the initial stages of the study is sufficiently important that it should take priority over other considerations.

A fourth point to be made is that it is all right to let some early data gathering go. These tasks will present themselves soon enough. Some facts can and should be obtained in the early stages, however. Routine, nonthreatening types of questions or observations of the sorts an investigator should be expected to be interested in can speed the process of acceptance. Furthermore, they help to define the situation as one in which research will be taking place. As a result, the observer can become part of the natural setting more readily.

Problems of Recording Observations

Unless some feasible way is found to record the volumes of data cascading over the observer's perceptual field, all else is wasted effort. Even the most seasoned investigators do not go into the field to observe with the intention of recalling everything from memory. Consequently, one or more methods of data compilation will have to be designed. Actually, the range of alternatives for recording observations is quite restricted. Minor variations may occur in their use, but observers must choose between either mechanical methods or note taking.

Mechanical methods include the use of tape recorders, cameras, and so on. Their use, according to McCall and Simmons (1969, p. 73) should be restricted to "more important, complicated, or information-packed situations." Expenses incurred in purchasing the machinery plus those required to retrieve the data from the tapes or films usually place these types of devices out of the reach of most investigators. Besides, in many observation studies, the researcher is not interested in obtaining the full range of information provided by the studies raising questions about their efficiency.

Note taking in some form is the most frequently relied upon method. Several points must be made about this form of recording information obtained from observations. First, notes have to be written up as soon as possible after the observation. As a facility for recording observations in this matter is developed, researchers usually find that much more is remembered than they thought possible. Recording which is done as the observations are occurring is usually less desirable than that accomplished later because the note taking done as the social behavior is occurring tends to supplant the observing. One popular way to record observation is by using a log or diary. That permits data to be recorded chronologically and enables researchers to more readily detect changes over time in the behavior being observed (McCall and Simmons, 1969, 74–75).

In an effort to integrate the day-to-day recording of information and the development of an indexing system, McCall (in McCall and Simmons, 1969, p. 76) suggests the following procedure:

> Each day's field notes are typed directly upon mimeograph stencils and multiple copies are run off and filed in labeled folders, each of which pertains to a single topic, category, variable, or hypothesis. The verbal material pertinent to the subject matter of a given folder is circled in red and only those pages which contain circled material are inserted in that folder. A complete copy of the day's field notes are placed in chronological order in a cumulative file folder which then serves the purposes of an ordinary field diary. The stencils and a few extra copies are labeled and filed separately in chronological order so that, should further categories emerge later in the study, pertinent pages of field notes from the past can be added to the new files.

The second point to be made about note taking is that it must be designed in such a way to facilitate data analysis. This entails some procedure for the systematic classification of observation. More often than not, this will be done as the project develops. In all probability, the scheme will be revised and modified at various points in the study. Eventually, though, a carefully developed classification scheme or indexing scheme is indispensable to the ultimate analysis of the observations.

Even when an investigator is diligent in writing observations down as quickly as is feasible, some time will elapse between recording observations and their analysis. It is conceivable that there will be less than accurate recall about whether the information was directly observed, based on inference, or what. Strauss (quoted in McCall and Simmons 1966, p. 74) suggests how verbal observations can be recorded:

> Verbal material recorded within quotations signified exact recall; verbal material within apostrophes indicated a lesser degree of certainty or paraphrasing; and verbal material with no markings meant reasonable recall but not quotation. Finally, the interviewer's impressions or influences could be separated from actual observations by the use of single or double parentheses.

Although Strauss' comments were specifically directed at interviewing, they are applicable to observation as well. And even though confined to recording verbal data, the remarks point a way for researchers to develop a technique for more refined coding of nonverbal types of observation. Such a notation procedure has the added advantage of providing readers of the material with a plausible basis for assessing the relative value of the data presented.

In sum, although others can rely on some form of assistance from computers, calculators, card-sorters, and key punch machines, observers must do enormous amounts of recording and retrieving data by hand. If it is not undertaken systematically, such work can be frustrating and time consuming. In addition, considerable quantities of relevant data can be lost or, perhaps even worse yet, inaccurately presented. There is no substitute for the orderly accumulation and analysis of data, even those obtained by observation.

SOME QUESTIONS FOR REVIEW

1.   Review the major characteristics of observation. In what ways do these characteristics render observation unique as a method of data collection?

2.   What are the major types of observation? Compare and contrast them in terms of the ways they contribute to the objectives of observational research.

3.   Outline the factors which influence the selection of observation as a data-collection device. Which, in your estimation, have the greatest bearing on its choice? Why?

4.   Design a study that utilizes observation as the primary (or only) method of data collection. What do you see as its major limitations? Merits? How could the study be improved?

5.   Review the problems associated with recording observations. Discuss the advantages of note taking as opposed to the use of a tape recorder.

NOTES

1.   McCall and Simmons (1969) take a more long-range view of the descriptive features of observation. They see the ultimate contribution as being that of "analytic description."
2.   Chapter 1 should be reviewed on these points.
3.   This and other types of interviews will be taken up in Chapter 10.

BIBLIOGRAPHY

Becker, Howard S., and Blanche Geer, "Participant Observation: The Analysis of Qualitative Field Data." In *Human Organization Research,* edited by Richard N. Adams and Jack J. Preiss. Homewood, Ill.: Dorsey Press, 1960: 267–89.

———, Blanche Geer, Everett C. Hughes, and Anselm L. Strauss. *Boys in White: Student Culture in Medical School.* Chicago: University of Chicago Press, 1961.

Hammond, Phillip E., ed. *Sociologist at Work: the Craft of Social Research.* New York: Basic Books, 1964.

Masters, William and Virginia Johnson. *Human Sexual Inadequacy.* Boston: Little, Brown, 1970.

McCall, George J., and J. L. Simmons. *Issues in Participant Observation: A Text and Reader.* Reading, Mass.: Addison-Wesley, 1969.

Reiss, Albert J., Jr. *The Police and the Public.* New Haven, Conn.: Yale University Press, 1971.

———. "Systematic Observation of Natural Social Phenomena." In *Sociological Methodology,* edited by Herbert L. Costner. San Francisco: Jossey-Bass, 1971.

Ruebhausen, Oscar M., and Orville G. Brim, Jr. "Privacy and Behavioral Research," *Columbia Law Review* 65 (1965): 1184–1211.

Stinchcombe, Arthur L. "Institutions of Privacy in the Determination of Police Administrative Practices," *American Journal of Sociology* 69 (1963): 150–60.

Vidich, Arthur, J. "Methodological Problems in the Observation of Husband-Wife Interaction," *Marriage and Family Living* 28: (1955): 234–39.

———, Joseph Bensman; and Maurice R. Stein. *Reflections on Community Studies.* New York: John Wiley, 1964.

Whyte, William F. *Street Corner Society.* Chicago: University of Chicago Press, 1955.

Wiseman, Jacqueline P. *Stations of the Lost: The Treatment of Skid Row Alcoholics.* Englewood Cliffs, N.J.: Prentice-Hall, 1970.

Zeldich, Morris, Jr., "Some Methodological Problems of Field Studies." In McCall and Simmons (eds.), *Issues in Participant Observation.* Reading, Mass.: Addison-Wesley, 1969.

CHAPTER 10
THE INTERVIEW

The interview is easily the most sociological of all research techniques. That is because its very form is derived from *verbal* interaction between the investigator and the respondent. Many insist that the best way to find out why persons behave as they do is to quiz them about their conduct directly by talking to them. The interview has some especially ardent admirers. They embellish it with even further qualities:

> But the interview is still more than tool and object of study. It is the art of sociological sociability, the game which we play for the pleasure of savoring its subtleties. It is our flirtation with life, our eternal affair, played hard and to win, but played with that detachment and amusement which gives us, win or lose, the spirit to rise up and interview again and again. (Benny and Hughes, 1956, p. 138).

Whether interviews ought to be approached with such an intense attachment is certainly open to debate. We doubt that one need go as far as Benny and Hughes to appreciate the value of interviewing as a data-collecting instrument. No one can deny, however, that the interview poses some very definite strengths and weaknesses, has particular adaptability to certain types of problems, and requires the acquisition of specialized skills not needed when using other tools. In addition, as with other forms of data gathering, the interview itself is frequently the subject of investigation. Variables that affect the use of various types of interviews and contribute to its refinement as a generator of scientifically relevant information are continuously sought and identified through research. These and related matters will be considered as we focus on:

1.   Characteristic features of the interview.
2.   Major functions of the interview.
3.   Factors affecting the use of the interview.
4.   Types of interviews and major problems in formulating and conducting them.
5.   Advantages and disadvantages in the use of the interview.
6.   Types of problems to which the interview is especially applicable.

CHARACTERISTIC FEATURES OF THE INTERVIEW

The interview is an act of verbal communication for the purpose of eliciting information. Beyond this universally recognized feature, a wide range of views on the essentials of interviews can be found. According to Denzin (1970, p. 195), "an interview is any face-to-face conversational exchange where one person elicits information from another." Benny and Hughes take what is in one sense a more restricted position. Although not confining interviews to face-to-face encounters, they stress *status equality* and *comparability* as central features of this form of interaction. Thus, an interview is defined by Benny and Hughes (1956, p. 142) as "a relationship between two people where both parties behave as though they are of equal status for its duration; whether or not this is actually so, and where, also, both behave as though their encounter had meaning only in relation to a good many other such encounters."

Neither these definitions nor others (Hyman, 1954; Maccoby and Maccoby, 1954; Theodorson and Theodorson, 1969) permit a view of the full range of characteristics embodied in the interview. Consequently, it is appropriate to examine the essential characteristics of the interview rather than confine ourselves to a formal definition. Its most salient features are as follows.

QUESTIONS ARE ASKED AND RESPONSES GIVEN VERBALLY

The verbal nature of the questions emphasizes three points about interviews that are not sufficiently stressed in the above definitions. First, interviews are not simply conversational exchanges. They are conversations in which the major thrust is obtaining verbal answers to questions put verbally.

Second, these verbal exchanges need not be on a face-to-face basis, even though they usually are. Interviews can be conducted over the telephone, for example. What is essential is that the interaction between the interviewer and the interviewee be verbal.

Finally, although it is certainly usually a conversation between two persons, interviews need not be limited to this number. It is not uncommon to interview husbands and wives together, for example, or parents and their children. Interviews can be conducted with groups of persons, such as delinquent gangs, as well as with individual members of the group. Recent innovations in telecommunications make this an even more likely occurrence in the future.

INFORMATION IS RECORDED BY THE INVESTIGATOR RATHER THAN THE RESPONDENT

Other types of data-collection techniques share this characteristic with the interview. Certain observational techniques and experimental procedures call for a similar recording of information. However, the verbal nature of the communication coupled with the fact that interviews are usually on a face-to-face basis make this a feature that must be considered in gathering scientifically useful data.

THE RELATIONSHIP BETWEEN THE INTERVIEWER AND THE INTERVIEWEE IS STRUCTURED IN SEVERAL SPECIFIC WAYS

It is, first of all, a *transitory* relationship. Both in terms of its duration and the question-and-answer form of conversational exchange, it is a relationship with fixed beginning and termination points. Regardless of what other ways the participants in an interview might interact, the interview proper is a fleeting, momentary experience for them.

Second, the relationship is one in which the participants are strangers. Even if they know each other in some unrelated context, although they probably do not, the relationship is distinguished by certain elements that combine to make the interview a new experience. Benny and Hughes (1956) put an emphasis on *equality* and *comparability* as unique features of such interaction that highlight this quality of strangeness. Regarding equality, they point out that "the interview is an understanding between two parties that, in return for allowing the interviewer to direct their communication, the informant is assured that he will not meet with denial, contradiction, competition, or other harassment" (p. 140). Comparability, on the other hand, is a recognition of the scientific demands to be placed on the data. They are a bow in the direction of the generalizability of findings rather than toward the respondents. The interview, no matter how much it plays on the subjective feelings of those being interviewed, is designed to obtain data that are, across many such contacts, capable of providing insights into *uniformities* in behavior. Ultimately, as Benny and Hughes (1956, p. 141) cogently observe, "it is the needs of the statistician rather than of the people involved directly that determine much, not only the content of communication but its form as well."

The net effect of these qualities is felt in two ways. First, they render the verbal interaction, with all its subtleties, meaningless as social discourse between two particular people. The interview is a kind of interaction that places stringent demands on the investigator and the respondent alike. Little wonder that effective interviewing requires special training. Anyone led to the deceptive view that interviews involve simply talking to people will deserve the fruits of his labors.

Furthermore, these qualities confine the use of the interview to cultural contexts in which this form of interaction can legitimately occur (Benny and Hughes, 1956). When social conditions are not sufficiently flexible to allow for such discourse or when knowledge of the immediate social context does not enable the investigator to be attuned to ways of construing conversations into interviews, they lose import as data-gathering techniques.

THERE IS CONSIDERABLE FLEXIBILITY IN THE FORMAT OF THE INTERVIEW

Few other data-collection tools offer such a large range of question-asking formats to the investigator. It would appear at times as though the only limitation is the ingenuity of the interviewer. Such an amount of structural variability allows for a greater degree of mutual understanding of both the questions and the answers on the part of the interviewers and interviewees.

It is not at all desirable to discuss various aspects of the interview in a "cookbook" fashion. Except for maintaining a constant sensitivity to some general problems, investigators who select the interview as a method of data collection do so precisely because it invariably affords a chance to take advantage of the unexpected or move into uncharted areas. Even the most standardized interview contexts do not prohibit such spontaneity of exploration before and after the data have been compiled through the interview.

Some of these characteristics are shared with other tools of social inquiry. Nearly all types of data-gathering instruments pose problems related to compiling and recording information. Then, too, relationships between investigators and the sources of their data are always transitory. Furthermore, insofar as persons are involved as the sources of data, the relationship between them and investigators will always be characteristically strange simply because of its scientific nature. Whether the persons are seen as "respondents", "subjects", "participants", or whatever, the information sought from them must meet the criteria of comparability. Finally, any kind of research technique is applied in culture-specific contexts. Questionnaires cannot be used with illiterate populations, documents cannot be perused in primitive cultures without written history, and so on.

What makes the interview distinctive is the same thing that makes any research method distinctive. That is how the *combination* of characteristics influences the accumulation of scientifically useful information. When combined, these features make the interview extremely useful as an instrument of data collection. But they also suggest that it is perhaps more valuable in the pursuit of certain objectives in the research process than of others.

MAJOR FUNCTIONS OF THE INTERVIEW

Those who select the interview as a research tool are provided with an instrument suitable for a variety of purposes. If for no other reason, their wide flexibility makes interviews suitable for numerous objectives. Two of their functions stand out from the rest: (1) description, and (2) exploration.

DESCRIPTION

As the above characteristics imply, information obtained from interviews is particularly useful in providing insights into the *discursive* nature of social reality. With the possible exception of certain types of observation, perhaps no other type of research tool performs this function as well. People spend most of their time with one another engaged in some form of verbal dialogue. Being able to capture the question-and-answer process as an unfolding dimension of this dialogue permits us to catch a glimpse of social life as it is lived (Forcese and Richer, 1973). A certain "gut-level" understanding of how people view the subject under investigation can be achieved which breathes life into what are otherwise abstract and stale statistical descriptions.

Knowing, for example, that the results of a given survey indicate that a certain percentage of the American public feel one way about an issue and a certain percentage feel another is one thing, but identifying what persons in the sample actually had to say is quite another. A Gallup poll conducted in the summer of 1973 illustrates our point vividly[1] (p. G.11). In this poll, carried out during a recess in the Senate Watergate Hearings, it was ascertained that 52 per cent of a sample of the American public were of the opinion that the Watergate Hearings were good for the country, whereas 41 per cent felt they were not. To enrich these data, comments by some of the sampled population were included. Among those comments were the following:

> "The people should know what's going on behind the scenes," said a 45-year-old public relations executive from Illinois. "The hearings will help create more discriminating voters in the future."

> A 66-year-old New York housewife commented: "The hearings are being dragged out and costing taxpayers a lot of money when there are other important issues to be brought to the nation's attention."

> A 46-year-old state politician from New Jersey had this to say: "The American people have learned more in a few months than they had in 12 years of school about how the Government operates and the dangers to a democratic republic."

> This is the view of a 39-year-old skilled worker from Anaheim, Calif.; "In my opinion, the members of the committee are using Watergate as a means of promoting themselves politically, and at the same time are hurting the chances of persons getting a fair trial."

By delineating in even this narrow way something of the *interactive* quality of social life, interview data can be an extremely useful descriptive tool. What is more, they enhance the understanding of sociological nature of facts among those exposed to such data.

EXPLORATION

Another valuable purpose of the interview is to provide insights into unexplored dimensions of a topic. A survey of the work done in an area as it is reported in the literature does not always produce the fresh, illuminating attack that a problem requires. Selective intellectual biases are usually more easily perpetuated than overcome. Regardless of the particular need, whether it be the identification of new variables for study, a sharpening of conceptual clarity, or whatever, the interview can serve as a highly effective exploratory device. Talking with people and gaining insights into their conduct from inquiries about their feelings, attitudes, and beliefs may provide just the right stimulation for the development of hypotheses for subsequent testing. Two examples will suffice to illustrate the usefulness of the interview in this regard.

Lane (1962, p. 8–9) found interviews useful in gaining numerous suggestive insights into the political views of the "American urban common man." He chose this opportunity for extensive exploration of the thinking of fifteen carefully selected respondents on a variety of research topics. In his words:

> Robert Redfield cautions the social scientist that he must understand the outlook of the men he studies, see things as they see them, before he can profitably employ the apparatus and objectivity of science. In this spirit I have sought in these interviews to understand these men as men, to understand the private import of what they say, to penetrate the latent meaning of their remarks, and then to see the social implications of what they have said.

In this same exploratory spirit, Komorovsky (1964) was able to interview both husbands and wives in an investigation seeking to shed light on blue-collar marriages. The practice of interviewing both marital partners is, interestingly enough, one that is seldom followed in research into the family. By talking with both husbands and wives and by using additional techniques that permitted her to probe their attitudes and beliefs in considerable depth, she was able to come up with some very interesting data about various aspects of working-class marriages. Among her numerous provocative findings were those dealing with different marital expectations among persons with different levels of educational attainment and what were detected early in the investigation as significant differences among working-class married people concerning ideal marital relations.

Such studies admittedly raise more questions than they answer.

Indeed, that is their purpose. But it cannot be overlooked that they are pivotal questions in the sense that they enable more pointed concentration in subsequent research. Hence, they lead to more systematically productive inquiries.

FACTORS AFFECTING THE USE OF INTERVIEWS

Several factors have a direct bearing on the usefulness of interviews in achieving the scientific objectives for which they are employed. Three of these are worthy of special attention; (1) the qualities of the interviewer, (2) the qualities of the interviewee, and (3) the nature of the problem being investigated.

QUALITIES OF THE INTERVIEWER

Broadly speaking, it is possible to distinguish between *subjective* and *objective* characteristics of interviewers. There is no way to determine ahead of time which will have the greater impact on the overall successfulness of a project. Some consideration must be given to both sets of factors.

Qualities of a subjective nature (i.e., those more or less peculiar to the individual) are extremely important. This is especially so if a major function of the research is exploratory. To be effective as instruments of exploration, interviews must be conducted by researchers who have highly inquisitive minds, who are capable of reorienting themselves quickly to newly emerging facets of a problem. Komorovsky displayed such a quality most effectively in being attuned at an early point in her interviews to the different responses being obtained to questions about marriage ideals. For Lane and others, this quality is best described as one of learning to "listen with the third ear" (Lane, 1962, p. 8).

By possessing such a quality, an interviewer can do any one or more of a number of things when interviewing. Sometimes the questions being asked are in need of sharper precision or require redirection and concentration on other matters. Perhaps the problem itself needs to be reconceptualized based on responses to questions being asked. Or it might be that different or additional persons need to be interviewed. No matter what is called for, the interviewer must have a facility for drawing together scattered and disjointed pieces of information into a uniform, integrated whole (Selltiz, Jahoda, Deutsch, and Cook, 1959, p. 60–65). More important, a keen sensitivity to exactly what it is that needs to be done is needed in the interviewing context.

In addition to these subjective factors, objective features of the interviewer usually have considerable influence on the effectiveness of the interview. As Gorden (1969, pp. 126–27) notes, "such characteristics as sex, age, race, ethnicity, social class, manner of dress and speech are important. Not only do they create an immediate impression and help determine whether or not the respondent will consent to be interviewed, but they also place certain limits upon the roles which the interviewer may successfully occupy." He goes on to point out that these overt or objective qualities are important because of ways in which they can interfere with the verbal interaction that takes place between interviewers and respondents.

There is not a sufficient amount of information available at the present time to accurately assess the impact of these variables on interviewer bias. Much more thought must be given to the connections between interviewers, respondents, and the problem being investigated before any consistent knowledge can be obtained (Gorden, 1969, p. 127). Any research design incorporating the interview as a data-collection device must include as much considered information on the possible effects of interviewer qualities as is available.

QUALITIES OF INTERVIEWEES

Interviewing, as we have already noted, is a special form of conversation. It is to be expected, then, that qualities possessed by interviewees would bear directly on the flow of communication. The factors that combine to make it possible for a person to respond candidly and freely to questions posed under interviewing conditions is not well known. Careful and continuous study of these factors has yet to be undertaken. Still, enough is known about the nature of social interaction generally to anticipate certain broadly influential factors.

Elementary among these is the relative capability of respondents to verbalize. Individuals selected as interviewees must be able to put their thoughts into understandable verbal form. As the likelihood of their inarticulateness increases, the feasibility of interviews for gathering information from them diminishes. The very young, the mentally deranged, and others with extremely limited communication skills are not suitable as interviewees. Those with little or no formal education will frequently present some problems in this regard. Finally, people living in relatively isolated personal conditions will often prove to be incapable of articulating their views in a meaningful way.

In addition to the problem of capability, there is the problem of the willingness of the respondents to be interviewed. Many investigators choose to circumvent this problem by seeking out respondents on a voluntary basis. Essentially, they reason that people who want to talk freely and openly will make excellent respondents; those who are unwilling to participate will present problems too bothersome to contend with. Lane (1962, p. 5–6), however, insisted that the unwilling must be interviewed along with the willing:

> Some were flattered and eager to participate; many were moved primarily by the cash consideration, which they and I both formally treated as irrelevant to our study; two were markedly reluctant, and would agree only after many efforts at persuasion and after it was settled that I would talk to them in their own kitchens and not in my office where I interviewed the others. These two men . . . were sufficiently different from the others so that the policy of not relying on volunteers and of making every effort to include exactly those selected by a randomization process was, I think, amply rewarded.

It is clear from Lane's comments that there are various ways to go about increasing the willingness of the respondent to be interviewed. Paying money for their services is certainly one way. A second way is to conduct the interview on the respondent's terms, such as Lane did when he interviewed two of his subjects in their own homes rather than in his office. A third way, one very familiar to students who must conduct interviews for class projects or research papers, is to convince the respondent that the interviewer's course grade or graduate degree depends upon his participation.

Willingness to be interviewed is also dependent to some extent on the respondent's knowledge of and familiarity with the topic being researched. There is no basis for assuming that persons who know about certain topics or have had experiences related to the questions being asked will be more willing to be interviewed, even though that is usually the way things work out. Sometimes, especially when the information sought is particularly sensitive or classified or may prove imminently troublesome to the respondent, those who know the most may have the least to say about a topic. Corwin (1970, p. 69), for example, found in a study of militancy among high school teachers that "for some interviewees the subject of conflict was too repugnant to discuss." Whether because of a personal dislike for such problems, a fear of being fired if they were discussed, a feeling that the researcher was encroaching on time and space that could be better utilized, or some other reason, people many times choose not to be included. Or if they are included, they select not to answer fully or truthfully.

Capability and willingness are not the only qualities of the interviewee that require attention. A third characteristic that can influence the communicative process and, eventually, the accumulation of scientifically useful data involves the status of the respondent vis-à-vis the interviewer. "Elite" or "specialized" interviewing refers to interviewees who are given "special, nonstandardized treatment" (Dexter, 1970, p. 5). Dexter pinpoints precisely what is meant by "nonstandardized":

1. Stressing the interviewee's definition of the situation.
2. Encouraging the interviewee to structure the account of the situation.
3. Letting the interviewee introduce to a considerable extent (an extent which will of course vary from project and interviewer to interviewer) his notions of what he regards as relevant, instead of relying upon the investigator's notions of relevance.

Interviewees, then, who are given a hand in directing the course of the interview, in shaping the problem according to their own views and experiences, can be considered "elite." They have something to say, and it may not fit in with the assumptions of the investigator about the topic being investigated. The well informed, whether they be mothers about child-rearing practices, lawyers about handling cases, doctors about medical practices, will usually feel unduly constrained by standardized interviewing procedures (Dexter, 1970).

Although the people handled in this manner are frequently the more prestigious, influential, and knowledgeable, such need not be the case. Lane (1962), for example, was not interested in the views of the politically sophisticated but in those of ordinary citizens. To the extent that he allowed his respondents to structure the course of the interview location, he was treating them as elites.

NATURE OF THE PROBLEM

Interviewing is also affected by the topic being investigated. Some subjects do not elicit much response no matter how much care is taken to have appropriate interviewers and interviewees. Most people, for example, simply do not want to reveal how much money they make in their work. It is considered a topic that is exceptionally private. At the same time, most individuals appear to be willing to discuss their sex lives quite frankly with investigators. It is difficult to pinpoint with accuracy those problems individuals find too delicate and private for scientific scrutiny. As problems crop up, great skill is needed to obtain the desired information.

Some problems are difficult to research through interviews because the respondents find it impossible to verbalize about the point being investigated. Cressey (1953) found that it was impossible for embezzlers to know precisely at what point they became consciously aware of what they were doing. Hence, he stated that it was not, in his estimation, possible to test empirically Sutherland's assertion that an individual becomes a criminal when that person has an excess of definition favorable to the violation of the law (Sutherland and Cressey, 1955).

There are no cut-and-dried rules of thumb to follow. Problems that touch those segments of persons' lives that they tend to regard as *private* and problems that create special difficulties in *verbal communications* for the respondent will have a bearing on the scientific quality of the information obtained. When interviews are used under such conditions, care must be taken to account for these factors and minimize their influence.

To contend with these and the related problems discussed in this and previous sections, social scientists have developed several distinctive types of interviews. A working familiarity with them is essential in regulating the intrusion of extraneous variables into the research process and in achieving the overall objectives of investigations built around the use of the interview.

TYPES OF INTERVIEWS

Any one of a number of approaches can be relied on to classify the various types of interviews used by investigators in gathering scientific data. Perhaps the simplest and most convenient way to distinguish among them is in terms of the degree to which they are structured.

UNSTRUCTURED INTERVIEWS

As their name suggests, unstructured interviews do little more than indicate to the interviewer what the general nature of the problem is and ask that interviewees be questioned about it.

Investigators might, for example, be charged with the task of finding out what they can about the generation gap by interviewing adolescents and/or their parents. There is no specification of time limits. As much or as little time may be spent with respondents as is felt necessary by the interviewer. Questions are not ordered in a particular way. What is asked first in one interview may come toward the middle or the end of another. In fact, the same questions may not be asked from interview to interview. And those that are asked may not be worded in the same way. No particular restrictions are placed on either the characteristics possessed by the interviewees or the number of interviewees to be contacted beyond their status as adolescents or parents. There are no particular qualifications that interviewers must have. Finally, the problem is not posed in such a way that particular facets of it are to be concentrated on. The interviewing context is as free of regulation and conscious constraint as possible.

There are special advantages to the use of this type of data-gathering technique. First, the interview can more closely approximate the spontaneity of a natural conversation. Second, those features of the problem central to the respondent's thinking are identified more readily. As a result, the interviewer is less prone to impose one or another bias that would slant the course of the conversation and restrict the flow of data. Third, there is a much greater opportunity to explore various aspects of the problem in an unrestricted manner. Each of these considerations makes the unstructured interview a potent research instrument. Still it is not without its limitations.

One of the major difficulties with the unstructured interview is the questionable comparability of the data obtained from one interview to the next. With no systematic control over the question-asking procedures, the reliability of the data is thrown into serious question. A second problem is that quite a bit of time can be wasted conducting interviews in which the respondents have little or nothing to add to knowledge already obtained. Without some attention to the selection of respondents, interviewers may be engaging in needlessly repetitious or unproductive conversations. By not concentrating in some detail on one or another facet of a problem, investigators run the risk of being led up blind alleys. There is, after all, no assurance that exploration will invariably lead to productive and fertile ground. The chances that research activities will not provide valuable insights are pronounced when the problem being investigated is not carefully conceptualized.

There is a third problem with the unstructured interview. To the extent that an investigator does not know how to decide in advance on procedures for the classification of responses, considerable time must be devoted to coding data once the interviews have been completed. The possibility that the same types of responses get coded differently at different times is increased. For these and other reasons, most investigators prefer to introduce at least some degree of structuring in their interviews.[2]

STRUCTURED INTERVIEWS

There are several ways for an investigator to maintain some control over the interview context. Regulating any or all of the dimensions of the interview will produce varying degrees of structure. Obviously, considerable flexibility is permitted in deciding the extent to which interviews are to be structured. There are no hard, fast rules to follow. A brief discussion of the most salient dimensions of the interview that are susceptible to control and that can affect research findings will enable the researcher to develop sensitivity to the range of factors that can be regulated in ways that will enhance the scientific utility of his findings. Among the most relevant areas to consider introducing structure into are the following: (1) the setting of the interview, (2) ordering of questions and limiting the range of responses, (3) regulating interviewer and interviewee characteristics, and (4) limiting the facets of the problem being scrutinized.

Specifying the Setting of the Interview

The place where an interview is conducted can have a great deal of bearing on the quality of the information obtained. Whether the investigator is interested in controlling for this dimension of the interview context will be determined by a number of considerations.

First, of what importance is the time element to the investigator? When it is important that respondents be located with a minimum of difficulty, it might be well to make plans for having the interview conducted in a place that will minimize the time needed to travel to and from the research setting. Researchers and correspondents do not usually have the time to waste going long distances. Nor do researchers have time to return again and again to places where respondents are supposed to be but aren't. If it is possible to find a convenient and suitable place where all interviews can be conducted, gathering data will probably proceed more smoothly than it will otherwise. If ease of location is important, do whatever must be done to structure the setting in such a way that the interests of both the interviewer and the respondent will be served.

Second, what must be done to assure respondents of their confidentiality in the research project? As nearly anyone knows, it is no simple task to get people to talk about things they consider "inappropriate" or "touchy" or "out of order." Intrusions into the normal working day of a business executive or a factory worker or housewife for the purpose of asking questions about things they may or may not want to discuss can be hazardous. People at work may well not want to say things about their superiors or about working conditions or politics or whatever for fear of being overheard. At the same time, meeting with them in a bar or at their home or somewhere else not closely identified with their work or with the topic under discussion may enable them to open up and more freely discuss various matters of interest to the researcher. Should there be some difficulty in convincing them that their comments are not being recorded surreptitiously, the researcher might well be advised to find a neutral location.

Controlling Questions and Responses

If enough is known about the topic under investigation, it is usually possible to structure the interview by regulating questions and responses. Insofar as asking questions is concerned, there are two major points to consider. The first has to do with the order in which questions are asked. To achieve more reliable results, it is advantageous to ask questions in the same order from interview to interview. To avoid complications and be assured of continuity, investigators usually develop interview schedules when such structuring is desired.[3] These can become as elaborate as the investigator wishes. In addition to asking questions in a certain order, for example, it is possible to specify in the interview schedule that the sequence of questions be dictated by the responses of the interviewee. An interviewer may be instructed to ask one question if a respondent answers one way and to ask another if the respondent answers differently. For example, an interview schedule may say:

> If the respondent answers yes to the above question, ask the following:

In highly structured interviews relying almost exclusively on a detailed interview schedule, the interview approaches the questionnaire in format, but that should not deter anyone from opting for highly structured interviews. Indeed, it should not be forgotten, as Gorden reminds us (1969, p. 56):

> . . . all of the above diagnostic concepts regarding the inhibitors and facilitators of communication and most of the tools described under the heading of strategy, tactics, and techniques are applicable to the

design and administration of a questionnaire as well as to interviewing.

It is also possible to structure the responses as well as the questions in an interview context. This is achieved by offering the interviewee his choice from one of any of several alternatives. For example, a question might be put as follows:

Would you say you strongly support, modestly support, slightly support, or do not support at all, the previous statement?

Or, as is frequently found in public opinion surveys:

Which of the following would you vote for for President? (list names).

When the occasion permits, interviewers are usually instructed to hand the respondent a card indicating the range of responses from which an answer is to be selected.

Some risk is involved in structuring responses in interview situations. Unless a sufficient amount of information is known about the views of the respondent toward the topic being studied, responses may be omitted that might be of importance from the perspective of the respondent. It is, in effect, the same problem encountered in all attempts by investigators to make assumptions about the perceptions of those being studied, whether the method of data gathering be interviews, questionnaires, or some other form of data compilation.

Interviewer-Interviewee Characteristics

Given the fact that the interview context is conversational and more often than not face-to-face, interviewer-interviewee characteristics can assume considerable significance in obtaining scientifically useful information. There are no fixed rules governing the structuring of the interview context according to these characteristics. However, both the subjective and objective features of interviewers and features associated with the interviewees (such as their willingness to be interviewed and the status of the respondent vis-à-vis the interviewer) must be examined carefully to see whether they can be controlled for in an effort to structure the context of the interview accordingly. As the conversational context of the interview is less and less affected by these considerations, interviews can be more highly structured along these lines. Unfortunately, little systematic research into this area of interviewing has been undertaken. Whatever techniques and procedures are selected will invariably have to develop out of the subjective expertise of the investigator.

An additional aspect of the interviewer-interviewee characteristics about which some advanced decision must be made concerns the extent to which the initiative in obtaining information rests with the respondent or with the interviewer. In most interviews, it is up to the interviewer to "pry" the information needed from a respondent. In some types of interviews, such as the nondirective interview, however, the respondent supplies information with a minimum of direct questioning from the interviewer. (Selltiz et al., 1959, p. 267). The task of interviewers is simply to encourage the respondent to continue talking. As Selltiz et al. (1959, p. 261) point out, "interviews tend to rely on such comments as: 'You feel that . . .' or 'Tell me more' or 'Why' or 'Isn't that interesting' or, simply, 'Uh huh'."

Limiting the Problem

As researchers give more thought to what it is they want to find out from respondents, there is a tendency to narrow the topic of original interest considerably. Several factors influence such decisions. Ubiquitous problems such as time and cost have to be considered. Hard decisions must be made by narrowing the range of items on which to obtain data. As more and more thought is given to the actual research questions on which data are being brought to bear, the questions become increasingly more refined in ways that can contribute to narrowing a study's scope.

One of the most effective forms of structuring the interview context in a way that limits the problem being considered yet retains most of the flexibility of the interview as a data-gathering technique is the use of the *focused interview*. Interviews are focused in the sense that the respondents have all been subjected to the same experience. Investigators, aware of this, conduct interviews to have respondents discuss various dimensions of the effect of the experience on them. All those who might have attended the same play or the same religious crusade, for example, might be asked particular questions relating to this common experience.

Merton, Fiske, and Kendall (1956) restrict the use of the term *focused interview* to an interview in which the respondents have shared some common experience that has, in turn, been carefully scrutinized by the investigator to generate hypotheses about the effects of the experience on the participants. The interview context focuses on the actual effects of the experience as viewed by the participants.

Selltiz et al. (1959, p. 256) broaden the definition of focused interviews to include shared experiences that serve as the basis for the interview. There is no stipulation that the investigator need be aware of the experience by having participated in or been intimately familiar with it.

There is nothing to prohibit a researcher from accepting either position. There is little disputing the fact, however, that precision is enhanced as knowledge of the situation or experience by the investigator is increased. Therefore, the more closely an investigator can approach the narrower conception of the focused interview, the greater the likelihood of obtaining more precise data. At the same time, there is a much better chance of being able to make full use of the advantages inherent in interviews.

If there is one overriding conclusion to be reached from our discussion of various types of interviews, it is that considerable latitude is permitted in reaching decisions about how to structure them. That there are no explicit, step-by-step procedures and rules to follow will probably prove frustrating to some. To others, however, it is just this feature of interviewing that encourages its selection as a data-gathering device.

Overall, there are three clear advantages to be gained from structured interviews. First, data from one interview to the next are more easily compared. Second, problems of recording and coding data are less intractable. Consequently, greater precision is achieved. In addition to these important advantages, a third is that the more highly structured the interview context, the less likely that attention will be diverted to extraneous, irrelevant, and time-consuming conversation.

As interviews become more structured, they tend to loose the spontaneity of natural conversation. In addition, there is the danger that the investigator has structured the interview in such a way that the respondent's views are minimized and the investigator's own biases regarding the problem being studied are inadvertently introduced. And, finally, the possibility of exploration, although not totally eliminated, is less likely to occur than when unstructured interviews are used.

ADVANTAGES AND DISADVANTAGES OF THE INTERVIEW

Regardless of the type of interview used, there are certain merits and shortcomings common to all of them. Although some of these have been alluded to already, it will be profitable to summarize them. At the same time, certain problems not yet touched on in any detail need to be explicated.

ADVANTAGES OF THE INTERVIEW

Gorden (1969, pp. 52–4) lists five major advantages of the interview:

1.   It enables the investigator to obtain desired information more quickly.
2.   It permits the investigator to be sure that respondents interpret questions properly.
3.   It allows, as we have mentioned frequently, for greater flexibility in the process of questioning.
4.   Much more control can be exercised over the context within which questions are asked and answers given.
5.   Information can be more readily checked for its validity on the basis of nonverbal cues by the respondent.

Other forms of data collection may share certain of these advantages with the interview. None, however, offers such a unique combination of advantages as the interview permits.

Still, the interview is not without its problems. Several disadvantages, some probably already detectable to the discerning reader, persist. Before selecting the interview as a major research tool, these limitations must be carefully weighed against the advantages.

DISADVANTAGES OF THE INTERVIEW

1.   The Validity of Verbal Responses

As is frequently mentioned in social science research writings, there is always the question of whether a person actually behaves the way he says he behaves. When attempting to obtain information from verbal responses regarding actual conduct, a serious question confronts investigators whether verbal responses can be relied on with any great degree of validity.

2.   Interviewer Variability

As we all know, there are times when a person is "up" for a given conversation and times when certain things which get said in the course of the conversation tend to elude us. We are tired, we are distracted, we find our mind wandering, and so on. Even in studies with a single interviewer, the problem of the variability in an interviewer's sensitivity to responses must be taken into account. An interviewer may from time to time look at similar responses differently and record them differently from interview to interview. The extent to which interviewers themselves tend to be a source of variation as they move from interview to interview is a matter for careful attention in assessing the overall utility of the findings from interviews.

3. Inter-interviewer Variability

When more than one interviewer is used on a study, problems tend to be compounded. This is especially true when the interviews are unstructured. Even as the interviews become highly structured, interviewers vary considerably between and among themselves regarding such matters as being able to obtain and maintain rapport with respondents, being able to project the proper kind of image, being able to elicit exactly the kinds of information needed and record the information appropriately, and so on.

In effect, as more and more interviewers are added, the problem of interviewer variability becomes compounded and becomes one of inter-interviewer variability.

4. Variations Inherent to the Interviewing Context

Aaron Cicourel (1964, p. 99) has observed with respect to the interviewing context that it cannot be expected to remain constant. In his words:

> The nature of responses generally depends upon the trust developed early in the relationship, status differences, differential perception, and interpretations placed on questions and responses, the control exercised by the interviewer, and so forth. The validity of the schedule becomes a variable condition within and between interviews.

Investigators cannot always be certain that the interview context will remain exactly the same as they move from interview to interview. What Cicourel points out is that the interview context itself becomes a variable that must in some way be accounted for in assessing findings from studies utilizing the interview as a major research instrument.

5. Time

Interviews usually take much more time to complete than is at first envisioned. This is especially so when one considers the additional time taken to transcribe information from tapes. Although it might permit an investigator to accomplish more interviews in a day, taping has the disadvantage of being time consuming. Estimates vary, but it is usually agreed that from six to nine hours are required to effectively transcribe one hour of recorded interview material.

Although some degree of efficiency can be obtained as the interview context becomes more and more structured, little can be done to offset the limitation of time.

6. Recording Information

Interviews also pose the problem of how to record the information being obtained from respondents. No foolproof system has yet been worked out to everyone's satisfaction. Some choose to jot down certain phrases or comments at crucial points, waiting to write up their notes when the interview is completed. If that is done, there is almost universal acceptance of the rule that an interviewer's notes should be written up immediately after the interview, if at all possible, while the conversation is still fresh in the mind of the investigator. It is also common practice to inform the respondent that you will be jotting down comments occasionally so that he will not be distracted unnecessarily by your actions. Because the questions conform to a more systematically developed schedule, note taking can be more organized and in all probability does not serve to disrupt the flow of communication between interviewer and interviewee.

Some investigators feel that note taking is invariably distracting to respondents and does not afford the investigator an opportunity to capitalize on nonverbal cues in the interview. It is maintained that people are naturally curious about what is being written down. Besides, investigators must devote some thought to what is being written down and, consequently, have less time to pay attention to the respondent.

When it is felt that such factors do come into play, investigators are likely to rely on some type of recording device for their interview. One advantage of recording interviews is that there is no problem with remembering the chronological sequence of the conversation later. Furthermore, when some doubt exists as to the inflection or emphasis given certain points, the recording can provide a ready check. And regardless of how diligent one is about reconstructing the commentary of an interview as quickly as possible after its termination, a series of interviews following on the heels of one another in the same day usually leave an interviewer's mind somewhat fuzzy. Finally, there is no interruption to the communication flow when recording devices are used.

However, just as people tend to be distracted by note taking, they can be intimidated by a microphone. Knowing that every syllable is being recorded can be as disconcerting as wondering what an interviewer is writing on a note pad. One of the major sources of respondents' nervousness in the presence of recording devices arises not from a fear of the devices but, instead, from the inept use of the devices by interviewers. All too frequently, the interviewer is not skilled in the use of the recording machine. The interviewer's own awkwardness is a major factor contributing to feelings of uneasiness on the part of the respondent. This observation underscores a point often neglected by interviewers who are prone to place too much emphasis on the effects of recording devices on respondents. Too often the *inter-active* nature of the interview context is minimized. As a consequence, the impact of their own behavior on respondents is overlooked. Interviewers should become experienced in the use of recording devices prior to conducting interviews so they can use them in an unassuming manner. Such preparation is far superior to recording no information at all. Should it come down to a matter of recording or not, researchers should not overlook the fact that respondents like to feel that their comments are of sufficient dignity and importance to warrant recording them in one or another fashion. To have that important fact ignored by viewing the respondent as the focal point of the interview rather than a participant in it (albeit in a specialized and restricted way) is an unfortunate and needless error.

USES OF THE INTERVIEW

The interview, in one or another form and given all its strengths and weaknesses, is especially suited for use with certain types of research problems.

It can be used, first, to study problems that rely on verbal expression for their comprehension. Not every problem of interest to the scientific investigator is one that elicits commentary from respondents. Many of the macrosocial interests of sociologists, for example, rely on data generated and dealt with in other ways. Such phenomena are empirically demonstrated by findings that do not rest on what respondents have to say about them. Interviews are invaluable research tools when the problem under scrutiny is one in which the respondents' own verbally expressed views are central features of the behavioral context being studied. These are, as a rule, problems of a more microsocial nature. When investigators are interested, in any study, in examining the views of respondents from the respondent's own vantage point and, insofar as possible, in the respondent's own words, the interview is an effective research device.

A second important use of the interview is as an adjunct to other methods of data collection. In discussing the interview as a research tool and assessing it as a generator of scientifically useful information, we have been treating it as if it were always used alone. That is not always the case. The use of the interview to obtain verbal data to augment other forms of data collection is a frequent practice in social science research. In instances where it is felt that the situation being examined can be more realistically portrayed by having interview data alongside scientific tables, graphs, and the like, the usefulness of such data is obvious. It is easier for an audience to grasp the behavioral context of the data when they are confronted with types of evidence with which they have a working familiarity. The verbal nature of interviews makes this possible because people more often relate effectively to situations that involve people speaking to one another than they do to tables that summarize views.

The interview data do more than add flesh to statistical information. Gorden (1956, p. 55), for example, discusses three ways in which interviews are useful as pretest devices for questionnaires:

1.   They permit an investigator to explore the clarity of questions with respondents.

2.   They enable investigators to structure responses along lines more realistically related to the range of views as seen by respondents.

3.   They bring to the forefront those questions that, for one reason or another, respondents do not want to answer.

These additional uses of the interview, when viewed alongside its use as an independent research tool, simply serve to enhance its overall appeal.

SOME CONCLUDING REMARKS

Interviews are extremely powerful research tools when used appropriately. More than any other social science method, the interview capitalizes on the most natural form of social communication—verbalizing. As a result, once the requisite skills have been mastered, interviewing is easily adapted to by almost any investigator.

However, questions of time and money, plus the possibility of a rather low yield of useful scientific information relative to these investments, force many researchers to opt for other methods. To resolve some of the dilemmas posed by interview data, a well-traveled path has been beaten to the door of the questionnaire. As the next chapter will indicate, the advantages of such a course do not always outweigh the disadvantages.

SOME QUESTIONS FOR REVIEW

1.   What are the characteristic features of the interview? Why is the interview the most sociological of all research techniques?

2.   To what ends do the features of the interview most notably lend themselves? Which types of interviews most appropriately achieve these objectives?

3.   What factors must be weighed in deciding upon the interview as a primary research tool? When is it more advantageous to use it as one of several data-gathering techniques?

4.   Distinguish among interviews on the basis of their structured nature. Compare and contrast the merits and limitations of each type.

5.   Design a study in which some form of interviewing is the major research tool. What are its major strengths? Weaknesses? Suggest ways to improve the study design.

6.   Is it always advantageous to consider relying on interviews as the sole means of data-colleciton? Explain.

NOTES

1.   Reported in the *Knoxville News-Sentinel,* Knoxville, Tennessee, September 2, 1973.
2.   For ways of incorporating unstructured interviews into research designs employing observation, consult Chapter 9.
3.   Gorden (1969, p. 51) distinguishes between interview schedules and guides. In his words:

> The interview guide, in contrast to an interview schedule, provides only an outline or checklist of the topics and subtopics to be covered but does not specify a sequence. In such cases, it might also include several ways of wording questions or various probes which might be useful in pursuing the subject.

> Interview guides are used in conjunction with all types of interviews, serving many useful purposes (Gorden, 1969, p. 51).

BIBLIOGRAPHY

Benny, Mark, and Everett C. Hughes. "Of Sociology and the Interview," *American Journal of Sociology* 62 (1956): 137–42.

Cicourel, Aaron V. *Method and Measurement in Sociology.* New York: Free Press, 1964.

Corwin, Ronald G. *Militant Professionalism.* New York: Appleton-Century-Crofts, 1970.

Cressey, Donald R. *Other People's Money.* New York: Free Press, 1953.

Denzin, Norman K. *The Research Act.* Chicago, Aldine, 1970.

———. *Sociological Methods: A Source Book.* Chicago: Aldine, 1970.

Dexter, Lewis Anthony. *Elite and Specialized Interviewing.* Evanston, Ill.: Northwestern University Press, 1970.

Forcese, Dennis P., and Stephen Richer. *Social Research Methods.* Englewood Cliffs, N.J.: Prentice-Hall, 1973.

Gorden, Raymond L. *Interviewing: Strategy, Techniques, and Tactics.* Homewood, Ill.: Dorsey Press, 1969.

Hyman, Herbert H., with William J. Cobb and others. *Interviewing in Social Research.* Chicago: University of Chicago Press, 1954.

Komorovsky, Mirra. *Blue Collar Marriage.* New York: Random House, 1964.

Lane, Robert E. *Political Ideology.* New York: Free Press, 1962.

Maccoby, Eleanor E., and Nathan Maccoby, "The Interview: A Tool of Social Science". In Gardner Lindsey (ed.). *Handbook of Social Psychology,* Vol. 1, Ch. 12. Reading, Mass.: Addison-Wesley, 1954.

Merton, Robert K., M. Fiske, and P. L. Kendall. *The Focused Interview.* New York: Free Press, 1956.

Selltiz, Claire, Marie Jahoda, Morton Deutsch, and Stuart W. Cook, *Research Methods in Social Relations.* New York: Holt, Rinehart and Winston, 1959.

Sutherland, Edwin H., and Donald R. Cressey. *Principles of Criminology.* New York: J. B. Lippincott, 1955.

Theodorson, T., and A. Theodorson, eds. *A Modern Dictionary of Sociology.* New York: T. Y. Crowell, 1969.

CHAPTER 11
THE QUESTIONNAIRE

Probably no other data collection tool is used more frequently in social research than the *questionnaire*. Many means of data collection are employed to elicit information from the targets of social inquiry, namely, social groups. But the questionnaire, used alone or in conjunction with other data collection methods, must be considered most popular.

This chapter will examine the questionnaire as a data collection device from several perspectives. Specifically, the major objectives are:

1. To identify and differentiate between several types of questionnaires.

2. To discuss some of the more important advantages and disadvantages of questionnaires as research tools.

3. To direct attention to situations for which questionnaires are best suited.

4. To delineate some of the problems associated with questionnaire construction and administration.

SOME IMPORTANT FUNCTIONS OF QUESTIONNAIRES

Generally, all types of questionnaires perform at least two functions:
(1) description, and (2) measurement.

DESCRIPTION

Information acquired through questionnaire administration may
provide descriptions of individual and/or group characteristics such as
sex, age, years of education, occupation, income, political affiliation,
religious preference and/or membership, membership or non-
membership in civic groups or fraternal orders, and the like.

Describing elements serves several purposes. For instance, a
knowledge of the age distribution of a group of factory workers may
provide the researcher with plausible explanations for certain group
behaviors on the job (e.g., clique formations, liberal or conservative
positions on political and/or social issues, and intra-worker *esprit de
corps*). A knowledge of the sex composition of social aggregates may
assist in accounting for such things as competitiveness, worker
productivity, or differences in expressions of interests and abilities.
The educational characteristics of groups may help to explain
particular attitudes manifested by them. In the industrial setting,
educational differences between employees may be associated with
differential assessments of job content and supervision.

It is observed, therefore, that accurate descriptions of elements in
any social setting can benefit the researcher in many ways. Insight,
explanation, and prediction are but a few of the many contributions
questionnaires make to social inquiry.

MEASUREMENT

Another primary function of questionnaires is the measurement of individual and/or group variables, particularly attitudes. Questionnaires
may contain single or multiple items (e.g., questions about things or
statements) that are designed to measure various attitudinal
phenomena such as social distance, perceptions of group cohesiveness, degree of racial prejudice, sexual permissiveness, religiosity,
anxiety, role clarity, and alienation. The list of attitudinal dimensions

that may potentially be tapped is virtually endless. Each year improvements are made on existing measuring instruments (in the form of questionnaires) and new instruments are constructed as well. In a later portion of this chapter, we will examine questionnaire construction in greater detail. Portions of measuring instruments in questionnaire form are shown in Tables 11-1, 11-2, and Table 11-3.

TYPES OF QUESTIONNAIRES

Questionnaires are not restricted to any particular length, nor are they limited to dealing with one specific topic. In social research, short questionnaires have been administered in postal card form through

Table 11-1. A Hypothetical Index of Group Cohesiveness

"Do you feel that other members of your work group give you ample consideration when issues concerning job matters are discussed?"
  (CHECK ONE)
____ My opinion is considered very important by other group members.
____ Group members are fairly interested in my ideas.
____ Group members are somewhat disinterested in my views.
____ Group members ignore my opinions when job matters are discussed.

"To what extent do you and/or other members of your work group refer to your group as "we" or "us"?
____ To a great extent (very frequently).
____ To some extent (fairly frequently).
____ To a small extent (fairly infrequently).
____ To no extent at all (seldom, if ever).

"How would you characterize the way the members of your work group get along?"
____ We get along better than most groups.
____ We get along about the same as other groups.
____ We get along less than other groups.
____ We seldom, if ever, get along well.

"To what extent do you feel other members of your work group would come to your aid if you were in trouble involving your work tasks?"
____ My work group members would come to my aid without question.
____ My work group members would be fairly indifferent about my problems.
____ I feel that I am on my own and cannot depend on other work group members if I happen to get into trouble.

Table 11-2. A Hypothetical Index of Desire for Change in Work Tasks

Each statement below is followed by the following responses (not reprinted here): "Strongly Agree," "Agree," "Undecided, but Probably Agree," "Undecided, but Probably Disagree," "Disagree," and "Strongly Disagree." *Select the response that best fits you.*

1. On my job it is important that I do new things frequently.
2. Changing my job to meet changing technology in the work place would be very disturbing to me.
3. I like a job where I can perform the same operations routinely every day.
4. Assembly-line type work appeals to me.
5. I dislike frequent disruptions in my work routine.
6. I like my present job and would feel bad about having to perform some other different task.
7. Doing a variety of different things on the job each day helps make me feel that time goes by more quickly.
8. I would tend to feel comfortable performing most any job at my place of work, should higher-ups decide to switch me around from one job to another frequently.

Table 11-3. Champion and Dager's Depersonalization Scale[a]

Each of the statements below is followed by the responses: "Strongly Agree," "Agree," "Undecided, but Probably Agree," "Undecided, but Probably Disagree," "Disagree," and "Strongly Disagree." *Select the response that best fits you.*

1. On my job it is possible to make errors without too much disruption.
2. The way I do my job is important to my fellow workers.
3. Many times they think getting the job done is more important than the people on the job.
4. If I ever stay home from work, this department would be in a real bind.
5. A person who likes to do work that requires thinking would like performing my job.
6. Things are really regimented around here.
7. When I come to work each day, I look forward to a new and challenging experience.
8. Sometimes I wonder just how important I really am around here.
9. I think my job is too mechanical.

SOURCE: Dean J. Champion and Edward Z. Dager, "Some Impacts of Office Automation upon Status, Role Change, and Depersonalization." *Sociological Quarterly,* 8:71-84, 1967. (p. 78)

[a] This is a partial replication of items from the scale.

the mail (Bock and Lade, 1963; Bradt, 1955; and Brown, 1965). In other instances, questionnaires have been as long as 100 or more pages. For example, at a small, southeastern liberal arts college in 1968, a 110-page questionnaire was administered to all full-time faculty. The purpose of the questionnaire was to obtain information about faculty academic and civic activities and to present a case for accreditation for a national educational organization.[1]

Presently, no universally acceptable standards exist to evaluate the appropriateness of specific types of questionnaires for specific target audiences. It is the primary responsibility of the social scientist to determine the length, nature, content, and method of administration of questionnaires in advance of proposed studies utilizing them.

Although questionnaires may be classified according to several dimensions, the major means of differentiating between them used here are (1) type of response required, and (2) type of questionnaire administration.

TYPE OF RESPONSE REQUIRED

Responses to questionnaires may be (1) fixed or closed, (2) open-end, or (3) a combination of types (1) and (2).[2]

Fixed-response Questionnaires

Fixed-response questionnaires consist of items (statements or questions) with a fixed number of choices. The respondent is asked to check the response that best fits him. Tables 11-1, 11-2, and 11-3 above are examples of questionnaires with fixed or closed questions and/or statements. Whether an investigator will use a fixed-response questionnaire in his research depends on a number of things. First, an assumption is made that the target sample has a knowledge of the subject matter of the questionnaire. A second assumption is that the researcher knows enough about the sample under investigation to be able to anticipate what kinds of responses will likely be given. For example, if the researcher is interested in obtaining information about political attitudes from a random sample of registered voters, it is logical to assume that most of the voters under study will manifest specific political party preferences (e.g., Democrat, Republican, or American Independent). Furthermore, it is assumed that they will reflect attitudinal positions of varying intensities on several political issues and/or topics. Most measuring instruments in questionnaire form are of the fixed-response variety.

Open-End Questionnaires

Open-end questionnaires are characterized by questions that require short or lengthy replies by respondents. Table 11-4 provides several examples of open-end questions. Rather than anticipate particular responses from the target sample, the investigator simply provides several pages of open-end questions requesting respondents to elaborate on their opinions and attitudes about things in varying detail.

Questionnaires Comprised of Fixed-response and Open-end Questions

Many questionnaires are made up of items with both fixed and open-end responses. The researcher will include various measuring instruments (sets of statements with fixed responses) in his questionnaire as well as items with fixed alternatives, but including an "other" category. In an unpublished study of a comparison of student attitudes toward on- and off-campus living conditions, Champion (1969) included both types of items in a questionnaire administered to a

Table 11-4. Some Sample Items of an Open-End Variety

1. What is the title of your present position in this company? Please specify.

2. What are your primary responsibilities or duties? Please specify _____

3. What are ·the chances for your advancement to a higher position with this company in the future? _____

4. Why do you feel this is so? Please specify _____

5. What are your recommendations for an "ideal" work setting? _____

6. Do you feel that the current method of nominating presidential candidates is fair? Check one: ____ Yes ____ No.

7. If your answer to question #6 was "yes," then go on to question #8. If your answer to question #6 was "No," would you please explain the reason or reasons for your feelings. _____

8. _____ etc.

random sample of seniors at a small college. One item dealt with those factors that students regarded as most crucial in determining whether they preferred living on or off campus.

Students were asked to check all responses associated with the item that favored living on campus. Similar lists of reasons were provided following items that were unfavorable to on-campus living, and items that were favorable and unfavorable toward off-campus residence. Several blank spaces were provided at the end of each list to allow the students freedom to list alternative reasons that had not been anticipated. Table 11-5 illustrates a single item taken from the questionnaire administered in the study.

A BRIEF COMPARISON OF FIXED-RESPONSE AND OPEN-END QUESTIONNAIRES

It should be apparent that some topics or items treated in questionnaires are most easily handled by fixed-response categories. Sex, years of education, and race almost always are confined to a limited number of fixed-answer alternatives. Political affiliation and religion are similarly easy to classify into a finite number of categories, provided that most people in a designated population to be studied can be defined as such. For example, utilizing Democrat, Republican, and American Independent as political party categories will usually cover most persons in the United States. Other categories could be constructed similarly to facilitate the classification of the political affiliation of Canadians or Australians, if such populations were to be studied. It is also likely that Protestant, Catholic, and Jewish will cover most United States citizens surveyed in a given study, and that few will fall into an "other" category. If the researcher were to study the Japanese or Turkish people, religious categories could be constructed in advance for these populations as well, and they would probably include most people surveyed.

Attitudinal measures on questionnaires are frequently restricted to fixed-response categories as well in order for the researcher to obtain a total score or raw score for the persons under investigation. This facilitates comparisons between people or groups based on the attitudinal characteristics they manifest as measured by their responses to the designated attitudinal statements.

Open-end questions are most frequently employed when the researcher does not anticipate probable replies from respondents. A general lack of familiarity with the population under study will tend to favor a greater use of open-end response categories. Some of the ad-

Table 11-5.   A Single Item from a Student Study of On- and Off-Campus Residential Preferences

1. What are some important advantages to living on campus? CHECK EACH WHICH APPLIES BELOW.
_____ a.   Enables students to become more involved in campus activities.
_____ b.   Helps students to develop close friendships with others through dormitory living.
_____ c.   Allows easy access to classes.
_____ d.   Eliminates having to prepare meals.
_____ e.   Enables students to develop independence from parental supervision.
_____ f.   Helps students to feel more a "part of the school."
_____ g.   Eliminates expense of operating an automobile and commuting.
_____ h.   Other. If you feel that there are other important advantages to living in on-campus facilities, please list then in the space provided below.

_____
_____
_____
_____

vantages and disadvantages associated with each type of questionnaire response are listed and discussed briefly below.

SOME ADVANTAGES OF FIXED-RESPONSE QUESTIONS

1.   Fixed-response items are easy to score and code.   (Coding is a procedure whereby the researcher assigns a number or numbers to particular types of responses—e.g., Democrat = 1, Republican = 2, American Independent = 3, and so on—in order to distinguish responses from one another in subsequent data analysis.) The researcher can more easily transfer the data from the questionnaire directly to an IBM card (using a key-punch machine) to the extent that fixed-response items are included.

2.   No writing is required of the respondent.   The respondent simply checks the response which applies to him (her). In cases where respondents cannot adequately express themselves verbally, the fixed-response item is a definite advantage.

3.   Fixed-response items facilitate completion of the questionnaire.   Lengthy questionnaires with fixed-response items are completed more rapidly than those questionnaires requiring written replies for the same information.

4. If the questionnaire is mailed to respondents, there is the strong likelihood that respondents will complete and return the questionnaire more frequently if little or no writing is involved.

SOME DISADVANTAGES OF FIXED-RESPONSE ITEMS

1. One major disadvantage of fixed-response items in questionnaires is the potential inability of the researcher to provide the respondent with *all* relevant response alternatives. Fixed-response items, as noted previously, require some familiarity with the population under study. If a respondent is forced to make a choice among several alternatives that do not fit him, the researcher may end up with misleading information.

2. Fixed-response items, especially those used in attitudinal measures, may lead a respondent to lapse into a response set. In order to "get it over with quick," the respondent may simply go through the entire questionnaire and check the first response he finds, regardless of whether such a response is true of him. Some measuring instruments have built-in lie factors to determine to what extent a respondent is at least being consistent in his replies throughout the questionnaire administration. Questionnaire length (to be discussed in a later portion of this chapter) sometimes creates the propensity to elicit a response set from respondents. The longer the questionnaire, the more patient the respondent must be to complete it. If it appears to be too long to the respondent, the likelihood of a response set increases.

SOME ADVANTAGES OF OPEN-END ITEMS

1. Open-end items are particularly useful when the researcher has little or no information about the sample to be studied. The respondent is less restricted in terms of possible choices he can provide as responses to particular questions.

2. In certain instances, open-end items are helpful to the researcher for gaining insight into the behavior of a particular group being studied. There is always the possibility that the researcher will be able to anticipate some probable responses in order to establish a limited number of fixed-response categories. But often, the flexibility of an open-end item will elicit unanticipated and insightful replies from respondents that will enhance the investigator's understanding of what is going on and why.

SOME DISADVANTAGES OF OPEN-END ITEMS

1.   A major disadvantage of open-end items is the difficulty of classifying and/or coding responses.   Different respondents may *appear* to provide similar responses to the same item on a questionnaire, but the importance and meaning each respondent attaches to his reply may be considerably different. Although several individuals are placed in an equivalent category for purposes of facilitating data analysis, the results of such analysis may be seriously misleading.

2.   A bias exists in open-end response items that stems from several sources.   At the outset, persons who cannot express themselves adequately on paper (and also orally) will be combined unfairly with more fluent individuals. Therefore, an educational bias exists initially, particularly if the target population from which the sample is drawn is quite heterogeneous in this respect. By the same token, questionnaires in the general case (i.e., those containing open-end and/or fixed-response items) are subject to a similar kind of educational bias. Not everyone who responds is equally adept in the art of self-expression.

Socioeconomic differentials may contribute to misleading results and incorrect interpretations of findings as well. Persons of different socioeconomic backgrounds do not necessarily see things the same way as everyone else. Nor do they use the same vocabulary to express themselves. Questionnaire wording at the outset has a built-in bias feature that must be considered in assessing the quality and meaning of the information obtained.

3.   A third disadvantage of open-end items is that they are time consuming to complete.   If the researcher mails questionnaires to respondents, the response rate will likely be lower where open-end response items are used compared to situations where fixed-response items are employed. Many individuals may feel that they do not have the time or the interest to sit down and complete a series of open-end questions. Face-to-face interviews appear to be more successful with better response than open-end questions on a self-administered questionnaire (See Chapter 10).

Summarizing this discussion briefly, questionnaires may contain fixed-response items, open-end items, or both. Many questionnaires are designed to include items of both types. This greatly enhances the flexibility of the questionnaire as a tool for description of a target sample and the measurement of salient variables, attitudinal or otherwise. Familiarity with the target sample, the heterogeneity of the socioeconomic characteristics of it, and the time and manpower limitations of the researcher dictate most frequently the nature and content of questionnaires along the dimensions cited above.

THE TYPE OF QUESTIONNAIRE ADMINISTRATION

There are basically two methods for administering questionnaires to a target sample. These are (1) the mailed questionnaire, and (2) the face-to-face questionnaire administration.

The Mailed Questionnaire

Much has been written about the mailed questionnaire method of administration (Andreason, 1970; Bradt, 1955; McDonagh and Rosenblum, 1965; and Vincent, 1964). This method consists simply of mailing a questionnaire of variable length to previously designated subjects. Instructions for completing the questionnaire are usually enclosed and a return envelope provided. The researcher waits one to two weeks until the questionnaires are returned. If he has devised a method whereby each respondent can be identified, he may elect to send follow-up letters to those who do not respond within a reasonable waiting period (e.g., two weeks). Although estimates of nonresponse to a mailed questionnaire vary, it appears to be a normal expectation that nearly 70 per cent of the questionnaires mailed will not be returned. A follow-up letter to nonrespondents may raise the response rate to some degree, but as we will soon see, there are many factors that influence questionnaire response rates generally. These will be discussed in the last section of this chapter.

Face-to-Face Questionnaire Administration

The face-to-face method of questionnaire administration requires that predetermined subjects be given questionnaires to complete in the presence of the researcher or his assistants.[3] Most persons reading this book are probably familiar with the experience of completing a questionnaire in a college class for a graduate student or professor during the course of their academic careers.

Champion and Dager (1967) administered questionnaires to bank employees during one afternoon and collected the questionnaires from the workers the following morning. Researchers will sometimes personally call on individuals at their homes in a particular city and request that the respondent complete the questionnaire while the researchers wait for them. In an unpublished study of East Tennessee National Guardsmen, Cramer and Champion (1975) administered questionnaires to successive groups of guardsmen in large classrooms early on Saturday mornings prior to their weekend drills.

A COMPARATIVE ASSESSMENT OF THE MAILED QUESTIONNAIRE AND FACE-TO-FACE ADMINISTRATION METHODS

It should be apparent that the major benefit of a mailed questionnaire is economy. Mailed questionnaires, therefore, are an inexpensive means of obtaining information about particular target samples. However, there is always the problem of nonresponse and what to do about it. Follow-up letters can be used, provided that the researcher has maintained a record of the identity of the nonrespondents, although in many instances, there is not a substantial increase in the original rate of response. Champion and Sear (1969, pp. 336–37) mailed 2,700 questionnaires to a random sample of residents in three southern cities and received an initial response of 802, or about 29.7 per cent. They varied the follow-up letter procedure by selecting another random sample from the nonrespondents in the first mailing ($N = 300$) and received an additional 151 responses. This increased the initial response from 802 to 953, or an increase of 42 per cent. However, the overall response percentage (953 out of 2,700) was only 35.3 per cent.

There are some important drawbacks to mailed questionnaires. One is that you never are sure who completed the questionnaire. If the husband in the family is the designated respondent and his wife completes the questionnaire for him for one reason or another, there is no way for the researcher to know for sure who completed it. If the assumption is made that the husband completed the questionnaire, the data obtained would not necessarily accurately reflect his opinions about things and would therefore be misleading. Another drawback is that there is no way to ensure that people will return the questionnaire received, and therefore, a high rate of nonresponse has become commonplace. A third drawback is that there is always the possibility of persons misinterpreting what is meant or intended by particular questions or statements. Without the presence of the researcher to clarify and explain things the respondent does not understand, a person's response to certain items may not be meaningful, and the investigator may be led to misinterpret the data he obtains.

A strong point for the mailed questionnaire, however, is that the respondent exercises the option of completing the instrument in the privacy of his own home with some degree of anonymity. Boruch

(1971a and 1971b), Pearlin (1961), Pelz (1959), and Reubhausen and Brim (1965) are some of the researchers who have discussed the significance of anonymity for eliciting cooperation from respondents. The logic is that persons will more likely respond to questions when they feel that their responses will be kept confidential and cannot be associated with them. It would appear that this argument is fairly sound, particularly if the questionnaire content consists of sensitive items, issues, and/or requests for respondents to divulge intimate details about their personal lives and habits. Relatively little research has been done in this area concerning the distinction between those topics deemed sensitive and those labeled innocuous. Certain topics take on variable value to different target populations. What is sensitive to one group may not be sensitive to another, and so forth.

The major advantages of administering a questionnaire to people in a face-to-face situation (e.g., in the classroom, on the front doorstep, and so on) are that (1) a high rate of questionnaire completion and return can be expected; (2) the researcher knows who is completing the questionnaire, and (3) the investigator is present to answer any questions respondents might have concerning the meaning of particular items. Of course, if the researcher must travel throughout the city to contact persons personally, or if he has assistants do the same thing, this questionnaire administration procedure becomes much more time consuming and costly contrasted with the mailed questionnaire. Student groups are often selected as the researcher's guinea pigs because of their accessibility and the convenience of gathering large amounts of data cheaply and quickly. But there does remain the question as to the generalizability of the characteristics of student respondents to the so-called normal adult population. Students tend to be atypical of the population at large. This factor must be considered particularly in the interpretation phase of a researcher's work. Generalizations to populations other than students must be tempered with conservatism and caution as must all generalizations from samples to populations from which they are drawn. (See particularly Chapter 8 for a discussion of sampling issues and problems.)

CONSTRUCTING THE QUESTIONNAIRE

To the layman a questionnaire is likely to be viewed as a simple device that anyone can create or throw together, given the time and interest.

To the social researcher, however, questionnaire construction is a complex task. And usually, before the final form of the questionnaire is determined, many revisions in wording, length, and content have been made. Most researchers will probably agree that the construction of a good questionnaire for any target audience is a tedious and an arduous task. Although it is a discouraging note to add, even the best of questionnaires suffer from numerous imperfections that neither the researcher nor his assistants recognized during the preparation of it.

This section will focus on some of the major factors that researchers must take into account in the construction of questionnaires for selected target samples. Let's begin by considering some of the questions that arise in the initial stages of questionnaire preparation.

1.   What is the definition of the population about which we seek information?
2.   What is the socioeconomic and/or educational level of the intended target of our inquiry?
3.   What kinds of facts do we wish to learn about them?
4.   How accessible are they?
5.   How will the questionnaire be administered?
6.   What kinds of response patterns will we use?
7.   How long should we make the questionnaire?
8.   How much control can we exert over ensuring their response to our questionnaire?

Ideally, every element in the population to be studied should be identified and given an opportunity for inclusion in our research (see Chapter 8). The socioeconomic level or educational background (if known) of the intended target population will enable the researcher to design questions or formulate statements at a particular level of readability commensurate with that of the respondents.[4]

The kinds of things we wish to learn about the sample will directly determine the content of the questionnaire. Some of the standard sociological items such as age, sex, occupation, and years of education are almost always included. Other items are added as needed. For example, a job satisfaction measure or an index of employee productivity or a scale of political conservatism or activity may be added.

The length of the questionnaire is a controversial subject in social research that has never been fully resolved. Some investigators argue (particularly in the case of the mailed questionnaire) that the shorter the questionnaire, the greater the response rate. They base their argument on the notion that people will be increasingly reluctant to spend time completing a questionnaire if it appears to be quite lengthy. Some research (Champion and Sear, 1969) has indicated just the opposite result. Three questionnaires of identical content were constructed with different spacing between items so that the items were spread over three, six, and nine pages respectively. The longer questionnaires were returned more frequently than the shorter ones.

Of course, if the questionnaire is to be administered on a face-to-face basis and the researcher is operating within certain time restrictions (a bank vice president may allow a researcher fifteen minutes to administer a questionnaire to his employees during the opening banking hours), the length will have to be designed to fit the existing situation.

Extremely lengthy questionnaires can cause some respondents to become test-weary. Tired respondents may become somewhat careless in the answers they provide. They may also drift into a response set, as discussed in an earlier section of this chapter.

The amount of control the researcher exerts over his respondents must also be considered an important factor. An army major may order his subordinates to complete a questionnaire of virtually any length. Similarly, an official of a company may make mandatory the completion of a questionnaire by subordinate staff members or workers. A teacher in the classroom can administer a questionnaire to the students and coerce them into participating and completing the questionnaire by saying that their refusal to cooperate may affect their course grade. Under these conditions, the length of the questionnaire almost becomes an immaterial consideration, although the researcher must bear in mind that the longer the questionnaire, the more weary the respondent may become. And it is extremely difficult to calculate the full implications for research validity and reliability of such questionnaires administered under these kinds of conditions.

SELECTING THE QUESTIONS

Because the primary functions of questionnaires are description and measurement, the researcher has a variety of options for selecting items for inclusion. Several excellent sources exist that either tell the researcher where to find existing measuring instruments in questionnaire form, or provide a compilation of the measuring instruments themselves.[3] The investigator will often want to combine existing measures with items of his own. Existing questionnaires may not be sufficient or adequate for dealing with particular aspects of a social situation being studied. If the investigator chooses to construct a measuring instrument in questionnaire form, he will usually follow certain scaling procedures, as discussed in Chapter 6. His instrument will usually undergo tests for validity and reliability as outlined in Chapter 7. The procedures presented in these two chapters are primarily geared to assist the researcher in assessing the accuracy and consistency of questionnaire measures.

Including items whose primary function is description is a fairly easy task for the seasoned researcher. But precautions need to be taken, particularly with reference to the question wording. For example, if an investigator wants to estimate the amount of marijuana consumption among an aggregate of college students, he might draw a probability sample of them and ask the following question:

"How often do you smoke marijuana per month?"

or,

"How many 'joints' do you smoke per week?"

Each of these questions is equally presumptuous in that it is assumed that the students who answer them actually smoke marijuana, when in fact none may do so. Such questions are comparable to the familiar exemplary inquiry, "When was the last time you beat your wife?" The ridiculousness of this question is quite apparent. First, it assumes the respondent is married (which may not be true). If the respondent *is* married, then it assumes that he beats his wife (which may not be true also). It is important that the researcher learn to refrain from assuming too much about a population under investigation.

Provided that the investigator obtains the confidence of the persons in the samples he studies (particularly where information concerning law violations is requested), a safer and more reasonable approach to the marijuana question would be:

"Have you ever smoked marijuana?"

If the respondent's reply is positive, then the researcher can follow up with:

"Do you smoke marijuana currently?"

Again, if the respondent's answer is affirmative, the researcher can ask a question concerning the frequency of marijuana usage (e.g., "How many times per week, month, etc. do you smoke marijuana?;" and/or "How many 'joints' do you smoke per week, month, etc.?").

By the same token, it is important for the investigator to know whether or not the sample selected has the necessary information he will request from them. It is interesting to ponder how often respondents give opinions about and express attitudes toward things that are unknown to them. Many communities throughout the United States are currently considering supplementing their water supplies with various kinds of chemicals. Fluoridating a city's water supply is a primary target of controversy. Referendums pertaining to fluoride in water supplies are supported in some cities and not in others year after year. It would be enlightening to know for sure just exactly what proportion of persons in these respective communities are familiar with the chemical and biological implications of fluoridation, regardless of whether they vote for or against it.

Caution is expected of the social researcher when it comes to interpreting answers persons give to questions or statements. For instance, several interpretations could be made concerning a person's religiosity based upon his response to the statement:

1. On the average, how often do you attend a church?
    _____a.   I do not attend a church
    _____b.   One to two times per month
    _____c.   Three to four times per month
    _____d.   More than four times per month

Does a person's church attendance necessarily reflect his degree of religious zeal or strength of beliefs? Also, can the amount one contributes to religious organizations in the form of donations or tithes necessarily be equated with his religiosity? Making the jump from a person's response to an inference about the person's attitudes and/or beliefs toward particular ideas or objects is risky business. The question of validity is paramount here. A review of Chapters 6 and 7 will emphasize several of the problems involved in making such inferences based on responses to questionnaires.

RESPONSE AND NONRESPONSE: SOME CONSIDERATIONS

Researchers utilizing questionnaires in their investigations are concerned about maximizing the number of respondents selected for questionnaire administration initially and assessing the potential effects and implications of any amount of nonresponse (particularly in mailed questionnaire situations).

SOME FACTORS THAT INFLUENCE RESPONSE RATES

Below are listed some of the more important factors that affect the rate of response to questionnaires generally. Many of the factors identified are particularly relevant for mailed questionnaires, although most pertain to all types.

Questionnaire Length

Much attention has been given to the effects of questionnaire length on response in the methodological literature (Champion and Sear, 1969; Levine and Gerald, 1958; Roeher, 1963; Robin, 1965; and Linsky, 1965). A common belief is that shorter questionnaires will be returned or completed more often than longer ones. At present, no standards exist for determining precisely what is a "short" questionnaire and what is a "long" one. In an earlier portion of this chapter we briefly discussed a study by Champion and Sear (1969) that investigated factors potentially influencing response rate to mailed questionnaires. Although their initial literature review on the subject revealed inconclusive evidence to support the "shorter-questionnaires-are-returned-more-frequently" contention, findings from their study indicated that longer questionnaires were associated with greater response. They controlled for questionnaire content in their investigation, spacing the identical questions differently so that apparent questionnaire length would be three, six, and nine pages respectively. One interpretation of these findings could be that these page differentiations are inadequate expressions of short and long questionnaires, whatever they are. Again, no standards exist currently whereby to judge the length variable.

However, it is reasonable to assume that persons eventually get tired of answering questions or responding to statements in questionnaires as the length increases.

Questionnaire Content

A questionnaire containing controversial material or requesting respondents to reveal intimate details of their personal lives may elicit both high and low response rates, depending on the topics investigated and the target audience. It is entirely likely that some individuals will find material on some questionnaires to be offensive and "immoral," whereas others will find the same material interesting or "arousing." It would be logical to expect differential response rates from such diverse groups.

Some people may define questionnaires as an invasion of their privacy and refuse to respond on such grounds. Others may see the questionnaire as an opportunity to express their feelings to others, and therefore, the instrument functions as a means of tension release or frustration reduction, as well as a data-gathering tool.

Anonymity

Another common assumption is that persons are more likely to respond to a questionnaire to the degree that their anonymity is maintained or guaranteed. Sensitive items related to racial or religious attitudes or to sexual behavior may appear to be less threatening to the extent that respondent anonymity is preserved. On the other hand, because of certain psychological and/or social factors presently unidentified, persons may derive some gratification (to ego, to sexual prowess, and the like) from disclosing things about themselves to others. No consistent pattern is evident in the literature concerning the degree of anonymity on response rates (Andreason, 1970; Bennett, 1967; Boruch, 1971a, 1971b; Conrad, 1967; Hoch, 1967; Pearlin, 1961; Pelz, 1959).

Other Factors

If a questionnaire is to be mailed, such factors as type of postage used (i.e., metered, personally stamped, special delivery, and so on), type of cover letter attached as an explanation of the purposes or objectives of the questionnaire (appeals to respondent egoism or altruism), rewards for responding (money, turkeys, opportunities to express opinions), and the socioeconomic status of the target sample are considered to be influential to different degrees for eliciting greater rates of response. If the questionnaire is administered on a face-to-face basis (as discussed in an earlier portion of this chapter), such factors as the appearance and/or ethnic and/or racial origin of the investigator or questionnaire administrator, the readability of the questionnaire, and the type or types of responses required must be considered important in determining the response rate. When questionnaires are administered on a face-to-face basis, many problems paralleling those encountered by interviewers are found. For an extended treatment of such problems, Chapter 10 should be consulted.

WHAT ABOUT NONRESPONSE?

Two of the most frustrating questions a researcher must deal with are: "Who are the nonrespondents?" and "What would be the outcome of my results if they were to be included as a part of the data analyzed?"

There are various ways of identifying nonrespondents, particularly in a mail survey. Lists of individuals are compiled to whom questionnaires are sent. Those who respond and return the questionnaire are checked off the list. Those who do not return the questionnaires may be sent follow-up letters to remind them to return the questionnaires. Under such conditions it is ethical to notify potential respondents that their identities are known in advance and that the researcher will know if they have responded to his questionnaire.

Another method is to use a code number on each questionnaire and/or on the return envelope enclosed. Most respondents will observe the code number, however, and this apparent absence of anonymity may inhibit their response. An alternative that raises an ethical issue is to use invisible ink or some other such recognition medium on questionnaires as means of identifying those who respond. In instances where such practices are employed, the respondent may or may not be told that he can be identified or that the response is an anonymous one (which it is not). The ethics of such data-gathering practices (regardless of how harmless the researcher believes them to be) are presently being scrutinized by various social and psychological professional associations (Catton, 1968; Conrad, 1967; Colfax, 1970; Hoch, 1967; Katz, 1967; Miller, 1968; Nikelly, 1971; Riemer, 1950; Rutstein, 1969; Reubhausen and Brim, 1965; Sawyer and Schechter, 1968; Schultz, 1969; Westin, 1967).

If the researcher has made no provisions for identifying nonrespondents, he has little or no hope of being able to delineate their characteristics (social, psychological, economic, and the like) and contrast them with those who did respond. Obviously, the respondents and nonrespondents differ on at least one dimension—some returned the questionnaire and others did not. Why not? Would the addition of the information obtained from the nonrespondents to the data initially obtained from the respondents change or alter the researcher's findings to any significant degree? There is virtually no way of answering this question. Some people even question the inclusion of respondents who have required a second stimulus (a follow-up letter) to respond. Because response rates to mailed questionnaires are in the 30 to 40 percent range usually, this leaves a considerable chunk of a random sample unaccounted for. When the researcher draws (hypothetically) 5,000 persons randomly from a population of 50,000 and obtains a response of 1,500 (30 per cent), what can the resulting sample be called? Seventy per cent of the original random sample could potentially reverse a researcher's original findings if it were possible to include them ultimately. From a philosophical viewpoint, the question of the effect of nonrespondents on the original research outcome is, more often than not, purely a speculative matter.

A CONCLUDING NOTE

Questionnaires are used alone or in conjunction with other data-gathering techniques in social research. They are useful when economy is an important consideration (which it usually is). Mailed questionnaires are particularly useful for collecting information from individuals who are spread over a wide geographical area. Social surveys utilize questionnaires extensively because they are an inexpensive and rapid method for obtaining information.

As a research tool, a questionnaire is subject to various kinds of contamination from several sources (social desirability, anonymity, socioeconomic and educational differentials, and so on). Nonresponse (in mailed questionnaire situations) is a significant factor that seriously limits the generalizability of findings from any study using the questionnaire as a primary data-gathering instrument. It is suggested, therefore, that the researcher use a variety of data-gathering methods that can act as validity and reliability checks on one another. In any event, the questionnaire remains the most widely used data-collection method in social research today primarily because of convenience and economy. But its popularity should not deter one from neglecting its shortcomings, which this chapter has sought to reveal.

SOME QUESTIONS FOR REVIEW

1. What are several important functions of questionnaires for social research? Discuss.

2. Discuss some weaknesses and strengths associated with open-end and fixed-response type questionnaires. Can both types be used together in a single questionnaire instrument? Why or why not? Discuss.

3. What appear to be some problems associated with the mailed questionnaires? What do you see at its major strengths in relation to other forms of questionnaire administration?

4. If a person administers a questionnaire to another person and remains in the other persons presence, in what ways might the

presence of the researcher affect the nature of the respondent's replies? Discuss.

5. What kinds of factors influence nonresponse? How much overt control does a researcher exert over nonresponse? Discuss.

6. How does nonresponse influence the validity of information obtained by the researcher? Discuss briefly.

NOTES

1. One of the authors, Dean J. Champion, was teaching at the college on a part-time basis when the lengthy questionnaire was administered.

2. The distinction is sometimes made between "structured" and "unstructured" questionnaires. We believe that this distinction is misleading. The notion of "unstructured" may convey the idea that the questionnaire has little or no continuity or coherence. Fixed-response and open-ended questionnaires are structured to acquire specific information about things. Open-end questionnaires lack structure only to the extent that pre-determined, fixed-alternative responses are not provided the respondent. Other than that, the respondent's attention is directed toward particular issues with specific research objectives in mind.

3. This method of administration parallels closely the interview schedule method of data collection. See Chapter 10 for a more extensive treatment of this method.

4. If a sample of illiterate persons is to be studied, an interview and/or observation of their behavior may be the best means of acquiring information about them.

5. For example, the *Handbook of Research Design and Social Measurement,* 2d ed., by Delbert C. Miller (David McKay Company, Inc., New York, 1970) is an excellent source for questionnaires as measures of such things as group dimensions, social distance, occupational prestige, employee satisfaction, community solidarity, and alienation. Another valuable source which includes *where* to find hundreds of measures in the social scientific literature is *Sociological Measurement: An Inventory of Scales and Indices,* by Charles M. Bonjean, Richard J. Hill, and S. Dale McLemore (Chandler Publishing Company, San Francisco, Calif., 1967).

BIBLIOGRAPHY

Andreason, Alan R. "Personalizing Mailed Questionnaires Correspondence," *Public Opinion Quarterly* 34 1970: 273–288.

Bennett, Chester. "What Price Privacy?" *American Psychologist,* 22 (1967): 371–374.

Bock, Walter, and James Lade. "A Test of the Usefulness of the Post Card Technique in a Mail Questionnaire Study," *Public Opinion Quarterly,* 27 (1963): 299–302.

Boruch, Robert F. "Assuring Confidentiality of Responses in Social Research: A Note on Strategies," *American Sociologist,* 6 1971a: 308–311.

Boruch, Robert F. "Maintaining Confidentiality of Data in Educational Research: A Systematic Analysis," *American Psychologist,* 26 1971b: 413–430.

Bradt, Kenneth. "The Usefulness of a Post Card Technique in a Mailed Questionnaire Study," *Public Opinion Quarterly,* 19 1955: 218–222.

Brown, Morton L. "Use of the Postcard Query in Mail Surveys," *Public Opinion Quarterly,* 29 1965: 635–637.

Catton, William R., Jr. "Social Responsibility of the Sociologist," *et al.,* 1 1968: 9–10.

Champion, Dean J. "A Comparison of On- and Off-Campus Student Perspectives toward Living Conditions." Unpublished study, Knoxville: The University of Tennessee, 1969.

———, and Edward Z. Dager. "Pressures and Performance: Automation and the Bank Employee," *The Banker's Magazine,* 150 1967: 97–102.

———, and A. M. Sear. "Questionnaire Response Rate: A Methodological Analysis," *Social Forces,* 47 1969: 335–339.

Colfax, M. David. "Knowledge for Whom?: Relevance and Responsibility in Sociological Research," *Sociological Inquiry,* 40 1970: 73–79.

Conrad, H. S. "Clearance of Questionnaires with Respect to Invasion of Privacy, Public Sensitiveness, Ethical Standards, etc.," *American Psychologist,* 22 1967: 356–359.

Cramer, James A., and Dean J. Champion. "Factors Associated with the Intention of National Guardsmen to Participate in the Control of Civil Disorders," *Journal of Political and Military Sociology,* 3 1975: 43–55.

Hoch, E. L. "The Privacy Issue and the Professional Response at the Departmental Level," *Journal of Educational Measurement,* 4 1967: 17–22.

Katz, Martin. "Ethical Issues and the Use of Human Subjects in Psychopharmacologic Research," *American Psychologist,* 22 1967: 345–348.

Levine, Sol, and Gordon Gerald. "Maximizing Returns on Mail Questionnaires," *Public Opinion Quarterly,* 22 1958: 568–575.

Linsky, Arnold. "A Factorial Experiment in Inducing Responses to a Mail Questionnaire," *Sociology and Social Research,* 49 1965: 183–189.

McDonagh, Edward C., and A. Leon Rosenblum. "A Comparison of Mailed Questionnaires and Subsequent Structured Interviews," *Public Opinion Quarterly,* 29 1965: 224–236.

Miller, R. I. "Invasion of Privacy by Computer," *Lex et Scientia,* 5 1968: 18–24.

Nikelly, Arthur G. "Ethical Issues in Research on Student Protest," *American Psychologist,* 26 1971: 475–478.

Pearlin, Leonard R. "The Appeals of Anonymity in Questionnaire Response," *Public Opinion Quarterly,* 25 1961: 640–647.

Pelz, Donald C. "The Influence of Anonymity on Expressed Attitudes," *Human Organization,* 18 1959: 88–91.

Reubhausen, O. M., and O. G. Brim. "Privacy in Behavioral Research," *Columbia Law Review,* 65 1965: 1184–1211.

Riemer, Svend. "Values and Standards in Research," *American Journal of Sociology,* 55 1950: 131–136.

Robin, Stanley. "A Procedure for Securing Returns to Mail Questionnaires," *Sociology and Social Research,* 50 1965: 24–35.

Roeher, G. A. "Effective Techniques in Increasing Response to Mailed Questionnaires," *Public Opinion Quarterly,* 27 1963: 299–302.

Rutstein, David D. "The Ethical Design of Human Experiments," *Daedalus,* 98 1969: 523–541.

Sawyer, Jack, and Howard Schechter. "Computers, Privacy, and the National Data Center: The Responsibilities of the Social Scientists," *American Psychologist,* 23 1968: 810–818.

Schultz, Dean P. "The Human Subject in Psychological Research," *Psychological Bulletin,* 72 1969: 214–228.

Vincent, Clark E. "Socioeconomic Status and Familial Variables in Mail Questionnaire Responses," *American Journal of Sociology,* 69 1964: 647–653.

Westin, Allan F. *Privacy and Freedom.* New York: Antheum Publishers, 1967.

CHAPTER 12
SECONDARY SOURCES

It is not always necessary or even advisable for social scientists to generate the original data needed to expand knowledge. Frequently, information has already been compiled by others that can be put to scientific use by enterprising investigators. To cite just one example, voluminous amounts of materials are collected regularly by federal, state, and local governmental units, businesses, educational institutions, law enforcement agencies, and countless other organizations. And these sources do not begin to exhaust the list, as this chapter will demonstrate. All are waiting to be tapped by those researchers interested in taking the time and trouble to learn their whereabouts.

Obtaining information from other sources is no panacea, however. Although a veritable gold mine of data exists, research that begins with data that have already been collected calls for a keen sensitivity to the problems as well as the prospects accompanying such an undertaking. In that respect, using data from other sources is like all research activity. There are other respects, of course, in which it poses unique problems. Among the range of topics that serve as a guide for projects utilizing these sorts of data are the following:

1. Major features of secondary sources.
2. Major types of secondary sources.
3. Important uses of secondary data.
4. Advantages and disadvantages in the use of secondary materials.

MAJOR FEATURES OF SECONDARY SOURCES

There is practically no limit to the sorts of materials that can serve the purposes of scientific exploration. From the most private of items such as personal letters, diaries, logs, and appointment books to the most systematically accumulated and distributed documents such as the publications of the United States Census Bureau, an almost bewildering array of information awaits investigators. Diverse as they are, however, these sources share certain common characteristics.

First, they are *ready-made*. That can prove to be both a great strength and a severe drawback at the same time. Still, not having to take the time to construct and administer a questionnaire, conduct interviews, or spend hours observing and writing up field notes can be very inviting. Finding existing data suited to the resolution of scientific problems can be enormously time saving.

Besides being ready-made, these are types of information over which investigators have practically no original control with respect to how they were collected and classified. Both the form and the content of secondary sources are shaped by others. Clearly, this is a feature that can limit the overall scientific value of secondary sources. Because of it much of the hard work connected with research projects involving secondary sources revolves around restructuring and reclassifying information in ways designed to extract their scientific insights. Some researchers find it so restricting that they choose to collect their own data. Others see it as a challenge that affords them an opportunity to obtain data that might otherwise not be researched at all. Occasionally, of course, whether by luck or sheer perseverance, an investigator can find information that is precisely the sort needed to answer the research question at hand.

Finally, secondary sources are not limited in time and space (Festinger, 1953, p. 301). By that is meant that the investigator using them need not have been present either when or where they were gathered. Originally gathered information, whether obtained by interviews, questionnaires, observation or some combination thereof, is restricted to the special and temporal context of the researcher. Only when others can use them do such data become free of this restriction. No such limitations are found when using secondary sources. Data are collected for scientific purposes independent of the spatial and temporal context in which they were originally gathered.

With these features in mind, it is possible to arrive at a definition of secondary sources. When speaking of secondary data sources, what we have reference to is *any information originally collected for a purpose other than its present scientific one.*[1] Such a definition has the advantage of being broad enough to cover examination of previously collected scientific as well as nonscientific information. As the discussion of each type of source in the following section will indicate, what distinguishes secondary sources is the fact that their present use departs from the use for which they were originally intended.

MAJOR TYPES OF SECONDARY SOURCES

Various approaches have been used to classify secondary sources of data (Festinger, 1953; Forcese and Richer, 1973; and Hyman, 1972). Forcese and Richer for example (1973, p. 180) distinguish between expressive documents, mass media reports, and official records. They go further, placing these along a continuum on the basis, first, of their reliability and, second, their prequantification. Expressive documents have low reliability and low prequantification, mass media reports lie somewhere in the middle range of reliability and prequantification, whereas official records are seen by them as having high reliability and, of course, high prequantification. No effort is made by them to assess their classifications on the basis of validity or representativeness, however. For that matter, their categories leave the impression that the *overall* reliability of official records is high. In fact, numerous questions have been raised about the reliability of official records from a scientific standpoint, quite aside from their reliability relative to one another.[2]

Because one scheme is no less satisfactory than others, secondary data sources can also be arranged according to their accessibility. From such a vantage point, secondary sources can be appropriately classified as private or public.

PRIVATE SOURCES OF SECONDARY DATA

Data from private sources cover an immense range of materials, some of which are regularly used by investigators and others of which apparently hold little value. First among this type of data are strictly personal documents. Letters, diaries, and other bibliographical materials such as individual life histories are included among these. Earlier sociologists found such materials more suitable than contemporary sociologists have found them in examining social conduct. Studies such as Thomas and Znanieki's, *The Polish Peasant in Europe and America* and Shaw's *The Jackroller* made significant contributions to our understanding of human conduct by relying extensively on them. In an introductory comment to the reissued edition of Shaw's work (1966, p. 3), Howard Becker points directly to several of the important aspects of materials such as life histories. In his words:

> We have found that the "own story" reveals useful information concerning at least three important aspects of delinquent conduct: (1) the point of view of the delinquent; (2) the social and cultural situation to which the delinquent is responsive; and (3) the sequence of past experiences and situations in the life of the delinquent.

Still, personal documents are not easily accessible to most investigators. Besides, there are all sorts of questions that can be raised about them when they are available. Their authenticity is sometimes open to question, as is the accuracy of the information they contain. In addition, it is especially difficult to assess the representativeness of personal documents. For these reasons, they do not enjoy a central place in the design of much contemporary social science research although there is a continued interest in their use on the part of some researchers.

A second type of private data exists in the files and published materials of the multitudes of bureaus, agencies, and voluntary organizations that characterize American society and other societies as well. They are also found in personnel records and business files of American industry and in similar organizational settings in other countries in the world. Such data are frequently available to investigators exercising the necessary precautions in seeking access to them. Probably the most influential factor affecting the accessibility of such data is the lack of knowledge of their existence. They remain out of the reach of researchers because it is not known that they are available for the asking.

Another factor that weighs heavily has to do with the ingenuity and creativity of the investigator who is seeking factual information to test crucial scientific points. It is not at all uncommon to find that information handled in a routine, day-to-day fashion fails to illuminate its scientific utility to those doing the handling. Researchers are just as susceptible to this human fallibility as anyone else. Some researchers simply fail to see the worth of data that others capitalize on in a seemingly easy manner. Consequently, even when the whereabouts of these types of private data are known, it is not always possible to benefit from them.

By and large, these data sources suffer from weaknesses similar to those found in using personal documents. It is not by accident, given these limitations, that researchers have begun paying much closer attention to sources that are more directly attuned to procedures of scientific data gathering. In this connection, there are two ways for investigators to go about gaining access to information. The first is for investigators to have raw collected data given to them by others or data that are available from their own previous research.[3] It goes without saying that access to such private data banks depends largely on close personal proximity and cooperation of the researchers. Such a practice speeds the process of satisfying degree requirements. At the same time, it provides important training in the data analysis phase of social research.

The secondary use of data collected by others is fraught with problems. The limitations of the original studies necessarily restrict the research questions that can be posed as well as the operational procedures that can be employed in extracting useful information from them.

PUBLIC SOURCES OF SECONDARY DATA

A second way for investigators to use data collected from other studies is to rely on the information available in various data archives. Researchers not fortunate enough to have developed a personal data bank or to be in a position to capitalize on the accumulations of others need not turn away in dismay from the possibility of using other data sources. Opportunities for using existing information are numerous. What is more important, they do not demand that investigators rely so heavily on the winds of good fortune. In referring to these data sources as public, what is meant to be underscored is the fact that they are more or less available to all social scientists on an equal basis. That some scientists have availed themselves of the opportunity to use such data more frequently than others simply shows their willingness to make the most of information available to all. It is that quality of equality of accessibility that distinguishes public from private data sources. Thus, about the only thing that keeps researchers from using such information is their relative lack of knowledge of them (or, of course, a deliberate decision not to use them). To help interested students determine the whereabouts of such data sources, three general types can be singled out for discussion. These include (1) data archives; (2) selected government data; and (3) other published material.

Data Archives

To make data from studies available to a larger number of people and, at the same time, guarantee their more exhaustive use, data archives have been developed in many countries (Bisco, 1967; Council of Social Science Data Archives, 1967; Hyman, 1972, pp. 331–33.) These house data obtained by and large from surveys but, as Hyman notes, they are not always restricted to such information (1972, p. 330). Data archives serve several purposes (Bisco, 1967), the most important of which is to locate and house data for secondary analysis. Some appreciation for their general uses is contained in the opening comments of the Council of Social Science Data Archives publication (1967):

> Social science data archives are depositories of data that scholars, policy-makers, and others may use for scholarly research or for other purposes. The Council is a voluntary association of social science data archives. Through the Council, the member archives exchange information about new data sources, methods of data management and retrieval, and promising lines of secondary analysis. In addition, the Council is a vehicle for the exchange of information and experience among persons conversant with the new methods of managing, retrieving, and analyzing social science data by computer.

Investigators interested in sharpening their analytical skills, critically examining the works of others, or engaging in some type of cross-cultural research should check the range of possible sources mentioned in this and the other sources cited above. What might prove to be some very exciting and productive surprises (Forcese and Richer, 1973, p. 189) await those inclined to take advantage of archives.

In 1967, for example, there were 25 voluntary members of the

Council of Social Science Data Archives. In 1970 Hyman provided the following selected list of archives in existence then.

1. Bureau of Applied Social Research, Columbia University, New York City.
2. Carleton University Social Science Data Archives, Ottawa, Canada.
3. Columbia University School of Public Health and Administrative Medicine Research Archives, New York City.
4. Data Repository Section, Survey Research Laboratory, University of Illinois, Urbana.
5. International Data Library and Reference Service, Survey Research Center, University of California, Berkeley.
6. Inter-University Consortium for Political Research, University of Michigan, Ann Arbor, Michigan.
7. International Development Data Bank, Michigan State University, East Lansing, Michigan.
8. Laboratory for Political Research, Social Science Data Archive, University of Iowa, Iowa City, Iowa.
9. Louis Harris Political Data Center, University of North Carolina, Chapel Hill, North Carolina.
10. Public Opinion Survey Unit, University of Missouri, Columbia, Missouri.
11. Roper Public Opinion Research Center, Williams College, Williamstown, Massachusetts.
12. Social Science Data and Program Library Service, University of Wisconsin, Madison, Wisconsin.
13. Social Science Research Council Data Bank, University of Essex, England.
14. Steinmetz Institute, University of Amsterdam, Netherlands.
15. UCLA Political Behavior Archives, University of California, Los Angeles.
16. Zentralarchiv fur Empirische Sozialforschung, University of Cologne, Cologne, Germany.

But knowing that archives exist and utilizing their holdings are two different matters. Unless investigators themselves assume the initiative for making use of these data sources, such facilities are of little value. How does one go about moving beyond the knowledge that archives exist to actually using them in scientific investigations? There are numerous ways to become familiar with the various data banks in the United States and other countries.

One way is simply to write the archives of interest. If an investigator knows what type of information is needed, the inquiry can be direct and to the point. If, on the other hand, there is an interest in finding out what sort of data are available, information should be requested along these lines. Either way, researchers can learn much about what data there are, how they are categorized, what is involved in retrieving information, what, if any, charges there are for using the data, and so on.

For those who like to see their data first-hand, another way to assess the relative usefulness of archive data is to visit the archives and browse through their holdings. Frequently, it is difficult or awkward to put into a letter precisely what it is that is needed in the course of conducting a research project. Letters cannot be exhaustive, and there is no substitute for direct access to archives. It may well be that a worthwhile and workable project will come to mind during the course of such perusals.

Finally, investigators should not ignore the leads that can be obtained from others who use data archives in their own research. Relying, as Elder did (Hyman, 1972, p. 84) on a knowledgeable informant (the assistant director of an archive) saved valuable time and effort. As Hyman comments, "Perhaps it does not require great sagacity to think of this simple procedure and some would naturally avail themselves of an informant, but for those who might neglect this avenue and think only of machines as aides, it is worth stating" (1972, p. 84–85).

Selected Governmental Data

Probably no other nation in history has accumulated such a massive amount of data through its various federal bureaucratic agencies as has the United States. Some, such as the census, are required by the Constitution. Most, however, have developed as a product of the normal recordkeeping and reporting that is engaged in by governmental units. Many of the most important of these data are summarized in the *Statistical Abstracts of the United States*, which has been published annually since 1878. Contained in it is information of the "social, political, and economic organization of the United States. It is designed to serve as a convenient volume for statistical publications and sources" (1973, p. iii). Many states have similar documents summarizing statistical data from state agencies and bureaus.

To suggest to investigators how such data can be useful in answering some of their research questions, it is advantageous to describe at least one or two of these sources briefly. Because there is probably no other compilation of data relied on so extensively by social scientists, the United States census certainly must be placed at the top of any list. Certain kinds of useful information can almost always be found there, especially in connection with projects seeking aggregate data on population characteristics.

Basically, the census is a de jure method of enumerating various population characteristics. That is, it counts people according to their place of residence rather than on the basis of where they are when they are being counted (Kammeyer, 1971, pp. 27–30). Prior to 1960, the census was taken by canvassers who went to homes to find answers to questions of interest to the census bureau. Since that time, however, it has essentially utilized self-enumeration. Information is collected by sending questionnaires to households and either having them returned through the mail or picked up by a canvasser.

Information is collected from a vast majority of Americans with respect to items such as name and address, relation to head of household, race, age, sex, marital status, and other population and housing items (Kammeyer, 1971, pp. 162–68).[1]

Policy makers and planners as well as social scientists have, in effect, enormous amounts of data collected for them in advance and ready for their use (Kammeyer, 1971, pp. 162–68). But even a source that is highly sensitive to the needs and demands for quantification in social science data collection procedures is not without its problems.

For one thing, to those not acquainted with the numerous census publications, it is difficult to learn what data are actually contained in them. Although Census Data Finders are available, they are not themselves easily comprehended without considerable study. In fact, that they are even needed underscores the problems related to comprehending and making full use of the entire range and nature of all the information compiled.

Another problem is that the data are not as free of errors as might be thought, given the range and quantified nature of the data. As Kammeyer notes, there is a certain amount of underreporting of information on certain groups in the population. Nonwhites in general and male nonwhites in particular are underrepresented in census figures (Kammeyer, 1971, p. 28). Although this largely stems from inherent shortcomings in the data-collection procedures, it means that generalizations to the entire United States population from census data must be made cautiously and with some reservations.

Finally, there is evidence that some information gets classified in different ways by the same canvassers at different times and that canvassers, even when highly trained, differ among themselves in classifying data. Kammeyer (1971, p. 28–29) illustrates the point well by noting

Table 12-1. Subject Items: 1970 Census

Population Items	Housing Items
100 per cent	*100 per cent*
Name and address	Number of units at this address
Relationship to head of household	Telephone
Color or race	Private entrance to living quarters
Age and sex	Complete kitchen facilities
Marital status	Number of rooms
	Water supply
	Flush toilet
	Bathtub or shower
	Basement
	Tenure
	Commercial establishment on
	property
	Value
	Contract rent
	Vacancy status
	Months vacant
20 per cent	*20 per cent*
State or country of birth	Components of gross rent
Years of school completed	Heating equipment
Number of children ever born	Year structure built
Employment status and hours	Number of units in structure
worked	Trailers
Weeks worked last year	Farm residence
Last year in which worked	
Occupation, industry, and class	
of worker	
Activity 5 years ago	
Income	

the different results obtained with respect to educational attainment levels of the population.

These limitations do not keep census data from being extremely valuable sources of information to the social scientist. There are few areas of substantive concern in these disciplines that do not employ at least some basic demographic information obtained from them. What is important about the limitations is that an awareness of them permits investigators to interpret findings more realistically when using this data source.

Table 12-1   (Continued)

Population Items	Housing Items
15 per cent	*15 per cent*
Country of birth of parents	Source of water
Mother tongue	Sewage disposal
Year moved into this house	Number of bathrooms
Place of residence 5 years ago	Air conditioning
School or college enrollment	Number of automobiles
Veteran status	
Place of work	
Means of transportation to work	
5 per cent	*5 per cent*
Mexican or Spanish origin or	Number of stories
descent	Elevator in structure
Citizenship	Fuel for heating, cooking, water-
Year of immigration	heating
When married	Number of bedrooms
Vocational training completed	Clothing washing machine
Presence and duration of disability	Clothes dryer
Occupation-industry 5 years ago	Dishwasher
	Home food freezer
	Television—Radio
	Second home

SOURCE: Kenneth C. W. Kammeyer, *An Introduction to Population* (San Francisco: Chandler Publishing Co., 1971), pp. 162–68.

A second source of public information frequently relied on by social scientists, public officials, journalists, and others is the *Uniform Crime Reports.* It is worth examining briefly if for no other reason than that some rather sharp similarities and contrasts can be drawn between this publication and those of the Census Bureau. It is hoped these will serve to alert the sensitive investigator to certain basic questions that must be asked about *all* selected governmental data. Established by the Federal Bureau of Investigation in 1931 to compile information useful in assessing the overall effectiveness of police activities throughout the country, these annual reports contain data on both offenses known to the police and arrests actually made by them. Information is obtained on police activity with respect to approximately 30 different types of offenses. In addition, there is

descriptive material on the number of full-time law enforcement officers, patrol data, patrol and shift assignments, assaults on police officers, and a variety of related topics.

Each annual report consists of information voluntarily submitted to
the Federal Bureau of Investigation by local police departments
throughout the country. Although the FBI provides guidelines for
completing forms used in submitting information, it exercises no
direct control over the reporting practices of the agencies compiling
the data. Compliance with its appeals for uniformity has improved
over the years but is still difficult to obtain in some instances. Numerous changes have been made in recent years to upgrade the
reporting and compilation procedures, but social scientists especially
have found the data contained in the *Uniform Crime Reports* to be of
questionable scientific value. Several points are usually made in this
regard (Caldwell and Black, 1971, pp. 49–62).

First, the voluntary nature of the data collection process has resulted
in the underrepresentation of police departments in certain locales,
especially rural areas. In addition, some sections of the country, such
as the South, have a consistently lower reporting rate than others.
Other factors as well, such as local political pressures, internal organizational demands of police department bureaucracies, and so on have
been known to affect reporting practices.

Second, the data reflect only officially recognized crime. How much
crime there is that does not get reported or result in an arrest must be
ascertained in different ways. Recently, surveys have been conducted
that suggest there is considerably more criminal activity in the United
States than documented in the *Uniform Crime Reports* (President's
Commission on Law Enforcement and Administration of Justice, 1967).
Although such an observation should perhaps be no surprise,
developing techniques for measuring the extensiveness of crime has
proven to be a difficult task.

Third, because of the frequent changes made in reporting practices,
it is difficult to compare data from one report with those from
another. In fact, comparisons cannot easily be made within the same
annual report owing to the fact that at least two types of data, offenses
known to the police and arrests made by them, are presented. Great
care must be exercised, then, whenever comparative data are desired.
That does not mean that comparisons cannot be made with other data
sources. But as Hindelang (1973, p. 32) suggests:

> . . . it is not surprising that inter-relationships across sources of
> criminal justice statistics (e.g., information regarding the relation-

ship between offenses known to the police and commitments to prison) remain essentially unexplored because compatible information from more than one source has rarely been drawn together for analysis.

Finally, whether the report contains information useful in assessing the seriousness of offenses is open to question. One important feature of the report is the Crime Index. Fluctuations in rates of crime from year to year in the United States are determined by comparing information on offenses known to the police per 100,000 population for a selected group of seven crimes including murder, aggravated assault, rape, robbery, burglary, auto theft, and larceny of $50 or more. Not only are the offenses not weighted in terms of their relative seriousness, few acceptable reasons can be given for the selection of these particular crimes. Dissatisfaction with the Crime Index has been instrumental in efforts to devise more scientifically appropriate measures of crime seriousness, but these measures, too, are not without their critics (Blumstein, 1974).

For all their shortcomings, the *Uniform Crime Reports,* because they represent the only nation-wide, systematic compilation of data on the crime problem, remain an important source of data for the social scientist. As with other data sources, they should not be dismissed in a cursory fashion. As Hindelang (1973, p. 32) notes:

In many ways it seems as though most researchers have forsaken the use of official statistics without really attempting to examine them.

Emerging from this brief discussion of two governmental data sources are some questions that can serve as guidelines when using any such documents.

1. Are the data contained in a central source and are they retrievable in a systematic, easily accessible way? Census data are usually available in machine-readable form on tapes. Statistics on crime, whether in the *Uniform Crime Reports* or elsewhere, are seldom, if ever, available in such a way.

2. What are the stated reasons for collecting the data? The Constitution stipulates that some form of census must be taken periodically. No such authority lies behind the collection of police statistics on crime. Whether uniformity in data gathering is being established by law or by voluntary compliance can seriously affect the representativeness of the information.

3. How comparable are the data from one report to the next and within the same report? Census data are much more likely to provide

comparable information than documents like the *Uniform Crime Reports.*

Although not an exhaustive list, these are the types of questions that need to be asked prior to using governmental documents for social science research projects.

Other Published Materials

Beyond data found in archives and selected governmental publications are a host of potential sources from which information can be obtained for social science investigations. These range from highly classified and codified materials, such as those contained in the Human Relations Area Files,[5] to the contents of newspapers, magazines, books, professional journals, radio and television program tapes, and so on. In fact, included here could be all remaining types of documents to which social scientists have public access.

Effective use of these data sources depends on the ingenuity of the investigator as well as the nature of the research question being posed. Becker (1963, p. 141), for example, relied on articles indexed in the *Reader's Guide to Periodic Literature* to document a contention that the Federal Bureau of Narcotics was influential "in the preparation of journalistic articles" to assist in its campaign to enact legislation against marijuana. Both the number of articles appearing and the specific contents of articles were examined.

Especially interesting is the methodology employed by Useem in his study of draft resistance during the Vietnam era (1973, pp. 29–34). He relied on· practically the full range of secondary sources available to scientific investigators, as well as the primary data collection technique of structured interviewing. In this way, both the context surrounding the movement and the movement itself could be more comprehensively grasped. It is instructive to note the sorts of materials utilized, even though they embrace a broader range of documents than specifically addressed in this section. Particularly useful to his research (1973, pp. 29–30) were:

1. Federal government studies and reports, including the annual statement of the Selective Service System; congressional hearings on extension of the draft and the volunteer army; research conducted in the offices of the Department of Defense and the Veterans Administration; reports of several national commissions concerned with compulsory military service; and federally sponsored studies conducted by external organizations, such as the National Opinion Research Center and the University of Michigan's Institute for Social Research.

2. Journals and newsletters of the Resistance, as well as publications of radical student organizations, draft counseling and antidraft groups, pacifist organizations, and various leftwing groups, plus independent periodicals concerned with antiwar, leftwing, and pacifist developments in the United States. Among the several dozen helpful publications were *Win Magazine, The Guardian, The Peacemaker, Liberation, Resist, New Left Notes, Final Draft, Downdraft, Draft Counselor's Newsletter,* and *AMEX-Canada.*
3. Academic studies of military manpower and the student movement, ranging in focus from the administrative practices of the Selective Service System to the economic costs of being drafted and the individual and institutional correlates of student activism.
4. Surveys of opinion on the draft and the Vietnam War and secondary analyses of trends in these national and special polls.
5. Historical studies covering the Resistance, reaction to conscription in previous American wars, and movements similar to the Resistance in other societies (Britain, France, and Australia).

When an investigator is interested in ascertaining broad trends, detecting a shift over time in the type of attention paid to a particular topic, suggesting potential future developments or needs based on previously published materials in an area, or some related integrating problem, reliance on the published works of others becomes especially relevant. Feldman, in fact, correctly maintains that the writings of others become original data for the integrator (1971:87). It is unfortunate that so much of the time devoted by researchers to "surveys of the literature" has been conducted without the realization that they could have borne fruitful scientific results. The orderly accumulation of scientific knowledge is, after all, predicated at least in part on such activity.

Of course, the same kinds of concerns must be displayed when engaging in this sort of data-collection as are used in connection with other forms. Problems of selection, coding, indexing, and retrieval procedures, comparability, and reporting of findings are all just as real when engaging in this form of research as in any other (Feldman, 1971, pp. 88–94). As is so frequently the case, there is no step-by-step protocol for doing these things. Each investigator must learn to develop procedural tactics for contending with these problems more or less independently. By far the most important lesson to be learned at this point is that of *viewing the published works of others as data in their own right,* not simply as sources from which material can potentially be abstracted.

SOME MAJOR USES OF SECONDARY DATA

Anyone who takes the time to carefully appraise the nature of data already available to him should do so within the context of an appreciation of the major uses to which those data can be put. Broadly speaking, these uses can be viewed in two ways. First, they can be examined from the standpoint of how they can actually be used to generate scientific information. Second, they can be looked at in terms of the ways they promote the overall objectives of the scientific enterprise. Because the two are closely intertwined, the distinction is largely one of the relative emphasis given one or the other.

For those social scientists who increasingly find it advantageous to use secondary data in generating scientific findings there are, as a rule, three ways to proceed. First, such data can be used to demonstrate original scientific findings. Numerous examples of this are found in Hyman's (1972) review of the works of secondary data researchers. In this connection, Feldman (1971, p. 95) makes it clear that documents used for integration can achieve many of the objectives of primary research:

> . . . testing hypotheses; lending (or not lending) support to extant propositions; offering new information and generalizations; generating theoretical issues to be explored; and suggesting future research.

Second, they can serve as auxiliary documentation, that is, they can complement original data being accumulated by the investigator. To a certain extent, that is what Useem's study of draft evaders relied on these sources for. It would have been impossible for him to have originally accumulated all the data housed in the numerous sources of information already at his disposal. And it is quite likely that his study would have been less thorough in terms of his sensitivity to the original data collected without these secondary sources.

Finally, secondary data can be used to verify previously established findings. Put another way, when appropriately used they can provide a relatively crude form of replication.

With respect to the uses of secondary sources in pursuing the overall objectives of the scientific enterprise, all the above mentioned applications come into play. Addressing the larger context to which particular investigations relate, Feldman (1971, p. 99) indicates their relevance to the accumulation of scientific knowledge:

> If one believes in the cumulative nature of science, then periodic stock-taking becomes essential for any particular arena of scientific

endeavor. The cumulation of knowledge in an area may, of course, occur more or less haphazardly—but this does not, and should not, preclude more systematic attempts by laborers in a field to determine when they have arrived (and, consequently, where they might go). It is as this kind of systematic attempt that large-scale reviews and integrations are important.

Still, even under the most optimal conditions, secondary sources pose difficult problems for researchers. Those who hope to save time, reduce the amount of tedium connected with procedural details such as coding and classifying, or otherwise short-cut the hard work of empirical inquiry will soon be disappointed. And those who impose unduly harsh standards of perfection on secondary data will find, if they become involved in primary data collection, that no piece of scientific research is without flaws of one or another kind.

Ultimately, whatever uses secondary data sources have for scientific activity depends on the subjective ingenuity of the investigator in making use of them to demonstrate a point. This subjective quality, related as it is to the investigator and pertaining to nothing inherent in the sources themselves is, at one and the same time, a major strength and weakness. It is to a more systematic review of these matters that we now turn.

MAJOR ADVANTAGES OF SECONDARY ANALYSIS

For those who have yet to sense the benefits that can be derived from the use of other sources of data, it might be well to summarize some of their major advantages. First among these, and perhaps so obvious that its positive nature might be overlooked, is the enormous saving in time and money. As was seen in Useem's (1973) research, it is frequently not possible to accumulate all the data bearing on a problem. What better way to expand scientific knowledge efficiently and still satisfy intellectual curiosity than by capitalizing on information already in existence?

That brings us to a second advantage, namely, the very real possibility of using the work of others to broaden the base from which scientific generalizations can be made. This is especially so when information from several cultural settings is being examined. Although a variety of obstacles stand in the way of obtaining data that are comparable on a cross-cultural basis, the potential for such research brought about with secondary sources should not be ignored.

A third advantage to be gained from relying on other sources is found in using them to verify findings already obtained in primary research by an investigator. The need for additional empirical support need not await the time when additional primary data can be collected. By turning to sources already containing relevant information, the verification process is more rapidly enhanced.

Finally, an advantage frequently overlooked stems from the frustration so often encountered by researchers who turn to such sources for their information. Out of the disillusionment and dissatisfaction with the quality of data available, more useful *scientific* measures of the problem are frequently developed. This is precisely what has happened with respect to measures of the seriousness of delinquency and crime, for example. Scholars long dissatisfied with official data sources have turned to what they regard as more suitable measures of seriousness. What is important is that the measures originated in the scientific community *in response to* disappointment with data suiting the needs of law enforcement agencies (Sellin and Wolfgang, 1964).

SOME DISADVANTAGES OF SECONDARY SOURCES

As the preceding points attest, there are numerous reasons why ready-made data can be turned to in the conduct of social research. But the price is high and the stakes, as revealed in a delineation of some of the major disadvantages of such sources, are not always worth the venture.

For one thing, it is hard to avoid the tendency to acquire the facts before knowing what the scientific problem is that is in need of solution. Such raw empiricism is encountered frequently enough as it is, even where primary data are being collected. Special care must be taken to guard against using data simply because those are the ones that are available.

The difficulties do not stop there. Even when they speak to issues of some scientific import, data collected for other purposes must be classified in ways consistent with the objectives of the present research. Several technical problems present themselves as a result. It is probable that many researchers considering the use of secondary sources abandon their projects at this point. Finding that the data as they exist do not conform to the categories and classifications envisioned by the investigator, that crucial variables are missing or not recorded in ways that render them useful as data, and so on can raise serious doubts about the overall worth of the source. Unless an investigator is capable of compromise and adjustment in the project objectives, design, and procedures, secondary sources can prove too frustrating. But compromise, adjustment, and modification are inherent to the research process no matter what the source of data.

That brings up a third and closely related disadvantage in the use of other sources. Problems encountered in gaining access to and preparing them for analysis sometimes pose sufficiently intractable problems that these sources are ignored. At worst, they are simply defined out of existence as potentially useful for empirical work.

Another problem with these sources is that it is sometimes not possible to comprehend the process of the original data gathering. Just because data are available does not mean that reasons are given for why they were gathered. Likewise, factors affecting procedural decisions are usually not spelled out. Because of this, a feel for the data is lacking. It is a condition that contributes, in part, to the inability of many to intuitively grasp ways in which other sources might be used in their own studies.

Finally, knowledge of the whereabouts of sources, even those labeled earlier as "public," is not necessarily available to all social scientists on an equal basis. Anyone familiar with the social organization of scientific research knows that accessibility depends to a degree on proximity. Being long distances from archives, library holdings, facilities for processing data and related conditions can do much to hinder the potential accessibility of secondary information. And that, in turn, can affect the knowledge an investigator might have of the types of sources. The dissemination of information about secondary sources, although improved over the past decade, is an important priority if such sources are to play a prominent role in scientific research.

CONCLUDING REMARKS

There are three underlying themes in this chapter. The first is that there are many types of data already available to investigators that can be of enormous use in the solution of research problems.

A second theme is that the use of secondary sources is no different from other social research. Problems of collecting, codifying, analyzing, and reporting findings are encountered throughout investigations utilizing these sources that are similar to those found in any empirical investigation. Furthermore, they involve decisions that bear directly on the basic structure of the data-collection process. Questions about sampling, reliability and validity, comparability of findings, and so forth are no more easily avoided here then elsewhere. Any sound research must address such problems head-on. They simply cannot be ignored if the project is to have scientific utility.

Finally, emphasis is placed on recognizing that attention to detailed procedural concerns is not enough to guarantee a study's scientific import. Only when data are viewed within the larger context of the scientific enterprise can they be expected to have much lasting cumulative value.

In a sense, therefore, our last chapter brings us full circle. Having started out stressing the fundamental dimensions of social research, proceeded to a consideration of the basic structure of the research process, and moved finally to specific methods of data collection, it is easier to view them as inextricably intertwined stages. At no point has it been easy to separate one basic concern from the rest. It is especially fitting that it was not possible to by-pass these issues when using secondary sources.

Furthermore, it underscores the basic thrust of the entire text, which is that scientific research necessitates the resolution of recurring problems and continuing issues at every juncture. Only when the entire range of problems is kept in sight can one expect to think and act effectively as a researcher. And only then can the systematic accumulation of scientific knowledge be expected to develop in an orderly fashion.

SOME QUESTIONS FOR REVIEW

1. What is a secondary source? What features make them distinctive from other types of information? What common qualities do they share?

2. List the various private sources of secondary data available to investigators. What problems are encountered in using them for scientific research?

3. What is it that distinguishes public sources of secondary data from private sources? What major types of public sources of secondary data can be identified?

4. Design a project in which data archives are the central source of information. What must be done to become familiar with the holdings of archives? Suggest how researchers can utilize these data sources more

effectively. If possible, visit an archive in the area and list a series of research questions which could be examined from its holdings.

5. Utilize data contained in either the *Uniform Crime Reports* or the census in a research project. Examine the sorts of problems encountered in their use and suggest ways in which these data sources could be improved for scientific purposes.

6. Discuss possible ways in which other published materials can be used effectively in research.

7. Delineate the major advantages and disadvantages of secondary data sources.

NOTES

1. Similar definitions can be found in Festinger (1953), Forcese and Richer (1973), and Hyman (1972).
2. An excellent discussion of these can be found in Robin Williams' *American Society,* 3rd ed., Alfred A. Knopf: New York, 1970.
3. This is a practice frequently followed, for example, by established researchers who are anxious to have full use made of their data. Often they do not have the time or lose interest in "milking" their data fully. Students or junior investigators working on papers, theses, dissertations, and the like are thus given access to raw and frequently valuable data.
4. Kammeyer lists many types of information collected from various samples of the population, along with the year in which each item was first included in the census and brief explanations for the importance of each item.
5. Researchers unfamiliar with the Files are urged to consult the *Nature and Use of the HRAF Files* by Lagacé (1974). In addition to providing a brief overview of their contents, he suggests specific research and teaching topics.

     As Lagacé indicates, "the HRAF files are a collection of primary source materials (mainly published books and articles, but including some unpublished manuscripts) on selected cultures or societies representing all major areas of the world. The materials are organized and filed by a unique method designed for the rapid and accurate retrieval of specific data on given cultures and topics, and are produced in formats which enable convenient handling and compact storage." (1974, ix).

Although more than two hundred university libraries and research organizations participate in the HRAF, they vary
considerably with respect to the extensiveness of their holdings.

BIBLIOGRAPHY

Becker, Howard. *Outsiders: Studies in the Sociology of Deviance.*
New York: Free Press, 1963.
———. "Introduction" in Clifford R. Shaw's *The Jackroller.* Chicago:
University of Chicago Press, 1966.
Bisco, R. "Social Science Data Archives: Progress Prospects," *Social
Science Information* 6 (1967): 39–74.
Blumstein, Alfred. "Seriousness Weights in an Index of Crime,"
American Sociological Review 39 (1974): 854–64.
Caldwell, Robert G., and James A. Black. *Juvenile Delinquency.* New
York: Ronald Press, 1971.
Census Data Finder. Rosslyn, Va.: National Data Use and Access Labo-
ratories, 1970.
Feldman, Kenneth A. "Using the Work of Others: Some Observations
on Reviewing and Integrating," *Sociology of Education* 44 (1971):
86–102.
Federal Bureau of Investigation, United States Department of Justice.
Uniform Crime Reports for the United States. Washington, D.C.:
Government Printing Office. Issued yearly.
Festinger, Leon. *Research Methods in the Behavioral Science.* New
York: Holt, Rinehart & Winston, 1953.
Forcese, Dennis P., and Stephen Richer. *Social Research Methods.*
Englewood Cliffs, N.J.: Prentice-Hall, 1973.
Hindelang, Michael J. "The Utilization of Criminal Justice Statistics,"
Review of Public Data Use 1 (1973): 29–33.
Hyman, Herbert. *Secondary Analysis of Sample Surveys: Principles,
Procedures, and Potentialities.* New York: John Wiley, 1972.
Kammeyer, Kenneth C. W. *An Introduction to Population.* San
Francisco, Cal.: Chandler, 1971.
Lagacé, Robert O., *Nature and Use of the HRAF Files,* New Haven,
Conn.: Human Relations Area Files, Inc., 1974.
President's Commission on Law Enforcement and Administration of
Justice. *The Challenge of Crime in a Free Society.* Washington, D.C.:
Government Printing Office, 1967.
Sellin, Thorsten, and Marvin E. Wolfgang. *The Measurement of Delin-
quency.* New York: John Wiley, 1964.

Shaw, Clifford R. *The Jackroller*. Chicago: University of Chicago Press, 1966.

Social Science Data Archives in the United States. New York: Council of Social Science Data Archives, 1967.

Statistical Abstracts of the United States. Washington, D.C.: Government Printing Office, 1973.

Thomas, W. I., and Florian Znanieki. *The Polish Peasant in Europe and America*. New York: Alfred A. Knopf, 1927.

Treinen, H. "Notes on an Experience with Secondary Analyses of Survey Data as a Teaching Device," *Social Science Information* 9 (1970): 123–32.

Useem, Michael. *Conscription, Protest, and Social Conflict: The Life and Death of a Draft Resistance Movement*. New York: John Wiley, 1973.

Williams, Robin M. *American Society* (3rd ed.). New York: Alfred A. Knopf, 1970.

APPENDIX A

A Table of Random Numbers

10 09 73 25 33	76 52 01 35 86	34 67 35 48 76	80 95 90 91 17	39 29 27 49 45
37 54 20 48 05	64 89 47 42 96	24 80 52 40 37	20 63 61 04 02	00 82 29 16 65
08 42 26 89 53	19 64 50 93 03	23 20 90 25 60	15 95 33 47 64	35 08 03 36 06
99 01 90 25 29	09 37 67 07 15	38 31 13 11 65	88 67 67 43 97	04 43 62 76 59
12 80 79 99 70	80 15 73 61 47	64 03 23 66 53	98 95 11 68 77	12 17 17 68 33
66 06 57 47 17	34 07 27 68 50	36 69 73 61 70	65 81 33 98 85	11 19 92 91 70
31 06 01 08 05	45 57 18 24 06	35 30 34 26 14	86 79 90 74 39	23 40 30 97 32
85 26 97 76 02	02 05 16 56 92	68 66 57 48 18	73 05 38 52 47	18 62 38 85 79
63 57 33 21 35	05 32 54 70 48	90 55 35 75 48	28 46 82 87 09	83 49 12 56 24
73 79 64 57 53	03 52 96 47 78	35 80 83 42 82	60 93 52 03 44	35 27 38 84 35
98 52 01 77 67	14 90 56 86 07	22 10 94 05 58	60 97 09 34 33	50 50 07 39 98
11 80 50 54 31	39 80 82 77 32	50 72 56 82 48	29 40 52 42 01	52 77 56 78 51
83 45 29 96 34	06 28 89 80 83	13 74 67 00 78	18 47 54 06 10	68 71 17 78 17
88 68 54 02 00	86 50 75 84 01	36 76 66 79 51	90 36 47 64 93	29 60 91 10 62
99 59 46 73 48	87 51 76 49 69	91 82 60 89 28	93 78 56 13 68	23 47 83 41 13
65 48 11 76 74	17 46 85 09 50	58 04 77 69 74	73 03 95 71 86	40 21 81 65 44
80 12 43 56 35	17 72 70 80 15	45 31 82 23 74	21 11 57 82 53	14 38 55 37 63
74 35 09 98 17	77 40 27 72 14	43 23 60 02 10	45 52 16 42 37	96 28 60 26 55
69 91 62 68 03	66 25 22 91 48	36 93 68 72 03	76 62 11 39 90	94 40 05 64 18
09 89 32 05 05	14 22 56 85 14	46 42 75 67 88	96 29 77 88 22	54 38 21 45 98
91 49 91 45 23	68 47 92 76 86	46 16 28 35 54	94 75 08 99 23	37 08 92 00 48
80 33 69 45 98	26 94 03 68 58	70 29 73 41 35	53 14 03 33 40	42 05 08 23 41
44 10 48 19 49	85 15 74 79 54	32 97 92 65 75	57 60 04 08 81	22 22 20 64 13
12 55 07 37 42	11 10 00 20 40	12 86 07 46 97	96 64 48 94 39	28 70 72 58 15
63 60 64 93 29	16 50 53 44 84	40 21 95 25 63	43 65 17 70 82	07 20 73 17 90
61 19 69 04 46	26 45 74 77 74	51 92 43 37 29	65 39 45 95 93	42 58 26 05 27
15 47 44 52 66	95 27 07 99 53	59 36 78 38 48	82 39 61 01 18	33 21 15 94 66
94 55 72 85 73	67 89 75 43 87	54 62 24 44 31	91 19 04 25 92	92 92 74 59 73
42 48 11 62 13	97 34 40 87 21	16 86 84 87 67	03 07 11 20 59	25 70 14 66 70
23 52 37 83 17	73 20 88 98 37	68 93 59 14 16	26 25 22 96 63	05 52 28 25 62
04 49 35 24 94	75 24 63 38 24	45 86 25 10 25	61 96 27 93 35	65 33 71 24 72
00 54 99 76 54	64 05 18 81 59	96 11 96 38 96	54 69 28 23 91	23 28 72 95 29
35 96 31 53 07	26 89 80 93 54	33 35 13 54 62	77 97 45 00 24	90 10 33 93 33
59 80 80 83 91	45 42 72 68 42	83 60 94 97 00	13 02 12 48 92	78 56 52 01 06
46 05 88 52 36	01 39 09 22 86	77 28 14 40 77	93 91 08 36 47	70 61 74 29 41
32 17 90 05 97	87 37 92 52 41	05 56 70 70 07	86 74 31 71 57	85 39 41 18 38
69 23 46 14 06	20 11 74 52 04	15 95 66 00 00	18 74 39 24 23	97 11 89 63 38
19 56 54 14 30	01 75 87 53 79	40 41 92 15 85	66 67 43 68 06	84 96 28 52 07
45 15 51 49 38	19 47 60 72 46	43 66 79 45 43	59 04 79 00 33	20 82 66 95 41
94 86 43 19 94	36 16 81 08 51	34 88 88 15 53	01 54 03 54 56	05 01 45 11 76

SOURCE: The RAND Corporation, *A Million Random Digits*, Free Press, Glencoe, Ill., 1955, pp. 1–3, with the kind permission of the publisher.

```
59 58 00 64 78    75 56 97 88 00    88 83 55 44 86    23 76 80 61 56    04 11 10 84 08
38 50 80 73 41    23 79 34 87 63    90 82 29 70 22    17 71 90 42 07    95 95 44 99 53
30 69 27 06 68    94 68 81 61 27    56 19 68 00 91    82 06 76 34 00    05 46 26 92 00
65 44 39 56 59    18 28 82 74 37    49 63 22 40 41    08 33 76 56 76    96 29 99 08 36
27 26 75 02 64    13 19 27 22 94    07 47 74 46 06    17 98 54 89 11    97 34 13 03 58

91 30 70 69 91    19 07 22 42 10    36 69 95 37 28    28 82 53 57 93    28 97 66 62 52
68 43 49 46 88    84 47 31 36 22    62 12 69 84 08    12 84 38 25 90    09 81 59 31 46
48 90 81 58 77    54 74 52 45 91    35 70 00 47 54    83 82 45 26 92    54 13 05 51 60
06 91 34 51 97    42 67 27 86 01    11 88 30 95 28    63 01 19 89 01    14 97 44 03 44
10 45 51 60 19    14 21 03 37 12    91 34 23 78 21    88 32 58 08 51    43 66 77 08 83

12 88 39 73 43    65 02 76 11 84    04 28 50 13 92    17 97 41 50 77    90 71 22 67 69
21 77 83 09 76    38 80 73 69 61    31 64 94 20 96    63 28 10 20 23    08 81 64 74 49
19 52 35 95 15    65 12 25 96 59    86 28 36 82 58    69 57 21 37 98    16 43 59 15 29
67 24 55 26 70    35 58 31 65 63    79 24 68 66 86    76 46 33 42 22    26 65 59 08 02
60 58 44 73 77    07 50 03 79 92    45 13 42 65 29    26 76 08 36 37    41 32 64 43 44

53 85 34 13 77    36 06 69 48 50    58 83 87 38 59    49 36 47 33 31    96 24 04 36 42
24 63 73 87 36    74 38 48 93 42    52 62 30 79 92    12 36 91 86 01    03 74 28 38 73
83 08 01 24 51    38 99 22 28 15    07 75 95 17 77    97 37 72 75 85    51 97 23 78 67
16 44 42 43 34    36 15 19 90 73    27 49 37 09 39    85 13 03 25 52    54 84 65 47 59
60 79 01 81 57    57 17 86 57 62    11 16 17 85 76    45 81 95 29 79    65 13 00 48 60

03 99 11 04 61    93 71 61 68 94    66 08 32 46 53    84 60 95 82 32    88 61 81 91 61
38 55 59 55 54    32 88 65 97 80    08 35 56 08 60    29 73 54 77 62    71 29 92 38 53
17 54 67 37 04    92 05 24 62 15    55 12 12 92 81    59 07 60 79 36    27 95 45 89 09
32 64 35 28 61    95 81 90 68 31    00 91 19 89 36    76 35 59 37 79    80 86 30 05 14
69 57 26 87 77    39 51 03 59 05    14 06 04 06 19    29 54 96 96 16    33 56 46 07 80

24 12 26 65 91    27 69 90 64 94    14 84 54 66 72    61 95 87 71 00    90 89 97 57 54
61 19 63 02 31    92 96 26 17 73    41 83 95 53 82    17 26 77 09 43    78 03 87 02 67
30 53 22 17 04    10 27 41 22 02    39 68 52 33 09    10 06 16 88 29    55 98 66 64 85
03 78 89 75 99    75 86 72 07 17    74 41 65 31 66    35 20 83 33 74    87 53 90 88 23
48 22 86 33 79    85 78 34 76 19    53 15 26 74 33    35 66 35 29 72    16 81 86 03 11

60 36 59 46 53    35 07 53 39 49    42 61 42 92 97    01 91 82 83 16    98 95 37 32 31
83 79 94 24 02    56 62 33 44 42    34 99 44 13 74    70 07 11 47 36    09 95 71 80 65
32 96 00 74 05    36 40 98 32 32    99 38 54 16 00    11 13 30 75 86    15 91 70 62 53
19 32 25 38 45    57 62 05 26 06    66 49 76 86 46    78 13 86 65 59    19 64 09 94 13
11 22 09 47 47    07 39 93 74 08    48 50 92 39 29    27 48 24 54 76    85 24 43 51 59

31 75 15 72 60    68 98 00 53 39    15 47 04 83 55    88 65 12 25 96    03 15 21 92 21
88 49 29 93 82    14 45 40 45 04    20 09 49 89 77    74 84 39 34 13    22 10 97 85 08
30 93 44 77 44    07 48 18 38 28    73 78 80 65 33    28 59 72 04 05    94 20 52 03 80
22 88 84 88 93    27 49 99 87 48    60 53 04 51 28    74 02 28 46 17    82 03 71 02 68
78 21 21 69 93    35 90 29 13 86    44 37 21 54 86    65 74 11 40 14    87 48 13 72 20
```

```
98 08 62 48 26    45 24 02 84 04    44 99 90 88 96    39 09 47 34 07    35 44 13 18 80
33 18 51 62 32    41 94 15 09 49    89 43 54 85 81    88 69 54 19 94    37 54 87 30 43
80 95 10 04 06    96 38 27 07 74    20 15 12 33 87    25 01 62 52 98    94 62 46 11 71
79 75 24 91 40    71 96 12 82 96    69 86 10 25 91    74 85 22 05 39    00 38 75 95 79
18 63 33 25 37    98 14 50 65 71    31 01 02 46 74    05 45 56 14 27    77 93 89 19 36

74 02 94 39 02    77 55 73 22 70    97 79 01 71 19    52 52 75 80 21    80 81 45 17 48
54 17 84 56 11    80 99 33 71 43    05 33 51 29 69    56 12 71 92 55    36 04 09 03 24
11 66 44 98 83    52 07 98 48 27    59 38 17 15 39    09 97 33 34 40    88 46 12 33 56
48 32 47 79 28    31 24 96 47 10    02 29 53 68 70    32 30 75 75 46    15 02 00 99 94
69 07 49 41 38    87 63 79 19 76    35 58 40 44 01    10 51 82 16 15    01 84 87 69 38

09 18 82 00 97    32 82 53 95 27    04 22 08 63 04    83 38 98 73 74    64 27 85 80 44
90 04 58 54 97    51 98 15 06 54    94 93 88 19 97    91 87 07 61 50    68 47 66 46 59
73 18 95 02 07    47 67 72 52 69    62 29 06 44 64    27 12 46 70 18    41 36 18 27 60
75 76 87 64 90    20 97 18 17 49    90 42 91 22 72    95 37 50 58 71    93 82 34 31 78
54 01 64 40 56    66 28 13 10 03    00 68 22 73 98    20 71 45 32 95    07 70 61 78 13

08 35 86 99 10    78 54 24 27 85    13 66 15 88 73    04 61 89 75 53    31 22 30 84 20
28 30 60 32 64    81 33 31 05 91    40 51 00 78 93    32 60 46 04 75    94 11 90 18 40
53 84 08 62 33    81 59 41 36 28    51 21 59 02 90    28 46 66 87 95    77 76 22 07 91
91 75 75 37 41    61 61 36 22 69    50 26 39 02 12    55 78 17 65 14    83 48 34 70 55
89 41 59 26 94    00 39 75 83 91    12 60 71 76 46    48 94 97 23 06    94 54 13 74 08

77 51 30 38 20    86 83 42 99 01    68 41 48 27 74    51 90 81 39 80    72 89 35 55 07
19 50 23 71 74    69 97 92 02 88    55 21 02 97 73    74 28 77 52 51    65 34 46 74 15
21 81 85 93 13    93 27 88 17 57    05 68 67 31 56    07 08 28 50 46    31 85 33 84 52
51 47 46 64 99    68 10 72 36 21    94 04 99 13 45    42 83 60 91 91    08 00 74 54 49
99 55 96 83 31    62 53 52 41 70    69 77 71 28 30    74 81 97 81 42    43 86 07 28 34

33 71 34 80 07    93 58 47 28 69    51 92 66 47 21    58 30 32 98 22    93 17 49 39 72
85 27 48 68 93    11 30 32 92 70    28 83 43 41 37    73 51 59 04 00    71 14 84 36 43
84 13 38 96 40    44 03 55 21 66    73 85 27 00 91    61 22 26 05 61    62 32 71 84 23
56 73 21 62 34    17 39 59 61 31    10 12 39 16 22    85 49 65 75 60    81 60 41 88 80
65 13 85 68 06    87 64 88 52 61    34 31 36 58 61    45 87 52 10 69    85 64 44 72 77

38 00 10 21 76    81 71 91 17 11    71 60 29 29 37    74 21 96 40 49    65 58 44 96 98
37 40 29 63 97    01 30 47 75 86    56 27 11 00 86    47 32 46 26 05    40 03 03 74 38
97 12 54 03 48    87 08 33 14 17    21 81 53 92 50    75 23 76 20 47    15 50 12 95 78
21 82 64 11 34    47 14 33 40 72    64 63 88 59 02    49 13 90 64 41    03 85 65 45 52
73 13 54 27 42    95 71 90 90 35    85 79 47 42 96    08 78 98 81 56    64 69 11 92 02

07 63 87 79 29    03 06 11 80 72    96 20 74 41 56    23 82 19 95 38    04 71 36 69 94
60 52 88 34 41    07 95 41 98 14    59 17 52 06 95    05 53 35 21 39    61 21 20 64 55
83 59 63 56 55    06 95 89 29 83    05 12 80 97 19    77 43 35 37 83    92 30 15 04 98
10 85 06 27 46    99 59 91 05 07    13 49 90 63 19    53 07 57 18 39    06 41 01 93 62
39 82 09 89 52    43 62 26 31 47    64 42 18 08 14    43 80 00 93 51    31 02 47 31 67
```

```
41 84 98 45 47    46 85 05 23 26    34 67 75 83 00    74 91 06 43 45    19 32 58 15 49
46 35 23 30 49    69 24 89 34 60    45 30 50 75 21    61 31 83 18 55    14 41 37 09 51
11 08 79 62 94    14 01 33 17 92    59 74 76 72 77    76 50 33 45 13    39 66 37 75 44
52 70 10 83 37    56 30 38 73 15    16 52 06 96 76    11 65 49 98 93    02 18 16 81 61
57 27 53 68 98    81 30 44 85 85    68 65 22 73 76    92 85 25 58 66    88 44 80 35 84

20 85 77 31 56    70 28 42 43 26    79 37 59 52 20    01 15 96 32 67    10 62 24 83 91
15 63 38 49 24    90 41 59 36 14    33 52 12 66 65    55 82 34 76 41    86 22 53 17 04
92 69 44 82 97    39 90 40 21 15    59 58 94 90 67    66 82 14 15 75    49 76 70 40 37
77 61 31 90 19    88 15 20 00 80    20 55 49 14 09    96 27 74 82 57    50 81 69 76 16
38 68 83 24 86    45 13 46 35 45    59 40 47 20 59    43 94 75 16 80    43 85 25 96 93

25 16 30 18 89    70 01 41 50 21    41 29 06 73 12    71 85 71 59 57    68 97 11 14 03
65 25 10 76 29    37 23 93 32 95    05 87 00 11 19    92 78 42 63 40    18 47 76 56 22
36 81 54 36 25    18 63 73 75 09    82 44 49 90 05    04 92 17 37 01    14 70 79 39 97
64 39 71 16 92    05 32 78 21 62    20 24 78 17 59    45 19 72 53 32    83 74 52 25 67
04 51 52 56 24    95 09 66 79 46    48 46 08 55 58    15 19 11 87 82    16 93 03 33 61

83 76 16 08 73    43 25 38 41 45    60 83 32 59 83    01 29 14 13 49    20 36 80 71 26
14 38 70 63 45    80 85 40 92 79    43 52 90 63 18    38 38 47 47 61    41 19 63 74 80
51 32 19 22 46    80 08 87 70 74    88 72 25 67 36    66 16 44 94 31    66 91 93 16 78
72 47 20 00 08    80 89 01 80 02    94 81 33 19 00    54 15 58 34 36    35 35 25 41 31
05 46 65 53 06    93 12 81 84 64    74 45 79 05 61    72 84 81 18 34    79 98 26 84 16

39 52 87 24 84    82 47 42 55 93    48 54 53 52 47    18 61 91 36 74    18 61 11 92 41
81 61 61 87 11    53 34 24 42 76    75 12 21 17 24    74 62 77 37 07    58 31 91 59 97
07 58 61 61 20    82 64 12 28 20    92 90 41 31 41    32 39 21 97 63    61 19 96 79 40
90 76 70 42 35    13 57 41 72 00    69 90 26 37 42    78 46 42 25 01    18 62 79 08 72
40 18 82 81 93    29 59 38 86 27    94 97 21 15 98    62 09 53 67 87    00 44 15 89 97

34 41 48 21 57    86 88 75 50 87    19 15 20 00 23    12 30 28 07 83    32 62 46 86 91
63 43 97 53 63    44 98 91 68 22    36 02 40 09 67    76 37 84 16 05    65 96 17 34 88
67 04 90 90 70    93 39 94 55 47    94 45 87 42 84    05 04 14 98 07    20 28 83 40 60
79 49 50 41 46    52 16 29 02 86    54 15 83 42 43    46 97 83 54 82    59 36 29 59 38
91 70 43 05 52    04 73 72 10 31    75 05 19 30 29    47 66 56 43 82    99 78 29 34 78
```

AUTHOR INDEX

SUBJECT INDEX